Navigating the Sermon

for Cycle B
of the Revised Common Lectionary

A Compilation of "Charting the Course" Columns from
Emphasis: A Preaching Journal for the Parish Pastor
a Component of **SermonSuite.com**

CSS Publishing Company, Inc.
Lima, Ohio

NAVIGATING THE SERMON

FIRST EDITION
Copyright © 2011
by CSS Publishing Co., Inc.

For more information about CSS Publishing Company resources, visit our website at www.csspub.com, email us at csr@csspub.com, or call (800) 241-4056.

ISBN-13: 978-0-7880-2670-6
ISBN-10: 0-7880-2670-4   PRINTED IN USA

Table of Contents

Introduction

Over forty years ago, CSS Publishing Company was founded by two pastors and a Sunday school superintendent who had a vision to assist pastors "on the front lines" in their efforts to share the gospel of Jesus with people over the entire United States. The lectionary was taking hold over the country in an effort to bring a common message to people, no matter where they worshiped.

Over the years, CSS has published many different products. Of the more than 1,700 publications that have been produced in the history of the company, **Emphasis: A Lectionary Preaching Journal** has been one of the most popular. In its history, thousands of pastors and their congregations have benefited from the commentaries and insights found within its pages.

Navigating the Sermon is a collection of commentaries from "Charting the Course," which is at the core of what **Emphasis** is about. For each Sunday in the Cycle B lectionary, the writers who contributed to these columns have provided thematic guidance drawing together the lessons for each Sunday in the church year. Not only have they provided one idea for each Sunday, but most days have multiple themes from which to choose.

We are excited to offer this new resource to the readers of **Emphasis**, both old and new, and pray that this book will be a blessing to you and an invaluable aid to your preaching ministry.

The editors of CSS Publishing Company

Drowsy disciples

I watched with amusement, recently, as a gentleman across the table from me at a church committee meeting struggled to stay awake. Our meeting came at the end of what had apparently been a tiring day for him, and now the meeting itself was running long. No one there would question this member's devotion to the church or his commitment to its work. But he simply could not keep himself awake. His eyes would blur and begin to flicker, his head would start to bob, and finally his chin would sink into his chest.

As is so often the case in settings of involuntary sleep, he did not slumber for long. A few moments would pass, his body would jerk and his eyes would pop open again. Just as his naps did not last long, however, neither did his intermittent awakenings. Soon he was back into the familiar cycle, and his chin was back in his chest.

I have experienced that struggle. We all have. Perhaps we've fought it in a classroom or a committee; while trying to enjoy a movie, a concert, or a play; while driving at night, which is a particularly frightening experience. Or, perhaps we have even felt the struggle to stay awake while in the midst of a one-on-one conversation.

Sometimes, sleep simply seems irresistible. And no matter how hard we try, we cannot manage to stay awake. What's a person to do?

Isaiah 64:1-9

The book of Isaiah is readily understood as a three-part book, and our passage comes from the third part. The first 39 chapters of Isaiah are generally associated with the pre-exilic period of Isaiah himself. Chapters 40 through 55, meanwhile, reflect and address a different context: the period of the Babylonian exile rather than the earlier era of the Assyrian threat. And, finally, the last eleven chapters of Isaiah seem to be addressed to the post-exilic inhabitants of Jerusalem. That, then, is the context of our Old Testament lesson.

The scene that Isaiah imagines — indeed, invokes — anticipates the kind of scene that Jesus later describes when teaching about the end of time (a part of which is reflected in this week's gospel lesson). Isaiah's picture of mountains quaking and nations trembling resonates with Jesus' images of stars falling and the heavens being shaken. This climactic day is both global and cosmic. When this particular act in history comes to an end, it will not be merely with a curtain closing. No, but rather the scenery will topple, the stage will crumble, and the entire theatre will be shaken.

The lectionary linking of this Isaiah passage with the later Mark passage suggests to us a backdrop of New Testament eschatology against which to read Isaiah. As such, Isaiah's plea that the Lord "would tear open the heavens and come down" has a layer of meaning for us as Christians that it would not have had for Isaiah's original audience.

Likewise, the assurance that God "works for those who wait for him" has added meaning for us. Waiting for him is precisely the current condition of Christ's followers, and it is the setting of so many of Jesus' end-of-time teachings. The servants wait for their master's return, the bridesmaids wait for the bridegroom's arrival, and the vigilant Christian watches and waits for the coming of the Son of Man.

While the look and feel of a tumultuous spectacle is not unique to Isaiah's picture, he offers a clearer insight into the cause-and-effect than we may find elsewhere. "That the mountains would quake at your presence," he prays, and "that the nations might tremble at your presence." The turbulence in Isaiah's vision, therefore, is not merely some natural upheaval of human events or cresting wickedness. Rather, all the quaking and trembling is in response to the very presence of the Lord. As the soldiers in the barracks scramble into place and stand at attention when the commanding officer enters, so, too, with the earth and its people when the Lord tears open the heavens and comes down.

In stark contrast to the tremors that accompany God's presence, meanwhile, is Isaiah's later portrait of God's absence. "Because you hid yourself we transgressed," the prophet observes. And "you have hidden your face from us, and have delivered us into the hand of our iniquity." The tumult surrounding his presence may seem daunting, but see the trouble and despair that occur in his absence. We may sweat uncomfortably in the summer sun, but if the sun disappeared we would be lost altogether.

Meanwhile, a contemporary audience may miss the boldness of the prophet's statement that "we have all become like one who is unclean." The phrase seems merely poetic to a modern reader, but within the context of Old Testament Israel the prophet is saying a profound thing.

First, the Hebrew word for "unclean" (*tawmay*) is the same word used to describe Dinah's condition after she had been raped by Shechem (Genesis 34:5). She had been defiled, and that is the strong language the prophet uses to describe his people's condition.

Furthermore, the distinction between clean and unclean is a significant theme in the Old Testament Law. The people were to religiously avoid contact with unclean things, they were forbidden from eating unclean foods, and they were to be thorough and merciless in dealing with uncleanness, whether in skin, clothing, houses, or the community. "You are to distinguish," God says, "between the holy and the common, and between the unclean and the clean" (Leviticus 10:10).

We are familiar with the leper law in scripture — the requirement that a leper had to call out "Unclean, unclean!" (Leviticus 13:45). The concern, of course, was to maintain the health of the community at large. The lepers, while perhaps many in that time and place, were still a tiny minority of the community, and the laws were designed to keep the disease from spreading as much as possible. But see how the prophet has painted a dramatic picture: "We have all become like one who is unclean." There is not, then, a community of clean and whole people with a few unclean ones to be ostracized. Rather, the whole lot of us is unclean — defiled, to be avoided, and to be dealt with mercilessly.

Finally, the prophet expands on the uncleanness of the people by exclaiming, "all our righteous deeds are like a filthy cloth." While the human stage of an awakened conscience is to recognize how filthy our filth is, there is another level: the before-God recognition that even our cleanness is filthy. The prophet is not here decrying how shameful is the people's wickedness, but rather how shameful is the people's righteousness. The image is reminiscent of Paul who, after itemizing his proud accomplishments and asserting his righteousness (Philippians 3:4-6), reevaluates it all as rubbish (3:8; the Greek, *skubalon*, refers to the excrement of animals). So it is that our righteousness is like dirty laundry and our best accomplishments are like the stuff we're careful not to step in.

1 Corinthians 1:3-9

In topical teaching and preaching, this passage is the kind of material that never gets dealt with. American Christians typically engage in such a rush to relevance, so eager for personal application, that a passage like this goes largely overlooked. This is "flyover country" for most Bible reading and study. The lectionary, however, forces us to land here instead of flying over it. What others choose to bypass we make our destination.

These early verses found in most of Paul's letters are commonly known as the "thanksgiving section" of an ancient epistle. For our purposes in the New Testament, however, the importance of this section may best be illustrated not by its presence in most of Paul's letters but by its conspicuous absence from one of Paul's letters.

Galatians is clearly the angriest of Paul's epistles, and he noticeably passes the traditional thanksgiving section in order to go straight to his lament: "I am astonished that you are so quickly deserting the one who called you" (Galatians 1:6). While they are customary, therefore, thanksgiving sections should not be dismissed as empty or meaningless. Paul does not write the same thing to every church in this section, and he does not include this section at all when writing to the Galatians.

I have been in a number of settings over the years where some variation on this question has been asked: "What are you thankful for?" Folks share the matters for which they are most grateful, and that typically results in a list of things, people, and circumstances. Somewhat in contrast to those familiar answers, however, Paul's thanksgiving section is all about God. Even though this passage is addressed to the Christians in Corinth, and even though it is ostensibly about them, still there persists this theme that reveals Paul's true orientation. One-fifth of all the words in this brief passage are nouns or pronouns referring to God. The apostle, who elsewhere said that for him to live was Christ (Philippians 1:21), bears witness to that fact by the way the Lord saturates his thinking and his language even when talking about other people.

Paul's language presents us, meanwhile, with a kind of fill-in-the-blank opportunity. Take his initial sentence — "I give thanks to my God always for you because..." — and consider how that phrase might be followed. If the apostle were writing to your church or mine, how would he complete that sentence, that thought?

Paul's claim that he gives thanks always because of the Corinthians becomes remarkable as we read the two Corinthian letters that follow. Every church has its issues, of course, but the church in Corinth seems to have more than its fair share. Most of 1 Corinthians is devoted to answering their questions and addressing their problems, and 2 Corinthians reveals a genuinely painful struggle that Paul and the Corinthians have experienced in their relationship. Yet, still, he is always thankful for them.

This introductory passage includes allusions to subjects that will be recurring themes in the letter. "Speech" and "knowledge" are recognized here as goods, but later qualified as not the greatest goods (see, for example, 8:1, 11; 13:1-2; 14:9-19). Paul also references here their "spiritual gifts," which becomes a major topic later.

Finally, Paul looks to the future — "the day of our Lord Jesus Christ" — which ties this passage to our other two lections. He is eager that they should be "blameless" on that day, and he recognizes — as we have seen in Isaiah and will see again in Mark — that the present involves waiting ("you wait for the revealing of our Lord Jesus Christ").

Mark 13:24-37

All three synoptic gospels include a collection of end-of-time teachings of Jesus during the extended narrative between the events of Palm Sunday and Easter. In Matthew, the teachings with an end-of-time theme occupy most of chapters 24 and 25. Luke devotes somewhat less of his Holy Week account to this material than Matthew, giving most of chapter 21 to it. In Mark, the key chapter is chapter 13. Specifically, Mark 13 corresponds substantially to Matthew 24 and Luke 21, though the three chapters are not identical.

Mark's use of this material is perhaps the most striking of the three inasmuch as he has so much less "red letter" material than the other two. For Matthew and Luke, these end-of-time teachings are a comparatively small percentage of the overall collections of Jesus' teachings that they include in their gospels. Mark, on the other hand, is very sparing in his sayings of Jesus, focusing more on his deeds than his words. This end-of-time section, therefore, represents a significant percentage of the total teachings of Jesus recorded and reported by Mark.

In regard to our particular passage, verses 24-32 are represented in the same contexts in Matthew 24 and Luke 21. Verses 33-37, however, are not found in the corresponding portions of Matthew and Luke. If Mark's brief reference to a man going on a journey and leaving servants in charge is an abbreviated form of the parable of the talents, as some have argued, then we find it elsewhere in Matthew (ch. 25) and Luke (ch. 19). In both Matthew and Mark, therefore, this entire teaching is found in the midst of the Holy Week narrative. In Luke, meanwhile, the parable of the master leaving his servants in charge while he goes on a journey appears just prior to Jesus' triumphant entry into Jerusalem.

Within the larger context of Jesus' end-of-times teachings, it is worth noting the three very different themes that are developed. On the one hand, the nature of life prior to the coming of the Son of Man seems to be so ordinary as to be innocuous (for example, Matthew 24:37-44 and Luke 17:26-30), though Mark does not echo that theme. On the other hand, there is the cautionary note that extraordinary events should not be easily mistaken for his coming (as in Mark 13:5-10, 21-23). And then, finally, there is the theme of truly cataclysmic events that will accompany his return (such as Mark 13:14-20, 24-25).

Likewise, the end-of-times teachings leave us with different impressions about the timetable of these events. What Jesus teaches for the first half or more of Mark 13 adds up to suggest a long process. Don't jump to quick conclusions, we hear him saying, for many things will need to take place and be fulfilled before the Son of Man appears. But then, in verse 30, he makes the remarkable claim that "this generation will not pass away until all these things have taken place."

The convergence of these competing themes leaves readers shrugging their shoulders. How, then, are we to know when Jesus will return? Well, frankly, we don't know. And, notably, we discover that we have significant company in that lack of foreknowledge: such as the angels in heaven and Jesus himself (Mark 13:32).

Finally, the underlying Greek word here for generation (*geneya*) is used numerous times by Jesus (exclusively in the synoptics). Examining that broader context of Jesus' use of the word, it's hard to dispute the plain meaning of the text: Namely, Jesus seems to be saying that the aforementioned signs will all occur within the lifetimes of his contemporaries. On the other hand, a careful look at Jesus' use of the term also reveals an entirely negative connotation. "This generation" is impossible to satisfy (Matthew 11:16-19), "evil" (Matthew 12:45), "faithless and perverse" (Matthew 17:17), "adulterous and sinful" (Mark 8:38). "This generation" will persecute and reject the Son of Man (Luke 17:25), will be "charged with the blood of all the prophets shed since the foundation of the world" (Luke 11:50), and will be condemned by the people of Nineveh and the queen of the South at the judgment (Matthew 12:41-42).

Given that larger context of Jesus' references to "this generation," therefore, it stands to reason that the guarantee in Mark 13:30 is a prediction of judgment. It's not merely that the present generation will get to witness, like spectators or bystanders, the prerequisite signs of his coming. No, but rather they will be the victims of the unfavorable and portentous events.

Application

The conclusion of the gospel lesson strikes a note that is typical of Jesus' end-of-time teachings: "be on the watch" and "keep awake." Acknowledging that no one knows "that day or hour," he warns that it may come "in the evening, or at midnight, or at cockcrow, or at dawn." This is a deliberately inconvenient assortment of times. Lest we assume that the big event will occur at an opportune time — when we are paying attention, when we are naturally awake and alert, when we are open for business — Jesus cautions that he may come while we are sleeping, and he concludes, "Keep awake."

I don't take Jesus to mean, of course, that all of his followers for the past two millennia were expected literally to go without sleep until they finally cracked and died. I do take seriously, however, the profound challenge we face: to maintain an attitude of alertness and readiness when it is so tempting to change into something comfortable, fluff the pillows and call it a day. Our appetites and our culture conspire to distract us, and we are tempted to set aside the work of our long-delayed master in favor of something else — something more immediate, more pressing, more comfortable.

But let the rest of the world scramble to get into line and stand at attention when he suddenly arrives. We should be found already in place, fully attentive, and ready to go.

An Alternative Application

Isaiah 64:1-9. "For People Who Are Going to Pot." As we have illustrated above, this passage from the last third of Isaiah paints a grim picture of the condition of the people. They have "transgressed" and "become like one who is unclean." Even their "righteous deeds" are "filthy," and they are blown away by their iniquities. And, in a particularly damning critique, the prophet observes that "no one ... calls on your name, or attempts to take hold of you."

Then, in the next breath, the prophet recalls the basic nature of the people's relationship to God: he is "our Father" and "our potter," and that is the trump card. In Jesus' beloved parable of the prodigal son, it is that relationship — a father and his son — that trumps everything the son has wasted and done wrong. And, for as filthy and undeserving as the people are in this passage, God's special relationship to them will have the last word.

The use of "our Father" here, incidentally, may come as a surprise to some. In every church I've served, I have encountered folks who carry a night-and-day distinction between the Old and New Testaments. The fact that this warm, familial understanding of God appears in the Old Testament, therefore, may be news to some people in our pews.

It is the image of the potter, however, that I want to devote my attention this Sunday. It is something of a theme in scripture (see also Isaiah 29:16; 45:9; Jeremiah 18:1-12; Romans 9:19-21), as well as a meaningful image in the familiar Adelaide Pollard hymn, "Have Thine Own Way, Lord."

The potter-and-clay picture of our relationship with God, and the fact that "we are all the work of your hand," recalls the fundamental truth of our creation (Genesis 2:7). It affirms the ultimate sovereignty of God and his purpose in our lives. It reminds us of God's ongoing recreation of us, and it challenges us to a posture of submission, humility, and responsiveness to the potter's hand.

Changing times

Advent reminds us of the flow of time. We are all bound by time. Time is our teacher, our boss, our constant companion. Time locks us into the march of life and forces us to wake up each morning in a place we've never been before, in a place we can never return to again.

All our lives we struggle with time. When will we ever have enough time? When will I be old enough? When will time stop long enough for me to love you? One woman went through a great period of depression when her husband died. The grief slowed time for her. A year later, somewhat recovered, she talked with her pastor. "How long did it last for you," he asked, "these months of loneliness in the wilderness of your grief?"

She said, "Longer than I had hoped, but not as long as I feared." Bound by time, she wrestled alone in the deserts with it, captive to its march of dictation. We can call it "Wilderness Standard" time, the time of struggle, the time of depression, the time of empty hands. Some of us linger in that time zone today.

But today's lectionary passages remind us that there are many kinds of time. "Time marches on," we say. Sometimes it paces. Sometimes it races. The poet (attributed to Henry Twells) put it like this:

When as a child I laughed and wept, Time crept.
When as a youth I dreamt and talked, Time walked.
What I became a full-grown man, Time ran.
When older still I daily grew, Time flew.

We know what he is talking about. Time that flies when we're having fun. Time that races and teases and stalls and hurries. Time that lingers during the week, but rushes through a Friday night of partying. Time that charts the weeks of courtship and organizes the plans for the wedding. Time that counts nine months meticulously in pregnancy and steps year-by-year through the grades of school. Time that changes babies into children, and children into teens, and teens into young adults, and young adults into newlyweds, and newlyweds into parents, and parents into middle-aged folk, and middle-aged folk into seniors.

Along with calendar time, the Bible also calls us to face something we might call "crisis time." It is the time of significance in our lives; the kind of thing Billy Graham has termed "The Hour of Decision." T. S. Eliot said this kind of time is "the moment that gives the meaning." It is the sense of time held by the prophets of the Old Testament when they spoke about the coming day of the Lord.

Isaiah helps us think about the blessing of having our times in God's hand. Peter urges us to make the most of that time, especially in days of Advent when we expect another divine invasion. Mark's gospel opener bridges Old Testament and New, pointing to the intrusion of Jesus as at least one fulfillment of the prophetically announced day of the Lord. Sometimes it is in the unlikely places of our lives that we begin to find time stopping or moving or changing, and then we know that God's time is both the moment of opportunity for us, as well as the moment of judgment, but it is also always the moment of choice. Whoever we are and whatever we will be is found in the choices we make in the moments of our lives. This preaches well during Advent.

Isaiah 40:1-11

This passage stands at the beginning of the second part of Isaiah. All of the prophecies gathered into our book of Isaiah chart the fortunes of Israel from the eighth through the sixth centuries. For this reason many scholars think there were different people who championed the "Isaiah" cause over several hundred years, and their writings comprise either two books (pre-exilic Isaiah, chs. 1-39; exilic Isaiah, chs. 40-66) or three books (splitting exilic Isaiah between chs. 55 and 56, forming post-exilic Isaiah as well). Others believe that the Isaiah of historical contexts who makes appearances through chapters 1-39, wrote all of the prophecies in this book, seeing from a distance those future events predicted in chapters 40-66.

One's stance on these issues of authorship need not enter the pulpit. Instead, the distinctions between sections ought to inform homiletic intent and style. Whereas Isaiah 1-39 speaks much of coming judgment, the theme and tone changes markedly here at chapter 40. Whether seeing the judgment and its aftermath in a future trance, or experiencing it firsthand in the person of "Second Isaiah," the prophet begins to depict the changing times when violence and destruction give way to restoration, reconciliation, and rebuilding.

This passage cannot be understood apart from two major themes of the Hebrew Bible: covenant and the day of the Lord. The prophets spoke out of a covenant context. They never envisioned Israel as a nation similar to her neighbors. Invariably they saw Israel as formed and nurtured out of the redemptive events described in Exodus. Israel was wrestled from Pharaoh by Yahweh, bought through the bloody battle of the "ten plagues," married to Yahweh at Mount Sinai, and guarded through wilderness wanderings until life could begin again in the promised land of Canaan. Whether one views this as a historically accurate picture or not, the careful biblical exegete cannot escape the normativity this perspective holds over the prophetic imagination. The prophets saw Israel as the special nation of God, bound to God by the suzerain-vassal covenant of Exodus 20-24, and elaborated in the rest of the Pentateuch.

Thus Israel was expected, by covenant strictures, to live in a particular way. Violations of covenant lifestyle or loyalties would result in the coming of the curses that made up one section of the covenant document (see Exodus 23:20-33).

In this setting, Israel's recent experiences pushed it directly into the path of covenant judgment. The northern kingdom rebelled openly against Yahweh and lost both its place in the land and its identity (see 2 Kings 17). Now the southern kingdom was following the same path. This is the reason for all of the judgments expressed in Isaiah 1-39. Under Hezekiah's recent leadership, bringing about a national repentance, the curses of covenant disobedience were averted for a time. They would, however, return as subsequent kings lost sight of Yahweh's unique place in the national identity.

Over the years, the prophets developed some code phraseology. Most widespread was the term, "Day of the Lord" (*yom Yahweh*). It had come to denote the impending violent interruption of Yahweh into history, similar to Yahweh's stirring appearance when Israel was still enslaved in Egypt. This time around, however, Yahweh would strike with anger against Yahweh's wayward people. Thus, the day of the Lord would come in vengeance.

Over time, three specific dimensions of this terrible day of the Lord began to emerge in prophetic utterances. It would be, they said, 1) the time of judgment when God would address the evils of both Israel and the surrounding nations; 2) the time of salvation for a faithful remnant; and 3) the time of the messianic kingdom, when peace and prosperity would be restored, and Yahweh would live in harmony with the people in the glorious kingdom that would never end.

While Isaiah 1-39 had much to say about the first of these three "Day of the Lord" attributes, Isaiah 40 launches into both of the latter dimensions. The remnant is to be pardoned and comforted, and a path leading toward the growing eschatological messianic kingdom is to be prepared. Verses 6-8 are a brief recollection of the judgment dimension of the day of the Lord, but spoken in a way that serves to remind Israel that condemnation and punishment are not God's last word to them.

2 Peter 3:8-15a

It is not helpful to probe too far into theories of origins with this letter. If tradition stands, this is a communication from the apostle Peter in his last years before being executed at the hands of Nero around 64 AD. There are a number of challenges to this view (none insurmountable), and any good commentary can provide highlights. Still, the similarities between 2 Peter and Jude add mysterious questions surrounding the writing of this letter.

What is clear, however, is that external persecution, the death of the church's first leaders, growing moral challenges, and the expanding delay of Jesus' return have stirred a restlessness among the original readers of this letter. They want action — either from Jesus by way of coming quickly, or in divine judgment on the wicked around them, or some easing of lifestyle restrictions that keep them on edge.

Peter's words do not really help. Instead, he affirms all the difficulties these people face. Then, however, he reminds them that the ultimate source of reality is not these passing circumstances but the eternal plan and love and promises of God. If Peter's readers keep this in mind, although the current concerns threaten, they will not overwhelm or undermine (see also Isaiah 43:1-7).

When we know that our times are in the hands of God we understand that every moment is a moment of opportunity (v. 14). Malcolm Muggeridge understood that. Shortly before he died, he penned a book called *Confessions of a 20th Century Pilgrim*. This writing includes a reflection that returned to him often as he faced the prospect of death. He was not so troubled, he says, about the many things that he did wrong, and the sins that he wished he had not done. Instead he regretted that he had not lived out all of the opportunities that God had set in front of him during the times of his life. "Let me tell you the worst thing that haunts me," he wrote. "It is that when I could have had the first rate, the very best, when that's the thing that God wanted to give me, I took tenth rate."

Peter is trying to nurture the same reflection. Peter's master, Jesus, pledged at one point in the gospels, "I came that you might have life, and that you might have it abundantly." Yet, so often, we fritter away the times of our lives with second- or third-rate stuff. We take processed cheese when we could have had cheddar. We wrap our shoes in brown paper bags instead of receiving the family shoes of the kingdom. We ask for artificial flowers when primroses and crocuses and tulips are in bloom.

Like the prodigal son in Jesus' story we always look for the good things of life in the wrong places. Yet the time of God never leaves us. In the moment of opportunity God always comes to us to offer again a choice between good and ill, between grace and gravel, between heaven and hell. Of the prodigal son Jesus said, "But when he came to himself...." And when we truly come to ourselves in the moment of God's time, there is only one place to go — back to the Father.

Mark 1:1-8

Mark grew up in the city of Jerusalem (see Acts 12). His father may well have been a priest. That could be why his family was counted in the wealthy, upper class of society. Early Christian traditions say that when Mark was only a teen, his father died. For a time, according to one early source, Mark planned to become a priest like his father, but then things began to change very rapidly. First, Mark's mother, Mary, became enamored with a rabbi named Jesus, who had caught the nation by storm with his teachings and healings. Then Jerusalem was turned upside down by news of a successful assassination plot that ended with Jesus' execution on a cross. The killing was followed by more chaos when reports circulated that Jesus, who had been crucified, was now alive again. It wasn't long before Mark's mother decided to invite those who believed that Jesus was alive to use her home for a meeting place and headquarters.

Next, cousin Barnabas from Cyprus came to town and brought along a former terrorist named Paul, who now spoke of his devotion to Jesus. Suddenly the energy swelled again when Barnabas and Paul asked Mark to travel with them on a mission trip to distant lands (Acts 12:25). Although he was excited at first, Mark soon left the travelers and returned to Jerusalem (Acts 13:13). Paul got very angry, calling

Mark a runaway (Acts 15:36-40). Maybe Paul was right. It did take Mark a few years to grow up, and to gain the courage of a leader, and to travel once more as a Christian missionary. Finally Mark ended up in distant Rome, where Paul claimed him again as a valued friend (Colossians 4:10; 2 Timothy 4:11), and where Peter called him "my son!" (1 Peter 5:13). When Peter was executed by Emperor Nero, tradition has it that the church in Rome asked Mark to write down his recollections of Peter's teachings about Jesus. The result is with us today in the gospel called by Mark's name. It begins with the good news ("gospel") of changing times.

God's time is both the moment of opportunity and of judgment. This is why the writer of Ecclesiastes balances the times of our lives (Ecclesiastes 3): "a time to be born and a time to die... a time to kill and a time to heal... a time to build and a time to tear down." Missed times of opportunity turn against us in judgment. That is also why Mark ties the coming of Jesus specifically to a prophecy about the day of the Lord. Both dimensions of time are found in it. And John's appearance as a prophet emerging out of the wilderness further confirms this connection.

This tension was symbolized well by the ancient Greek sculptor, Lysippus, who carved a statue of marvelous beauty — a man with wings. Most striking was the man's hair. A great wave of hair flowed down the front of his head, cascading in a single hooked lock over his forehead. But the back of his head was completely bald.

On the pedestal, Lysippus had chiseled the figure's name, "Opportunity," and a series of questions and answers: "Why do you have a lock of hair on your forehead? *So that people might seize me as I come.* And why are you bald on the back of your head? *Because, when I am gone, no one can lay hold of me again.*"

Once the moment of opportunity is missed it becomes a moment of judgment. As Whittier put it: "*Of all sad words of tongue or pen,* the saddest are these, 'It might have been.' "

This mirrors the urgency of Mark's opening words. While some hoped for the day of the Lord to bring joy and meaning and blessing, those who ignored it would find themselves facing a future of terror. At the same time, the "good news" is that Jesus broke into our times to bring the blessings of the kingdom long before any hint of judgment would darken the skies. This is why we can know that death is coming and yet face it unafraid. We know that Jesus went through the blackness for us, and that his light beckons from the other side. Even the moment of our death can also be the moment of God's good grace.

Application

Harry Emerson Fosdick once said that it would be nice to find God in all the beautiful things of life — poetry, music, gorgeous sunsets, and the like. Yet, so often we don't give it a thought when life rolls along through sunlight and smiles. We're too busy enjoying ourselves at that time to look at the clock and hear the urgency of God's time. Unfortunately, it is often only when a crisis grinds us to a halt, or when death takes a friend, that suddenly time stops and we must face God.

Where did Charles Colson find God? Not in the White House, but in a prison cell when his life was shaken apart. When did Martin Luther write "A Mighty Fortress Is Our God"? He wrote it when he was on the run for his faith and his life. Listen to Helen Keller, blind and deaf from her early years. She wrote, "I thank God for my handicaps, for through them I have found myself, my work, and my God."

As Advent unrolls this year, it might more clearly measure God's time for us. Today might be the day that Jesus breaks into our tick-tock time and rides into the middle of our lives. We have let the clock on the wall carry us along, but now, in this moment, comes the call to find the meaning of our lives.

An Alternative Application

Isaiah 40:1-11. The Isaiah passage carries with it so many good themes for Advent. One is God's care and the need for people to know it even as they live through changing and challenging times. A second is the anticipation of eschatological blessing. Isaiah's poetic words point in a future direction, but do not fully flesh out that picture. Part of the vision is, of course, the ministry and message of Jesus. But much is still to come, as Peter reminds us, and in the anticipation itself there is growing energy and hope. This is what people need every Advent season.

Third, there is in this passage the dynamic call to participation in the process. We hear voices over distances engaging in urges toward action. "Prepare!" "Cry out!" "Make a road!" This section of Isaiah's prophecy has a very engaging feel. How are we invested in the process of the coming of the Messiah? What is your task? What is mine? How do we know when we are doing it, and who can help us assess the ongoing outcome? This is Advent in motion.

Advent 3
Isaiah 61:1-4, 8-11
1 Thessalonians 5:16-24
John 1:6-8, 19-28
Craig MacCreary

We are not the light

By now, most congregations are in the home stretch of their pre-Christmas preparations. There is much at stake for the life of any church. Try and imagine what a bad or indifferent Christmas would do to the morale of your church. We want if not a "Currier and Ives" Christmas for our families at least enough joy and good cheer to override any past enmity. Hopefully tinsel, garlands, and ornaments will chase away any seasonal affective disorder we may be suffering. Most of us are determined that the retelling of the story will bring at least enough peace of mind to help us deal with a world that often seems to be tearing itself to pieces. There is much on the line here and we want to get every carol, tradition, and pageant just right.

The struggle of getting the holiday lights up and running has often stood between me and the fullness of the Christmas spirit. Some of us are old enough to remember the strings of lights in which if one bulb went out they all went out... sounds like some churches and families I know. Some of us can remember the bulbs that radiated so much heat that they could smelt steel. Christmas often meant burnt fingers and singed limbs. Like much of church life, the ratio of heat to light in these bulbs made you wonder whether it was worth the effort. It has never added much to my Christian character to be scouring for an open hardware store on Christmas Eve to replace an exotic numbered fuse for the string of lights that is embedded near the top of the tree. It comes down to... find the fuse or find the strength of character to redo the tree ... or the courage to leave town.

Sociologists and other scholars remind us that there have always been ways of looking for and celebrating divine light. Humankind could not get along without such celebrations. The darkness of the winter night is too great to bear not to have some way of fighting it off. Our most ancient ancestors gathered in hope that the light would shine in the darkness and that the darkness would not overcome it.

My father-in-law is an electrical engineer. He understands the might as well as much of the mystery of electricity. He spent his career designing high-energy towers that carried electricity across America. Though he is certainly not the light, he probably brought as much light to so many people as any other person I know. One thing he understood about electricity is how dangerous it can be if you don't make the right preparations. You can wind up with more heat than light; or you find an energy drain sucking the life out of the power grid; or you find yourself blowing a fuse and facing meltdown. We need Advent to make meticulous preparations for the light that is coming into the world.

The texts for this Sunday affirm this truth as they point to what the light reveals, how the light can be magnified, and the danger of thinking that we are the light. In each case the coming of the light is not a solitary personal matter but a communal challenge. The Hebrew exiles of sixth century BC find the light revealing a new path for a weary people. The church in Thessalonica finds itself in the dark, as things do not seem to be going according to plan. The gospel lesson reflects some of the conflict between the followers of Jesus and John as they sort out their roles in the midst of the religious upheaval of the first century. Followers of the Baptist and the early disciples of Jesus struggled with each other's claims. The conflict between early Christians and other faith communities gives some indication of how faith claims of religious communities can plunge us into darkness by going too far.

Isaiah 61:1-4, 8-11

I have had the dubious distinction of having lived through two power blackouts in New York City and one in Toronto. I know from these experiences that there is no greater ecstasy than the first nanoseconds when the lights come back on. Nevertheless, for some it is not so heartening to find that nothing has changed, or to find in many cases, following some serious looting, that things have gotten considerably worse.

It seems that in the midst of the joy of the return of the exiles, where there might be some light at the end of the tunnel they find themselves facing some stiff challenges. In a church I served, we had a project to improve the lighting system in stages. Unfortunately, we also wound up painting the church section by section as well because the lights revealed how much painting we needed to do. The return from exile revealed ruined devastations that needed to be repaired, a religious life that needed to be re-established, and a community that needed to be rebuilt. If anything, the light revealed just how far the Hebrews had to go. The light can be depressing before it is enlightening. Chapter 60 of Isaiah captures the ambiguity of the moment well, "Arise, shine; for your light has come and the glory of the Lord has risen upon you. For darkness shall cover the earth and thick darkness the peoples; but the Lord will arise upon you, and his glory will appear over you." As in many psychological theories of human experience, the light and the dark dwell very close together. As the Chinese character for crisis has it, this moment is a combination of danger and opportunity. Certainly, it was a theologically challenging moment to realize that God was saving God's people through the actions of Cyrus the Persian king. Whatever the future may hold it will be determined more by the greatness of God than the goodness of the people. This is not the message of the Santa who is checking "his list twice to see who has been naughty or nice."

Things do not get any more doubtful or hesitant. Yet chapter 61 of Isaiah proclaims that this is the time to "bring good news to the poor, proclaim liberty to the captives, release to prisoners and the year of the Lord's favor." The message seems quite problematic at the holiday season when we wait for the news that the latest fad plaything is in the local toy store; when our children are evermore captivated by the toys our society has to offer; and when in many settings the oppressed must settle for a Christmas basket from the local charity.

Even more than this maddening announcement is the statement that the exiles shall be called a planting of the Lord to display his glory and that "they shall be called oaks of righteousness." This does seem to be a very tall order. Is there any good news here? The prophet does not say that they shall be a bastion, or fortress, or army of the Lord but plantings that are grounded in the earth — breathing and capable of transforming light energy into nourishment, shade, and growth.

In many ways, oaks, as well as other plants, have the light business down pat. Plants have an ability to take decayed matter and turn it into new life. They can even take animal fertilizer and turn it into new life. To me, in many ways, this begins to look like the task of the church. How do we take the light that we have, mix it with decayed matter and what God's creatures leave behind, and turn it into something that is a further approximation of the kingdom? Plants also take carbon dioxide, a waste product from the rest of creation, and turn it into life-giving oxygen. Oaks are even able to give shade and oases from the burning sun. I suspect that such activity will be in a deep sense vital to any repair of the "former devastations" that we may have to do.

1 Thessalonians 5:16-24

I become a mass of anxiety when the electric lights begin to flicker. Does it portend a long-range problem that will plunge the neighborhood in darkness for what will seem an eternity? On the other hand, perhaps we have just a minor problem that is susceptible to a little jiggling and jury-rigging. Things will be up and running in no time. Often in church the problems seem of the latter kind, amenable to a reassignment here or there, a shuffle of agenda, a more severe application of the appropriate muscle power. I shudder at the inventiveness and circuitous methods I have used over the years to keep the Christmas tree lit. Candles would have been safer than the wiring, plugging, and jiggling that I did. Yet, like the church, we somehow managed to survive during the years.

On the other hand, there is the more dangerous problem of a flickering light that may mask something seriously wrong. Short-term solutions may even add to the problem. That seems to be the kind of crisis that the Thessalonians were facing. They were among the earliest of Paul's church plantings and the letter we have is perhaps the earliest book in Christian scripture. The church at Thessalonica has a flicker in the light because things are seemingly not going according to the eschatological schedule that the Thessalonians have in mind. More than a theoretical classroom issue it is a matter of the loss of those they loved before the return of the Jesus who loved them. "But you, beloved, are not in darkness, for that day to surprise you like a thief." Things may be on the blink, but for Paul no one need be in the dark as to the final outcome. The conclusion of human history is beyond doubt. There is no need for any theological jury-rigging, "for you are all children of light and children of the day; we are not of the night or of darkness." However, the Thessalonians seem to have given into the impulse to live as if they are completely in the dark. According to the first part of the chapter 5, idleness and drunkenness, as well as quarrelsomeness have broken out as a way of passing the time until things become a bit clearer.

In our own times, the day of the Lord seems far away. While some search for lifestyles of the rich and famous, others seem to pass the time locked in theological and political standoffs, and many overmedicate their lives. People in the mainline churches did not expect things to go the way they have. Those churches find themselves on the outside looking in at the levers of power and prestige they formerly held. For some, the world of science and the globalization of economic and political life have challenged verities of faith and belief. In today's lectionary reading, Paul outlines his program for those who find themselves trying to read the signs of the times by flickering light.

"Rejoice always" is a tall order in our day, just as it must have seemed a great challenge to the first-century church. Of course, I do not rejoice at having had cancer. I do rejoice that it has made me a better, more sympathetic pastor. I do not rejoice that my denomination has experienced yearly decline or that we are no longer invited to the White House on a routine basis. I do rejoice that we have found ourselves focusing a lot more on what should be primal in our common life. I do not rejoice at all the bumps and grinds that come along in a marriage. I do rejoice that the ones that have come along have often been the source of personal growth. All this may seem to be nothing more than looking on the bright side or for the silver lining. Yet, it is more than that when you exercise the discipline of looking for the ways that God might turn stumbling blocks into stepping-stones.

Praying without ceasing seems beyond our reach. Do I have that much to say? However, I find that I don't have much worthwhile to say if it is not in some sense a prayer. I pray until I find my voice. When the light is flickering, test everything, but do not quench the Spirit. There will be enough light to avoid living in the dark by keeping the energy flowing through rejoicing, praying, giving thanks, and devoting oneself to the words of the prophets.

John 1:6-8, 19-28

I believe it was Carlyle Marney who said that since the birth of the Christ child the church has been in postpartum depression. I think that he is on to something here. It certainly seems that the events following the birth of the Christ child were difficult and onerous. This text in all probability reflects, as does other parts of the Christian Testament, the conflicts between the followers of Jesus and John who were trying to perpetuate their teachings. Some suggest that a John community existed into the fourth century. Christian-Jewish relations did not get off to a stellar start when the conflict between the Pharisees and the early Christians moved to the center of the gospel. In part, John's gospel is written to explain why many in the Jewish community just didn't get it. John's answer is that the wind blows where it blows. Of course, the divide must have severed families and communities. When Christians have not been in conflict with others, they have found plenty of opportunity to go at each other claiming their own truth as the only truth. In some ways, Christmas can feel like a first-class disaster or an accident waiting to happen.

In this context, John the Baptist is given some pretty refreshing lines for a religious figure. He confessed to not being the light and did not prevaricate that beyond a shadow of a doubt he was not the messiah. With more than our share of messiah complexes in religion and politics this is quite a statement to hear. He does not stop there. He is not Elijah, either. Nor is he the prophet. He rejects the tag of being part of any religious ideological plan or movement of history. With no credentials, just why anyone should listen or be interested in John at all seems a mystery. With so many ways to mark our days to Christmas why is John trotted out to be part of our Christmas preparation?

John's claim, echoing the Isaiah experience, is that he is one who is crying in the wilderness, "Make straight the way of the Lord." Note that he does not say "the one," rather just one. For the writer of the gospel, John the Baptist seems to reflect the role of the gospel writer's church. While knowing they [the church] are not messiahs, they can point to the messiah. Though John baptized with water, the implication is that there is the greater baptism through immersion in the Holy Spirit.

In the midst of the wilderness, this is what we can do. We can point to the one who is the Messiah who has led us through the desert, who like Moses, has sustained us with thirst-quenching water and nourishment enough for each day. He is the one who gives even more than water. If we can point to him it might even get us through the spiritual and commercial wilderness than can be Advent and the Christmas season to come.

Application

Here we are as church people with two weeks to go before Christmas and we have all been here before. There is always a temptation to attack the surrounding cultural myths and methods of finding the light. I recall one New Jersey priest a few years ago who decided at midnight mass, in a career-ending moment, to explain to the children that there is no Santa Claus. He soon found out that he was not the messiah. We often find ourselves looking for ever more inventive and clever Christmas pageants or programs to get to the light, or we pray that the ones we have will be serviceable enough to outlast the dark. We invest a lot of energy in the ritual and rights of the holiday season to get us through personal and communal darkness. The foolishness of some seasonal office parties reflects the lack of authentic community. As we go through the Advent cycle, our hopes grow stronger and our anxieties grow deeper.

The texts the lectionary gives us for this Sunday speak to people caught in the build-up to Christmas, who are perhaps worried that the season might not deliver. Remember we are not the light but we can point to the light. Rejoice always, make all things a prayer, and don't get in the way of the holiday spirit. Get it down that plantings can take light (and what life throws at you) and turn it into enough oxygen to make breathing easier. This is a holiday checklist worth following.

An Alternative Application

John 1:6-8, 19-28. I am a John the Baptist person! He is my patron saint. He is the man in the middle. Caught between two epics he should be the emblem of all clergy who find themselves caught in the middle! In my church office I have an icon that tells his story. He looses his head but in heaven has it sewn back on! He should be the patron saint of all clergy. He should be the patron saint of the middle-aged who might be losing their mind raising children and caring for aged parents. He should be the patron saint of middle managers that in discovering their limits and strengths are uncertain of where their career might take them.

John knew his limits and in accepting them he could point to the unlimited power of God. It is perhaps at the boundaries and in the middle where we can most effectively point to the light.

Advent 4
2 Samuel 7:1-11, 16
Romans 16:25-27
Luke 1:26-38
David Kalas

Dust off the throne

When I was a kid, my parents would host several Christmas parties each year — one for each of the adult Sunday school classes from our church. In preparation for each party, my mother would employ me in vacuuming the living room, mixing the punch, lighting the candles, and such.

One task that invariably came before the first party of each Christmas season involved the silver tea set. It was a lovely set, but we seldom used it apart from the annual Christmas parties. Consequently, when December rolled around, the set looked dark and tarnished, and so it became my job to polish the silver set before the first party each year.

We all have things like that. Things that we don't use very often. Things that we bring out only for special occasions, and when we bring them out, they need to be dusted off, cleaned out, and polished up.

The angel that came with Christmas news for Mary said that God was going to give her son "the throne of his ancestor David." Talk about something that hadn't been used for a while! The Jews had been living under Roman occupation for the past sixty years. A century prior to that, they were the ping-pong ball between competing foreign interests that followed in the wake of Alexander the Great. And, for the centuries before Alexander, Jerusalem had been assaulted by the Assyrians, demolished by the Babylonians, and supported by the largesse of the Persians.

Just one generation after David sat on his throne, his grandson alienated and lost ten of Israel's twelve tribes. Subsequent heirs to his throne included an assortment of weak and wicked men. Some stripped the gold from the palace and temple to pay off regional bullies. Some introduced idolatry and pagan practices into Jerusalem. Some who weren't so overtly bad still did not show the strength to oppose and undo what evil predecessors had done.

It had been a long time since David's throne had been used. An even longer time since it had been used well. Now, at Christmas, it was time to get it out and dust it off for Mary's son.

2 Samuel 7:1-11, 16

Our scene opens with a remarkable bit of initiative by King David. He "said to the prophet Nathan...." As we read the biblical accounts of prophets and kings, it is usually the prophets who go knocking on the kings' doors. Typically the Lord has some message for the king and his nation, and the prophet is employed to communicate that message. It is far less common, however, that we see a king knocking on the prophet's door to find out what the Lord has to say. Still more rare is David's move here: the king initiates the conversation, not because of what he wants from the Lord, but because of what he wants to do for the Lord.

David's sensitivity is exemplary. He saw for himself precisely the kind of thing that we usually need someone else to point out to us. Indeed, David saw for himself essentially the same thing that the prophet Haggai was required to point out to the Jews of post-exilic Jerusalem 500 years later (see below).

Nathan's reflexive response is a positive one. He no doubt sensed the fundamental goodness of David's plan, and he recognized that the Lord was with David. But Nathan's seal of approval proved premature, for "that same night the word of the Lord came to Nathan."

David is to be commended for not running ahead with his plan before consulting the prophet of the Lord. That prophet, however, may be questioned for giving the green light to David's plan without himself consulting the Lord. In any case, the Lord did not permit the project to get very far down the road at all before he corrected it.

"Are you the one to build me a house to live in?" the Lord asked David. God had not asked David — or any of his predecessors among Israel's leadership since the days when Moses first constructed the tabernacle according to God's design — to build him "a house of cedar." So David's proposal did not match God's purpose. Instead, however, God graciously turned the tables and revealed that his purpose was to build a house for David.

The Hebrew word (*bayith*) for "house" is, not surprisingly, a very common one in the Old Testament, and it occurs seven times in just the verses of our passage. But the ordinary word takes on a new meaning in the message that God gives to David through Nathan. While David intended to build for God a structure, God intended to establish for David a dynasty.

God also intended to establish a reputation for David: "I will make for you a great name, like the name of the great ones of the earth." It's hard to dispute that that promise and purpose of God has been fulfilled. In later Old Testament prophecy, David's name, reign, and throne became the emblem for Israel's past and future glory, a symbol for God's messianic age. That in itself is remarkable, since Solomon's reign was arguably more notable, at least in human terms. And yet, when we arrive at the New Testament, "son of David" is the loaded term the expectant crowds use when welcoming Jesus into Jerusalem.

Beyond the confines of ancient Israel, meanwhile, David's name and reputation continue to be great 3,000 years after the youngest son of Jesse tended to sheep on the hillsides near Bethlehem. It is a symbol of David — not of Solomon or Moses, not of Joshua or Judas Maccabeus — that flies on the flag of the modern state of Israel. And David has been known for generations and around the globe as the author of one of the most famous and beloved poems in the world (Psalm 23).

Finally, the twice-mentioned "rest" from all of David's enemies is attributed to the Lord. The statement reflects a faith perspective that is quite foreign to the world in which we live. If a political and military leader in our day came to a point where he was free from the harassment of enemies, how would we score that? We might think in terms of his strategy, his military might, his political acumen. We might consider the effectiveness of his advisors, his assistants, his generals. We might look at the national and international landscape to see what favorable circumstances permitted him to achieve such a position of security, but we would not naturally think to attribute the matter to God.

David himself, however, would be inclined to give the credit to God. After all, he knew, even as a boy facing his first enemy that "the battle is the Lord's and he will give you into our hand" (1 Samuel 17:47).

Romans 16:25-27

Our New Testament lesson may be viewed as either a very short passage or as a very long sentence. It qualifies as both. The length and convolution of the sentence can be off-putting for many readers, and so a part of our task this week may be simply to walk our people through some characteristically Pauline complexity.

We gather from 16:22 that Paul probably dictated this letter to the Romans. Tertius briefly peeks up from his otherwise anonymous desk to greet the Christians in Rome. It may be, then, that the failure to break Paul's words into more manageable sentences is Tertius'. Or, it may be that Paul, like many of us when leaving messages on answering machines and voice mails, spoke rapidly without apparent punctuation. Personally, however, I am most inclined to attribute this kind of sentence to a sort of childlike enthusiasm on the apostle's part.

We know how an excited child can babble on breathlessly with their enthusiasm flowing faster than their words can accommodate. That is how this closing passage from Romans reads to me. Not all of

Paul's writing is like this, after all. Not every sentence of his is three verses and (in the Greek) 53 words long. I credit this verbosity to Paul's excitement. I see here a crescendo of praise, and it bubbles forth faster than either Paul or Tertius can punctuate.

The sentence alludes to so many, many different subjects. Each one deserves consideration. "My gospel" and "the proclamation of Jesus Christ" is worthy of elaboration. "The revelation" could be exposited, and "the mystery that was kept secret for long ages" should be. We might say more about that mystery being "now disclosed," about "the prophetic writings," and about the central issue for Paul of it being "made known to all the Gentiles." Likewise, we might meditate for some time on the weighty subjects of "the command of the eternal God" and "the obedience of faith."

In my years of writing essays as an English major, I was frequently challenged by a professor's red pen, underlining some point in my paper with the comment: "Elaborate on this" or "Explain this more fully." We want to say that to Paul here. He has raised so many profound subjects, but he limits each to a mere reference, and we wish that he would elaborate, that he would explain these things more fully. He has left that heady task, however, to those of us who exposit the word.

Paul's reference to "my gospel" is neither unique nor common. He uses that same phrase in two other places: once earlier in this same letter to the Romans (2:16), and once in writing to Timothy (2 Timothy 2:8). He also uses the phrase "our gospel" on two occasions (2 Corinthians 4:3; 1 Thessalonians 1:5). While the phrase is not unique to this passage, it is unique to the apostle Paul. No one else in the New Testament makes that kind of personal, possessive reference to "my" or "our" gospel.

It's interesting, meanwhile, that Paul should credit "the prophetic writings" with the mystery being "made known to all the Gentiles." The Hebrew prophets of the Old Testament, after all, would have no natural appeal, familiarity, or credibility outside of Judaism — certainly not, we would think, in the Gentile world outside of Israel. If anything or anyone, we'd be inclined to point to Paul as the vessel through which the mystery was "made known to all the Gentiles."

Paul's phrase "the obedience of faith" is packed with beauty and meaning. It puts to rest the false contrast between Paul and James on the issue of faith and works. Paul doesn't use this exact phrase anywhere outside of this letter, but he uses the phrase "to bring about the obedience of faith" essentially to bookend what he writes to the Romans (1:5; 16:26).

Meanwhile, as we consider the variety of significant topics that Paul mentions without elaboration, there may be a method to his madness. He has assembled such a constellation of important truths, and then he has subordinated them all to a doxology. The sentence seems to have so many subjects, yet from beginning to end God is the real subject of the sentence — all the others only serve to say something about him. While each jewel may deserve its own focused study and appreciation, they are all linked together by Paul and employed in the larger crown of praising God. For that is the real meaning and message of this long sentence: glory to God!

Luke 1:26-38

An understanding of this week's Old Testament lesson from 2 Samuel will add a new layer of meaning to the gospel lesson for members of our congregations. That Joseph was "of the house of David" is not merely a quaint way of referring to genealogy or family tree. Rather, the image deliberately echoes the marvelous truth of the Old Testament lesson: namely that, while David intended to build a house for God, God instead promised to establish a house for David. Joseph was of that house, and his son would become the fulfillment of that millennium-old promise. And, of course, the angel's explanation of God's plan and purpose for that son of Joseph and Mary plainly echoes the explanation of God's plan and purpose expressed to Nathan concerning David.

Mary's initial response to the angel's news, meanwhile, is so marvelously human. He has told her that she will have a son, but not just any son. No, this will be "the Son of the Most High," suggesting his divinity. Her son will sit on the throne of David, who has been dead for a thousand years and whose throne must have seemed like a long-ago memory to a conquered and occupied people. He will rule over Judah, which at the time was just one province belonging to the vast Roman Empire; and his kingdom will never end, which must have sounded like pie in the sky given that the Jews' latest experience of independence (the Maccabean revolt and Hasmonean dynasty) lasted little more than a century. It is a fabulous picture, full of broad strokes and big promises. Yet Mary's concern rewinds all the way back to the most tiny and initial matter: "How can this be, since I am a virgin?"

How often do we doubt the big thing God might do because of some little fact about ourselves, about our condition, about our limitations? That was surely Moses' objection at the burning bush (Exodus 3:11; 4:10), as well as Gideon's reflex reaction to what God wanted to do through him (Judges 6:15).

The preposterousness of Mary's question, of course, can be found in hypothetically changing her condition. Would the plan of God articulated by the angel suddenly become so much more plausible if Mary were not a virgin? Would it be so very much easier to believe that she would give birth to the Son of the Most High, who would resurrect David's throne and reign over Judah forever, if only she had had sexual intercourse? Such myopia, however, is a common obstacle to faith.

The angel is marvelously patient with Mary — much more so, it would seem, than he was with Zechariah in a similar situation some months earlier (see Luke 1:19-20). Gabriel explains to Mary — to the extent that such a thing can be explained — how it will come to pass that a virgin will conceive. And, as a kind of reassurance to nurture her small and fragile faith, he tells her about her relative, Elizabeth. Since she found it hard to imagine a virgin giving birth, then perhaps she would be encouraged to know that God had enabled an old woman — barren her whole life, and now presumably well past her physical ability to have children — to have a son. Then comes the summary statement: "Nothing will be impossible for God."

Our preaching emphasis at Christmas time may tend to be on God's love and God's gift. We may, however, neglect the theme of God's power until the story turns to Jesus' ministry and, later, his resurrection. But the angel's parting words to Mary remind us that the Christmas story is also a display of his power — his potency to fulfill his purpose in any situation and against all odds. We recognize it when he calms storms, heals lepers, and rises from the dead. Likewise, we should also see it in the Christmas picture of a barren old woman and a young, virgin girl both giving birth to special baby boys.

Application

Our familiar Christmas carols speak often of Jesus' kingship. In fact, it's one of the great themes we sing each year: "Come and worship, come and worship, worship Christ the newborn king" ... "Come to Bethlehem and see Christ whose birth the angels sing; come, adore on bended knee, Christ the Lord, the newborn king" ... "Hark! the herald angels sing, 'Glory to the newborn king' " ... "Noel, Noel, born is the king of Israel" ... "Joy to the world, the Lord is come! Let earth receive her king" ... "And the star rains its fire while the beautiful sing, for the manger of Bethlehem cradles a king" ... "Born a king on Bethlehem's plain, gold I bring to crown him again, king forever, ceasing never, over us all to reign."

The promise that God had made to David in our Old Testament lesson must have seemed like a cruel joke for so many intervening years. Then the promise was renewed to Mary in the gospel lesson.

In the hymn "Come, Thou Long-Expected Jesus," Charles Wesley encourages us to see that the King who came at Christmas has a broader and deeper reign in mind than just the old boundaries of David's jurisdiction. "Born thy people to deliver, born a child and yet a King, born to reign in us forever, now thy gracious kingdom bring." And so we are invited to bring out our own throne for him. Perhaps it has been a long time since he has had his rightful place in our lives. Perhaps never. And so we dust off the throne, and we welcome the king.

An Alternative Application

2 Samuel 7:1-11, 16. "What's wrong with this picture?" We noted earlier that David showed uncommon sensitivity in the concern that he expressed to Nathan. His perception stands in stark contrast to the people of Haggai's day, and probably, also, to many people of our day.

Just as the writer of Samuel reports that David was "settled" and enjoying peace, so the people of Haggai's day had resettled and established themselves in the land. But the Lord sent Haggai to observe, "Is it a time for you yourselves to live in your paneled houses, while this house (the Lord's house, the temple) lies in ruins?" (Haggai 1:4).

What Haggai's contemporaries did not see for themselves, David did see. While the people of Haggai's day needed a prophet to come and correct their manifestly misplaced priorities, David went to the prophet to lament the impropriety of his situation. He recognized that he was pleasantly ensconced in a house of cedar while the ark of the covenant, symbolizing God's presence, was still in a tent. That, he sensed, was not right.

Children's puzzle books sometimes include drawings that contain subtle irregularities — mittens on a summer day, a bird flying upside down, a fish in a tree, and the like. The challenge, then, is to discover "what's wrong with this picture?"

David looked at the disparity between his accommodations and God's, and he went to Nathan to say that something was wrong with the existing picture. We would do well to look carefully over the picture of our lives — with the sensitive heart of David — to discover what may be wrong with our picture.

Christmas Eve / Christmas Day
Isaiah 9:2-7
Titus 2:11-14
Luke 2:1-14 (15-20)
Timothy Cargal

Night of light

One of the great cultural traditions of modern American Christmas observance is the use of lights. Everything that doesn't move is decorated with lights. Christmas trees are recognizable by their lights, and indeed as more and more types of trees are used as Christmas trees, the more it is the presence of the lights that identifies them as such. Lights are put around lampposts. We hang lights from the eaves and awnings of our homes, and around windows and doorframes. Lighted fixtures and images are arrayed in front yards, and those that are not self-lighted are bathed in spotlights. Without a moment's embarrassment at the brazen self-interest, electrical power companies promote contests for the best and most elaborate seasonal displays. Terms like "Sparkle Christmas" are entering the vocabulary of some regions, and almost everyone would recognize "the Season of Light" as a non-sectarian — indeed secular — term for Christmas time.

The tremendous irony of calling Christmastide "the Season of Light," at least in the northern hemisphere, is that it is of course the darkest time of the year. Shifts and adjustments in the western calendar system have only slightly obscured the fact that Christmas Day originally coincided with the date of the winter solstice, the date with the longest period between sunset and sunrise in the entire year. It seems more than likely that one reason that we so eagerly embrace all this use of artificially generated light for a celebration during this particular season of the year for us is in order to deal with the depression in energy and often in mood that accompanies the shortening of daylight hours.

Yes, the association between light and Christmas is tremendously ironic when considered in the context of the calendar in the northern hemisphere. But both the Old Testament and the gospel lessons appointed for Christmas Eve emphasize an important spiritual reason for the association of Christmas, light, and the deepest of darkness. It was precisely because of the tremendous darkness that the light of Christ needed to shine into the world. Even though it is impossible to know the time of year at which Jesus of Nazareth was actually born, from a spiritual perspective, nothing could better capture the significance of the time of Christ's birth than to call it "the Night of Light."

Isaiah 9:2-7

This oracle attributed to Isaiah of Jerusalem was not originally a prophecy at all, at least not in the sense that we typically now use the word "prophecy." That is to say, Isaiah did not compose this poem in order to predict long distant events (the birth of Jesus lay some seven centuries in the future) or even for that matter to predict events in the much shorter term of his own lifetime. Rather, this oracle is properly a celebration of the coronation of a new Judean king. Given Isaiah's close relationship with the Davidic house during the reign of four such kings (Uzziah [6:1], Jotham, Ahaz, and Hezekiah), it is difficult to know which king is being celebrated. Clearly the Book of Isaiah and the relevant portions of 2 Kings indicate Isaiah was most supportive of Hezekiah, and so he would be the most likely candidate. But given the general nature of the references to the Davidic house within the oracle (see especially v. 9) certainty is impossible.

But if Isaiah was most likely writing about Hezekiah in this oracle, why do Matthew (see Matthew 4:12-17) and later Christian tradition associate it with Jesus? The answer to that question lies in a proper understanding of how Matthew and his contemporaries understood the relationship between ancient prophecies and their own time. First, Matthew would have been the first to admit that Isaiah's words did not refer exclusively to Jesus. Isaiah spoke God's word to his own contemporaries and did so to help them understand what was happening in their own lives and not what would happen centuries later. But Matthew would also have argued that Isaiah's oracle was just as helpful to people of the first century in understanding what God was doing in their own time through Jesus. For Matthew, the oracle did not refer either to Hezekiah or to Jesus; it referred to both Hezekiah and to Jesus. What God had done for God's people in the eighth century BC, God was now doing again (in a deeper and fuller way, Matthew would no doubt have argued) for God's people in the first century AD. The same pattern of interpreting prophetic oracles can be found in the pesher commentaries from Qumran.

One clear indication that Matthew indeed took the original context of Isaiah's oracle very seriously (and in some ways more so than later Christian writers who began the association of this oracle with the circumstances of Jesus' birth) lies in where he places the "fulfillment" of the oracle in Jesus' life. Although the oracle specifically refers to a birth ("a child has been born for us, a son given to us," v. 6), Matthew said that the oracle's relevance to Jesus was fulfilled not at his birth but at the beginning of his ministry (see again Matthew 4:12-17). Thus, just as Isaiah's oracle was originally associated with a king's coronation and the beginning of his reign, Matthew associates it with the beginning Jesus' reign through his ministry.

The historical setting and background to this celebration of the coronation of a southern, Judean king is the fall of the northern Israelite kingdom to the Assyrian empire. The imagery of "deep darkness" (v. 2) is then used to express their desperation and hopelessness. That they have "seen a great light" that has shined upon them is that they have witnessed the survival and continuation of the Davidic dynasty despite the subjugation of their own homeland. Isaiah's hope and expectation was that these members of the northern tribes would see in this God's faithfulness to the covenant with David and all the Israelites more generally. He also apparently hoped that Judah would be able to roll back the Assyrian hegemony over the region and bring it back under Davidic rule (see especially vv. 4-5), but alas, despite Judah's continued existence for another century (until its own subjugation to Babylon), it was never able to reincorporate the northern tribal areas into a reunited kingdom. That harsh reality became itself a reason why latter Jews would look for a fuller and more complete "fulfillment" in a future messianic figure.

As already noted, the reference to the child's birth in verse 6 does not indicate the actual occasion for the writing of the oracle. Following a standard practice of Hebrew poetry, there is a synonymous parallelism between "a child has been born for us" and "a son given to us," and here it is the second line that has the primary emphasis. The sense is essentially that at the moment of the king's coronation the people look back upon his birth as a time of special blessing.

The more modern translations have properly recognized the pairing of qualifiers with each title and so corrected the translation of the old and still quite familiar King James Version. Thus, the king is "wonderful counselor, mighty God, everlasting Father, Prince of Peace." If it should be objected that some of these titles are not appropriate to a purely human regent, then the objection is to be answered by noting their original context. The king is "mighty God" not because he is himself divine, but because he was thought of as God's earthly co-regent over the people. He is "everlasting Father" because he is the latest heir to the everlasting covenant with David regarding the right to rule over God's people. The imposition of later trinitarian concepts to these terms is not so much wrong as applied to fulfillment in Christ (as explained above) as it is anachronistic as applied to the Judean king about whom the oracle was originally composed.

To summarize, the point is not that this oracle is only improperly applied to Jesus as opposed to say Hezekiah. Rather it is to stress that properly understanding its relation to Hezekiah is key to understanding its application to Jesus. The evangelists and others are telling us that what God had said in the past is an important lens for understanding what God has done in Christ. But if that lens is to provide clarity rather than distortion, then we must understand its original context rather than imposing on it our yet later ideas about Jesus Christ.

Titus 2:11-14

One of the great values of the epistle lesson assigned by the lectionary for Christmas Eve is that it reminds us that this night stands as the threshold between Advent and Christmastide. As more and more congregations adopt the practice of only Christmas Eve services rather than both Eve and Christmas Day services (Christmas morning being considered first and foremost "family time"), the Christmas Eve service is having all the liturgical functions of Christmas Day foisted upon it. Whatever one's feelings about that development, it is good to be reminded that Christmas Eve is also about the final preparations to make ourselves ready for Christ's advent.

Those preparations are in this passage understood primarily in terms of repentance. Even as we recognize that "the grace of God has appeared, bringing salvation to all" (v. 11), the lesson we are to draw from that grace is that we need to "renounce impiety and worldly passions, and ... to live lives that are self-controlled, upright and godly, while we wait for the blessed hope and manifestation of the glory of our great God and Savior, Jesus Christ" (vv. 12-13). The stance taken in this text is one that simultaneously looks back to Christ's first advent ("grace ... has appeared") and forward to his second advent ("while we wait"). It is thus the perfect stance for the threshold that is Christmas Eve in the life of the church.

But the end purpose of our repentance and redemption is not merely personal piety or even salvation understood as escape from God's eternal judgment. Christ has redeemed and purified us so that we might become "a people of his own who are zealous for good deeds" (v. 14). Christmas is not supposed to be just a time to recognize and celebrate God's gift to us. That gift is always to be a challenge to act in such ways as to extend God's grace to others. Even as we are busy driving back the physical darkness with all our decorations, we need to be busy driving back the spiritual, emotional, and social darkness from the lives of others. Doing so requires eager actions to accomplish good things and not simply season's greetings for best wishes.

Luke 2:1-20

The difficulties with correlating the various historical allusions in this gospel lesson with the records of Greco-Roman history and the account in Matthew are by now well-known. Quirinius became "governor" (legate) of the Roman province of Syria about a decade after Herod the Great's death, and there is no evidence that the Romans ever required people to return to their ancestral homes to be registered in a census (then as now, the point of a census was to determine current population patterns for taxation and other purposes). Matthew 2 has Mary and Joseph living in Bethlehem at the time of Jesus' birth with special circumstances leading to his being raised in Nazareth, whereas in Luke 2 Mary and Joseph's relations to Bethlehem and Nazareth are reversed. Here in Luke, shepherds visit Jesus on the night of his birth in response to an angelic visitation; Matthew recounts a visit by Magi approximately two years later (see Matthew 2:16) in response to an astral event.

For those interested in delving into the details and some of the suggestions for sorting out this tangle, almost any recent critical commentary will suffice. The Christmas Eve service, however, is probably not the occasion for exploring these matters. It is best to do that in Christian education settings, or if you must treat them homiletically, to do so when the Matthean texts are appointed for the First Sunday after Christmas in Year A or at Epiphany. Without suggesting that these problems do not exist (remember, they are well-known even to people without seminary training), simply stay with the details of the Lukan text. Don't homiletically re-create the crèche in your sermon. The preacher's task is to preach the gospel lesson, not some hybrid story that exists only in our minds.

Most of the historical problems in this lesson arise in verses 1-7. What is most important homiletically in this passage, however, is really not affected by any of those difficulties. Luke has set up a marked contrast between where the focus of attention lies in the world and where it should properly lie. Caesar Augustus decides he wants some information, and "all the world" is set in motion to respond to his whim. The Savior of the world is born to two Galilean peasants, and "there was no place for them in the inn." In the juxtaposition of that use of imperial power and the inability to recognize God's presence with and for the powerless (see Luke 1:46-55), there is a vivid description of the darkness that has blinded the world.

But God pierces the darkness with the blinding light of the glory of the Lord (v. 9). The angel announces to shepherds that a new shepherd-king like David has been born. This child will be the "Savior" (one of a number of titles that Gaius Octavius had appropriated for himself along with Augustus ["revered"] and Pontifex Maximus [the bridge between the material and spiritual worlds]) whose coming is "good news of great joy for all people," not a threat. They have to be told precisely where they will find the child because he is in fact in the last place that anyone would look for newborn royalty ("lying in a manger"). The angel is then joined by a multitude of angels who proclaim to the physical world what only the spiritual realm can yet recognize: God is to be praised because the Lord has favored the world with peace.

While it is still night ("Let us go now," v. 15b), the shepherds go to seek out the child and his parents and discover them in precisely the circumstances that the angel announced. That fact is not coincidental. If the angel's message has been demonstrated true in the details that could easily be confirmed, then all of the message is to be accepted — even those parts that still seem to verge on the outlandish. The message was trustworthy beyond all reasonable expectation in announcing where the child would be found, and so the message is trustworthy in announcing what the child will ultimately accomplish. And so those of the physical world who have seen the light shining in the darkness join in the praises with the spiritual realm (v. 20).

Application

For many who gather for worship on Christmas Eve, Christmas is a time of joyous light both literally and figuratively. They have the material resources to join in our cultural "Season of Light" by decorating their homes if they wish, sharing in the parties, traveling to be with family members, exchanging gifts — all the things we do to brighten our lives in the midst of the onset of winter. The fact that they make the commitment to attend church in this prime "family time" shows that they understand as well that a spiritual light has shined into their lives. They have seen the light of the glory of the Lord and have felt the warmth of God's grace and peace.

All of that is as it should be. Those who have been blessed by God should recognize and rejoice in that blessing and share its benefits with others. To paraphrase the first question and response of the Westminster Catechism, the highest purpose of human life is to glorify God and to enjoy God forever. But truly understanding and appreciating the light that God has shined on our lives requires that we never forget as we bask in its warmth that "the people who walked in darkness have seen a great light" (Isaiah 9:2a), that "the light shines in the darkness" (John 1:5).

We remember and celebrate Christ's birth in the midst of one of the longest nights of the year. We drive back the darkness with candlelight services and every manner of lighting we can devise. But it is still in the night that we cause all this light to shine. Like the Christmas house lights that are hard to see in the full sun of day but illuminate our yards in the blackness of night, we only can see the light because we see it shining in the night.

In the same way, we need to see the figurative and spiritual night that still shrouds the world. There are still oppressive political and social structures that oppress people. There are still people shrouded in the darkness of depression rather than bathed in the light of joy. There are still people whose lives are more characterized by what they genuinely need — not just what they lack — than by what they have. As the letter to

Titus challenges us, we have received the blessings of God to make us "zealous for good deeds." Just as we use our resources to drive back the darkness of the longest nights, so we need to use our spiritual and material resources drive back the darkness of these nights as well. Then Christmas Eve will truly be a night of light.

An Alternative Application
Luke 2:14. The praise of the angelic multitude is only one of several poems in the Lukan infancy narrative that have been construed liturgically as songs. There are as well Mary's Magnificat (1:46-55), Zechariah's Benedictus (1:68-79), and Simeon's Nunc Dimittis (2:29-32). Taking the Gloria, then, as a point of departure, one might construct a sermon on the "songs of the season" comparing and contrasting these songs from the gospels not only with the themes of secular Christmas carols but even with the carols of the church. What are the different Christmases that are reflected in the lyrics of these songs?

Still surprised after Christmas

The Christmas story is so familiar to us and to our people that we may no longer see it clearly. Specifically, I wonder if we can fathom how full of surprises was that event — and the days preceding it — for Joseph and Mary.

Between the two Christmas accounts (both Matthew and Luke offer versions of the story), we see both Joseph and Mary having angelic visitations and communications. Likewise, the shepherds outside of Bethlehem and Zechariah in the temple were visited by angels. Assuming such appearances were an uncommon thing, the story and the period are full of surprises.

Of course, for Mary and Joseph the surprise of angelic visitors is quickly eclipsed by the shock of the news that the angels brought: Mary is pregnant. She immediately knew that this was not humanly possible, and so was duly surprised. Joseph's surprise was apparently experienced first at the more predictable human level before he was introduced to the higher surprise of Mary's condition.

In keeping with the theme of things unexpected, I assume that stable accommodations for them and for Jesus' birth were unhappy surprises to Joseph and Mary. And while every new mother expects to have visitors — eager to congratulate, anxious to hold the baby — they are usually family and friends, but Mary and Joseph found themselves visited by complete strangers. First came the shepherds with their fantastic tale, and then, later, the Wise Men came — exotic guests from a faraway land following a cosmic sign. Mary and Joseph must have been constantly marveling at events as they unfolded.

And then, even after Christmas, the surprises just kept coming.

Isaiah 61:10—62:3

Perhaps the chief characteristic of Hebrew poetry is its parallelism. A single thought is expressed two or three times in slightly different forms — a rhyming of ideas rather than a rhyming of sounds, as has sometimes been observed.

Sometimes the parallelism is a purely literary technique: the idea is not necessarily advanced or nuanced by the repetition, just reinforced. More often, however, the repetition adds another layer of imagery and insight, while still expressing basically the same idea. For example, in the case of the first verse from Isaiah 62, "For Zion's sake I will not keep silent" and "for Jerusalem's sake I will not rest" are two phrases that say essentially the same thing. Nevertheless, not keeping silent and not resting are two different images, and the combination of the two strengthens the point that God is making.

Meanwhile, within the context of that parallelism, an idea that is expressed only once — not repeated, just stated — has a kind of emphatic quality. It stands in contrast to the pattern, and thus it stands out.

In our selected lection, two statements are given that kind of emphasis.

In the verses from the end of chapter 61, the rhyme pattern, such as it is, goes A-A, B-B, C-C, D-D, E. The "E" line is the one idea that is expressed without repetition: "The Lord will cause righteousness and praise to spring up before all nations."

Likewise, in the first two verses of chapter 62, we are presented with a A-A, B-B, C-C, D, E-E scheme. In this case, the "D" line is the idea that is expressed without repetition, and therefore is emphatic: "And you shall be called by a new name that the mouth of the Lord will give."

Names are an immensely important business in scripture. The Old Testament emphasis on the name of the Lord (see Genesis 4:26b; Exodus 3:13-15, 20:7; 1 Kings 8:14-29; Psalm 113:3; Proverbs 18:10) and the New Testament emphasis on the name of Jesus (see Matthew 18:20; John 16:23-26; Philippians 2:9-11) illustrate the profound importance of God's name. Earthly names, likewise, are vested with power and significance.

Throughout the pages of the Old Testament, we see God's people giving meaningful names to places — names, so often, that identify places as intersections with God (such as Beersheba, Bethel, Gilgal, Peniel). Likewise, we watch Eve, Rachel, Leah, and others name their children with great meaning, even at times with a sense of testimony. In Jacob's two efforts to get blessings (Genesis 27:18-36; 32:22-29), we witness something of the significance of names.

It is against that larger backdrop, then, that we see the importance of being given a new name. The promise of a new name that appears here in Isaiah is echoed in Revelation (2:17), and it is revealed on a kind of case-by-case basis as we see the Lord giving new names to Abram (Genesis 17:5), Jacob (Genesis 32:28), and Simon (John 1:42).

The scripture theme and personal appeal of a new name manifested itself for many generations in the giving of a new name at baptism. The so-called "Christian name" symbolically affirmed the spiritual truth of becoming a new person in Christ. In the case of our selected passage, Isaiah does not reveal what the promised new name will be. We intuitively recognize, however, the beauty of a new identity that comes from God, the consequence of an intersection with him, and ever after a testimony about him.

Galatians 4:4-7

A group of folks in my church are endeavoring to read through the Bible in a year, and we are meeting together monthly to discuss what we've been reading. Recently, I took the opportunity of our monthly meeting to provide for the group an overview of the inter-testamental period. As we put together the puzzle pieces of the Diaspora, the Hellenism that followed in Alexander's wake, the translation of the Septuagint, the network of roads in the Roman Empire, and the larger context of the *pax Romana*, we were impressed anew by "the fullness of time."

Presumably, God could have sent his Son at any point during human history. He is sovereign, and he didn't need much, if any, cooperation from us in order to enact his plan. In his famous retort in *Jesus Christ Superstar*, Judas questions the Lord's timing, asking why Jesus came in such a "backward time" when there was no mass communication. Yet the timing of God is impeccable — far beyond the comprehension of Judas' manifest misunderstanding.

Moffatt takes a somewhat different view of the timing issue. "But when time had fully expired," he writes, "God sent forth his Son." Reminiscent of judgment and eschatological passages, Moffatt sees the matter not so much as the time being right but rather as the time being up.

The expressed purpose of God's carefully timed action was to "redeem those who were under the law, so that we might receive adoption as children." If we were to separate the two phrases in this sentence and ask Paul's original audience to whom each referred, we might get two different answers. "Those who were under the law," of course, is clearly a reference to the Jews. Those that "might receive adoption as children," however, might have been construed as a reference to the Gentiles. After all, they are the ones who need to be adopted, right? Not the chosen people. Not the children of Abraham.

The whole impetus for the letter to the Galatians, you recall, was to answer the influence of the Judaizers in the midst of the Galatian churches. While Paul's opponents were urging dependence on and conformity to the law among the Gentile Christians, Paul contended that even those who had had the law needed a new relationship with God.

The great signature phrase from this passage, of course, is Paul's expression, "Abba! Father!" Paul uses the same expression in a similar context when writing to the Romans (8:15). Meanwhile, the only other New Testament occurrence is in Mark's account of Jesus praying in Gethsemane (14:36).

Barclay notes that "the proof that we are sons comes from the instinctive cry of the heart." The reflex is quite a different matter from the deliberate act. The latter may be a calculation; the former is what comes naturally. And this is the great evidence of our adoption: that it becomes our reflex to cry, "Abba! Father!"

Finally, sports fans are fond of borrowing one fairy tale character and applying her name and reputation to certain teams: Cinderella. A "Cinderella team" or a "Cinderella season" refers to the phenomenon of an improbable rise. Here was a team that no one took seriously, a team that was nobody's preseason pick to make the playoffs, and here they are in the championship game. In the most dramatic cases, it's a story of "from worst to first."

That is something of the drama suggested by Paul's imagery at the conclusion of this passage. Paul suggests a movement along a spectrum: from slave to child, and from child to heir. The jump from slave to child is enormous. Both persons can be said to "belong" to the one who is the head of the household, but see how different those experiences of belonging are.

A slave belongs to a master. He belongs in the same way as a field, a house, or a cow. He is a commodity. He has a price — a limited, identifiable value. As he ages, he is a depreciating asset. And, to some extent, he is expendable.

A child, by contrast, belongs to a parent. And the child's experience of belonging is not that of a possession but that of a member. He is priceless — of inestimable value — and he is nurtured and protected by the one to whom he belongs.

In the end, therefore, Paul manages to juxtapose two potent images: "slave" and "heir." From slave to heir is the quintessential "worst to first" story. To go from slave to heir is to change from the one who is property to the one who inherits property, from one who is a belonging to one who belongs.

Luke 2:22-40

Each of the four gospel writers has his own characteristic style, themes, and emphases, and this passage from Luke's gospel is characteristic of its author.

First, it is commonly observed that Luke pays more attention to female characters in the telling of his story than the other gospel writers do, and we see that tendency demonstrated here. Of the four adult characters who cross the stage during this scene, two are women. Joseph is never mentioned by name, while Mary is. While Simeon evidently blessed both of them, he went on to speak a special word addressed personally to Mary. Furthermore, while Luke's identification of a woman, Anna, as a prophet is not unique, it is uncommon. Yet it fits with his egalitarian understanding of the church and of the Spirit's work (as evidenced by his record of the early church in the book of Acts).

Second, Luke is particularly attentive to the theme of the Holy Spirit. His companion volume has sometimes been nicknamed "the Acts of the Holy Spirit" because of that unmistakable emphasis within that book. And, even within the gospel, Luke is mindful of the Spirit's work. The most notable indication of that thematic emphasis in Luke's gospel can be found in a comparison of Matthew 7:11 and Luke 11:13. In our selected lection, the Spirit is explicitly referenced three times, each in connection with Simeon.

Simeon's famous exclamation — "my eyes have seen your salvation" — is remarkable in its context. Standing on this side of Jesus' ministry, death, and resurrection, it is rather easy for us to behold Mary's baby and recognize him as God's salvation. But for Simeon to see this anonymous couple of nobodies and recognize that their infant was God's salvation — this is an astonishing identification. How does one look through the nursery glass at the hospital and point out, from among the collection of almost indistinguishable infants, which one is destined for greatness? How does one perceive, in a crowd, which parents are carrying a special child?

Luke wrote that Simeon was "guided by the Spirit," and so it must have been. For it is always and only God that enables us to recognize God. So it was for Peter in his recognition of Jesus (see Matthew 16:16-17), for all who come to Christ (John 6:44-45), for all who come to know the Father (Matthew 11:27), and as Paul wrote in our New Testament lection for all who come to know God as Father (Galatians 4:6).

Simeon's identification of Mary's baby with God's salvation is reminiscent of Jesus' words to grieving Martha outside Lazarus' tomb. She affirms a belief in a resurrection that is an event — "on the last day" (John 11:24). Jesus' response, however, suggests that the resurrection is not found in an event or a point in time, but in a person — "I am the resurrection and the life" (11:25). Likewise, Simeon recognized that God's salvation was not found in an event, an action, or a point in time; rather, God's salvation was embodied and found in a person — in a little baby, no less.

At first, one senses in this scene and in Simeon a profound joy. He is the embodiment of the Israel that awaits the long-awaited Messiah, and indeed "the whole creation (that) has been groaning" (Romans 8:22). Now the promise is fulfilled. Now Simeon may depart in peace. But then, into that joy and peace, Simeon inserts an unsettling word: "A sword will pierce your own soul, too." Who says that to a new mother? Yet such is the pervasive, intrusive shadow of the cross. On the heels of Peter's grand recognition comes the first foretelling of the cross (see Mark 8:27-33). Only days after the beauty and celebration of Palm Sunday comes the pain and blood of Good Friday.

Meanwhile, we do not have an account of Anna's words recorded, but her appearance seems to echo much of what we had seen in Simeon. As a prophet, we presume that it is the Spirit working in her that enables her to know something about this child. She, too, seems to perceive that God's work is embodied in a baby. And then she goes a step further than we see Simeon go: "speak(ing) about the child to all who were looking for the redemption of Jerusalem." While it seems that Simeon spoke solely to God, Joseph, and Mary, Anna spoke to other people about Jesus. And so it is that Luke, who records for us the spread of the gospel in the book of Acts, shows us in the shepherds (2:17-18), and here in Anna, the very first evangelists.

Application

A person jaded by experience within a given relationship might say disparagingly, "Nothing you do surprises me anymore." A human being, perhaps for his own sanity, seems to build up a certain resistance to surprises. After we have been repeatedly surprised, shocked, stunned, or disappointed in a given situation, we become somewhat impervious to the surprises, for we come, in some sense, to expect them.

After all the astonishing things that Joseph and Mary had experienced in Bethlehem and the months leading up to it, you might think that a kind of immunity would have developed. After all they had been through, nothing could surprise them anymore, right?

But there in the temple, fresh off of their out-of-the-blue encounters with the shepherds and the Magi, Joseph and Mary are met by Simeon and by Anna — two more strangers with unusual interest in their child. And, as they listen to Simeon speak about their baby, "the child's father and mother were amazed at what was being said about him."

Still they are surprised. Even after all they had seen, heard, and experienced during recent months, they seem still to be surprised by the things Simeon was saying.

But then that comes with the territory, doesn't it? We keep being surprised by God. The disciples were continually surprised by what Jesus said and did. Even though he had explained in advance three times what would happen in Jerusalem, still they were surprised by both his death and his resurrection. Beyond Jesus' earthly ministry and into the book of Acts: the Pentecost crowd was surprised to hear the message being preached in their own tongues; the assembled believers were surprised by Peter's miraculous release from prison; and the apostles themselves seemed to be surprised by the Holy Spirit coming upon Gentiles.

Christmas was a time full of surprises: the incarnation, virgin birth, star, and angels. But the surprises keep coming long after Christmas. If we have known his power and his goodness, we might say that nothing he does would surprise us. Yet, we leave the manger and are filled with wonder and awe day after day, year after year, as we keep being surprised by our marvelous God.

An Alternative Application

Luke 2:22-40. "Patron Saint of Hope." Luke reports that "it had been revealed to (Simeon) that he would not see death until he had seen the Lord's Messiah." What we don't know, however, is how long Simeon had waited between the time when that guarantee was revealed to him, on the one hand, and the day he encountered Mary and her baby in the temple, on the other hand.

We know that there was considerable time between God's first promise of an offspring to Abraham and the birth of Isaac. We know, too, that there were centuries between God's promise that Abraham's descendants would receive the land (Canaan) and the days of Joshua when they finally conquered and settled it. And we know there were 700 years between Isaiah's promise of a sign to Ahaz — "The young woman is with child and shall bear a son, and shall name him Immanuel" — and Mary giving birth to Jesus.

It may be, therefore, that Simeon had waited for many years between his special assurance and the day he held and beheld the baby Jesus.

Some number of people in our congregations may feel that they have been waiting for God for a long time. Waiting for a promise to be fulfilled. Waiting for a prayer to be answered. Waiting to behold some part of his salvation. And the turning of another calendar page may be, somewhere inside, a grim reminder for them of the passage of time.

For the sake of people who are waiting on this first day of a new year, I would try to help them climb into Simeon's shoes. Help them experience his patient hope as they wait for the good thing that they know God has in store and help them refresh their own hope, recognizing that the next year may be when their eyes finally see and their hands finally hold the answer to their prayers.

What time is it?

One of my favorite bands is Chicago. They have a song that asks, "Does anyone really know what time it is? Does anybody really care?" I think the writer of Ecclesiastes would have liked this song, for it expresses a realistic view of the fleeting nature of time. That song and this well-known poem from Ecclesiastes would have us take some time this new year to think about time, to ask, "What time is it, really?"

Perhaps it is time to think back to our birth, to give thanks for the gift of life.

That might lead us to think ahead to the time of our death and that life will one day end (Ecclesiastes 3:2).

Perhaps it is time to plant some new thing, to go after some dream we have always had, to take a risk.

That might lead us to harvesting and enjoying things already long planted (Ecclesiastes 3:3).

Perhaps it is time to do in that thing that is taking the life out of us. To kill it. That old habit. That attitude that brings more death than life.

That might well lead us to taking time to open ourselves to healing, to the love and the forgiveness someone is offering us — even God (Ecclesiastes 3:4).

Perhaps it's time to sit down for a good cry, to look around us at the pain and hurt in this world and let our hearts be touched and broken, our eyes overflow with tears.

That might well lead us to taking time to laugh, to giggle, to see all the funny, wondrous, blessed things that are also in our world, God's world (Ecclesiastes 3:5).

Perhaps it is time to seek some solitude, some alone time to recollect ourselves, to seek that quiet place where all that would divide and scatter us must flee in the presence of a holy peace and calm.

That might lead us back to those places and people who most need our embrace, our hugs, our hands to hold, our voices to cheer, our hearts to love (Ecclesiastes 3:6).

Perhaps it is time to seek that thing we have long desired, that peace of mind, that love, that forgiveness, that new insight, that new job, that closer walk to the One who created us.

That might lead to taking time to look through the cluttered closets of our minds and lives, to take out and discard all the junk that has accumulated there, taking up space, tripping us, keeping us from having something far better in its place (Ecclesiastes 3:6).

Perhaps it is time to find that silence is truly golden and to not feel that we must always be heard or always have the last word.

That might well lead us to taking time to listen not just with our ears but with our hearts (Ecclesiastes 3:7).

Yes, perhaps it is also time to go to war. To get into our battle gear. To oppose and even hate all that which would harm, maim, and destroy, beginning inside our own selves.

And that might well lead us to a time peace within and without (Ecclesiastes 3:8).

Ecclesiastes 3:1-13

It may seem a little strange, at first, that this is a reading for New Year's. I mean, it, along with Psalm 23, is probably read more often than most Bible passages during a funeral service! Note also that another well-used funeral passage is also one of the readings today — from Revelation 21. If we are not careful, this service to begin the New Year could become quite gloomy!

To be sure, the whole book of Ecclesiastes isn't exactly the most optimistic of books. Just look at how many times the writer says, "Vanity. All is vanity." It's about 38 times!

Maybe the writer was having a bad day or a bad life for that matter. Is he just being pessimistic or realistic?

One could understand the reason for the pessimism. Most scholars believe this book was written sometime after the terrible exile to Babylon and during the great turmoil of oppression from those who succeeded Alexander the Great (around 250 BC). There wasn't much to be optimistic about after such events.

We do not know much about the writer. Although it has been traditionally attributed to King Solomon, most scholars are doubtful he penned it since much of it fits much better the syntax and style that developed later. In Hebrew his name is "Qoheleth," but that comes over in Greek as "Ecclesiastes." That literally means, "Book of the Teacher" (or "Preacher"). Ecclesiastes is counted among the "wisdom literature" of the Bible. In other words, it has words of wisdom for us. But it might be difficult to find them in a book that at first and even second reading seems so very dreary and world weary.

However, there is wisdom and even encouragement here if we look for it.

First, perhaps part of the wisdom the preacher is trying to convey is a realistic view of life. He refuses to go through life wearing rose-colored glasses. Life does not consist of a bed of roses without any thorns. Anyone who thinks otherwise is in for a rude surprise.

Second, the writer argues, or so it seems, for a balanced view of life. Sometimes it seems the glass is at least half empty — because it is (if it has even that much water in it). Other times it will seemingly be overflowing. Wisdom is realizing that there is an ebb and flow to life and that sometimes you will be up, sometimes down. Sometimes you walk through a dark valley. Other times you find yourself before a burning bush on a holy mountaintop. The great constant in life is change! It's like that hit song the Byrds sang in the 1960s based on this passage: "Turn, Turn, Turn." Life is always turning. The clock always ticking. The river flowing, changing. Seasons coming and going. It's like a friend of mine once said where he lived, "If you don't like the weather, wait a few minutes." Life is like that. Understanding and accepting this is wise.

Third, with a realistic and balanced view of life, the best you can hope for is to enjoy the life you have, to work, to live, to take whatever each moment brings to find happiness and enjoyment. That, to the writer, is about the best you can hope for in this life. "Look for the joy," he seems to be saying, "in the simple ebb and flow each day of life — in your work, in even the everyday things like eating and drinking. Take pleasure in the present. That is a gift from God."

Revelation 21:1-6a

John sees a new heaven and new earth. He is not the first to do so. In fact, as you will notice when you read this book, John draws heavily upon many teachings and passages from the Old Testament. Here this image of the new heaven and earth comes from Isaiah (65:17; 66:22).

These new heavens and earth replace the old ones that have vanished. This is something that John has hinted at earlier in the book (for example, see 2:17; 3:12; 5:9; 14:3). He also draws heavily from other books like Enoch and Esdras, which talk often about a new heavens and earth. It's interesting that the "sea was no more." The sea is often seen in the Bible as a enemy or a metaphor for chaos, destruction. It was the place out of which the beast had arisen (see 13:1; 12:12; Mark 5:13). Not being a sea going people, the Jews saw the seas as more threat than blessing. Besides, it was salty and of no use for drinking. Perhaps more than one of them, however, had experiences with the sea and did not live to tell it. But the meaning is that this threat or enemy is now one that can no longer threaten.

Next a new Jerusalem is seen coming down from heaven (this is also referred to in 11:2). This is the holy city, pure now as a bride is for the groom. It is perfect this time because it does come from God, from heaven. It is the ideal. The real Jerusalem never really matched this. Indeed, because of the Roman-Jewish Wars of AD 66-70, the temple had been destroyed. It was the dream of every Jew to see it restored. John sees this only coming as an act of God and from heaven. It is contrasted with the evil city, the great harlot (called "Babylon" but which is really a reference to Rome). Because it descends from heaven, it will be a source of blessings for all humanity. It is a city "from God." God is its creator and giver.

John hears a loud voice from heaven announcing or explaining what all this means — that God is now dwelling among humanity. The image of "tabernacle" is used here and refers, once again, to the Old Testament stories about how the tabernacle of God was carried with Moses and the people, that is, God was with them now wherever they went. Also, the image from that period of Israel's history is used to say that now they are "God's people" (Leviticus 26:11-12; Jeremiah 31:33; Ezekiel 37:27). The meaning is that now there is restored to God's people the greatest blessing of all — fellowship with God, intimacy with God. It is as if paradise is restored.

One result of this is the promise made in Revelation 7:17 is fulfilled — death is destroyed and therefore with it no more reason for tears, for grief. There will be no more pain (see Isaiah 35:10; 51:11; 65:19). The old world, the old life is truly replaced by a whole new one.

Now, for the first time, God personally speaks — the one "seated on the throne." What God says is that now all things are made new. This, too, is a dream rooted in the Old Testament (Isaiah 43:18-19). Paul sees it fulfilled already in Jesus (2 Corinthians 5:17). Not only is human life made new again but all creation. And God says, "It is done!" All of this and more is done, will be accomplished. God promises it. Just as surely as God said, "Let there be light" and let there be this and that of creation, so God's word carried the power to accomplish whatever God desires.

God desires a whole new beginning for humanity. God can do this as the "Alpha and Omega" that is really saying God is the source of all life and all things. Though God is transcendent and above all creation, God is still immanent, present, and concerned with all of creation as is evidenced in John's writing, "To the thirsty I will give water as a gift from the spring of the water of life." The promise is that God will meet all the physical and spiritual needs, even the gift of eternal life.

Matthew 25:31-46

This parable is about the judging of the nations. It is only found in Matthew. Maybe it is not even correct to call it a parable. The NEW Interpreter's Bible calls it an "apocalyptic drama." It does fit well the theme of Christ the King Sunday as Christ sits in judgment as king over all nations brought before him. His court is made up of angels. But is also uses the shepherd-like image of this king who takes tender care of the needy. If one thing is clear about Jesus, he was a champion of the poor, the needy, and the outcast. Among them he spent much of his time, for he said, "The sick are the ones who need the physician." This then becomes the criteria for judgment — how well have his followers followed that example of compassion for others.

The idea of judgment or separation has been present in the earlier parables, for example, the story of the wheat and weeds growing together. They are allowed to grow together until separated at harvest. Now, in this drama, that separation comes (yet it is still in the future), though a different image is used — the sheep (those who loved their neighbors) from the goats (those who may have professed to love God and neighbor but you couldn't tell it from how they lived).

As Jesus said earlier, "Not everyone who said, 'Lord, Lord,' will enter the kingdom of heaven but only those who do the will of God." What separates the sheep from the goats is those who have not separated piety from practice, faith from works, hearers of the word from doers of the word.

Perhaps the judgment is based on how people responded to the messenger who shared the gospel, that is, how they treated them and their message. These messengers were often poorly clothed, sick and hungry, and even imprisoned. So maybe this has to do with how one receives the gospel and its messengers (who are "the least of these" and "these bothers of mine" v. 40). So this is not just a general ethical lesson about how to treat everyone but how one treats the gospel and the servants of that gospel. For in them Christ himself is present.

One of the things that really stands out to me in this story is that no great thing is required of the sheep, that is, they are not asked to give great sums of money. They are judged based on the simple, little things like giving a glass of water, visiting someone in prison, giving a coat to a needy person. Sometimes we think that unless we can do something grand and great, we might as well not give anything at all. Jesus says that even cups of cool water given in his name to someone thirsty will not go without reward.

These things are not done or given out of calculation of gain or what they can get from it. To the contrary, those who Christ honors here did not even know they were doing these things. It was just instinctive, natural for them.

One of the kindest, most giving people I have ever known like this was my father-in-law. He was a quiet, unassuming man who had this instinctive goodness about him. He would have been embarrassed to be told so. He helped me and so many others never asking or expecting anything in return. He died a few years ago and I know the Good Shepherd welcomed him into that fold in heavenly places.

Application

Comings and Goings... From time to time I like to go to a restaurant and just sit. If available, I choose a booth with a large, wide table to spread out a book, newspaper, or notebook. I turn it into a mini office. I also try to choose a spot as far from the hustle and bustle as possible, an increasingly difficult endeavor.

One day I thought I had found such a place. True, there was an empty booth behind me but I dared hope for the best. Alas, it was not to be. For as I sat there that day many people came and went. No sooner did one leave than another and then another arrived. Much coming and going the whole time. Indeed, an endless stream of arrivals and departures.

I thought of earlier in the day when I made a visit to the hospital, only to arrive in the room and see a sheet over the person and bereaved family members arriving and each being told the sad news.

As I left the hospital that day I walked by the newborn unit, beholding a harvest of wiggling, wrinkled, sleeping, crying infants making their first appearance to the world.

Comings and goings…

That day in the restaurant I collected my materials, got up, and walked outside, only to look back through the window and see that my booth had been taken and done so without any knowledge that it had once been mine, if only for a little while...

Comings and goings…

I got in my truck. Yes, I drive an old green Ford Ranger that my daughter has named, "The Green Goblin," and even before I could back out, two cars were waiting in line to take my parking place.

Comings and goings…

I drove out to the airport to pick my daughter up arriving from college, embracing her with a longer hug than usual while all about us there was much coming and going, tearful good-byes and tearful greetings.

Comings and goings…
Arrivals and departures…
Waxings and wanings…
Ebbings and flowings…
Waves flow in and flee away…

Beginnings and endings…

Hellos and good-byes…

Springs and summers…

Winters and falls…

Rain that falls and then leaps again into the sky…

Sunsets and sunrises…

Days into nights into days…

Indeed, "for everything there is a season, and a time for every purpose under heaven."

Depressing, glum observations, you may think. Not the kind of thing you like to think about at the beginning of a New Year? Sounds like something that depressing writer of Ecclesiastes would say. But comings and goings fill our days. Do not despair or begrudge them, but embrace and cherish them. They make up the stuff of life. They fill our days with opportunities to know and be known, to love and be loved, to learn and unlearn, to discover and become lost in mystery, to receive and to give. And in so living I dare to believe and hope, indeed, I know that somewhere in all the comings and goings and in-between them, God is always coming, never going. God sees that we sat in that booth, that we walked, talked, loved, and lived. God sees all our comings and goings, whatever the season, whatever changes each moment brings. Sure, there is a Great Going some day for all of us, but it just leads to the Great Coming into God's presence for all eternity (see the Revelation 21 reading for today).

As the Psalmist sang, perhaps as a blessing to each person coming and going from the neighboring booth in his favorite restaurant: "The Lord will keep your going out and your coming in from this time on and for evermore" (Psalm 121:8). Amen.

An Alternative Application

Matthew 25:31-46. "Martin and the Visitors." Tolstoy's wonderful little story based on this passage has been told many times. The actual book is, *Where There Love Is, There Is God Also* (not a bad title for a sermon). A powerful sermon or meditation would be reading or telling that story. It can also be found as *Martin the Cobbler*. Sharing this story will be a powerful way to present the theme in this parable from Jesus. It might also be related to a new year in which we, too, look for ways each day to be the love of Christ to those around us. There are many opportunities to do that, if we just look and love.

Epiphany of Our Lord
Isaiah 60:1-6
Ephesians 3:1-12
Matthew 2:1-12
Bass Mitchell

What gifts can we bring?

I can never think of the story of the wise men without remembering something two little children said concerning it.

One was asked by his Sunday school teacher, "What gifts did the wise men bring the Christ Child?" He replied, "Uh, gold, frankinstein and mermaids."

Another little boy, "Gold, frankincense, and myrrh? I bet he really wanted a puppy."

What does the Christ Child really want from us? What gifts can we bring?

I think the gift we can give the Christ Child that he really wants is the gift of receiving.

You see, we get things a little backward at Christmas time. So much of our time and effort goes into us giving gifts and this is good. The older I get the more joy I get giving gifts rather than getting them. The heart of Christmas is not about us giving, but GOD giving, and us receiving. The gift Christ wants from each of us this new year is accepting him, receiving his love, his grace, his forgiveness into our hearts and lives... of reaching out with hands of faith to receive him as Savior and Lord.

What gifts can we bring to the Christ Child?

The wise men brought costly gifts —

Gold, the king of metals and metal of kings...

Frankincense, expensive incense used in worship

Myrrh, costly ointment used as perfume...

Let us offer him OUR gold this year... our tithes and offerings with which he has so richly blessed us, that the work of his kingdom might grow and prosper...

Let us offer him OUR frankincense this new year... our worship together each Sunday and each day of our lives...

Let us bring to him OUR myrrh... our own gifts and talents and abilities to be used in his service as sweet smelling perfume.

Isaiah 60:1-6

Many scholars today believe that much of the passages in Isaiah chapters 40-55 should be dated during the Babylonian exile period (roughly 587-538 BC). They likewise think that much of the materials in chapters 56-65 are dated after the exile (after 538 BC) when some of the people returned to Jerusalem, having been released by Cyrus, king of Persia who conquered the Babylonians. Of course, what they found was a city and temple in ruins. It must have seemed like a hopeless and overwhelming task, even though they were back home. In the readings for today, it's almost as if the prophet is echoing many of the promises made in chapters 40-55, for the themes here are very much the same — of God's deliverance, God's glory and light coming to them, enabling them to be a light to the nations. The message is pretty clear — the future was a bright one for Jerusalem because God was coming to dwell among them again. This re-sharing of the promises seeks to bolster a discouraged people with tremendous tasks before them. Those promises made years before had not all come true (especially see Isaiah chs. 56-59). They had waited for them but perhaps had grown weary of waiting. Maybe they still saw themselves, especially sitting back among the ruins of Jerusalem, as a people God had forsaken. The vision shared is so glorious and so hope-filled that it surely did serve to lift their spirits and give them the strength to continue.

Verses from this chapter lend weight to the dating of these passages to the time after 538 BC. For example, the temple seems to have been rebuilt but was poorly furnished (see Isaiah 60:7; 62:9). It appears that the walls of the city have not yet been built (see 60:10; 61:4). The people were back home. They were seeking to rebuild but they faced many obstacles outside and within. Could there really be a future for them? Was it possible for a people who had seemed like a valley of dry bones to come alive again? Dare they believe the promises of their prophets? Was God's glory to shine in the midst of them again?

Isaiah 60:1. "Arise." That's the first word. It is a command, an order. Who is to arise? Zion, Jerusalem, the people. They must "arise" because they have been laying down, discouraged. What do they see when they dare stand and look up? Light. The image is that of a sunrise over the hills around the city. They had been in a seemingly endless dark night of the soul. That night was over now. The sun was rising upon them. This very same image is used also in Isaiah (58:8,10; 59:9, 19).

Often light is used as an image for God in the Bible. It is the very first gift of creation — "Let there be light," God commands, and there was light. God appeared to the people in the midst of a cloud of fire (see Exodus 19:16ff; 24:16ff; Deuteronomy 5:22-27). God comes to them in brilliant, dazzling light (see Isaiah 6:1-30; Psalm 18:8ff; Habakkuk 3:1-17; Ezekiel 1:1-12). God speaks to Moses from a burning bush. The light of God's presence shone on the face of Moses, so much so that he had to wear a veil.

But there is still darkness. Where? Still perhaps in the hearts of the people. It has been a long period of darkness. Many have been discouraged of ever seeing the light again. But the image here seems to be from the standpoint of standing on a hill, maybe even Mount Zion itself, and seeing the first rays of the sunrise, but there are still places in the valleys and ravines that are dark — that have yet to feel the touch of the sun. So it was with the people. But the sun was rising! Soon all the darkness would have to give way to the light.

The darkness here is also primarily among the other nations of the world. A theme we see often is that the world is in darkness, that is, blinded to the truth about God. They do not know God. They walk in darkness. But not for long. Why? For Jerusalem, for the people who now bask again in the light and glory of God are to be so illuminated, so reflecting God's light that it will shine forth into all the world. So much so that the kings of other nations will be drawn to the light, to the knowledge, love, and service of the one, true God. (Note that this passage and others like it are often used around Epiphany — when the wise men from representing other nations come to adore and worship the light of the world in Christ. Indeed, later tradition pictures them as kings, kings coming to the light!)

Ephesians 3:1-12

This passage comes straight from the very heart, the soul of Paul. He reminds the Ephesians, mostly Gentile Christians, about his calling — to be a missionary to them! Because he did this, he was now under arrest (most likely in Rome). Paul does not feel bitter. His calling, as are all things, was by "God's grace" (v. 2). I think we have to look at all Paul writes from that standpoint — grace — and his own experience of it. It was so radically different than how he was reared, than what he had always thought and believed. But on the road to Damascus and afterward, he came to know something far more wondrous — the loving, accepting grace of God in Christ given freely, not because of our merits or works or goodness, but in spite of our lack of any of them. Once he had felt so worthy, so righteous because of his own works of obedience. Now he feels the opposite — see verse 8. He knows he was not worthy and still isn't. He's the least among the apostles. But God's grace took him, accepted him, empowered him for the greatest work of all — sharing the good news.

Now this good news he talks about here as being a "mystery" for a long time. It had been a mystery to him surely. God had revealed it to him. For so long he had lived and believed passionately that God was the God only of his own people. They were the chosen ones. Everyone else was outside the covenant and the promises, lost with no hope. But Paul, through his calling and experience, came to realize that this was not who God was at all or what God was about. In Christ, God was reaching out to the whole world, even the Gentiles, to let them know they were loved, they were included in God's family as well. They are "fellow heirs, members of the same body, and sharers in the promise in Christ Jesus through the gospel" (v. 6). This had been the plan of God all along (vv. 9, 11). But it took him so long to see it.

Are we any different? We still deal with a spirit of exclusivity, of wanting to build walls, of drawing up lists of who's in and who's out.

But you see none of that in the gospel. God's love is unconditional. It's all about grace. "Just As I Am," the old hymn says. God accepts us just as we are. Of course, that grace then changes us, transforms us. We do not stay as we are when grace fills our lives. Just look at the life of Paul after his experience of and growing in the grace of God. But our changing first is not a prerequisite for God's grace. God's grace accepts us though we are not worthy and never can be.

Matthew 2:1-12

One could spend a lifetime studying this passage. There's just so much in it that leads to so many other things. But let's hit some of the highlights.

First, there's Herod, called "Herod the Great." He ruled from 40 to 4 BC. He ruled at the will of Rome. A half Jew, he was mostly hated by the Jews. He did bring some good things — the rebuilding of the Temple (finished in 20 BC) and was one to make help available during times of famine. But mostly he was a power-mad ruler, suspicious of everyone. He had a number of his own relatives killed as he feared they were plotting against him. Herod was an evil, paranoid man. When it says here that all Jerusalem was troubled with him as he heard this tale of a new born king, we understand the reason for the fear — it would most likely mean pain and suffering for someone, maybe everyone.

Second, this tells us a great deal about the date of Jesus' birth. If Herod died in the spring of 4 BC, then we know Jesus must have been born before that. Most scholars say sometime between 7 to 4 BC.

Third, the wise men here in Greek are called *magoi* or Magi. They are said to be from the "East," mostly likely meaning Persia (modern-day Iran). They were learned men, men who studied the stars and thought that from there they could learn about events on earth. They were often advisors to kings, so it was not unusual that they would go to see King Herod upon arriving in Jerusalem. They were, to say it a little differently, seekers, seekers after truth. They were also Gentiles. Later tradition gave them names, even said they were kings and rode camels (of course, none of this is in the biblical account).

Fourth, they see a star, presumably identifying it with some significant event in Palestine. That event they come to believe is the birth of a great king. Many people have tried to determine just exactly what this was that they saw. Some suggest it was Halley's Comet (visible in 11 BC) or more likely the conjunction of three planets — Jupiter, Venus, and Saturn — in 7 BC. Or some other celestial event about which we know nothing.

The important thing is not to get lost in such details or sidetracked by them so that we miss the message here. What is that message?

This story is yet one more bit of proof, given by the gospel writer, that Jesus is indeed the royal Messiah they had been longing for. Even at his birth the learned Magi knew this and thus came to worship and adore him. This is the kind of response the gospel writer wanted from his readers then and now.

This is also a story that goes so well with the epistle reading for today — Paul talking about the inclusion of the Gentiles in God's family. This passage tells the "Epiphany," that is, the appearance of bringing the light of God to Gentiles! These Magi were not Jews. The point? Even as a child the good news was shared with Gentiles. These were but the first of many more who would come to worship and adore the Christ, for they found in him God's own presence and love. Wise people still do this.

Application

Arise, shine! Isaiah 60:1-6. It was the longest night of my life. I was but a boy. We lived on the banks of the Neuse River in North Carolina. A storm was coming. Little did we know that it was much more than any mere storm — it was a hurricane. It came upon our little town, wind toppling trees, lightning like I have seldom seen, thunder that makes you shake, and when there it was not lightning, everything was pitch black. Electricity had been one of the first casualties. Then we saw the river rising up over its bank, moving toward our house. It was going to flood us. We had time to evacuate to the city fire station. When we got there, it was already crowded. I still remember a kind man giving me a lukewarm cup of coffee. Then I noticed that my parents and some others were kneeling on the floor. At first I thought they were praying. But no, my little sister, about five years old at the time, had slipped on the wet floor and hit her head. She was rushed to the hospital where they discovered she had cracked her skull. For a time that long dark night and the next day we thought we were going to lose her.

Much of the rest of that experience has long sense faded from my memory. Just as well. But there is one other thing. The days that followed I recall going back home and seeing the sun rise over the river. Only a few clouds were left and the sun seemed to chase them away. Our house, like so many others, was damaged. Great damage was done to the town. Trees were down everywhere. Some houses looked like they had been bombed. How would we ever recover from that darkness, from that storm? But I remembered the sun rising. I felt its warmth on my face. It seemed to bring new life and hope to all of us. We did rebuild. It took us a long time, but we did it. To give thanks, we had a special service in our town for all the churches. We knew God had seen us through it and was with us.

How many times I have felt like I was in a similar situation. Maybe it was not a hurricane but some trial, some burden that was weighing heavily upon me, some darkness that wanted to crush me. But then the light came. The sun rose! I arose. I rebuilt. I felt God renewing me.

How often I have been with others through such darkness — a car accident, a death, a serious illness, troubles stacked on top of troubles. Then the light of God's presence and power somehow shone through it all and lives that seemed shattered, started to become whole again.

Many centuries ago the people of God found themselves devastated by a storm of exile and oppression. The storm ended. They went back home only to find it in ruins. But one stood among them and said, "Do not look on these ruins. Look higher! Look up! The sun is rising! That sun is the light of the glory of God, coming to lift you up, to renew you, to rebuild you into a people God can use. So, arise! Shine!"

An Alternative Application

Ephesians 3:1-12. "The Two Signs." One of the things I like to do to pass the time while driving is to read church signs. Here are some of my favorites:

"Try our Sundays. They are better than Baskin-Robbins."

"If you can't sleep, don't count sheep. Talk to the Shepherd."

"Can You Hear Me Now? — God"

I saw another couple of interesting ones this week, although they were not humorous, they did get me to thinking.

The first one was a large white sign planted down by the highway. I could not see the church itself as I suppose it was up the gravel road beside the sign, high up a steep hill. So all I or anyone else not familiar with the church could tell about it was on that sign. They had everything they believed on that sign in short, pithy, large dark words. No welcome, just the name of the church. No times of the services listed, just what they felt they wanted us passersby to know. Perhaps others might feel differently, but the sign did not give me a warm and fuzzy feeling. It didn't entice me at all to wish to come there, to climb up that steep hill. To the contrary, it made me wish to pass it by as quickly as possible.

46

Not too far down that road, I spied another church sign. It, too, was large and white. At the top of the sign was the name of the church and at the bottom was the time of the services. But between these in large, bold red letters was this: EVERYONE WELCOME HERE!

I got the feeling, you see, that the first sign was into raising walls.

The second was into extending bridges.

The first, excluding.

The second, including.

The first was written in the large dark letters of the law.

The second was composed in the bold, red letters of grace.

Baptism of Our Lord
Genesis 1:1-5
Acts 19:1-7
Mark 1:4-11

~~David Davis~~

Wayne Brouwer

Baptism's stage

Several years ago, I flew to Edmonton, Alberta, for a meeting. Someone was supposed to pick me up at the airport, so when I arrived, I tried to make myself obvious. I searched the waiting crowd for someone alone, someone who might be looking for me, someone who was as intent as I was about finding the right connection. One man seemed to fit the caricature of an informal chauffer, but as I approached him and our eyes locked, he turned away and left. When the crowds dissipated I was standing by myself, and no one seemed to want me.

After a while I called my contact number. Someone had indeed been sent for me, I was told. But since time was marching on, maybe it would be best for me to grab a cab. So I hailed a taxi and made my way to the meeting address, only to find there the man whom earlier I thought might have been sent for me. He was even more surprised to encounter me. "I looked at you," he said, "and I thought to myself, 'No, he doesn't look like a minister.'" So he left the airport without me in tow.

I'm not quite sure what a minister is supposed to look like. Nor am I certain why I don't look like one. And I can imagine, in the world that buzzed on while Jesus was being born, that few people had any idea what features an incarnate God might take on. How does deity reveal itself in our world? What accommodation must the transcendent use to become immanent? Is there a disguise that filters out enough glory to make the holy bearable, while at the same time suffusing sufficient radiance to tell an awe-inspiring tale? The scripture passages on this Epiphany Sunday are meant to help us think a bit about how God appears among us.

In some ways it seems like we have to gain another dimension of perception. Two-dimensional objects are flat and lifeless compared to the fullness of those things that add depth to height and width. Cartoons are transformed into creaturely beings when flat gives way to holographic expansion. Some filmmakers cash in on this phenomenon by creating 3-D movies that require special glasses to lift the characters off the screen and provide new dimensions of depth to viewers' perceptions. Many theme parks make the most of this in rides and features, which create an impression of interaction with fictional beings inhabiting weird and wonderful worlds, while actually remaining confined to safe entertainment havens. We are able to understand two-dimensional expressions, and, for most of our bigger experiences, three dimensions (even when created artificially by special glasses) are enough.

But not so when spirituality needs to secure transformed eyes. Three dimensions are insufficient to see God. Isaiah needed the heavens to rend in order to add a new dimension to heart vision. Paul stumbled with words that could not convey enough when pushing his friends to read between the lines. Similarly, the ancient astrologers who interpreted the physical phenomena of the heavens and then pursued the spiritual phenomena thus revealed, saw things that Herod, with his acute royal vision, was completely blind to. On this Epiphany Sunday they all urge us to sharpen our perspectives in order to truly see.

Isaiah 60:1-6

What some call "Third Isaiah" is comprised of chapters 56-66. Whether the book is from a single author or is a compilation over years (or even centuries), there are definite changes of tone at chapter 40 and again at chapter 56. The tirades of condemnation against both the surrounding nations and also the people of God found in chapters 1-39 are ended. Similarly missing are the introspective ruminations about the pathos and powerless victory of the suffering servant (chs. 42-53). In these eleven chapters the world is made new as Israel is gathered from the far reaches and God's glory is re-established in Zion. These chapters resonate with a global view of both God's realm and Israel's significance. God's design is not merely to restore the tiny nation of Israel (Isaiah never does seem to limit his focus only to Judah) to the spine of hill country that forms the backbone of Palestine. Nor is the God of Israel content with limited significance among the deities of the nations. In this final section of Isaiah's prophecy, Israel becomes the cornerstone of a worldwide hegemony in which righteousness flourishes and God is supreme ruler.

Here Isaiah sounds the royal trumpets that demand that the people stand. Gloom and darkness (remember Isaiah 9:1-2) were the result of spiritual alienation. Nations became blind in their quest for domination and in their search for utopia. Projecting into a future time when the failures of the past have been cleansed from the slate, Isaiah pictures the dawn of a new creation (see Isaiah 65:17). As God's Spirit brooded over the murky, dark, and chaotic waters at the beginning of time (Genesis 1:1) and then brought light and life, so now God is doing it again in the middle of human politics.

This time, Israel is already formed as a (restored) nation, so several steps in the Genesis process of organizing the nations can be skipped. In fact, it seems that the nations themselves are wandering in the fog of desperation, and the new light of recreation provides them with the ability to regain structure and purpose.

The recent trilogy of movies based upon J.R.R. Tolkien's *Lord of the Rings* novels seems to capture the sense of this passage well, especially in the second (*The Two Towers*) and third (*The Return of the King*) episodes. Evil as engulfing darkness and righteousness as life-giving light are powerfully painted across the screen. There are several scenes from the films that might well serve to illuminate this passage.

Interestingly, Israel becomes the center of the universe. All other nations begin to bring to her their richest treasures (v. 6). Richard Mouw, in his wonderful reflections on this final section of Isaiah, *When the Kings Come Marching In* (Eerdmans, 2002), offers helpful reflections on understanding this passage alongside the eschatological paintings of Revelation 21-22.

Ephesians 3:1-12

When Paul was in Rome around 60 AD, awaiting a hearing before Caesar for the charges pressed against him in Jerusalem (see Acts 21-22), he was given a modest amount of freedom (see Acts 28). His house arrest lasted for about two years, according to Luke. During this time, Paul received visitors and carried on correspondence with some of the churches and individuals who had become his special acquaintances during the three mission journeys outlined in Acts 13-20.

One of his visitors was a slave named Onesimus, whose acquaintance Paul had made during his three-year stay in Ephesus. Onesimus belonged to Philemon, a wealthy estate owner who had come to know Jesus and the salvation he brought through Paul's forays out from Ephesus. Philemon's estate was near Colossae, a short way up the Lycus River valley in Asia Minor.

For some reason, Onesimus ran away from Philemon's employ and wandered until eventually turning up in Rome. There, Paul and Onesimus were brought together, and Onesimus began to function as a personal attendant to Paul. Finally, however, Paul realized that he could not keep Onesimus with him and also carry on a meaningful relationship with Philemon. So Paul arranged for Tychicus to chaperone Onesimus on his way back to Philemon's estate. Paul wrote a short but powerful letter outlining these matters to Philemon, and also calling on his friend to establish a new relationship with Onesimus that now brought them into the family of Christ on equal footing, and required a rethinking of the master/slave dynamics.

Paul also wrote at least two other letters to be carried along the way by Tychicus. One went to the church in Colossae (nearby Philemon's estate) and addressed a particular cult of ritualistic Christianity that seemed to be troubling that congregation (see Colossians 2). The other letter appears to have been a more general epistle, built on some of the same framework as the letter to the Colossians and certainly containing many of the same themes and references (note the clear parallels between Colossians 3-4 and Ephesians 4-6), but intended more as a letter of broad encouragement. Earliest manuscripts do not have the designation "in Ephesus" in the greeting of chapter 1:1. Furthermore, Paul's letter to the Colossians contains a reference to another of his letters which was supposed to be in the hands of "the Laodiceans" (Colossians 4:16). Many scholars think that this could well be the letter now known as Ephesians, and that it ended up in Ephesus as part of its circulation among the churches of the Lycus River valley. The church in Ephesus, after all, seemed to become the prominent congregation among them, and could well have served as the storage depot for any important documents.

In any case, Paul gives, in these verses, a brief history of God's revelation (vv. 2-6) and also a brief recapitulation of how the latter stages of this revelation coincided with Paul's unique calling and appointment as an apostle (vv. 7-12). The chapter begins with a kind of literary "stutter." Verse 1 is interrupted by Paul's need to rehearse the divine revelatory sequence and his own part in it, and the theme of Paul's prayer is not picked up again until verse 14. The uniqueness of God's revelation moves from its former more hidden phase as emanating from Israel into its recent phase when it was concentrated in the person and work of Jesus. This recent expression of God's revelation provides the basis for a new age in which Gentiles share with Jews God's power and care. Furthermore, this revelation is in progress, unfolding through the mission journeyings of Paul, and beginning to effect the course of world politics. All nations will come under the sway of God's power, and this will be effected through the mysterious administration of the revelation of God through the church.

How does one preach this? A helpful analogy comes from the Second World War. In a particular German prisoner of war camp, the soldiers from various nations were kept somewhat isolated. A fence ran down the middle of the camp separating American POWs from those under British command. At noon each day, the ranking officers of each group could briefly meet at the fence, under guard, to exchange news and information. While their German captors understood English, the prisoners of rank were able to sneak in some secret communications by way of the Gaelic language, which each of them knew.

One day when the officers approached one another with the stiff formality required by their German overlords, the British general slipped in a Gaelic report that came by way of a smuggled crystal radio set. They had learned of the successful Allied invasion of Normandy, and the news that the war had turned tide against the Axis powers. Soon liberation would come; it was already in process and the outcome was guaranteed.

Without breaking a smile, the two men retreated back to their communities. But soon the mystified Germans heard a whoop and holler from the American POW barracks. For the next six months, the prisoners ate starvation rations, went about in tattered clothing, and seemed confined and limited by their German guards. But in their hearts they knew already that the world had been turned upside down, and the powers that claimed superiority would soon be wasted before the greater power that was being unleashed.

The report of heaven's great victory has arrived, according to Paul, through the revelatory communication of Jesus. In the church, often battered and beaten by the powers of this world, the message lives, and we know the sure and secure eternal purposes of God (v. 11) giving us the overwhelming freedom and confidence that come only to those who have this faith (v. 12).

Matthew 2:1-12

Matthew's gospel is designed to help Jewish Christians understand the continuity of the new covenant with that of the older one. Jesus is the family heir to the covenants with both Abraham and David (Matthew 1:1-17), he was miraculously born like many of the greatest Hebrew leaders (Matthew 1:18-20), and his coming was announced by divine messengers (Matthew 1:19-25). Throughout the gospel, Matthew takes pains to show the royal bearing and authority of Jesus (culminating, for instance, in the great kingly pronouncement of the Great Commission in ch. 28). He also shows how Jesus relives the life and history of Israel in order to fulfill and perfect what was left incomplete by Israel's near disastrous covenant-breaking.

Matthew is the only gospel writer to tell of the Magi and their conversations with Herod, which would precipitate the great crisis of the slaughter of the innocents. Matthew's purpose in selecting this material seems quite clear. Jesus is born into the royal family of David and therefore has a right to rule. His kingly stature is written by divine revelation in the heavens, and seen by those attuned to such informative displays, even from other nations. Within the boundaries of Palestine, however, those who are closest to the new revelation of God are blind to it.

The battle between Herod and Jesus mirrors that between the Pharaoh of Egypt and Moses in the first sections of Exodus. It is a kind of doppelganger reverse image, however, in that Herod ought be on God's side, while the Pharaoh was definitely God's enemy. In Exodus, the Pharaoh seeks to destroy the male babies of Egypt, including the divinely appointed deliverer. Here Herod sets himself to the same task and, like Pharaoh, accomplishes only the first, not the latter. Meanwhile, those who understand the divine revelations, even though they are from distant nations, begin to see in Jesus the coming universal rule of God. They bring their gifts to honor him in Bethlehem, and are willing even to obey divine direction that will thwart Herod's plans.

The revelation manifesting God on this Epiphany Sunday is sometimes seen best by those who are at a distance, and sometimes least accessible to those who live in the community of faith. When religion gets self-serving, the first focus of attack is God himself, for God has a way of distributing out carefully crafted spiritual power plays that set us at the center of our universes. Only when we pay careful attention to the revelation of God do we bow in wonder.

Application

Epiphany happens, in the Northern Hemisphere, during the shortest days of the year and the longest, coldest nights. There is a line in C.S. Lewis' first Narnia Chronicles book, *The Lion, the Witch and the Wardrobe*, that captures our fervent need for God's special revelation during these often bleak times. Mr. Beaver is musing with the children from the other world about what life has become in Narnia. It is "always winter," says Mr. Beaver, "but never Christmas."

So it is with the liturgical year of the church. Advent signals something about to happen. Christmas tells the warm story of the incarnation. But Epiphany reminds us that we live in an alien environment, and that this new manifestation of God's presence does not make life easier. Too long it has been winter in Narnia, but we have gotten used to it. Too long we have been content to hunker down "in the bleak midwinter," with no promise of spring, and certainly no holidays to party. But when God appears, things begin to change. Those who will not see this new revelation of God are dooming themselves to alienation and defeat. And those who begin to see in Christ a glimpse of God's world yet waiting to be born, also start to feel the agony of terrifying transformation that must take place both within our hearts and throughout the fabric of our godless society until the kingdom, the power, and the glory are once again recognized as ruling from heaven's throne.

Perhaps, through worship and preaching today, those who gather can obtain a new pair of glasses: glasses that reach behind, through, and around the ordinarily perceptible and enrich our vistas with glory and grace.

An Alternative Application

Isaiah 60:1-6. The Isaiah passage is marvelous in its image building. It might be well to review Richard Mouw's book and preach on the themes of eschatological transformation as they are both anticipated and already experienced.

Much could be made of the power of light over darkness, and the coming of sight to those who were blinded. Especially since we are very early in January, and many may have missed the grand opening of the New Year last week because of partying, today might be a good day to recite and rehearse some of the great "resolutions" of the Christian church. There are creeds and confessions that sizzle with significance, and they might be used effectively today to give the transitioning world's feel that Isaiah tries to portray. For some really great words that might be used as congregational confessions, see "Lord's Days 1, 9, and 10" of the *Heidelberg Catechism*.

Epiphany 2 / Ordinary Time 2
1 Samuel 3:1-10 (11-20)
1 Corinthians 6:12-20
John 1:43-51
Craig MacCreary

Getting on the right frequency

One of my proofs for the existence of God is that as a child I neither set the neighborhood ablaze nor did I manage to burn down our home. I don't believe that I had any more pyrotechnic propensities than other children. However, property within my vicinity was under constant threat of incineration by my constant experimentation with sunlight, optics, basic chemistry, and the electromagnetic properties of radios. There is a thin line between being a young Leonardo da Vinci and a juvenile delinquent of the first order. Only the larger hand of a God that was all merciful as well as almighty spared my fellow neighbors and me from serious harm.

Like many youth, I was not so much trying to blow up the world as to get into harmony with its deeper mysteries and rhythms. If I could penetrate the veil that seemed to separate me from the adult world of privileged power, which could only come from maintaining a monopoly over such secrets, it seemed well worth the risk. My particular specialty was the alchemy of trying to get FM and shortwave frequencies out of AM radios. It seemed to my child's mind a simple task of merely rearranging a few tubes. Many can recall that pre-transistor electrical innards emitted enough heat to smelt steel. Undeterred by singed fingers, I went at it with an aplomb that resulted in few meltdowns and considerable acrid smoke in the midst of minor pyrotechnics... but no major damage to life, limb, and property.

Such child's play became the theme of an adult life and a career in ministry. Trying to get on the right frequency with God, others, and the mood of the moment has proved no less arduous than my childhood play. Certainly there has been an equal amount of heat produced and not a few misses with catastrophe. Yet, there have been several moments when I felt something like well-modulated frequencies. From time to time in my life, I have known the joy of experiencing the crackling hardness of signals that took a great deal of time and distance to cover before they were decipherable.

The Second Sunday after the Epiphany presents us with three texts that signal God's presence in the world and challenge us to see if, by getting in tune with what God is doing, we can be on the right frequency. The Hebrew lesson tells the tale of the struggle of a young apprentice and an old priest to decipher the message and get on the same frequency together. In the Corinthian text, Paul struggles to hear God's message in a world that is on a different wavelength in regard to human sexuality and the meaning of embodiment. In the gospel lesson, Phillip and Nathaniel find that they are making serious adjustments in the range of self-understanding as they seek to fine tune their theological understanding of Jesus. Nathanial is drawn to Jesus precisely because of Jesus' high definition, full-color imaging of Nathaniel's whereabouts and activity.

It seems that nowadays we have a wider range of reception than ever before. Yet I wonder if we will be anymore successful in picking up on the message and meaning that God is trying to convey to us. Frankly, having been born in a pre-television era, I am still amazed by color television. I am no less astounded when now and then the background static of life is penetrated and we find God coming in loud and clear. The season of Epiphany suggests that from time to time in our adjusting and fine tuning we may pick up a presence and power far beyond our usual wavelengths. We may even discover that in the fullness of time, God overrides all the background noise and comes through loud and clear even on the most humble crystal AM sets.

1 Samuel 3:1-10 (11-20)

When are you likely to get it wrong and miss the message? Two things cause my reception to drift off frequency. I begin to pick up static when I over or under theologize. I have probably missed a lot by simply failing to ask these questions "What does God want with me in this moment? What does God expect of me in this time and place? What is it that I need to respect that God is trying to do with and through others?" Sometimes it is not just the floorboards creaking, or two branches rubbing against each other, nor is it the noise of the gardener. Such incidental moments just might turn out to be the signals of a God trying to hone in on us and remind us that the original intention was that home be in a garden. Then there are times when I am off the beam by doing too much theologizing attempting to draw meanings and find revelation with more certainty than is available to human reception. Sometimes it is just the gardener to talk with, and two branches to watch, or floorboards broadcasting the need for some basic carpentry.

The word having been rare in those days, we can suspect either end of the broadcast spectrum here. The time is ripe for hearing or the human ear is overripe for being plucked by too much imagination. In either case, the lamp of God had not gone out and perhaps the voice of God will now be heard, less in the official voice of the system than in the nocturnal wonderings of a youthful apprentice. Yet, it is the voice of the experienced Eli that recognizes that Samuel might not just be hearing things but could be tuned into what God is doing. At any rate he tells Samuel to stay tuned. Oftentimes I jump around on the dial when I would benefit from simply staying on one frequency.

It was a time when, no doubt, many were tempted to give up listening. A time when things are not clear; certainty is rare; clarity unusual; direction infrequent. The light of the Lord has dimmed, but not completely gone out. These are often the times when we find it hard to stay tuned. It does seem that such times become opportunities for people who do not usually talk with each other to find themselves on the same wavelength, having a conversation about the shared experience of God's silence! Stay tuned. Eli and Samuel find themselves having a discussion that they might not otherwise have had. Stay tuned when youth and experience have a conversation about shared need. Who knows what God is up to here in letting both Eli and Samuel find their voices? Perhaps only God's silence can provoke such a conversation.

Stay tuned when a congregation finds itself at a moment in which the congregational plot thickens and folk must write a new chapter. Stay tuned and see what God is up to in a life that discovers that the usual reruns are no longer sufficient and they are signaling the need to rethink his or her living. We tend to tune out the way Jesus' followers initially responded to Good Friday. As human possibilities have exhausted themselves, human imagination grows dim and human reception becomes lost in background static. Yet the light that is the energy of God has not gone out.

What should we fine tune here? We ought to hone in on the conversation between youth and experience. We ought to sharpen our attentiveness to those like Samuel who find the strength to speak a difficult truth in love and power. Stay tuned to those folks. Stay tuned to those like Eli who find they are coming to the end of a chapter in life and in the life of his or her community. Not knowing where things are headed they keep their antenna up. Stay tuned to those folks.

The Samuel saga signifies some significant changes and transitions in the life of Israel as they move toward monarchy, to the centralized role of worship in Jerusalem, and to the rise of prophets, like Elijah and Elisha. The silence and rarity of the word of God has prepared the way for a new conversation. Stay tuned.

1 Corinthians 6:12-20

As Paul puts it elsewhere, "What then are we to say to this?" Preachers are to be on your guard here; we are getting down to "where the pedal meets the metal and the rubber hits the road." We have to be concerned here not with theoretical issues dealing with the names of Christ or the return of Christ, but with the basic questions of understanding the body and what it means for humans not just to have a body but to be embodied.

In a way, the modern church has found itself revisiting many of these same issues that challenged and divided the Corinthians. The dietary issues surrounding what was permissible to eat in the Christian community were viewed in my seminary experience as the quixotic preoccupation of people who had not reached the existential heights of modern theological discourse. In my current congregation, we now struggle over the common meal. For many, we do not discern the Lord's body, eating, and drinking judgment to ourselves, if we do not provide vegetarian alternatives. No one in America can escape awareness of the intense emotions that swirl around the issues of human sexuality in many congregations today. The question of "for whom" the body was made now dominates denominational meetings, ordination councils, and judicatory deliberations. Many of us have had a grand time reflecting on and commenting about the nature of the Hollywood version of the Passion as it involved the price paid for our redemption. Just what emphasis should be placed on the role of the bodily suffering of Jesus? Many struggle now with whether the glory in the body should mean principled self-sacrifice or self-fulfillment. The Corinthians would no doubt find our struggles familiar.

As one approaches any practical question of ethical concern, part of the process is discerning what the "controlling authority" is. In this case, the underlying ethical norm that permeates Paul's writing is love. For him, the bodily issue involved in eating is whether we have gotten things out of sync with the love that "never ends." Those who are on the right wavelength know that "food is made for the stomach and the stomach for food." Love asks of us: "Do we eat to live or live to eat?" When it is the latter we tend to do unloving things. The unloving situation in the Corinthian church was to eat up the fellowship meal before everyone arrived. In our case it might be to enjoy the ham and bean supper without attending to the needs of those who find such eating and drinking repulsive. In our time, loveless consuming might mean failing "to live simple that others might simply live." Paul's vision is expressed in 2 Corinthians 5:14-15: "For the love of Christ urges us on, because we are convinced that one has died for all; therefore all have died. And he died for all, so that those who live might live no longer for themselves, but for him who died and was raised for them." Does "living for him" mean suppression of the body or expression of the body in a way that does not merely take more punishment but rather takes away the sin of the world? The potential for exciting sermons hangs on such questions.

John 1:43-51

Ernest Campbell, former preaching minister at Riverside Church in New York City, tells the story of the startup of color television in Germany. The initial response was frustration at not being able to pick up the color signals. Intense investigations led to the discovery that many did not know that they had to buy color sets to pick up the new advance in televised entertainment. In some sense, the gospel of John deals with the difficulty in picking up God's signals that something new is about to happen. We may have to reorient and redirect our minds and hearts in order to understand what God is doing if we are to get beyond our "black and white" thinking.

This gospel lesson describes two disciples whose ability to interpret things is somewhat behind the curve. Similarly, in trying to change frequencies, the church has always played catch-up. It took several hundred years for the church to gain clarity on the nature of Jesus and the meaning of the Trinity. From time to time, we have to make considerable adjustments to pick up the frequency on which God is broadcasting. Sometimes we can only find the frequency by changing *where* we frequent. Either way adjustments are going to occur. Nathanael seems, like many of us, to have the wrong geographic fix: expecting little good to come out of a minuscule backwoods town such as Nazareth. Tourist guides in modern Nazareth point out that the entire town, in Jesus' day, would fit inside the current Roman Catholic Basilica. Perhaps we don't do any better at discerning what God is doing because we have our own "frequent frequency" problem.

Nathanael is astounded that Jesus already knows where he has been frequenting. Like many of the characters in John's story, Nathanael is amazed but he still does not quite pick up on where Jesus is coming from. Calling him "rabbi" is a good start, yet falls short, in John's understanding, of adequately bringing the picture of Jesus into focus. "Son of God" is very, very good, but Nathanael seems to have spun the dial just a bit too far. In the next breath he says, "You are the king of Israel." This poses problems in John's story. Jesus withdraws when the crowd wants to make him king by force.

In a sense, Nathanael "ain't seen nothing yet." What he does see is not yet fully in focused. The story will have to progress so that we can see that Jesus is not only a teacher but also a "new Moses." It will take some movement in the plot before we know that Jesus' throne will be a cross, and that the Spirit will pour forth from his life and from these events in a saving act that will take away the sin of the world.

There is no doubt that at a certain level we can see that Jesus is special and that he is a teacher who merits our attention. However, if we stay at this level we have not seen anything yet. We may have to change our "frequency" if we our going to get this story live and in living color.

Application
Tuning in... adjusting the color... picking the radio station... rarely do these activities seem to be a joint venture. Actually, family fights over which station to watch, how loud the volume should be, and what tint the color should have are basic familial "lore." Churches as well have had their share of fights over bathroom color, carpet texture, and organ volume. If anything, it seems that getting on the right frequency is best achieved by benevolent dictatorship. Yet in these texts, honing in on God's voice is a joint enterprise. Paul invites the church to test the Spirit and his witness. Nathanael and Philip approach Jesus together. Eli and Samuel worked together to receive God's message. Can we come into focus that all have been given a voice and are heard? Can we get a clear picture without developing the kind of relationships that can allow many hands to be on the dial?

An Alternative Application
1 Samuel 3:1-10 (11-20). "The Lord said to Samuel, 'See, I am about to do something in Israel that will make both ears of anyone who hears of it tingle.' " Now there is a moment in living stereo. When have you found your ears tingling? Was it at the response to a proposal of marriage? Was it something like the words, "That's the ballgame and the Boston Red Sox are the World Champions"? Or maybe your moment came when your oncologist said, "I see that your CEA level has dropped markedly. I think that we can talk longevity in your case."

Let us contrast these moments with Sunday morning worship. Do we get within hailing distance of such joy? In John's gospel, Jesus says that he has come that our joy might be complete. That sounds like tingle time to me. Yet all too often we fall short of such worship and common life, or we reserve such "let loose" moments only for Christmas, Easter, and Pentecost. Is this why mainline churches have greater worship attendance at these times and why Pentecostal churches are growing?

Is it that we have not learned to do that dance well — of standing up to and with people? Do we miss tingling ears because we do not know how to speak the truth in love? Is it that we have grown tone deaf to what we are missing because many have grown too used to speaking in academic, philosophical, or psychological terms? Perhaps we cannot distinguish between lecture and a sermon in a way that excites.

Of course, there are those who say that the way forward is not through the ear at all and that it is time to get out the PowerPoint presentation and have at it. Yet Paul ponders how people can be saved without a preacher. Having grown up near New York's Riverside Church I was exposed to terrific preaching early in my faith journey: Harry Emerson Fosdick, Robert McCracken, Ernest Campbell, and William Sloan

Coffin. I am a Christian partly because of the sermons I heard. Not that they answered all my questions, but they did make my ears tingle. I knew early on that this was a form of communication that moved me and touched me, and was not found in other places in our culture.

In the season of Epiphany this might be a Sunday to celebrate the ministry of ear tingling. Preaching defined as "truth through personality" opens the question of sharing your story. How has your preaching changed through the years? Where do sermons come from? How does the rhythm of sermon preparation shape your life? What might it be like to live with someone who, in some form, measures themselves by the answer they give to the question, "Do you have anything to declare?" This could be a lot of fun. It might even get the congregation's ears to tingle at the weekly miracle of preaching that, amazingly, has gone on for well over 2,000 years.

All the time in the world

As a rule, you can tell how much time a person has by how quickly they move. Of course, there are also some idiosyncrasies of personal temperament that factor into how quickly a person moves. All else being equal, though, a person will move and act with a manifestly greater sense of urgency when he has little time.

It's a rare traveler who runs down the concourse at the airport when he has a long layover ahead of him. And, it's an equally rare person who drives casually, even ponderously, when he's running late for an appointment.

One of the great tests of personal patience comes when we are in more of a hurry than the people around us. If we are short on time as we drive, it's a great frustration to be behind someone who seems to be in no hurry at all. Likewise, we may become fidgety and unpleasant if we are in a hurry while the clerk, cashier, or server is functioning slowly, as though they had all the time in the world.

When the football team that is ahead has the ball during the final two minutes, the players move very deliberately, taking their time. When the football team that is behind has the ball during the final two minutes, however, the players move with speed, urgency, and efficiency.

In most instances, it is a relatively simple read of body language to identify whether a person is in a hurry or not. The question, then, is what our body language as Christians communicates about how much time we have.

The prevailing conviction in the New Testament is that time is short. Jesus' followers, therefore, are challenged to live with a corresponding urgency and purposefulness. After two millennia, however, we may be hard to convince that the time is short. Consequently, we may live and serve like people who have all the time in the world.

Jonah 3:1-5, 10

The first verse of our selected Old Testament passage inadvertently reveals one of the great themes of the book of Jonah: "The word of the Lord came to Jonah a second time." In that "second time" we are confronted by God's grace.

The word of the Lord had already come to Jonah once, and he responded with blatant disobedience. What should be done about that? When the soldier is insubordinate, does his commander just give the order a second time? Not likely. The insubordination results in a different kind of order being given.

Yet, this commander, deserving more, tolerates less. He does not dismiss the prophet who tried to dismiss him. He does not smite Jonah, but graciously harasses him back into obedience. Twenty-seven hundred years before, poet Francis Thompson wrote "The Hound of Heaven," Jonah lived it...

I fled Him, down the nights and down the days;
I fled Him, down the arches of the years;
I fled Him, down the labyrinthine ways
Of my own mind; and in the mist of tears
I hid from Him ...

Still with unhurrying chase,
And unperturbed pace,
Deliberate speed, majestic instancy
Came on the following Feet,
And a Voice above their beat —
"Naught shelters thee, who wilt not shelter Me."

Like the unforgiving servant in Jesus' parable (Matthew 18:23-34), however, the Lord's attitude toward Jonah does not seem to influence Jonah's attitude toward the Ninevites at all. Though he himself had been the beneficiary of God's gracious "second time," Jonah resented the same mercy being extended to the hated people of Nineveh (Jonah 3:6—4:2).

The writer reports that "the people of Nineveh believed God." The phrase itself reveals a bit of the Old Testament's understanding of the role of a prophet. Technically, the people of Nineveh had not met, seen, or heard God. Yet they believed him. How? By believing what was proclaimed to them through a prophet of God — even a severely flawed one.

The other noteworthy thing about that phrase — "the people of Nineveh believed God" — is that it is essentially the same phrase that Paul hangs his doctrinal hat on in Romans (see 4:3) and Galatians (see 3:6). He makes his case about the primacy of faith for salvation by pointing to the account from Genesis that Abraham "believed the Lord, and the Lord reckoned it to him as righteousness" (15:6). So, too, in Nineveh. The people believed God, and that became their salvation.

Finally, while we embrace the familiar truth of this passage — that God was merciful, both to his recalcitrant prophet and to the wicked but ignorant Ninevites — we may be less comfortable with the accompanying truth: namely, that "God changed his mind."

As post-enlightenment Christians in the west, we are naturally disposed to think of the deity in more philosophical terms, emphasizing his otherness. The down-to-earth testimony of scripture, however, is often embarrassing in its emphasis on the essential sameness of God — that is, typically human emotions, motivations, and actions that are attributed to God. We call the phenomenon anthropomorphizing — projecting our human attributes onto God. What we cannot say with certainty, however, is where the anthropomorphizing leaves off and where the "created in his image" begins. Are these qualities attributed to God by human beings? Or are these qualities found in human beings because they are originally a part of God?

I expect that we human beings are impossible to please on this difficult point. If we affirm that God changes his mind (see Exodus 32:12, 14; Jeremiah 18:8-10; 26:3, 13, 19), then we are inclined to question his omniscience and immutability. If, on the other hand, we affirm that God does not change his mind (see Numbers 23:19; 1 Samuel 15:29), we may fall into an undesirable fatalism and question the purpose of intercessory prayer.

Commenting on the occasion in Exodus when "God changed his mind," John Wesley wrote: "See the compassion of God toward poor sinners, and how ready he is to forgive." For God to change his mind is not for him to change his nature. Neither circumstances nor our prayers will prompt him to divorce his character or his will. Yet within his will it seems there may be more than one option, more than one plan. His plan for Nineveh in Jonah's day clearly changed; his will did not change, at all.

1 Corinthians 7:29-31

The larger context of this brief excerpt from 1 Corinthians 7 is Paul's discussion of Christian marriage. The whole epistle is arranged around a series of questions and problems: problems within the Corinthian church that have been reported to Paul, and questions from the believers there that he endeavors to answer. Here, the apostle addresses himself to the people's questions and concerns about marriage.

The striking thing about the movement of Paul's teaching, as reflected especially in our lection, is the presumption of an end-of-time context with its attendant implications. Situational ethics supposes that how we should behave depends upon the particulars of our situation, and in a sense that perspective was a part of Paul's thinking, too. That is to say, how we Christians live, ought to reflect the fact of our situation: namely, that "the appointed time has grown short."

A few Christian friends of mine, who were attending college in Ohio, had spent their spring break in Florida. They returned predictably tan. After only a few days back in the frozen north, however, their tans began to fade and peel. I remember two of the girls mournfully singing a dc Talk chorus as they looked in the mirror: "Things of this world are passin' away / Here tomorrow, but they're sure not here to stay."

Not all the things of this world seem so fragile and temporary as a tan, but I suppose that from eternity's perspective they are. The problem for us, trapped in our mortality and finitude, is that we do not always perceive this world's passing. "Every day the world gets older," wrote Ambrosiaster. The tanned skin may change unmistakably before our eyes. Other things of this world, though, may seem much more permanent to us. Still, Paul assures the Corinthians that "the present form of this world is passing away." It is fading and peeling all around us, whether we perceive it or not.

At first blush, Paul's counsel seems impossible. In matters of marriage and possessions, in both our grieving and our rejoicing, we are called upon to be whatever we are not, or not to be whatever we are. What a strange and unreasonable ethic, but then we observe the logic of the pattern.

This is not a typical ethic: an exhortation to be good rather than bad. Instead, it is a challenge simply to be other than what we are: to replace whatever our present prevailing reality may be with a different one. Our present reality may not be a bad thing. It may, in fact, be a good thing, like marriage or rejoicing. Still, something else endeavors to eclipse it.

In the larger context of New Testament teachings, we might label that new reality as "kingdom reality." That is the great resonance between this passage from Paul and Jesus' beatitudes (Matthew 5:3-12). All across the board — from Jesus' out-of-this-world ethical instructions... to Peter's counsel to suffering Christians... from Revelation's encouragement... to persecuted believers... to Paul's instructions here to the Corinthians — we are invited to live in light of the truth that "the present form of this world is passing away."

Mark 1:14-20

John the Baptist appears by name in all four gospels. That, incidentally, is more than some of the disciples can claim, as well as the Wise Men from the east, any of the notables such as Herod, Lazarus, Caiaphas, and assorted others. Indeed, while John's appearance in Mark's gospel is comparatively brief, he is the one with whom Mark begins the whole gospel story (see Mark 1:2-9).

Mark suggests a more sequential relationship between John's ministry and Jesus, while other gospel accounts report more of an overlap. In any case, Mark summarizes the beginning of Jesus' public ministry with several significant phrases.

"Proclaiming the good news" might also be translated "preaching the gospel" (as it is, for example, in the King James Version). So it is that Jesus' followers, in this and many other ways, carry on our master's ministry.

"The time is fulfilled" is a compelling image. In Matthew's gospel, we are more acquainted with the scriptures, or prophecy, or the law being fulfilled. But here we bump up against the New Testament's theology of time, if you will. Just as a parent will announce that it's time to eat, or time to take a bath, or time to go to bed, the preaching of John and of Jesus presumes that the Father has announced that "it's time...."

"The kingdom of God has come near" is, in my experience, one of the great neglected themes in so many churches. Ask most church folks what the central themes of Jesus' teachings were and I suspect that love, forgiveness, and the golden rule would top the lists. They might list a half-dozen other themes still without getting around to the kingdom of God, and yet that is a central issue in Mark's summary of Jesus' message. It is also prominent in the Lord's Prayer, and it is the recurring subject of Jesus' parables.

"Repent" is Jesus' first imperative. "Believe" will come next. "Follow me" will come soon. And variations on "love" will recur. But the first instruction is to repent. It is the necessary first step, for it is the step away from our sin and toward our God.

"Believe the good news" is the grand invitation. Sometimes a friend or coworker will preface a conversation by saying, "I've got good news and bad news." Jesus, meanwhile, comes along and says, "I've got good news, and you are invited to believe it." As we saw above with the Ninevites (and elsewhere with Abraham), believing is the key. On the other hand, there is an undeniable human tendency not to believe good news (see, for example, Exodus 6:9; 2 Kings 7:1-2).

Finally, Mark reports the call of the first disciples. It is the familiar scene along the shores of Galilee — two sets of brother-fishermen, all responding to Jesus' call to follow and to fish anew.

These first disciples stand in dramatic contrast to other, would-be disciples, and by comparing the sad stories of other men — men who failed to follow Jesus — we see more clearly the hallmarks of true disciples. Simon, Andrew, James, and John, for example, have an immediacy to their response. Jesus calls, and they come. There is not the hesitation or delay that characterizes the would-be followers of Luke 9:59-62. Likewise, the account of these fishermen who followed Jesus makes explicit the people and things that they left behind in order to follow him. The aforementioned would-be's could not tear themselves away from the people, and the rich young ruler (Matthew 19:16-22) was too attached to his things. "But first" is the motto of all those who end up not following Jesus, while the true disciples demonstrate by their actions that Jesus is first of all.

Application

As I sit intently watching the end of a football game, my wife knows better than to try to engage me in conversation. We have been married long enough for her to anticipate that I will be a distracted conversationalist during the crucial final minutes of a game. Wondering how long she will have to wait to have her husband back, she will ask, "How much time is left in the game?" "Just two minutes," I might respond. "Yes," she says, "but how much time is really left?"

When there are two minutes left in the first or second half of a football game, the officials will give a "two-minute warning" to each team. Theoretically, that means there are just 120 seconds left until the end. In reality, however, those final two minutes might last for fifteen or twenty actual minutes.

Likewise, when John the Baptist and Jesus came on the scene proclaiming that the kingdom of God was near, they were sounding a kind of cosmic two-minute warning. "The time is fulfilled," Jesus announces. "The appointed time has grown short," Paul echoes. And thus we hear the referees blowing the whistle to signal that the game is coming to an end.

The final two minutes, of course, are the end of the game. Not "the end" as a point, but as a period, a final phase. The two-minute warning, therefore, marks the beginning of the end. And this was, in effect, what John, Paul, and Jesus all announced.

At another level, of course, that is the same sort of warning that Jonah was giving to the people of Nineveh. It was a local rather than a cosmic two-minute warning, but it was, nonetheless, a signal that this was the beginning of the end for them and their town.

As a fan, there is nothing quite so maddening as seeing your team acting sluggish when they ought to be hustling. And, when it's the final two minutes, you particularly want to see a sense of urgency in the players.

With the prevailing theme of "time" in this week's passages, it is time to ask ourselves whether the church is acting sluggish. Are we moving with purpose, efficiency, and urgency? Or have we slowed down because these final two minutes have taken so very long? Are we living and behaving like people who have heard the two-minute warning, or like people who have all the time in the world?

Alternative Applications

Mark 1:14-20. "Following Orders." In our treatment of the gospel lesson above, we noted the series of imperatives expressed by Jesus. That series could be given a fuller treatment in a sermon, for the order is significant.

We identified "repent" as the proper first step. Likewise, "believe the good news" is elemental to our salvation. We do not arrive at belief and park there, however. Faith is followed by discipleship — "follow me." And even that personal relationship and loyalty is not the end of the matter, for there remains the calling to "fish for people."

If your congregation either needs to learn or to be reminded of the basic steps of the Christian life, the imperatives in the Mark passage provide a good opportunity.

Jonah 3:1-5, 10; Mark 1:14-20. "What to Believe." Jesus' exhortation in the gospel lesson is this: "Believe the good news." We have noted above the sweetness of that invitation, as well as the fallen human tendency to disbelieve good news.

Meanwhile, as we set this week's passages side by side, we are struck by the faith of the Ninevites. They, too, believed and were saved, but we can't really say that they believed the good news. Jonah — partly because of his assignment, and perhaps partly also because of his preferences and prejudices — did not bring "good news" to Nineveh. Indeed, he brought quite bad news: "Forty days more, and Nineveh shall be overthrown!" Nevertheless, the news came from God, and the people believed God.

Whether the doctor tells me that I am in excellent health or that I need some serious surgery, I do well to believe him. Whatever he tells me — whether the message is welcome or not — I can be assured that it is for my good.

I counseled recently with a married man who was contemplating an extra-marital affair. I trust that, in coming to me, he had some sense of what he was likely to hear, and that his coming was some proof of what he wanted to hear. Still, what I told him could not have been an easy message to receive. Even so, whether the news is good or bad on the surface, if it comes from God, then we should believe, and we can be assured that it is for our good.

Looking for a leader

Leadership is a hot topic in business and society. Dozens of new books on leadership appear in print every week. Leadership tracks at conferences are the first to fill. Executive coaching with the purpose of creating confident leaders is a mushrooming industry. Even in the church, a seminary education is not complete until leadership has been taught and caught, and congregations are looking for pastors who can function at least in part as CEOs.

Kouzes and Posner, in their book, *The Leadership Challenge*, and the seminars that have been developed around it, declare that there are five primary investments that leaders must make, and that the better they do these things, the stronger their leadership quotient will be: 1) challenge the status quo; 2) inspire a shared vision; 3) enable others to act; 4) encourage the heart; and 5) model the way. These leadership activities sound like they might be lifted from the Bible. The prophets of the Old Testament (and New, for that matter) certainly challenged the status quo in their communities. Kings like David and Solomon were gifted in their abilities to inspire shared visions that captured the minds and passions of the nation in a quest for greatness. The entire priestly system was designed to enable others to act by resolving the brokenness in people's relationships with God and with each other. Elders of both Old and New Testament times were informally selected on the basis of their ability to wisely encourage the hearts of the people. Deacons of the New Testament were put in place to model the way for the community of grace to express its care in meaningful ways.

In our lectionary passages for today, the idea of leadership is probed and developed. As Moses helps Israel transition from his role at the helm of the national ship to the next generation of captains, the promise is given that God will provide the next generations with the gifts and qualities necessary to carry the torch and blaze the trail. In his conversations with the church in Corinth, Paul explains how a fractured community can function holistically when positioned well, under effective leadership, and Mark's gospel makes clear that unusual leadership competence was evident even in the early days of Jesus' public ministry.

Part of the task of preaching today seems to be to call out leaders and leadership development among the people of the congregation. The other part is probably to reiterate that the church is never leaderless — it is always the church of Jesus Christ, the truest leader of leaders on both sides of eternity.

Deuteronomy 18:15-20

Deuteronomy is the fifth and final book of the Pentateuch (the Hebrew *Torah*). If one arranges these five books around the theme of covenant which is constantly expressed throughout them, Exodus serves as the pivotal expression of the covenant establishment at Mount Sinai; Genesis provides the background in a kind of covenant prologue; Leviticus mandates the character and qualities of covenant lifestyle; Numbers explains what happens when the covenant is stretched and tested and broken, and whether it can survive the tensions of its partners' relations with one another; and Deuteronomy serves as a bridge to the next generation of those who will live under the covenant. Deuteronomy is developed as a kind of last will and testament of Moses, a final declaration of the identity of Israel as God's people, and a summary of earlier covenant expressions.

Here, Moses eases the worries of the people. He has been their only national leader since they emerged from slavery into freedom four decades previously. Now he is talking about his life coming to an end, and there is fear in the camp that no one will be able to fill his shoes, no one will emerge as the next warrior and elder statesman who has the ear of the mighty, but hidden, deity that has provided for them during these wilderness wanderings. As he announces his imminent departure, Moses assures the people that God will not leave them leaderless, and that others will be called and equipped to function in this role.

What is not certain, in this passage, is whether Moses and/or the people understood this promise as something to be fulfilled immediately, or only in some distant future. The people are in need of leadership, and would want, hope, and pray for an immediate divine election that would quickly and firmly establish the next phase of community safety, development, and history. Does Joshua fit this criterion? Is he the next Moses? The first chapter of the next biblical book, called Joshua, seems to lean backward on this passage to highlight the significance of Joshua's emerging leadership presence. Yet there is no question but that the New Testament church understood Jesus as the truest fulfillment of this pledge (see the reference Stephen gives to this passage in his speech in Acts 7:37).

What is clear in the text of Deuteronomy is that the divinely called leader of God's people would be confirmed in his presence and performance by declaring truth that is in harmony with God's unfolding plans and designs. The true leader will speak and act out of a confident relationship with the all-seeing and powerful deity, and their important collusion will be evident from the raw data of experience.

This theme of prophetic leadership has been given contemporary shape by Frank Peretti in his novel, *The Prophet*. While there are various responses to Peretti's theological and eschatological stance, his story is insightful as it imagines how a prophet would function in society, not merely in the safety of historical distance, but in our contemporary setting. The book and the movie that was made about it may provide illustrative material helpful in explaining the important but challenging nature of prophetic identity in any culture, past or present.

1 Corinthians 8:1-13

It was probably in the year 53 AD that Paul carried on the bulk of his correspondence with the congregation in Corinth. Late in the previous year, he and Silas had embarked on their second mission journey together (Paul's third, according to the book of Acts; see especially chs. 18-19). While the previous trek had established their primary base in Corinth, this one focused on a long-term commitment to Ephesus. But Paul's strong leadership with the Corinthian congregation would not dissolve easily. Around the turn of the year from 52 to 53 AD, as Paul was getting established in Ephesus, he wrote a rather sharply worded letter of chastisement and instruction when he found out that immorality seemed prevalent and unchallenged in the Corinthian congregation (see 1 Corinthians 5:9). The response from Corinth was mixed at best. Stephanas, Fortunatas, and Achaicus (see 1 Corinthians 16:17) brought news of challenges against Paul's leadership (see 1 Corinthians 4 and 9), word of ongoing immorality in the community (see 1 Corinthians 5-6), and a list of questions (see 1 Corinthians 7:1) that may have been legitimate queries from those who missed Paul's personal leadership presence or secret attempts to undermine his credibility from those who despised him.

Chapter 8 is found in the section of this letter that responds to the questions from Corinth in serial fashion. Evidently someone had asked whether it was permissible for members of the congregation to purchase the more inexpensive cuts of meat in the marketplace that were left over from ritualized pagan sacrifices. It is clear from various references in this letter that the population of the church in Corinth included both rich and poor, both free and slave. While wealthy members of the congregation would have no problem purchasing whatever meat and other food items they wished, the poor would always be stretched by the cost of staples. After the daily and seasonal sacrifices at the pagan temple shrines, leftover meat that was neither burned in the offering nor roasted to feed the priests and other temple workers was dumped in the marketplace cheaply for a quick sale. Some Christians believed this flesh was off limits because it had undergone ritual dedication to other gods during its sacrificial process. Others believed that the great God of Paul's preaching was powerful over all other gods and therefore counteracted any ritualistic magical powers that others might have superstitiously applied to the leftover meat, and that it was thus available for consumption by Christians, especially at the lower prices it was offered.

Paul takes a middle road, endorsing neither position strongly. He recognizes the motives that drive both the abstainers and the takers, and then posits an ethic based upon mutual respect. He encourages people to eat or not eat this meat based upon their understanding of the power of those pagan rituals that have entered the food preparation chain process. More importantly, he says, is for all to understand that the work of Christ has brought all into a new relationship with the creator God, and that no one has a right to use these secondary issues to drive a wedge between people and the deity or between segments of the uniformly redeemed community.

Paul's response must have satisfied no one in its immediate context. Those who ate freely of the meat would find Paul lacking leadership courage to declare things the way they truly are. Those who refused to eat on spiritually superstitious principles would resent being called "weaker" in their understanding of the impact of Christ's work.

Nevertheless, Paul's answer is a brilliant and helpful leadership model. Thinking again of Kouzes and Posner's leadership tasks, Paul challenged the *status quo* among all who were wrestling with this issue; he inspired a shared vision as to how Jesus trumps the entire question with a superior authority; he enables others to act by removing some of the community stumbling blocks that have stymied authentic engagement between members of the church with different views; he encourages the heart by speaking with passion and compassion of his care for all who are part of the congregation; and he models the way when he concludes his teaching by revealing his own practices in the matter.

There are at least two ways to preach on this passage (and probably many more). One is to focus on Paul's specific instructions and make the application to other debated behaviors in the Christian community (use of alcohol, Sunday observance, devotional practices, involvement in the entertaining arts, political leanings, tithing, and similar behaviors, have all been hot ticket items in such debates at one time or another and may well linger in many congregations). Another approach would be to take this passage in the context of today's other lectionary passages and unpack more fully the qualities of leadership that are stated briefly in Moses' promises about future great prophets and are always evident in the popular reaction to Jesus' teachings and ministry style.

Mark 1:21-28

According to the early testimony of the church, Mark wrote this gospel account based upon the teachings of Peter during his last years in Rome. There is no question that in it Jesus is portrayed as man of action and power. The gospel opens with a declaration that Jesus is the "Son of God," a term used widely in the day as a reference to the Roman emperors who were senate — or self-declared as offspring of the deities. Moreover, Mark does not give any birth or infancy narratives. These would only show Jesus in a weak and vulnerable state. Instead, the Jesus of Mark's gospel bursts upon the scene as a full-grown man, divinely commissioned (1:9-13) and commanding immediate respect from others (1:14-20).

It is important to read this gospel with fresh eyes, cleansed of the accumulation of theological baggage that so often prejudices our understanding of what the text might be saying about the Jesus of our dogmatic declarations. Notice these things: first, "they" go to Capernaum. Jesus has already gathered a band of followers and they together are a visible force to be reckoned with. There is a scene in the movie, *The Last Temptation of Christ*, where Jesus (played by Willam Dafoe) walks toward the camera from the distance, across heated wilderness sands that shimmer and warp our vision in the dance of distortion. Cut by cut, as Jesus draws closer, a few at first and then many more people are added to his wake. It all happens in a few seconds on film, and here in Mark's gospel there is something similar taking place. Within a few strokes, Jesus the strong man divinely sent becomes the leader of an impressive "gang."

Second, the scene quickly moves to a sabbath service in the synagogue. By doing so Mark sets the stage for Jesus to be revealed as a leader of authority. Only men (not women or boys) could speak in the synagogue, and only men of stature and learning could teach there. Without telling us of Jesus' education or other influences, Mark immediately places Jesus front and center in the community. He has something to say and he deserves to be given the contextual podium from which to declare it. The people respond at once to Jesus' pronouncements by affirming his insight and authority.

Third, their confirmation is not the only that is given. Right at that moment a spiritual antagonist enters to challenge Jesus' authority. From a vantage point outside of the sensory limitations of humans, this devilish spirit not only recognizes the transcendent power and authority of Jesus but also clearly states the supernatural battle that must emerge. And, according to Mark, Jesus is able to assert his authority decisively in a manner that leaves no question about Jesus' clout.

Fourth, the immediate reaction is widespread dissemination of Jesus' unique stature and abilities. This becomes important in Mark's gospel because much of the rest of the book includes an underlying suppression theme. Jesus often warns those he heals not to tell others about it for fear of how the people might react. Meanwhile, Mark has set it up from the very beginning of the gospel that people will respond, and will churn out the gossip network buzz, and will refuse to allow Jesus to disappear into backwater oblivion.

The stage is set for Jesus to become the greatest leader of all time. What remains, in the gospel, is to outline the strange way Jesus will end up on top; first he must be misunderstood, then he must be slighted and shamed, and finally he must be murdered before Easter morning and they will provide a different context in which to apprehend and follow his divine and eternal leadership.

Application

Jim Collins' book, *Good to Great*, has become a new Bible for doing business. Collins outlines the results of his research into companies that have moved up from decent business results to spectacular growth over an extended period of time. Among the seven qualities or traits Collins and his researchers found exhibited in these breakaway companies, one of the most important is what Collins calls "Level Five Leadership."

The idea of "Level Five Leadership" begs us to ask what are the other four levels of leadership? In Collins' paradigm they exist as follows: Level One Leadership is personal competence. Those who display it give evidence of impressive skills and integrated performance that lifts them to distinction among their peers.

Level Two Leadership is that of a contributing team member. When people work on projects or are assigned to groups, people exhibiting this kind of leadership quality are recognized by the group for both their relational talents and also for the insights that they bring into the team dynamics.

Level Three Leadership is that of effective management. Those who reach this recognition and achievement generally give appropriate guidance to systems and divisions that have been set up by others. They may innovate, but primarily within the context of the business structures that have been put in place before their term of service.

Level Four Leadership occurs when people are given opportunities to take charge of groups or companies and they do so with grace, style, and ease. It is an expression of public leadership on terms we are usually familiar.

But Level Five Leadership is a gift owned within more limited circles. Level Five Leaders, according to Jim Collins, express all of the competencies of levels one through four. To these, however, they add two additional qualities. The first is a paradoxical humility that does not wrap up self-identity with the leadership position, and the other is a tenacious commitment to the outcomes of the enterprise. Level Five

Leaders own responsibility for the organization, but without egomaniacal posturing. They identify their life's purposes with that of the organization so that others understand the symbiotic fit. They are not here for a short while in order to make a name for themselves or to reap the windfall of profits and inflated salaries; they are in for the duration because they understand the needs and dynamics of the company.

These levels of leadership, even though derived from a business model, may help to explain the uniqueness of Moses in Israel and the model he established in Deuteronomy 18. They may also help people understand what it was that Paul sought to do in his relationship with the recalcitrant Corinthian congregation that sapped so much of his energies. And they may certainly create analogies through which Jesus' early impact on his community and his continued influence on the church and the world may be framed.

An Alternative Application
1 Corinthians 8:1-13. This is a great passage for exploring Christian behavior. It might be used on its own to probe contemporary issues of social and personal ethics and build a moral paradigm which moves beyond defining legalistic particulars to investigating responsible lifestyles.

The right lens, "A or B"

One thing that I don't look forward to is the periodic visit to the optometrist. It is not so much the thought of having air blown into my eye or a day spent in a visual fog from the numbing drops that puts me off. What really irritates me is the process of determining the new lens prescription. As the examiner goes through the run of lenses to find my best prescription, I do my best to determine the answer to the question: "A or B, which is clearer?" Too much reading, too much exposure to the sun, and just plain spending too much time using my eyes — leave me little choice but to work my way through the exam on an annual basis. I am well acquainted with the procedure. However, having been trained to look on all sides of a question and take into account a number of varied viewpoints, I have a hard time with the forced choices. My medical mentor expects more clarity of conviction as to what is clear than I am able to muster. "Well, yes... Oh... No, not exactly... I'm not sure," certainly does not speed things along. He has more patients to see, and I have things to do. But I just can't decide: "A or B." I hedge my bets. My frustration builds, and the doctor has his suspicions about ministers once again confirmed. It is a sorry story repeated annually.

Getting clarity even on the basics of vision is more complex than we think. It always seems like a trade off. One lens brings something into focus leaving other things in a slight blur. Another corrects for astigmatism while not doing much to bring into focus the fine print. Some lenses of study bring into sharp relief the seamier aspects of a congregation's history while leaving the strengths and potential a smudged blur. My glasses, now up to trifocals, are a miracle of twisted and molded plastic covering a multitude of eye maladies. I say, "Hats off," to the men and women in the lab who will bravely put all this together.

"A or B," which is clearer? When it comes to a particular congregation the answer will depend on the day you ask me. The world is going to hell in a handbasket, or we live on the cusp of some of the greatest potential in human history: depends on which newspapers I read and on what day I read them. I am God's gift to the world — a long-suffering saint... or I am a pimple on the face of progress, which is better, "A or B"? Of course, the truth is that the best results will come from some combination of the two. However my ocular inquisitor does not offer me that choice. In the end, one lens will have to do the job to bring the near, the far, and in-between into focus.

The lectionary texts offered to us for this Sunday provide lenses that function somewhat as trifocals, attempting to bring into focus human experience and divine reality. The Isaiah text asks us to lift up our eyes on high and see. It seems that the usual point of focus may be missing the mark. In the letter to the Corinthians, Paul tries on his own trifocals. He attempts to bring focus to his ministry by directing his gaze to the life and circumstance of those who are under the law, those outside the law, and the weak. In Mark's lesson, after meeting with initial success ministering at Simon's house, things fall out of focus because Jesus is nowhere to be found.

Like my trifocals it sometimes takes three different focal points in order to see the big picture.

Isaiah 40:21-31

The context of the Isaiah passage is the return from exile. Yet there are two focal points to be observed. It is "return" and "not return" at the same time. Of course, there is the physical reality that there is a homecoming to the promised land from the place of exile. Yet, it is "not return" as well. Can anything ever be the same again? There are new stories to tell of courage in the face of temptations to surrender your distinctiveness to the surrounding culture. There are stories to tell of families shamed by the surrender of some of their members to the surrounding culture. Getting these stories into focus will lead to the consolidation of most of what we know as the Bible. The air will be filled with past glories and future uncertainties.

In the midst of this time, the words of the prophet calls the Hebrews to look up and consider the larger picture of God's power and purpose. "Have you not known? Have you not heard? The Lord is the everlasting God, the creator of the ends of the earth. He does not faint or grow weary; his understanding is unsearchable." The prophet invites the reader to consider that something else might be up here; a return to something that will never be the same anyway. Rather than give this possibility the evil eye, give it a second look.

A recent trip to the newly opened War Museum in Ottawa, Canada, gave me a second look that brought things into focus. The museum looks like the prow of a ship that has somehow managed to wedge its way into downtown Ottawa. Then again, look long enough and it begins to look something like a jet airplane that has landed on the downtown. From the another angle, it appears to be a tank that is rolling through the streets of Canada's capital. Looking from above it appears to be a trench that some kind of giant earthmover has left in its wake. That is precisely the effect that the architect wanted to convey. The interior of the building, without straight lines, does a good job of conveying the chaos of war. I do not recall ever being lost in a museum for so long. The floor pattern keeps you alert, defies easy navigation, and robs you of an easy stroll.

The War Museum has its share of triumphant boasting. That Canadians were able to cart home Hitler's limousine is a particular point of honor.

Yet, as one goes about the various displays, you find a sense of tranquility replacing the awareness of the futility of war. What goes on here? I found myself in a conversation with the vice-president of the museum who explained the feelings that were overcoming me. He said that the museum was designed around the theme of regeneration. He could have said resurrection. The prow of the ship points to the Peace Tower on Parliament Hill. The roof is covered in green grass that shows evidence of reclaiming what looks like a WWI trench. In one area, that to date only a few visitors find, he showed me that on November 11 of each year the sunlight follows a marble line in the floor and at 11 a.m. hits the gravestone that had once covered the grave of Canada's unknown soldier (before he was interred in the national cenotaph). Of course, the date and time marks the end of the First World War.

In short, peace breaks out. Human hopes for rescue from the fierceness of life or our longing for return to something that looks like the "good old days" will not be satisfied. Neither complete return nor total rescue is in the cards; but something on the order of resurrection is possible. "Have you not heard?" Here is the essence of the biblical pageant that peaks in the good news of Easter morning. Those who wait upon or hope in the Lord shall find new things coming into focus for they will see with an "eagle eye."

"Have you not known? Have you not heard? The Lord is the everlasting God, the creator of the ends of the earth. He does not faint or grow weary; his understanding is unsearchable." God knows the story of those who will claim too much because they successively resisted the overtures of the surrounding culture. God knows the narrative of those who have hoped too little and surrendered too much. God will give power to the faint and strengthen the powerless. God is about something much more than return, or even rescue. Keep this in focus and much will become come clear: enough to continue the faith journey despite our weariness and weakness.

1 Corinthians 9:16-23

Obviously, Paul is struggling here with his authority and standing. It seems that, not unlike Jesus, Paul found that in his ministry he had to endure the attack of those who felt that his message was more threatening than liberating. The easiest way to undercut a preacher was, and is, to hack away at their credentials. His Judaism, his Christian qualifications, his learning, authenticity, and intensity were all maligned.

The gospel writers remembered that Jesus authoritatively cast out demons. People of authority, like chief priests and the scribes, questioned the authority of Jesus and tried to trick him with a question about the authority of John the Baptist.

Untimely born, yet experiencing the fullness of time; not prone, though capable of speaking in tongues; citizen of Rome, yet looking to heaven; taking no back seat to any Jew, yet able to live beyond the law — Paul lived with a double focus in his ministry. What does seem beyond him is looking at things through anything less than two foci. His "this on the one hand... but that on the other," approach would seem less than authoritative until we see that a third focal point is tri-angled into the picture in a way that gives authority to Paul's words and power to his life. "For Jews demand signs and Greeks desire wisdom, but we proclaim Christ crucified, a stumbling block to Jews and foolishness to Gentiles, but to those who are the called, both Jews and Greeks, Christ the power of God and the wisdom of God." Without the cross, the central experience of Paul's life cannot come into focus.

In this lectionary passage Paul takes up the cross of focusing on his life and the lives of others simultaneously in a way that reflects the meaning of Jesus' cross. He is a man who is not about the authoritative power to classify people, as worthy and unworthy, clean and unclean, free or slave, Jew or Gentile. Of course, our world wreaks of the authority to classify people by putting them in their assigned place in the various scheme of things. The sketch "Two Wild and Crazy Guys" performed by Steve Martin and Dan Akroyd on *Saturday Night Live* captured the pathetic attempt of two eastern European immigrants to slot themselves into the swingy lifestyle of the modern American empire. Teen magazines portray the clean and unclean body types of thinness and obesity. The historical statistician reminds us that we have a noticeable proclivity for voting for the tallest presidential candidate. We all carry around a hefty bag of slots in which to put people. Maybe there is neither Jew nor Gentile, but in some churches there is a premium on the right theological accent in their preacher, cultivated at the right seminary. Some can remember when some American churches even put a premium on the right Scottish burr on Sunday morning. Some sociologists suggest that we have something like upward of thirty seconds or so before we are slotted in place by our first impression.

In his ministry, Paul poses a new basis of authoritative power. If Paul casts out any demons it will not be because of his capacity to put people in their place, but by taking up the cross of putting himself in their place. "I have become all things to all people that I might by all means save some. I do it all for the sake of the gospel, so that I may share in its blessings."

I gravitate not necessarily to the teacher that knows all but to the teacher who knows me; who is willing to enter into and appreciate and learn from my world. I appreciate the physician who knows not only the latest medical protocols but who knows what it is to be sick. In a world of "Donald Trump and Martha Stewart wannabes," I relish people who have the common touch over and above the Midas touch. Paul demonstrates in this section of 1 Corinthians, that though he is free of legalism, though he is a man of considerable strength and theological acuity, he can enter into another's world in redemptive ways: the obsessive, the unrelentingly theologically obtuse, and the unquestionably weak.

Paul has found himself sharing in the blessings of this gospel by taking up *this* cross of Jesus. In some sense clarity has come through being "cross eyed."

Mark 1:29-39

The gospel writer indicates that Jesus and the disciples are headed toward serious success. With the curing of many diseases, the silencing of demons, the healing of Simon's mother-in-law, the early Christian movement is about to become a player in the affairs of Jesus' world. At least that is how it would appear. Yet, at the height of their early success Jesus withdraws, leaving Simon searching for him and the rest wondering if their hunt for the Messiah has only just begun. Just when things are falling into place, Jesus takes off to be alone and pray. While this may not be a career-ending moment, it is far from a smooth move as far as the disciples are concerned.

Of course, in Mark's gospel things might not be as they appear. For Mark, success of this kind is fraught with the danger of mistaking the surface appearance for the deeper reality. Things come into focus in three places in Mark's story: at the baptism of Jesus; during the transfiguration; and at the foot of the cross. We do not fully understand who the Son of God is until we can look upon the cross and join with the centurion in saying that this "was truly the Son of God" (Mark 15:39).

Of course, we look to other places in our search for Jesus. Despite Mark's testimony, the Jesus seminar searches for him in linguistic patterns of divergence and convergence. Others prowl the library for evidence that one can find in him the "teacher of wisdom tradition." Some claim that they have found Jesus to be the master therapist. All of these may have found some truth about him. Yet, for Mark, it is at the foot of the cross that we can make the most thorough theological statement about him.

Some scholars have described this vignette as Mark offering a summary of the typical day in the life of Jesus. However, the attempt to offer such objective accounts seems to be something beyond the range of the gospel writers. They can paint a picture, not offer us a photograph to view the life of Jesus. Nevertheless, it seems that they do offer us some hints at what a typical day in the life of the Christian community is like — healings happen, folks gather, service is done, demons are silenced, and Jesus remains elusive beyond all our theological attempts to capture him. He remains the master beyond our attempts to manage him to suit our needs and aims. "When they found him, they said to him, 'Everyone is searching for you.' " Of course, when we find him it is all too easy to turn him into a therapy, a philosophy, or something far more useful to us than the cross. The conviction that Jesus is the Son of God in Mark's gospel comes first from heaven and then mysteriously from a cloud at the transfiguration. The only time a human voice gives testimony to the dimensions of Jesus' relationship to God is at the cross — when a centurion gazing at the crucified Christ "gets it." Even Gentiles and a representative of the empire can get it when they know where to focus.

Application

When Paul writes, "If I proclaim the gospel, this gives me no ground for boasting, for an obligation is laid on me, and woe to me if I do not proclaim the gospel" ... I become a bit nervous. I chaff at the notions of obligation and woe. They are not the thoughts that I like to bring to the preaching process. This seems a bit obsessive. On the other hand, I do, on occasion, fall into patterns in which I wind up proclaiming something that is other than gospel. Does this "other" bring woe? Paul's scruples cause me to wonder about the times I have joined in the cultural celebration of marriage to the detriment of the gospel. In reading 1 Corinthians 13, I wonder if I have put too much emphasis on celebrating the wonderful, delightful, near nauseating love of the young couple? It is God's love that never ends; even when their love grows a bit fragile and frail. Woe to me.

Woe to me if I reduce the gospel to a self-help plan on how to live. No doubt I can meet the expectations of many and gain some social capital with those I serve by offering sermons on a typical day in Jesus' life that will help them get through their day. Something will emerge that will no doubt improve lives and may even resemble the gospel. Yet, I ponder. Is the gospel not only about how to live but also how to die? Do I reflect in my preaching and teaching that I need to give resentments, rage, and hostility something that looks like Christian burial?

In turning away from parts of scripture that I may find difficult, do I fail to proclaim the gospel? In dodging the Second Coming, in sticking to the lectionary and in avoiding the discipline of the lectionary; in seeking to be uplifting and in being down instead of looking up — have I failed to meet my obligation to preach the gospel?

Paul's words are haunting but they can be helpful. It is good to know that even in its early stage the church had enough strength to admit that it was struggling with the temptation to substitute something else for the gospel.

An Alternative Application

Mark 1:29-39. There is a red light on my panel. It comes on as Peter's mother-in-law rises from her fever to immediately serve them. I find myself in something more than a panic of political correctness. Do I hurry on by this part of the story as fast as I can? Do I resort to rational enlightened explanations and detailed cultural analysis? Neither seems promising because both alternatives invite me to crawl into my head and avoid what might be pulling at my heart. How have I related to the many people that do serve me? Have I been a good defender of the rights and obligations that I owe to support staff? Peter's mother-in-law makes me more than a bit uncomfortable. I look to staff for emotional support and sometimes treat people who do support me emotionally as staff — assuming too much, caring too little. I suspect that my prayer life, while embracing the concerns of the world, has all too often been unaffected by the needs of those who clean my office, pickup my garbage, proofread my work, and in general make it possible for me to function in a somewhat reasonable, faithful way.

I suspect that my dis-ease with Peter's mother-in-law is less a matter of high theological merit than the fact that I must face some serious sin in my life. I marginalize the people I distance from myself in ways that affront the rule and reign of God. I recall that Mahatma Gandhi was able to make some of his associates uncomfortable by serving them much as Peter's mother-in-law did. Hats off to her! The gospel is not all about maintaining my comfort zone.

Doing our part

My four-year-old daughter wanted to be near her daddy the other day, even though I was busy in the garage with a project that had no natural interest for her. Still, she set aside her toys, her bike, and her scooter in order to help me.

I was building a bookshelf, and I was working with some power tools. At times, therefore, she had to stand at a distance as a spectator. At other times, however, I found ways to include her in my work. Her greatest sense of participation and accomplishment came when I gave her shop-vac duty. Once she got over the noise of the vacuum, she really enjoyed the sight of sawdust magically disappearing from the workbench and garage floor.

My wife was very pleased by how the bookshelf turned out. "You did a great job with this," my wife said to me as she examined the final product. "Well, I had a great helper," I replied, beckoning toward my beaming daughter.

Now, of course, we all know that the assistance of a four-year-old girl in such a project is nominal, at best. Obviously, I could have completed the job without her help. At times, frankly, it would have gone more quickly for me to do it myself. And yet, for all the things I build or fix or paint over the years, I know that bookshelf will remain an especially fond memory for me, and probably a source of pride and accomplishment for her. We had a good time together, and in retrospect I wouldn't have wanted to do it without her help.

The heavenly Father does not need retrospect. He seems to have known from the beginning that he would rather do it — whatever it is — with the help of his children.

Our assistance, of course, is dubious. We require a great deal of instruction and correction. We do things more slowly than God would need to if he were operating on his own. We tire easily. We get discouraged. Our technique is usually flawed and our final product is often blemished. Still, it seems that the Father enjoys doing it with us, and he would rather not do it without us.

2 Kings 5:1-14

The biblical writer of this episode, right at the outset, presents us with a bit of theology that deserves our attention. He reports that Naaman was a great man "because by him the Lord had given victory to Aram."

The Aramaens were not God's chosen people, and so it may be somewhat surprising that the author saw the Lord's hand at work in their affairs — particularly their military victories. It was commonplace faith to credit God with Israelite victories in battle, but Aram was outside the conventional understanding of the circumference of God's interest and activity.

The attribution of agency is another interesting element in the writer's theology. It was "by him" that the Lord had given victories, you see. It is another subtle example of a prevalent theme in scripture: that the Lord gets his work done through human beings. The writer does not merely say that "the Lord had given victory to Aram," but rather that it had come "by him" — by Naaman.

Years earlier, young David had understood that "the battle is the Lord's" (1 Samuel 17:47), and yet still it was that human agent, David, who was the instrument of God's victory. Likewise, the children of

Israel have, for millennia, thanked God for delivering them from bondage in Egypt. Yet he did not operate unassisted: He called and used the reluctant Moses.

It is likewise here within our Old Testament lesson. The work of God is the healing of Naaman. Yet see how many human beings are essential to that work of God: a captured Israelite girl, two kings, a prophet, and several servants. It was "by them," you see, that the Lord healed Naaman.

The Israelite servant girl in Naaman's household, of course, is yet another instance of God's ability to use us wherever we are. Joseph was, arguably, used more by God as a captive and as a prisoner than he would have been as merely the pampered son at home with his father Jacob. It was Paul and Silas' imprisonment that resulted in the salvation of the Philippian jailor and his entire household.

Mordecai rightly encouraged Esther to believe that "perhaps you have come to royal dignity for just such a time as this" (Esther 4:14). But royal dignity is not the only setting of God's providence. Men and women of God have been appointed to everything from the dungeon to the throne "for just such a time" of God's provident purpose. And some little Israelite girl managed to be an instrument of God even as a captive in Aram.

The self-important Naaman eventually arrived at Elisha's door, conspicuously laden with gifts and no doubt accompanied by entourage and fanfare. It seems that he expected a fitting welcome from the prophet whose home he honored with his presence. But in what would have been regarded as a great diplomatic *faux pas* — and perceived by Naaman as a great insult — Elisha did not come out to greet the visiting dignitary at all. He sent a servant out, and with humiliating instructions, no less.

If Naaman had been greeted and treated with importance, and if the price required for his healing had been some act of great generosity or daring, then his ego would have been well served. But he was not treated as important, and he was not given opportunity to be either magnanimous or courageous. Instead, his assignment was to strip down and take a bath in Israel's ignominious little Jordan River. Naaman's healing, like our salvation, "is not your own doing; it is the gift of God — not the result of works, so that no one may boast" (Ephesians 2:8b-9).

1 Corinthians 9:24-27

Paul uses a word that we are unaccustomed to hearing — and certainly unaccustomed to embracing — in church. Compete.

We are more or less reconciled to the competitive environment that so characterizes the world in which we live. Our educational process is full of scores and grades, which in turn result in students being ranked. Top five, ninety-eighth percentile, valedictorians, and such, and the colleges and universities that accept only the highest ranking high school students we refer to as "highly competitive."

Meanwhile, that competitive environment continues well beyond our formal education. Competition is explicit in the work place — between employees of the same business, and between businesses in the same field. Employers don't need to keep the least productive worker, consumers don't waste their time on products that are not competitively priced, and investors don't show much interest in the companies or funds that perform below the market average.

In short, competition is the way our world works. We are not inclined to think, however, that competition is the way God's kingdom works.

I'm sure Paul does not sincerely believe that, in the Christian life or in eternity, "only one receives the prize." It is apparent, however, that he thinks we should live as though that were the case. The issue for him is not that he wants to win the prize himself instead of you or me winning it. Obviously not, since he is encouraging his readers also to "run in such a way that you may win." Rather, the issue for Paul is that he wants himself — and the Corinthians, as well as all of us — to run with the intensity, single-mindedness, and discipline that characterize a competition. After all, does Christ deserve less than a sporting event?

Paul goes on to illustrate how much more purposefully we ought to run by comparing the prizes that come at the end of the road. The ancient athlete was awarded a wreath for his victory, but Paul observes that such rewards were so very temporary. By contrast, our reward is ultimately and infinitely lasting. So, if the athlete works hard just to win something that withers, how much more should the followers of Jesus Christ work and strive?

Paul's use of an athlete's discipline as an example for Christians to follow is reminiscent of a part of God's message through the prophet Jeremiah. The Lord was so impressed by the devotion to a lesser allegiance demonstrated by the Rechabites (Jeremiah 35) that he challenged his own people to exhibit such a devotion to him. Likewise, if a runner will try so hard in order to receive only "a perishable wreath," how much harder should we try in order to gain "an imperishable one"?

An evaluation of possible prizes would be worth exploring from the pulpit. So many of our people are running hard in pursuit of the promise of something or other. What is their anticipated payoff? What is their hoped-for reward? What is the wreath that awaits them at the end of their road? And just how perishable or permanent is it?

Ironically, it may be that the great impediment to Paul's challenge to run is that so many American Christians have been crippled by grace. Convinced of some egalitarian heaven, we do not think much in terms of greater or lesser rewards, let alone "only one receiv(ing) the prize." Because we have been rightly persuaded that our guarantee of eternal life is in spite of what bad we have done in this life, and that our salvation cannot be purchased regardless of what good we do in this life, we may have cut completely any connection between this life and our eternal reward.

Mark 1:40-45

From its opening line, this is a passage filled with beauty, pathos, and power.

Mark reports that this anonymous leper came to Jesus. It's a simple, factual statement, and yet it paints a remarkable picture. In a time and place where the lepers themselves bore the responsibility to maintain their own ostracism from society in general and from specific public contact, this one has the boldness to cross the taboo boundaries and come directly to Jesus. And the next phrase — begging him and kneeling — do not suggest that the leper stood at a great distance and called out. It is a picture of proximity. He began, therefore, with some profound assumption about Jesus: that Jesus would neither run away nor send him away.

Indeed, Jesus does not. In fact, not only is Jesus apparently unfazed by this close encounter with one who was regarded as contagiously unclean, he later even makes the move to touch the leper. That touch was surely not necessary to the healing, for we see elsewhere that Jesus could just "say the word" (see, for example, Matthew 8:8-13 and Mark 4:39). Still "Jesus stretched out his hand and touched him."

How long had it been since someone had touched this untouchable? From the God who breathed into dust, to the incarnation, to the father who ran to embrace his fresh-from-the-pigsty son, God has never recoiled from getting close to us, even in our uncleanness.

Mark reports that Jesus was "moved with pity." The Greek word Mark uses (*splagxnizomai*) appears twelve times in the New Testament, all in the synoptic gospels. Six times it is said of Jesus by the narrator. Two other times, Jesus uses it to describe himself. One time, the verb is used by a father begging Jesus to help his tormented son (Mark 9:22). On the other three occasions, Jesus uses the verb in a story to describe the response of one person to another person and their need: the master who forgave a servant's great debt (Matthew 18:27); the Good Samaritan (Luke 10:33); and the father of the prodigal son (Luke 15:20). Noteworthy is the fact that, in every instance, the verb is followed by some specific action. It is not meant to be a mere feeling — an internal experience only. Rather, it must give rise to some external expression.

This episode comes from the very first chapter of Mark's gospel, and already we see here three elements that become well-established themes throughout the gospel.

First, there is the use of the Greek word *euthus*. This little adverb, translated here "immediately" (v. 42) and "at once" (v. 43), is one of Mark's hallmarks. By way of comparison, Matthew uses the word five times in the 28 chapters of his gospel. Mark uses it eleven times in this first chapter alone, thus giving rise to the characterization of Mark as "the gospel in a hurry."

Second, there is the command to silence. This is one of the well-known traits of the so-called "messianic secret," a phrase coined by William Wrede and a phenomenon widely recognized and explored by New Testament scholars. Demons (1:25), disciples (8:30), and beneficiaries of Jesus' miracles (5:43) are all enjoined to keep quiet about him and what he has done for them.

And that, in turn, leads to the third pattern that is typical of Mark's gospel and is evident in our selected passage: the uncontainable nature of the news about Jesus. Almost immediately after Jesus instructed the leper to "say nothing to anyone," he "went out and began to proclaim freely, and to spread the word." The result, which one senses in all four gospels, but which is most explicit and most early in Mark, is that Jesus experienced an almost suffocating popularity as "people came to him from every quarter."

Finally, Mark's account of this event comes full circle. At the beginning, "a leper came to (Jesus)." At the end, "people came to him from every quarter." The passage is framed with images of people coming to Jesus — seeking him out, pursuing him, bringing their needs to him — but the image has grown from an individual to a multitude. It is reminiscent of John's account of Jesus' conversation with the Samaritan woman (4:1-42), which also multiplies from a personal encounter to a regional impact.

Many of my generation will recall "Pass It On" as a staple of youth group events. The first line in the song observes, "It only takes a spark to get a fire going." Charles Wesley expresses the same truth somewhat more elegantly: "See how great a flame aspires, kindled by a spark of grace!" And the truth articulated by both songs is embodied and illustrated by this passage from Mark, as just one life touched by Jesus brings so many more to him.

Application

The pattern and preference are evident from the beginning: God creates a world, and immediately gives his human creatures responsibility for it. Can they keep the earth spinning on its axis, or in orbit around the sun? Can they guarantee seasons, growth, and fruition? No. The creation depends always upon the creator. Yet, still, he calls on them to do their little part: "to till it and keep it" (Genesis 2:15).

As we observed above, the work of God recorded in the Old Testament lection is the miraculous healing of the leper Naaman. Yet see how many people were employed in that work. None of them actually healed the man, but they were all instruments in what God did. And Naaman, in his pride, is even uncomfortable with how small a part he plays. He expected to spend more, to do more.

The apostle Paul, in his first letter to the Corinthians, urges them to do their part. He makes a great point elsewhere that our salvation depends not at all upon our works. Yet still he challenges us to work — to live with the urgency, purpose, and discipline of a runner in a race.

And in the gospel lesson, the leper, too, does his part. He cannot heal himself — the big work is always left for God to do, but he comes in faith and humility.

All that God does, he could do without us, but he prefers to do it with us. Our contribution may be small, and it may not serve either our egos or our works righteousness, but he calls us to do our part.

An Alternative Application

Mark 1:40-45. "Ready, Willing, and Able." The leper came to Jesus, kneeling and begging. That's a posture familiar to us. We have done that, too. Pressed hard by some urgent need, some problem without an answer, we, too, have come to Jesus begging on our knees.

The leper in this passage becomes a picture of prayer, and his prayer is an exemplary one: "If you choose, you can make me clean."

What the NRSV translates "you can" is a form of the Greek verb *dunamai*. Our English word "dynamite" derives from the same root as this Greek verb. It is a strong word suggesting real potency. There is no doubt in the leper's mind about Jesus' ability. He can do it. He is able. He has the power.

We must give this man great credit for his confidence in Christ's power. After all, God's people have often doubted God's ability through the years. Sarah laughed, the freshly freed slaves panicked between Pharaoh and the Red Sea, ten of the twelve spies fretted, and so on. And these folks had been given much more reason to be confident of the Lord's power than this leper, to whom Jesus appeared to be a man, not God, and who probably only knew Jesus by reputation, not personally.

Do we go to our knees before the Lord with the same confidence? Do we also affirm his dynamite ability to do it — whatever it is?

The question for the leper is not whether Jesus can do it. Rather, the question is whether Jesus will choose to do it. "If you choose," he says in preface to his statement of faith. I know that you can. What I don't know is that you will.

This, too, is a common point of insecurity for God's people. "Lord willing," we say, sometimes not so much in submission to his sovereignty as in uncertainty about his desire. "Thy will be done" is the qualifier we add to our prayers, as though reconciling ourselves to something less than what is best. Here is what I sincerely hope and pray for, but thy will — that mysterious, unexplained divine disappointment — thy will be done.

From the Garden of Eden, we have been tempted to suspect that God withholds good from us (see Genesis 3:1, 5). Even when we are confident that he is able, we doubt that he is ready and willing to do what we have fallen on our knees to ask.

"If you choose," we pray uncertainly, like the leper. And Jesus, even as he stretched out his arm to touch the untouchable, reassured, "I do choose." I am not only able — I am ready and willing!

Transfiguration of Our Lord
(Last Sunday after the Epiphany)
2 Kings 2:1-12
2 Corinthians 4:3-6
Mark 9:2-9
Craig MacCreary

Transfiguration or disfiguration

The transfiguration plunges us into the kind of text that many preachers would rather avoid if possible. There is neither law to interpret nor parable to enter into. Neither is there the warm fuzziness of Advent and Christmas. There are no healings to affirm or to water down. These genera of texts leave little room to romanticize their meaning into political agenda or to personalize their content into another twelve-step approach to life. We are left with very atypical events to decipher and proclaim. We find ourselves looking as much for the exits as for commentaries when we come to such passages.

Yet, there is opportunity here to receive insight into the glory of God and the purpose of our lives. I like the icon that shows the disciples tumbling down the mountainside at the gift given to them in being witnesses to the transfiguration. While there is something here that might cause us to stumble, we also may find ourselves gaining a new footing in our faith journey.

It is one of the great ironies of human history that the feast of the transfiguration is celebrated on some calendars on August 6 — a date that might cause us to fall to our knees in trembling for another reason. On August 6, 1945, the atomic bomb was dropped on Hiroshima, Japan. God once again sets before the human race the ways of life and death. The challenge before the world as never before, is transfiguration or disfiguration.

We may disfigure the garden we were intended to live in and the image we were made in. Given the possible contribution of human induced global warming to this past year's hurricanes, we may be facing, in dramatic ways, evidence of our choice of the methods of death. Given the contribution of religion to the world's misery, we may be as much on the side of disfiguration as transfiguration.

In the lectionary text from the Old Testament, the faith community faces a time when things can often be tipped in the direction of disfigurement. Some scholars point out that some eighty percent of church difficulties can be traced to times of transition in pastoral leadership. A recent television documentary, *Congregation*, told the tale of First United Methodist Church in Germantown, Pennsylvania, as they tried to transfer the mantle of leadership from a pastor of long standing to a newcomer. It came in the midst of change and upheaval in the community and the congregation. One sees the look on the faces of the people change as they move from high hopes, take a tumble, and come up knowing that this change will require more effort than they had originally thought. One longs to see all the participants transfigured by hope rather than so disfigured by their frustrations and fears.

It is rather telling that our political process seems to so disfigure our national leadership. Side by side, before and after photos reveal the toll the office has taken on them. Then one sees glimpses of transfiguration as the days of their term run out and they anticipate surrendering their responsibilities.

The saga of Elijah and Elisha invited us to ponder how we come down on either the side of transfiguration or disfiguration in the midst of transition and change in leadership.

The lection from Corinthians reminds us that when things are shrouded and veiled and we don't comprehend it, we are liable to disfigurement. We find that life gets twisted and distorted when we worship the gods that we have made rather than the God that has made us. The body can only stand so much disfigurement before it begins to perish. On the other hand, physical activity and care can lead to transfiguration — often offsetting the results of bad genes.

In Mark's gospel, Peter, James, and John hear the voice proclaiming Jesus' divinity from a cloud. In the midst of the cloud much remains a mystery. Yet one thing is clear: Jesus is to be listened to as the authoritative voice of God. Perhaps not until we are in the cloud do we perceive this.

2 Kings 2:1-12

Elijah's prophetic ministry is a call to a world that is disfigured by its political, economic, social, and religious structures. Building on the work of Walter Brueggemann in *Testimony to Otherwise: The witness of Elijah and Elisha*, I find in the Elijah passage a witness to structuring a world that chooses transfiguration over disfiguration. He is not dependent on competition for sustenance and survival. Rather in collaboration with the widow of Zarephath and with God's help he finds enough to feed the widow and himself in the midst of the surrounding scarcity. Present patterns of competition and consumption of the world's resources may leave the planet and our lives so disfigured that the sustainability of all life is called into question. At its deepest places the whole creation is growing in travail, waiting for the revelation of the sons and daughters of God. We are faced with transfiguration or disfiguration.

Elijah has not bought into the definition that the royal system has placed upon him and all other people. The disfigurement that can come from a slavish acceptance of the way things are — as opposed to the way they could be — is highlighted in 1 Samuel. Demanding a king, Samuel reports back to the people what God had told him: "These will be the ways of the king who will reign over you: he will take your sons and appoint them to his chariots and to be his horsemen, and to run before his chariots; and he will appoint for himself commanders of thousands and commanders of fifties, and some to plow his ground and to reap his harvest, and to make his implements of war and the equipment of his chariots. He will take your daughters to be perfumers and cooks and bakers. He will take the best of your fields and vineyards and olive orchards and give them to his courtiers" (1 Samuel 8:11-14). When nations send fourteen-year-old children to do their fighting, young lives are disfigured. Young teenage girls are being disfigured by resorting to bulimia and anorexia to achieve the cultural norm for body types. The powers that be will disfigure the retirement hopes and dreams of many into a hellish nightmare. This will happen while the few who had contacts at some royal court avoid disaster. Elijah objects to the governmental land use policy of Ahab that robs Naboth of his vineyard... which boils down to what is mine is mine and what is yours could be mine.

Much is at stake in the departure of Elijah. Does the end of his earthly career put an end to the meaning of his earthly ministry? There are several ways in which scripture makes clear that the meaning of his ministry will be expanded upon. His departure makes clear that like Moses we are dealing with an archetypical figure whose life gives us a handle on events to come. Elisha will be granted the inheritance of an elder son because he sticks around to see this moment. Certainly, the arrangement for Elisha to continue this prophetic witness leaves nothing to chance. The transfer of power itself partakes of the archetypical story of the parting of the waters and reminds the reader that this narrative is not a mere footnote to the larger historical meaning. Furthermore, the book of Malachi makes clear that we are not dealing merely with history. The meaning of Elijah's life has future implications: "Lo, I will send you the prophet Elijah before the great and terrible day of the Lord comes. He will turn the hearts of parents to their children and the hearts of children to their parents, so that I will not come and strike the land with a curse" (Malachi 4:6). This seems to describe a transfiguring moment if ever there was one. Children and parents will not be at each other's throats rather that they will be open to each other's hearts. I find parents often mourn their relationship with their children because it is often marred by the market forces of our society. The land is not to be considered a source of competition and curse, but blessing. A world struggling through climate change would be transfigured by such a self-understanding.

Christian people find Elijah reappearing in the figure of John the Baptist and giving meaning to the moment of Jesus' transfiguration.

2 Corinthians 4:3-6

Paul's division of humanity into those who are being saved and those who are perishing does not sit entirely well with many Christians. Certainly moderns find this notion disturbing as yet another reason to divide humanity into an "us verses them" scheme with the "us" being those who are saved. We long for unity and human divisions to be overcome. We live in a time when we need religion to be a source of harmony of the kind that can bridge the racial, class, and ethnic divisions that threaten our common life. It's a time when religious leaders and communities have found the strength to apologize to native people for the role played by many faith groups in the oppression and cruelty inflicted on the "other." Among the many sorrows of religious people is the disfigurement of religion by hate and elitism that have denied others their full humanity. Moderns should find themselves more than a bit nervous as they read Paul's words.

The Christian scriptures themselves puzzle over why it is that some accept Christ and others do not. John's gospel attributes the acceptance of Christ to the action of the Holy Spirit that blows where it blows. My ancestors in the Reformed and Congregational tradition, seeking some evidence of what group they were in, somehow took comfort in elaborate theories of double and single predestination. Such labors seem for many of us to be the result of a disfigured understanding of the meaning and purpose of religion. Yet, this has been a troubling question for Christians. It often seems that for many it is a concern that they had not reckoned on having to deal with. How it could be that so many would not "get it." Even today, many ponder why they have a sibling, uncle, neighbor, or someone else close to them that shows little evidence of saving grace in their lives.

I sense that I am most likely to avoid the disfiguring potential of Paul's words when I apply them to my own life rather than use them as a justification for my doubts about others' religious destiny. I find the great divide to fall within my life as much as between me and others. There is a Christ that habitually remains hidden to me because I have found myself all too comfortable with the god of this world.

Enraptured with success as a definition of my validity I am often blinded to the Christ who looked on the rich, young man with love when the young man did not understand what Jesus was telling him. Eager to please that god that measures life in quarterly reports and PowerPoint presentations, the Christ that suggested a plan for failure to the disciples remains hidden to me. He said to them: "Wherever you enter a house, stay there until you leave the place. If any place will not welcome you and they refuse to hear you, as you leave, shake off the dust that is on your feet as a testimony against them" (Mark 6:10-11). I find my life and my ministry often disfigured by the way that I internalize the failures, remember the criticisms, and obsess when things are not going well. Paul may be on to something here after all.

My inordinate attention to the god of the world not only disfigures me, but my anxious pursuit of positive outcomes and clear conclusions disfigures the lives of others as I lay my message on them. "For it is the God who said, 'Let light shine out of darkness,' who has shone in our hearts to give the light of the knowledge of the glory of God in the face of Jesus Christ" (v. 6). My problem is that many of the faces of Jesus remain hidden to me because of fear of, and enthusiasm for, the god of this world. I do not find myself focusing on the face of Jesus that must have been there in those places where scripture recounts that he was not able to heal. "And he could do no deed of power there, except that he laid his hands on a few sick people and cured them. And he was amazed at their unbelief. Then he went about among the villages teaching" (Mark 6:5-6). When that face remains veiled — the one that had to confront the unbelief of many — and had to continue on his mission being faithful rather than successful, then I am likely to add to the world's disfigurement.

There is no doubt that Paul's words hold the potential for contributing to the world's disfigurement. Yet in facing the question and considering the Christ that I keep hidden, there is transfiguration for me as well as for the lives I touch.

Mark 9:2-9

One way to enter into a text is to ask, "How would I write this story?" Of course most, like the disciples, would want to make sure that they had a solid factual basis to what was happening. Yet, I suspect that this is the kind of event that demands much more than factual reporting. The gospel writers exercise their own discretion as to what is to be included. Luke finds it necessary to mention that the disciples were overcome by sleepiness of the kind that was, perhaps, a foretaste of the drowsiness that overtakes them in the garden of Gethsemane. Mark and Luke mention the fear of the disciples while Matthew leaves it out. My selection for the cutting room floor is the cloud that enveloped the disciples. For me fear is fine; drowsiness is a constant companion; but being in a fog is a less than appealing image.

If I told the story it would run something like this: The disciples climbed the mountain... the clouds parted... the heavens opened... revelation occurred... and they felt they clearly had a future. Of course, it might conclude with: "They lived happily ever after knowing what would happen, knowing how they should live — yet without any uncertainty as to who they were." Now that is my idea of transfiguration. Of course that is the problem. This is *my* idea of transfiguration. As a matter of fact, my idea falls pretty short of what transfiguration means. Actually, when we seek certain outcomes, count on happiness rather than looking for joy, and when we stick with the plan no matter what... it can lead to disfiguration just as easily as to transfiguration.

The heavens do not open and the mists do not part, but we are left with the command to listen to Jesus. More often than not, life does remain a mystery, as we are mysteries not only to one another, but also to ourselves. Yet, out of the surrounding cloud comes a voice that calls us to love and cherish each other. Out of the cloud of uncertainty comes a voice that calls us to follow the way of Christ that clears a path through the mists. I have walked with many through terminal illness feeling helpless to affect a cure or to answer their question, "Why me?" Yet there is a voice that summons me to follow Christ by being present to those I cannot fix, in situations I cannot explain. It leaves both of us listening to the voice and is a transfiguring moment. I long for peace in the world. Yet, the transforming moment comes when I hear the voice that says, "There is no way to peace, peace is the way." In such moments I know why Peter wanted to hang on to the experience and make it last.

Many of my generation can remember the fog that we entered on November 22, 1963, and the events surrounding the assassination of President John F. Kennedy. Ernest Campbell tells the story of how in the midst of fog and shrouded in gloom the congregation he served made arrangements for Marina Oswald, the Russian wife of the assassin, to come to their community to learn English. Looking around in that transfiguring moment all you could see was the love of Jesus.

Application

Where do you see yourself fitting into this story? What question do you ask of scripture? It makes all the difference in the world. Perhaps, even more importantly, it is not the question you ask but of whom you ask it. When I am in a panic mode before writing the Sunday sermon, which is okay on Tuesday but is not okay on Thursday, I find myself slipping down a sort of ministerial "Maslow" scale of needs. Things are very good when I am entering into the world of scripture and are not so good when I am asking myself: "Just how in the name of all that is sacred am I going to be able to preach this?"

When it comes down to the latter I have achieved a high level of significant disfiguration. That is the time I start searching for the killer sermon illustrations that will crack this baby wide open. Looking for ways to preach the text before I enter it, I start mentally reviewing every sermon I have ever heard on the text. The next step is chants, voodoo, and entrails!

However, given enough time to start asking less of myself and more of the text, I find that God may actually have something to say about it. Once this concession is made, the hard part is over and I am on my way. Let us be clear, sin does cling tenaciously so that last month's concession speech does not seem to cover this month's attack of business.

Transfiguration begins to happen for me when I ask of the text "Where do I fit in?" and I try different places on for size. Before explaining the transfiguration to your congregation, try taking them on the journey. What would it feel like to be invited up the mountain with Jesus? Would you feel gratitude or responsibility for finding yourself part of the inner core? Would you grieve those who are left down at the bottom of the hill? The text leaves the disciples only seeing Jesus. I doubt that I would feel that was enough. To quote Bill Coffin, "I want theological hitching posts to tie my red wagon to more than sign posts for my journey along the way." I rather suspect that the appearance of Elijah and Moses would leave me somewhat flatfooted — I should have paid more attention in Hebrew Testament 101.

As I go up this mountain I find myself more transfigured than I thought possible. Even in the midst of the cloud I hear words of hope.

An Alternative Application
2 Kings 2:1-12. Three times Elisha repeats the words to Elijah, "I will not leave you." Such repetition seems pointless adding little to the narrative. Yet, as the story is told it seems that each time the words are repeated Elisha gains permission to touch one more base in the Hebrews story and move on. It is at Bethel where Elisha makes his first promise to see it to the end with Elijah. It is at Bethel that Jacob is named Israel. The compiler of this saga has tied the meaning of nationhood to the Elijah/Elisha story. The tale means that kings are not immune to the judgment of God. The meaning of national security is tied here to faithfulness as understood in the Elijah narrative. The second stop is Jericho, recalling the climatic battle with those outside the covenant before Israel can enter the promised land. Yet, Elijah goes to the widow of Zarephath who is marginalized by the social order. As Elijah rounds the bases before he can get home he touches base with Israel's self-understanding as occupiers of the promised land. The order has lost its basis in the covenant if it marginalizes the vulnerable and weak.

Finally Elijah and Elisha touch base at the river Jordan where an exiting from the land of oppression and entrance into the promised land is reenacted. In revisiting this foundational event the fundamental narrative is tied to a ministry that in the end defies death. The power to kill pales in the face of the power to raise up. Only after the basic foundational events are revisited is it time for Elijah to be taken up and for Elisha to move on.

This raises the questions for the preacher. What foundational events in your community, in your church, need to be revisited in the in light of Elijah's ministry?

Ash Wednesday
Joel 2:1-12, 12-17
2 Corinthians 5:20b—6:10
Matthew 6:1-6, 16-21
Timothy Cargal

Dust in the wind

Sometimes a song gets so deep inside your head that it can never be uprooted. Maybe it is the melody or the mood evoked by its musical qualities. Maybe it is the themes and ideas that find expression in its lyrics. If it happens to be both the music and the lyrics perfectly matched to each other, then the effect is particularly strong. Such songs have the ability to become a recurring soundtrack to our lives.

One such song for me is Kerry Livgren's "Dust In The Wind." Since I first heard this song more than 20 years ago, not an Ash Wednesday has gone by without that song being the tune I just could not get out of my head. "I close my eyes / Only for a moment, and the moment's gone / All my dreams / Pass before my eyes a curiosity / Dust in the wind / All they are is dust in the wind." Certainly no Christian hymn captures any better Ash Wednesday's liturgical refrain, "Remember that you are dust, and to dust you shall return." As I repeat those words with the imposition of ashes on each parishioner's forehead, playing inside my own head it's the "Same old song / We're just a drop of water in an endless sea / All we do / Crumbles to the ground, though we refuse to see / Dust in the wind / All we are is dust in the wind."

Certainly "Dust In The Wind" captured the existential angst of my generation. The culturally dominant materialist philosophy has told us that we were literally nothing more than cosmic dust shaped by physical and evolutionary forces. And even though Christian faith rejects materialist reductionism, the Ash Wednesday liturgy just as certainly intends to inescapably confront us — brow beat is probably not too harsh a description — with the harsh reality of our mortality and our utter need for redemption. But is the message of Ash Wednesday really that "all we are is dust in the wind"? Must we pass through this doorway to Lent and all its remaining 40 days until Easter before we hear any suggestion of good news?

Joel 2:1-2, 12-17

Nothing is known of Joel son of Pethuel other than that he was the author of at least the core oracles preserved in this prophetic work. That he locates the liturgical life of God's people at Zion (v. 1) suggests that he was probably from Judah, but whether he lived during the time of the Assyrian, Babylonian, Persian, or even Greek invasions has been the topic of on-going scholarly debate. His particular prophetic genius was his ability to use the experience of a devastating locust plague to symbolize the ravaging of the people by invading armies (see especially 1:4 and 2:3-11, the verses passed over in this reading by the lectionary committee). Yet for Joel neither natural nor military disasters are consequences of simple bad luck or even a failure of political leadership. By weaving together the natural and the political, Joel makes his case that such catastrophes are nothing other than judgments of the "day of the Lord."

It is with precisely that assessment, presented as a warning cry, that the selection assigned in the lectionary begins. The sounding of the trumpet in Zion in itself is ambiguous; it might either herald God's blessings for the people (1 Kings 1:34; Psalm 81:3) or be the harbinger of danger and destruction (Jeremiah 4:5-6; Amos 3:6). However, the poetic parallelism of the next line in verse 1 clearly associates this trumpet blast with the latter. God's coming in this instance is "a day of darkness and gloom" for those who are about to come under divine judgment. The darkness is gathering and the whole cosmic structure "quakes" in anticipation. "Truly the day of the Lord is great; terrible indeed — who can endure it?" (2:11).

Yet the purpose of the prophet's warning is not to announce inescapable judgment, but rather to call the people to repentance so that they might be spared. God's nature is not fundamentally one of wrath. God "is gracious and merciful, slow to anger, and abounding in steadfast love." God "relents from punishing" those who return to God "with fasting, with weeping, and with mourning" for their sins (vv. 12-13). Judgment may have already begun, "yet even now" it may be averted by calling forth God's gracious nature through genuine repentance. Judgment may yet be transformed into blessing (v. 14).

Joel is one of the most supportive of the rituals of the temple and priesthood among ancient Israel's prophets. So it is that he draws on yet another use of sounding the trumpet in Zion, namely the blowing of the shophar to call the people to religious assembly (v. 15). The whole of the society, from the "aged" to "even infants at the breast" (v. 16), are to gather in the temple. No other obligation is greater than the need to answer the call to repentance. Even the newly married who were exempted from answering a call to arms (Deuteronomy 24:5) are not exempted from this call to duty. They are to fast and perform the rituals of repentance as the priests intercede for them in the temple courts.

These are hardly empty rituals. By acting in accord with the sacred service (the liturgy) that has been given to them, the people will demonstrate that they are indeed God's people. Their past sinful actions may have called this association into doubt, but by sincerely entering into the rituals they will once again mark themselves as those whom the world will expect God to protect (v. 17). But simply going through the motions won't do. They cannot simply abstain from food, but must "sanctify a fast." They cannot simply gather together to commiserate, but must "call a solemn assembly." In these ways they reclaim for themselves the dignity of God's own people, and with that, God's protection rather than judgment.

2 Corinthians 5:20b—6:10

Whereas Joel's message to his contemporaries was fundamentally a call to repentance, Paul's appeal to the Corinthian Christians in the epistle lesson is to be reconciled to God. Their goals are thus the same — restoring the relationship between God and God's people — but their emphases are different. Repentance emphasizes what is required from the human side, reconciliation what God does to repair the relationship.

Paul's focus on the divine activity in this rapprochement is most clear in 5:21. It is what God has done in making Christ "to be sin who knew no sin" that in turn transforms us to "the righteousness of God." If the end results of Paul's theory of atonement are clear, however, the mechanism by which this reconciliation is accomplished is anything but. How is it that Christ is "made to be sin"? Is it simply by being incarnated in sinful human nature, or is all human sin somehow imputed to Christ on the cross? Does the sinless Christ suffer as an innocent sacrificial victim, bearing God's judgment in the place of the sinful ones who would otherwise have borne it themselves?

As the history of Christian atonement doctrine demonstrates, any of these explanations (and others as well) are possible. But Paul is less interested in unpacking the mystery of the means of salvation than he is in calling people to live in the reality of salvation. Salvation is the "grace of God" that we accept, but even having accepted it, one might have received it "in vain."

Paul's emphasis here on reconciliation rather than repentance leads him to draw on a different strand of the tradition regarding the "day of the Lord" than what we have seen in the Joel passage. Citing Isaiah 49:8, Paul emphasizes that the climax of this age is "a day of salvation" rather than judgment. As we have seen, Joel would not have disagreed with this — at least as a potential outcome for those who respond in repentance. Paul also insists that this eschatological moment has already begun: "See, now is the acceptable time; see, now is the day of salvation!" (v. 2b).

Paul insists that he is "working together with God" (v. 1) in such a way as to assure that no obstacle is placed in anyone's path and "no fault may be found with our ministry" (v. 3). Yet the Corinthians did in fact find fault with his ministry (see especially 2 Corinthians 11), and precisely because they perceived as "obstacles" some of the results of his ministry that he himself enumerates here. "Afflictions, hardships, calamities, beatings, imprisonments, riots, labors, sleepless nights, hunger" (vv. 4b-5) — do those sound like the marks of salvation to you? Shouldn't the expectation of these things be an "obstacle" to any reasonable person?

Of course, those were not the only marks Paul identified of his ministry. His ministry was also characterized by "purity, knowledge, patience, kindness, holiness of spirit, genuine love, truthful speech, and the power of God" (vv. 6-7a). Now here are things that truly do "commend [his ministry] in every way" (v. 4a). But one might ask, "Which is it, Paul? Does your ministry of reconciliation with God portend 'hardships' or 'the power of God'?"

To that question Paul answers, "Yes." The "day of salvation" may have begun but it has not been fully realized. Consequently, both what might seem obstacles and what might seem blessings go hand in hand. Yet those "obstacles" are not God's doing but the actions of those who yet fail to recognize the truth of what God has done. "We are treated as imposters, and yet are true" (v. 8b). Those who are not reconciled with God, or who have perhaps only received "God's grace in vain," may see death, punishment, sorrow, and poverty, but the truth before God is life, rejoicing, riches, and possessing everything that ultimately matters.

One final point: note that there is no indication that Paul was writing this letter to Corinthian citizens outside the fledgling Christian community. Thus, when Paul wrote, "We entreat you on behalf of Christ, be reconciled to God," this imperative is being directed at his converts. That they might have indeed "accepted the grace of God in vain" is not some idle possibility but rather Paul's diagnosis of their condition. Paul's letter, like the season of Lent, is a reminder that although our salvation in Christ is secure, the ministry of reconciliation with God continues through our repentance and "working together with God" so that others might also accept divine grace.

Matthew 6:1-6, 16-21

The theme of this portion of the Sermon on the Mount is clearly stated in its opening line: "Beware of practicing your piety before others in order to be seen by them." Three specific rituals of piety are treated: almsgiving (vv. 2-4), prayer (vv. 5-15, with the lectionary leaving aside the model prayer now known as "the Lord's Prayer" in vv. 7-15), and fasting (vv. 16-18). The unit is framed by the references to the rewards of piety (vv. 1, 19-21), specifically the "reward / treasure in heaven," that is, spiritual benefit, that accrues to those who ultimately direct their pious acts toward God.

The issue of for whom such acts of piety are performed, whether for God or for others, is key to properly understanding the epithet of "hypocrites" that occurs repeatedly in this passage and elsewhere in Matthew's gospel, particularly the discourse in chapter 23. In colloquial English, a "hypocrite" is someone who says one thing and does another so that there is a disconnect between how they want to be perceived and who they actually are by their actions. Yet as each of these examples makes clear, those charged as "hypocrites" here in the Sermon on the Mount are actually performing these rituals. They are giving alms, praying and fasting; they are not saying one thing and doing something else. So what is the meaning of "hypocrite" here?

In classical and Koinà Greek generally, the hypokrites was an actor who played a role in a theatrical production. Thus, in a very real sense his (all actors were male, even those playing female roles) actions were purely for show. They were not true of the person himself at all, but were done for the sole purpose of being seen by others. Applied metaphorically in these verses, then, the indictment is that people who make a show of their ritual piety are engaged in nothing more than a performance. It is empty ritualism that may be rewarded with applause by the audience but has no lasting spiritual benefit for the person of the actor.

One of the key structures of Greco-Roman society was the patronage system. Providing assistance either to individuals or underwriting important public projects were prime ways in which people could increase their honor in a culture dominated by concerns with honor and shame. It is easy to see how the ancient practice of almsgiving could be corrupted in such a situation. Rather than being about demonstrating God's concern for those in need and one's own gratitude toward God for provision, the giving of alms becomes a means of displaying one's greatness and demanding honor in return. Discrete acts of benevolence, on the other hand, are about preserving the honor and dignity of the recipient, not the donor. In such acts God increases the honor and blessing of both donor and recipient.

Similarly, the issue regarding public prayer is not its publicness, but rather whom it is directed toward. The prayers offered by the "hypocrites" in the synagogue and on the street corners are not actually being offered to God at all; rather, those prayers are offered so that the person "may be seen by others" (v. 5). If you pray to the crowds, perhaps the crowds will reward your rhetorical excellence. But if your desire is to have God answer your prayers, then your prayers must be directed toward God. The "Father who is in secret... [and] sees in secret" can just as easily hear and respond to prayers offered in total privacy as those proclaimed publicly.

Fasting (and all other ritual acts of piety) would follow the same pattern. Why should anyone need to know that you are fasting, unless of course you are fasting for the purpose of drawing attention to your piety? But if your fasting is for the purpose of strengthening your relationship with God, God doesn't need to see a haggard appearance to know that you have been skipping meals.

Just as it is important to recognize the metaphorical aspect of the epithet "hypocrites" (such people are like play-actors), so it is equally important to recognize that the "treasures in heaven" are not literal, material treasures like those that thieves steal and moths and rust consume here on earth. The true treasure that we have in heaven is our relationship with God that is strengthened by the practice of spiritual disciplines. Our "heart" should be with God, not with things either in this present world or in the world to come.

Application

Kerry Livgren had it right. All the things we do to build up treasures for ourselves on this earth ultimately crumble to the ground consumed by rust or are stolen away by thieves. The locusts that devour the stuff of our lives come in the form of both natural disasters and simple human evil. Even should you manage to safeguard your wealth, once you are confronted with the limits of your own mortality — in the words of another line from the song — "all your money won't another minute buy." Like these haunting lyrics, the words of the liturgy demand of us, "Remember that you are dust, and that to dust you shall return." Not just dust, but "dust in the wind."

That is not to say, however, that this song got it exactly right. We are dust, but it is not true that "all we are is dust in the wind." We are also the recipients of God's grace, mercy, and steadfast love. If we live out the responsibilities of that relationship, and repent of our past failures to do so, then God will spare us from being devoured or scattered into nothingness like dust in the wind. Indeed, by the reconciling work of God through Christ, the day of salvation has already begun now for those who can truly accept that grace.

That we are reconciled with God is wonderful, good news. But the fact remains that the day of salvation has only begun; it is not yet finished. Even though we have experienced the power of God, we still encounter afflictions, hardships, calamities, sleepless nights, and all the rest. We are yet dust, and our mortal bodies will one day return to the cosmic dust of which we are made. Ash Wednesday is a reminder that our reality is both harsh and blessed. We are "dying, and see — we are alive ... punished, and yet not killed... sorrowful, yet always rejoicing... having nothing, and yet possessing everything." Ash Wednesday is, after all, just the beginning of Lent, and the transformed, resurrection life of Easter will come.

An Alternative Application

It is customary in our society at the beginning of the year to ask others what New Year's resolutions they may have made. And it is not uncommon around churches as Ash Wednesday approaches to hear people inquire as to what others plan to "give up for Lent." But in the light of the gospel lesson, perhaps we should ask ourselves if we are not undercutting the whole point of Lenten rituals if we are comparing notes about them as we would about New Year's resolutions. After all, how many people keep their New Year's resolutions anyway?

Lent isn't primarily about giving things up in the first place. Like the ritual of fasting, the foregoing of something is secondary to the primary purpose of devoting more attention to one's relationship with God. Anything that shifts our focus away from God and onto ourselves or how others perceive our piety transforms Lent from a spiritual discipline into an empty ritual.

Lent 1
Genesis 9:8-17
1 Peter 3:18-22
Mark 1:9-15
David Kalas

A watery grave

A photograph of the earth from outer space reveals how much of our world is water. Indeed, that cosmic view prompted folks to refer to the Earth a "blue marble in space." Scientists report that approximately seventy percent of the Earth's surface is covered with water.

Genesis, meanwhile, reports an occasion when 100 percent of the Earth's surface was covered with water. This is the familiar story of Noah and the flood.

Archaeologists have discovered other ancient flood narratives that bear striking resemblances to the Genesis account of Noah. Biblical scholars ponder these comparable accounts, pondering what they mean for the version of the story we have in the Bible, as well as whatever event lies behind the similar traditions.

Meanwhile, in our popular culture — and even in our churches — the story of Noah does not seem to generate much serious attention. Instead, Noah is relegated to the ranks of one of the standard Bible stories for children, probably because of the appeal of all those animals. What is presented in scripture as an unprecedented and unparalleled act of divine judgment becomes, instead, the subject of children's puzzles and plush toys. While we wouldn't think of depicting the story of Sodom and Gomorrah in nursery wallpaper, the story of Noah has been tamed into a kind of ancient Dr. Doolittle with his boatful of happy pets.

The apostle Peter, however, has a different take on the familiar story. And so he provides the link between our Old Testament and gospel lessons, as we explore baptism together this week.

Genesis 9:8-17

The old rule of thumb for preachers and other public speakers went like this: Tell them what you're going to say, say it, and then tell them what you said. This excerpt from Genesis has some of that quality to it, for there's no missing the central theme here: God is establishing a covenant.

Covenants, of course, are a singularly important theme throughout scripture. From the high profile Old Testament covenants with Noah, Abraham, and David to the front-and-center symbolism of the Ark of the Covenant; from the prophetic promise of the new kind of covenant God had in mind (Jeremiah 31:31-34) to Christ's own reference to "the new covenant in my blood" (Luke 22:20); covenants are a motif that our people need to hear and recognize as they listen to scripture.

The covenant that God established with Noah in this episode represents the very first in the larger pattern of covenants found throughout the pages of scripture, and it includes several elements that are typical. First, God initiates. Second, the covenants that God initiates are broader than mere one-on-one agreements; future generations are always involved. And, third, the covenant is accompanied by some physical sign, which in this case is the rainbow.

A distinctive feature of this particular covenant is that it includes more than just human beings in the party of the second part. While the later covenants with Abraham, Israel, and David are all between God and people, this covenant with Noah extends to "every living creature that is with you." Inasmuch as the judgment of the flood afflicted all creatures, not just humankind, it is perfectly appropriate to include the animals in this promise never to flood the world again. It also serves as a very wholesome reminder to us that God is concerned with all of creation. It is easy — perhaps natural — for us to be anthropocentric in our reading and exposition of scripture. But God's gracious promise here is not to human beings alone; this special covenant is with the other creatures, as well.

The use of the word "remember" may deserve some attention, partly because it appears twice within our passage, and partly because its use in scripture may differ slightly from its use in our everyday speech.

Two times in this lection God assures Noah that he "will remember" the covenant between them. That language may seem strange to us because of our standard assumptions about God's omniscience. Of course he will remember, we reckon. What is the alternative? That God would forget? That it would slip his mind?

We set timers and alarms, put sticky notes on our mirrors and refrigerators, keep calendars and lists of things to do, all to remind us of things that we don't want to forget. Could it possibly be that a rainbow serves as God's sticky note in the sky? A multi-colored note from God to himself that says, in effect, don't forget that agreement you made with Noah?

The way that "remember" is used in the Old Testament, however, connotes a higher purpose than merely not forgetting. To remember is to do something. In our parlance, it would be comparable to what we mean when we "remember" someone's birthday or anniversary. In that context, to remember means more than merely having it occur to you that, oh yes, Grandma's birthday is next month. To remember her birthday means that we do something to honor her and to celebrate it.

So, too, with remembering in the Old Testament. "Remember" implies action. God's command to his people to "remember the sabbath day" suggests a certain behavior, as does Moses' recurring exhortation in Deuteronomy for the people to remember all of his words. Likewise, when God assures Noah that he will remember their covenant, he is making a guarantee about his actions that should be a great assurance to humankind.

1 Peter 3:18-22

This brief passage is thick with doctrine. And since so many American churches today are largely comprised of folks who have not been indoctrinated — that is, folks whose church involvement is informed only by duty, or by style of music, or by the activities offered for the kids, or by the portal of such-and-such a support group — this passage may require some deciphering.

We recognize, first of all, that Peter's language in verse 18 is the language of substitutionary atonement. This is not the only model in scripture for trying to describe the mystery of Christ's death on the cross, but it is a prominent and recurring one.

The immediate context for this passage is the suffering of the Christians to whom Peter writes. While the epistle does not offer many clues about the specific historical context, it is abundantly clear that Peter's audience is experiencing some considerable persecution. Contrary to the natural and just cause-and-effect of good deeds being rewarded and wicked deeds being punished, Peter's people are suffering for being good and for doing right. The apostle reminds those innocent sufferers, therefore, of the ultimate innocent sufferer. And not only did he suffer undeservedly, but more: He suffered what others deserved.

We also recognize, in this passage from Peter, the reference that lies behind an oft-forgotten line in the Apostles' Creed — "he descended into hell." Most people in our pews only know about the parts of Jesus' life, death, and resurrection reported in the gospels. This element of the story may be unfamiliar, therefore.

Peter's cryptic reference in our lection to "a proclamation was made to the spirits in prison" is generally thought to be related to his slightly later reference to "the gospel was proclaimed even to the dead" (4:6). Beyond that, however, the matter is not detailed in scripture. And without the benefit of explicit explanation, centuries of Christians have been left to interpret the matter for themselves. Those interpretations vary greatly, and there is not ample space to recount and evaluate them here.

Part of our frustration lies in the fact that Peter's passing reference here in chapter 3 appears only on his way to making a point about baptism. His purpose, it seems, is not to teach about Christ's mission "to the spirits in prison," but rather to draw a connection between the Noah event and our baptism. We borrow from the 4:6 reference, therefore, to get a sense for Peter's perspective on the whole event, and we discover there that his emphasis is on the redemptive work of God: that even those who were dead "might live in the spirit as God does."

Finally, we find in this lection a bit of baptismal theology that deserves explication. Given the over-arching theme of baptism in this week's lections, we will turn to that topic in more detail below.

Mark 1:9-15

Mark is well known for his brevity. Of the four gospels, his is the shortest. He moves through the story of Jesus with unparalleled speed. And, in his haste, he doesn't stop to talk much: that is to say, Mark does not record anywhere near the volume of sayings of Jesus that the other three gospel writers include.

Mark's characteristic terseness is evident in our selected gospel passage. While Matthew devotes sixteen verses to the stories of Jesus' baptism and temptation, and Luke's account has fifteen verses, Mark covers the material in a mere five verses. Mark does not have any of the dialogue between John and Jesus that Matthew includes, and he does not specify the three temptations Jesus faced as both Matthew and Luke do. Rather, Mark summarizes the whole affair in the brief phrase "tempted by Satan."

Lest we think of Mark's gospel as doodles on a napkin while Matthew and Luke paint with oil on canvas, however, we must observe how effectively Mark draws his picture with only a few strokes. "He was in the wilderness forty days," Mark reports, "tempted by Satan; and he was with the wild beasts; and the angels waited on him." Mark's writing style is not a lyrical as Luke's, but he does have a poet's touch for economy of words and effective imagery. For here, in just one verse, we are given a powerful portrait of Jesus' temptation experience. It lacks the dialogue of the other two synoptics, but it does set the stage: wilderness, Satan, wild beasts, and angels.

Taken with the previous verse, we are presented with a kind of metaphor of the Christian's experience. Inasmuch as the follower of Christ may expect to share in Christ's experiences, we are duly warned by this passage about what lies in store. He was driven by the Spirit, as we may aspire to be; but see where the Spirit drove him. Mark's wilderness is fraught with dangers and difficulties that are both physical and spiritual, both natural and supernatural. Yet, at both beginning and end, Christ and we are not alone, for the Spirit leads and angels minister.

The references to "wild beasts" is unique to Mark. While Matthew and Luke, on the whole, give us more details about these episodes than Mark, he does include this additional and compelling image in his account. And it stands in rather dramatic contrast to the dove mentioned just a few verses earlier. Thus, the range of Christ's experiences is symbolized — from the lush green fertility and fresh water of the Jordan River valley where a dove descended on him to the brown ruggedness of the arid Judean wilderness where wild beasts surrounded him.

Surprisingly — and significantly — it happens that the dove is more powerful than all of the wilderness' beasts. We know that in the context of this story. We need also to recognize it within the contexts of our lives.

Following his brief accounts of the baptism and temptation of Christ, Mark offers his thumbnail summary of Jesus' early ministry: he proclaimed the good news in Galilee, and that proclamation is expressed in three themes — repentance, the kingdom, and belief. Those are three rich and fundamental topics. If the Bible were a web page, each of those themes could be clicked on, and our people would be presented with a wealth of cross references, definitions, examples, and explications. Of course, that is what our preaching and teaching ought to provide.

Finally, there is beauty and significance in Jesus' initial declaration: "The time is fulfilled."

The word for "time" found in the original Greek is not the more pedestrian *chronos*, but rather the provocative *kairos*. The Greek *kairos* has a sense of a "decisive point," often "divinely ordained." This "time" is not merely the minutes and hours marked on the face of a clock. No, this "time" is an appointment on a calendar — indeed, on God's own calendar.

The word "fulfilled" is a frequent and important one in the New Testament. Matthew uses it often to bear witness to the way that the Old Testament dots were connected by the person and work of Christ. Jesus used it himself to express his own purpose in relation to the law and the prophets (Matthew 5:17). He also recognized certain scriptures being fulfilled in him and by him, most notably as he taught in the Nazareth synagogue (Luke 4:21). And Jesus, along with Luke and Paul, use the word to signal something that is complete, even at capacity (see, for example, John 16:24; Acts 2:2; Philippians 4:18-19).

Children associate the familiar tune of "Pop Goes The Weasel" with a jack-in-the-box toy. As they crank the handle and the music plays, they come to recognize the approaching moment — an expectation that is at capacity in the instant before the music reaches "Pop!"

According to Jesus' declaration, the music of history and time had come to that moment, the cranking was completed, and it was appointment time for the good news and the kingdom of God to "Pop!"

Application

The old fable imagines a handful of blind men positioned around an elephant. After taking a moment to explore with their hands the beast before them, each is asked to describe the elephant. Since one has the trunk, another the tail, another a tusk, and so on, however, they come up with very different descriptions of what an elephant is like.

The fable may be used for all sorts of mischief, of course, but it does provide a helpful image: Namely, that some truths are larger and more complex than any one person can fully understand or adequately describe.

Baptism may be one such truth. Such a variety of imagery is used in scripture and beyond to unpack the mystery of baptism. We meet a sampling here.

As our people read their Bibles, front to back, they may be startled by baptism's sudden and without introduction appearance at center stage. It does not appear as such anywhere in the Old Testament. Yet just three chapters into the New Testament, it is the centerpiece of John's notable ministry, and it becomes the first prominent recorded moment in Jesus' adult life.

As noted above, Mark does not furnish many of the details that Matthew and Luke include. Instead, in the mode of Sergeant Joe Friday, he gives us "just the facts." Jesus came from Galilee to the Jordan, where he was baptized by John. As he emerged from Jordan's baptismal waters, the Spirit came down upon him, and his Father's voice spoke to him from heaven.

While we understand that a baptism of repentance was not necessary for Jesus, that was the nature of everyone else's participation in John's baptism, and that is a part of the meaning and purpose Peter clearly has in mind. It is no mere bath, he insists. Its cleansing exceeds "the removal of dirt from the body," and results in "the pledge to God of a good conscience." As John Wesley observes, "Not, indeed, the bare outward sign, but the inward grace; a divine consciousness that both our persons and our actions are accepted through him who died and rose again for us" (*Wesley's Notes on the Bible*).

Furthermore, Peter goes beyond the image of washing and uses the language of saving. And it is at this point that he senses a resonance with the story of the Flood. Noah and his family, Peter observes, "were saved through water." And so are we — in the water of baptism.

Alan Stibbs effectively points out in *The First Epistle General of Peter: A Commentary* that "the flood spoke of a judgment, which those in the ark were both saved from, and saved by, in order to enjoy a new world." And, likewise, "the water of Christian baptism speaks of the death which fell upon Christ, a death due to sinners, which believers in Christ are both saved from, and saved by, and through which they enter into the enjoyment of new life before God."

Paul saw death and resurrection in the imagery of immersion (Romans 6:4; Colossians 2:12). Baptism, then, becomes a kind of watery grave — yet not because we perish, but because we come to new life there.

An Alternative Application

Mark 1:9-15. "It's Time." With three young children at home, my wife and I find ourselves continually announcing the time. Not necessarily the exact time — for example, 3:30 p.m. But, rather, we are constantly expressing what it is time to do.

"It's time to eat." "It's time to go." "It's time for bed." These are standard, daily parental pronouncements and they are not just informational. Each one implies some action on the part of the hearers.

To announce that it's time to eat is to say, "You need to stop what you're doing, go wash your hands, and come to the table." When the kids hear that "it's time for bed," they are expected to respond in very specific ways: put on their pajamas, brush their teeth, lay out tomorrow's clothes, pick out bedtime stories to read, and such.

In Mark's summary of Jesus' preaching, we hear the most profound "it's time" declaration. "The time is fulfilled," Jesus proclaims, and that is not merely informational. The announcement — the time — requires some action. Specifically, two things: repentance and belief.

The coming of the kingdom is a surprisingly neglected topic in most of our churches. Surprising, I say, because we routinely pray for it ("thy kingdom come") and yet seldom talk about it. Yet the coming of the kingdom seems to be the centerpiece of Jesus' proclamation in this passage. It has "come near" because "the time is fulfilled," and it is because the kingdom "has come near" that we are called upon to "repent, and believe the good news."

This week's gospel lesson affords us the opportunity to explore with our congregations these three basic themes: God's kingdom, our repentance, and believing the gospel. Indeed, perhaps it's time to talk about them.

Lent 2
Genesis 17:1-7, 15-16
Romans 4:13-25
Mark 8:31-38
Wayne Brouwer

Building a new team

When Vince Lombardi was hired as head coach of the Green Bay Packers in 1958, the team was in dismal shape. A single win in season play the year before had socked the club solidly into the basement of the NFL, and sportscasters everywhere used it as the butt of loser jokes. But Lombardi picked and pulled and prodded and trained and disciplined the players into becoming a winning team. They were NFL champions in three consecutive seasons, and took the game honors for the first two Super Bowls.

Lombardi was a drill sergeant and a strategist, finding and developing the best in each of his players individually and then crafting a team community that could visualize the prize. "Winning isn't everything," he was often quoted as saying, "It's the only thing!" And his Packers proved him true, time and again.

Coaching is nothing without a team that responds. Leaders are merely overblown egos if there is no one who will follow. During the tumultuous French Revolution of 1789, mobs and madmen rushed through Paris streets. One journalist reported a wide-eyed, wild-haired wastrel lumbering along one day, feverishly demanding from all he saw, "Where is the crowd? I must find them! I am their leader!"

But just as surely, there is no team without a leader. People will mill about, or wander aimlessly. Isaiah, and later Jesus, saw the Israelites as sheep scattered on a hillside with no shepherd to guide them. England without Churchill was a patchwork of competing ideologies, stymied at the crossroads of the twentieth century's critical international events. India before Gandhi lacked cohesive identity and played a game of competitive kowtowing to expatriate authorities, and was only turned around when he helped inspire a national common cause.

In each of today's lectionary passages, there is a new team being called into existence by a great leader. God lays claim on Abraham and his descendents, telling the patriarch that the entire world is the new playing field, and all its national teams will be shaped by the new forays Abraham's family team will run. Paul remembers this event in his letter to the Romans and uses it as the rallying cry that sends the Christian church on its global mission. And Jesus, when facing his own demise, calls to the crowds to join him in the greatest endeavor ever attempted on planet earth — the overthrow of the truly demonic "Evil Empire."

Genesis 17:1-7, 15-16

In the world of the Bible, Genesis functions as the prologue to the covenant God makes with Israel at Mount Sinai (Exodus 20-24). Modeled after the Suzerain-Vassal covenants widely used in that day to organize affairs between kings and subjects, these covenants had standardized parts. The prologue rehearsed the background to the making of the covenant, and gave the reasons why it was necessary. Genesis is built, literarily, in four major sections that each help Israel understand a portion of the historical necessity that brought about this treaty ratification. Chapters 1-11 tell of the good world God created and the nasty civil war that has threatened to destroy it. Chapters 12-25 speak of Abraham and the way that God selected him to head the team which would become the advance troops in taking back God's world from the evil intruders. Chapters 26-36 are a character study of how Jacob becomes "Israel" (one who struggles with God) and thus bequeaths the nation with a name and an identity. Chapters 37-50 focus on Joseph, and describe how the nation eventually wound up in Egypt, from which it has so recently emerged.

Genesis 17 is part of the second section of the book, and God is building a new team. God's covenant-making initiatives with Abram begin in chapter 12; this episode is actually the fourth such scene in just six chapters. That ought to alert the reader to the critical changes which surface in this new covenant-making event. Along with the parity agreements between individuals of similar social rank in the ancient world (think of Jacob and Laban forming their parity treaty at the end of Genesis 31), there were two forms of king-subject covenants. One was a "Royal Grant." This was essentially a gift bestowed by a person of power and political privilege upon someone down-caste a rung or more. Usually the king noticed an act of bravery in battle, or striking beauty in the ballroom, or uncommon beneficence in bearing, and gave a gift in public recognition (so Persian king, Xerxes, to Mordecai in Esther 3-4). In each case the grant was a one-way act, with no specific reciprocal deed required.

The second type of king-subject covenant, the "Suzerain-Vassal treaty," was quite different, however. It moved on a two-way street, and both gave and expected much. When ratified, kings would provide safety and food and shelter and relief and community building grants, while the people were obligated to pay taxes, offer troops for the regiments, send food supplies, and enlist in government work projects. Rather than merely a bequest awarded by one to the other as was true with the royal grant, the Suzerain-Vassal treaty ensured that both parties invest in the relationship.

Interestingly, in the series of covenants developed between God and Abram in Genesis 12-17, the first three (Genesis 12, 13, 15) appear to be "royal grants." Each time a gift is proffered — land (twice) and a biological heir who will help establish a great Abram-family nation. Strikingly, after each royal grant is spoken, Abram seems to lose confidence in the gift. Rather than stay in the land of promise, he runs to Egypt to find better grazing for his crops and food sources for his crew. Similarly, instead of mating again with wife, Sarai, to realize a biological heir, Abram and the younger Hagar bond to produce Ishmael. Three times God makes royal grants with Abram, and each time Abram takes matters into his own hands.

This time, however, God changes tactics, and Abram comes out of the deal with a transformed heart. It is a Suzerain-Vassal covenant that is being crafted here in chapter 17. God promises land and blessings and descendents, but God also calls Abram to respond with faith and fealty. Abram is not merely the target of a nice gift; now he is called to share the mind and the mission of the Maker. God declares name changes for Abram and Sarai, and also requires the act of circumcision which will publicly mark all the males of the family as "owned" by God.

The outcome to this fourth covenant-making event is strikingly different than that following the previous three. Most notably, when pushed to the limit of trust in Genesis 22, the new Abraham gives evidence that his covenant relationship with God supersedes all other loyalties and commitments. Because of the Suzerain-Vassal covenant established in Genesis 17, faith sticks in Abraham's life.

Of course, for the Israelites at Mount Sinai reviewing this history, the lesson would be clear. God's gifts alone do not bind us into God's redemptive enterprises. A faith response and loyal service round out the picture. Without investment on our part, no great blessing of God lingers for our enjoyment. Abraham and his descendents form a great team because they have a great coach who gives the right incentives and demands the right stuff in return.

Romans 4:13-25

Abbott and Costello entranced an earlier generation with their side-splitting routine "Who's on First?" Pretending to discuss the players of a baseball team, names were confused with positions until tracking the game became an exercise in futility.

Among the religious discussions of Paul's day there was a similar confusion of identities. For some, evil was inherent in the system like yin's twin, yang. For others, humans had incurred the wrath of the gods and were punished through the spread of vices that flowed out of Pandora's mythical box. Others still believed divine perfection was trapped by a mean-spirited creator into the corrupt and forgetful stuff of human flesh, awaiting magical gnostic liberation.

Paul penned this letter while spending the winter in Corinth at the close of his third mission journey. He was preparing to leave for Jerusalem with offerings collected throughout Greece, Macedonia, and Asia Minor which were intended to alleviate the needs of the poor in Palestine (ch. 15). Paul hoped to embark on another mission journey soon thereafter, and this time stop in Rome on his way to Spain and the western reaches of the empire.

Paul's design in the first part of this letter (1:19—3:20) is to give a different view of the origins of evil. God is good; creation is good; and human alienation from the good is a late introduction brought about by our sinful choices. For Paul's audience in Rome, made up of both Jewish and Gentile Christians, the message communicated is that neither has the religious advantage over the other. All of humanity had the same opportunities to remain in fellowship with the creator, and all are equally responsible for their distance from God.

But now, in chapter 4, Paul turns a theological corner and explains how God initiates a restoration of relationships with humanity. All are welcome to be part of the new team. The captain is Jesus and the most valuable player is Abraham. No player joins the team because of skills, nor is any drafted based upon a previous winning record. All are brought on in the same way that Abraham came: receiving a uniform as a gift and believing that the captain shapes the only winning team in spite of all odds.

Several things are particularly noteworthy in this passage. First, "righteousness" in Romans (beginning with Paul's great assertion in 1:17-18) can be interpreted either as the unattainable holiness of God by which we are judged as inadequate, or as the reassertion of God's intended good designs for God's creation. Here it becomes obvious that the latter approach seems more consistent with Paul's more fully developed message. "Righteousness" is God's way of restoring what was ruined by sin and placed out of reach by "law."

Second, the covenant promises made to Abraham in Genesis 12-17 and clearly intended there as unfolding biologically, are here spiritualized to describe a new people that transcends national boundaries or ethnic definitions. But this must not be taken as a new theology or a change in divine plans. After all, God's intent was to bless all nations of the earth through Abraham's family. Here is the outcome of that divine plan. This knowledge is important for the congregation in Rome, since it was made up of both Jew and Gentile believers. They must see themselves as co-equal in their stance before God, and Paul explains how this is possible.

Third, Paul affirms that all of this is possible because of Jesus. He is the expression of God's righteousness inserted recently into our world, and the means by which we are attached to the righteous endeavors of God. He is the glue that binds the team together and keeps them connected both to the *owner* and the *game*.

Mark 8:31-38

Mark's gospel (as is true for the other synoptic gospels, Matthew and Luke) seems to have three major sections. The first section focuses on Jesus' healing and teaching activity as it widely spread throughout Galilee. When Jesus speaks, his theme is most often the character of "the kingdom of God." Then, secondly, comes the recital of Jesus' more intimate conversations about discipleship. The third major portion is devoted to Jesus' final week in Jerusalem, culminating with his trial, death, and resurrection. The transitions from section to section are the same in all three gospels — between the first and second occurs Jesus' transfiguration; between the second and the third is Jesus' entry into Jerusalem.

With that in mind, it is clear to see that our lectionary reading for today concludes the first section of Mark's gospel. By this time, according to Mark, Jesus has clearly expressed his divine power and wisdom. Enough so, in fact, that he can begin to speak about the sacrificial death toward which he is heading.

The occasion of Jesus' new disclosure is striking. He and his disciples are in the far north of Palestine, wandering among the tree-lined streams on the slopes of Mount Hermon. Waters gush from natural springs at the foot of the mountain, and some bubble from caves. For centuries, people had considered this place a gateway into the underworld and a haunt of the gods. Among these sacred shrines, Jesus asks his disciples if they truly understand who he is. Prophets and priests appeared here regularly, and Jesus could well be just another face in that mixed crowd. Even the residents of Caesarea Philippi might assume such about Jesus, but Jesus cannot move to the next phase of his ministry if his own little band is uncertain. So Jesus asks the important questions, and proffers the affirmation of Peter's important answer (8:27-30).

Peter's confidence is raised by Jesus' public recognition of him, so when the master next speaks, and tells of his impending suffering and death, Peter feels the need to intervene. Jesus uses the occasion to declare the parameters of the new team he is creating. It is not Peter's insubordination that calls out the rebuke, but Peter's misunderstanding of the game plan and its goal. Winning, for Jesus, means playing by a set of rules that have not been used for a long time on planet earth. It is like the "deep magic" of Aslan in C.S. Lewis' great tale, *The Lion, the Witch and the Wardrobe*. Most don't understand it, but without it the game becomes a never-ending cycle of violence in which there are only losers.

For that reason, Jesus moves from his reprimand of Peter to a brief exhortation about the characteristics that mark those on his team. It is not self-preservation but service that counts. It is not superiority but selflessness that wins points. It is not stridency but sacrifice that finds recognition from the owner of the club.

Jesus is putting together a team that will change the world. Unfortunately, few people seem to show up at the try-outs.

Application

There is a scene in Tolkien's *The Fellowship of the Ring* where a partnership is forged among those who would accompany Frodo on his journey to destroy the ring of power. The movie version makes for a very gripping visual illustration, and the original literary text is equally as moving. What comes through is a sense of selflessness as the bond that unites these creatures. Furthermore, each subsumes his will to the greater cause, and trusts an unseen and transcendent good for an outcome that will bless all of Middle Earth, even if the trek itself causes the demise of any or all of the compatriots.

So it is in these biblical glimpses of the mission of God. In a world turned cold to its creator, in an age riddled by Delphic oracles and temple prostitutes and emperors claiming divinity, in a little corner of geography where messianic hopes ran high, God calls together a strange team to make its mark by playing a different game. Walter Wangerin Jr.'s, great allegory, *The Book of the Dun Cow* (as well as its wonderful sequel, *The Book of Sorrows*), captures both the scope of the divine mission as well as the underrated character of the team. It is well worth a read in preparation for today's message. If the focus remains on the team apart from the mission, the point is lost. God is reclaiming God's creation, but does so through human agency. The game is fierce and the playing field is rough. Only those who can tear up their personal score sheets in order to get into God's game will make the team. Only they are truly called. Only they are equipped to serve and follow and play on the greatest winning team of all time.

An Alternative Application

Mark 8:31-38. On this second Sunday in Lent it might be profitable to focus on Jesus' gospel teaching. He is on the road to the cross, and he calls others to join him in that pilgrimage. Lent is a time of self-denial, and Jesus' words are a strong call to that vocation, not as an end in itself or as a means to a self-help goal (like dieting), but rather as a counter-cultural missional testimony. Those who travel this Lenten road are not first of all focused on Easter but on Good Friday; they do not presume a glorious outcome that gathers the media like paparazzi vultures, but sense that the journey of service brings light in darkness, hope in despair, healing for pain, and faith where power corrupts and destroys.

It is important to remember, though, that the Sundays *in* Lent do not belong to Lent. They are not Sundays *of* Lent in the way that the Sundays of Advent are owned by that season. When counting the forty days of this season, beginning at Ash Wednesday, it becomes clear that the Sundays are not registered in the tally. Because we live in a post-Easter world, the Sundays during Lent are oases of grace in what could otherwise become a horrible time of flagellation without mercy. While the theme of discipleship must carry us down a path of self-denial, it must not lose sight of grace. Easter grace. Divine grace. Life-giving grace. This is why any who would echo Peter's plea for a nicer and more sanitized version of Jesus' biography actually undermine the power of divine favor. For, as Dietrich Bonhoeffer so eloquently wrote, "... grace is always free, but it is never cheap"; only those who understand *The Cost of Discipleship* revel in the songs of grace that ring even on these Sundays during Lent.

Craig MacCreary

Table manners

Perhaps it is the oddity that I am writing this on the Monday before Thanksgiving or it is my proclivity to identify food with each passing holiday that, as I approach these texts, I find myself thinking of another text from Psalm 23: "You prepare a table before me in the presence of my enemies." Thanksgiving, Christmas, and the Fourth of July and I am dreaming dreams of sugar plum fairies, turkey legs, chocolate bunnies, and barbecues. This is definitely a job hazard for clergy. Most congregations revel in putting together various feasts. Of course, I have it all wrong. This is an embarrassment. This is definitely not what the psalmist had in mind. Perhaps I should not be doing this after I have run six miles and before lunch. It does not help in fixing my thought on a more excellent way or to the higher things in life. Unlike Paul, I find myself all too easily looking to the things that are seen rather than the unseen.

Yet each of these lessons evokes the table that is prepared for us and how we react to it: in thanksgiving for both tables of the law, in acknowledgment that what we bring to the table might not be as important as who presides at the table, in recognition that perhaps the tables should be turned?

Of course, this had already come up in the Hebrew's life together. "Why do you spend your money for that which is not bread and your labor for that which does not satisfy? Listen carefully to me, and eat what is good, and delight yourselves in rich food." It came up in the Corinthian church as they made a mockery of the common meal: "For all who eat and drink without discerning the body, eat and drink judgment against themselves." Some of the strongest condemnation of Jesus in the gospels centers on his table manners and his ministry of the table: "And the Pharisees and the scribes were grumbling and saying, 'this fellow welcomes sinners and eats with them.' What manner of man is this?"

The table can be sumptuous, or it can be as sparse as a simple hot dog with your father at your first ball game. Either way, there is a sense that the meal can be either one in which we draw closer to one another and to God or one in which the distance between the dinners is barely overcome by civility. A few clergy meals lately have felt like the last meal of the condemned before controversy erupts around the latest blue state/red state theological battle. Many families will find only helpings of shame, guilt, and disgust served up with Thanksgiving turkey and Easter ham. I have known church Easter egg hunts to break down into a sea of tears when, despite the best adult supervision, the children act out the meaning of Matthew 25:29: "For to all those who have, more will be given, and they will have an abundance; but from those who have nothing, even what they have will be taken away."

The stakes are raised whenever we talk of coming to the table. The mood changes and either tension mounts or relaxation sets in. At the table, either folks open up, clam up, become terribly self-conscious, or wonderfully conscious of the love of God in their midst. Our dining room contains the table and buffet that have been in my family for four generations. Having been made by a long forgotten manufacturer from Lackawanna County, Pennsylvania, it will not be revealed to be a treasure of historic proportions on the *Antiques Road Show*. However, I treasure it because all of the extremes of human experience that have taken place around it. From time to time it has called into question why we labor for things that do not satisfy, reminded us that in our rush at life we have often eaten and drunk judgment to ourselves. Certainly, at times it reminds me of the certainties that need to be overturned in our lives. It has been a table in the presence of our enemies that has testified to God's love through all the years. Each of the texts this Sunday, in their own way, brings us to a table that is prepared for us.

Exodus 20:1-17

Oh boy. Here it is — the big ten! Is it any surprise that going up this mountain we get a case of vertigo? How do we preach all this? Going down this laundry list results in moralistic excess. I think it is easier to preach ten sermons on each commandment than to preach one sermon on the Ten Commandments. One year, I volunteered to call the whole thing off if anyone could name the Third Commandment. The congregation lost the wager. Maybe it would be a good thing after all to drill them in marble and put them up in as many public places as possible.

The commandments seem a bit overwhelming at best. They are like the great meals that my mother would serve up at holiday season. It required an expansion of our dining room table by the addition of a couple of boards just to accommodate it all. Child of an only child, married to an only child, we never had to accommodate a horde of relatives. Overwhelmed by abundance, each meal carried me back to my childhood memories of the holidays. Perhaps the best way to preach the commandments is from a more childlike naive perspective than weighing in with all the training and learning that one has received over the years. Trying to get all that in may lead to a homiletical disaster.

The feast here to my child's eye is clearly composed of two boards' worth of table. God and people: If I have this right, you don't come away from this table with much nourishment if you don't have both. It looks like Calvin had it right after all. Without knowledge of self, there is no knowledge of God. "Nearly all the wisdom we possess, that is to say, true and sound wisdom, consists of two parts: the knowledge of God and of ourselves... In the first place, no one can look upon himself without immediately turning his thoughts to the contemplation of God, in whom he or she 'lives and moves' " (Acts 17:28). Welcome to the table. However, it seems that is precisely the problem in our time. Some come down on the side of God without much human understanding and sensitivity. Others of us come down on the human side of the equation, soft peddling the God stuff lest it offend. This seems to be a delicate balance at best.

I once attended a service of installation of a pastor in a black congregation. The preacher for the day at one point leaned over the lectern staring over his glasses and railed against those who opted for self-fulfillment over self-sacrifice as the basis of their belief. Since he was glaring at the contingent of mainline pastors in the room, it was pretty clear that he thought that we had gotten things out of balance. Pastor Dale Rosenberger tells the tale in *Who Are You To Say* of being ripped from stem to stern by a nurse who was repulsed at his injection of God-talk into the conversation of a hospital board of ethics, on which they both served. Following an Easter sermon, one astute, highly socially-committed and active parishioner asked, "You don't really believe any of this stuff, do you?"

If nothing else, the commandments remind us that there is no nourishment from these tables if we do not keep both tablets in mind and seek to balance their offerings. It seems simple enough until you are slumping in your pew at an installation or serving on the ethics board, or headed for home after Easter service. I don't like the translations that render the meaning of not taking the Lord's name in vain as a matter of bad words. The truth is that my life is in vain when I don't get my relationship with God in order. When I am stuck vainly looking in the mirror, the rest of my life becomes futile. Such ineffectual living tends to push the true God out of my life.

The commandments require us to hold both tables of the law together and not to put asunder what God has joined together. Any of the commandments can be an entrance into this truth. All of the commandments invite us to feast at the table of the Lord that requires both boards to hold everything.

1 Corinthians 1:18-25

In American parliamentary parlance, "to table" something is to put it in limbo, to put it off, to put it on the back burner. It is the opposite in Canada. To table something is to bring it into play. Of course in the holidays we want to bring as much into play as we possibly can. Thanksgiving, Christmas, or Easter is not the time to stint on anything. Bring it on. Needless to say, this means in most houses that someone will spend a great deal of time in the kitchen trying to cook up something that will win the plaudits of all the invited quests. I remember one church I served where the committees rotated meeting in various homes. The process seemed to dictate that we were all in some sort of perpetual game of topper. By the end of my first year, we were eating full-course banquets before we got down to business. This was not a good formula for doing business. In a church in Pennsylvania Dutch country, the plan was often for the hostess never to sit down at the table. As a matter of fact, no place was set for her. In many of the churches I served early in my ministry, years were taken off my life because of the way that the tables were piled high with the gastronomic triumphs of the parishioners. In a few congregations, the common meal has been made a mess of by the frenetic struggle to get it all right and serve up a seamless spiritual moment. Things must be served in good order, after all. On the other hand, the Corinthians seemed to have made a mess of things by letting the chaos of the secular order to break out in the shared life. Those who worked on flex time, the white-collar folks, came in and gobbled things up first before the blue-collar and the slave-collar folks showed up.

It seems that folks get into trouble here because of what they think that they have to serve up. We get the mistaken notion that it is our recipe for success that matters whether people are fed or not. Often, if things go according to our plans, a lot of folks will go without, while many will wind up stuffing them-selves. I suspect that Paul's experience with the Corinthians and what they had served up as church was in his mind as he wrote these words, "Where is the one who is wise? Where is the scribe? Where is the debater of this age? Has not God made foolish the wisdom of the world? For since, in the wisdom of God, the world did not know God through wisdom, God decided, through the foolishness of our proclamation, to save those who believe." The wisdom of the age, as it does in our age, left many with more than enough and others going hungry spiritually and materially. This approach to things in the American sense needs to be tabled.

The Corinthians needed to see that they were not the chefs nor was life according to their recipe. The wisdom of the world would only serve up disaster. They simply needed, in the Canadian sense, to table their lives. To place on the table of the Lord their joys, their failings, their sins, their triumphs, their common life, and their private experiences, that the power of God might transform these offerings into building blocks of the kingdom of God. For it is written, "I will destroy the wisdom of the wise, and the discernment of the discerning I will thwart." Of course, there are those who will seek signs and those who will find this all a stumbling block. They will say they have found the secret recipe — vote democratic or republican, plastics, intelligent design, mindless living, of doing your own thing, twelve ways to make chicken soup of the mind. Yet, our work is taking up the cross, of putting our lives on the table for God's work, joining in the task of making sure all can come to God's table — tabling, in the American sense, our own grand designs in order that God's plan for us to grow in God's wisdom and stature will serve up the meal that will satisfy our deepest hungers.

John 2:13-22

The gospels invariably bring us to the moment when the table that is prepared for is the one that is turned, even overturned, for us. It takes some serious believing that the son of Joseph and Mary who can-not even save himself from the cross is the one who will be able to destroy the temple and rebuild it anew. If anything, it seems that the world will do a lot more deconstructing of Jesus than Jesus does of the world. Then it came in the form of crucifixion. In the modern age, it seems we want to put him under our micro-scopes and dissect his intentions and motives. With all due respect to modern scholarship, to which much is owed, it seems that having once dissected him we then proceed to reconstruct him in our image: wise "Yoda"-like one, therapist, revolutionary, motivational speaker, medical specialist in diseases of the skin, humorist, and literary stylist. None of these are without merit in and of themselves. Yet, this text from John proclaims that if we do not understand Jesus as the one who first deconstructs and then reconstructs, then all of our understanding of Jesus will be seriously flawed. In a very uncanny way, Jesus' encounter with the temple makes clear that his work is in alignment with the full body of scripture.

Walter Brueggemann points out in *Hopeful Imagination*, that scripture invites us into a world of relinquishing and receiving. We are invited to give up that which inhibits the kingdom so that we may receive what God will establish as his next line of brick in the "house not built with human hands."

John sets the seemingly chaotic scene of stampeding animals, coins ricocheting, and tables crashing as ironically when the Passover that leads to sabbath rest is near. The hands on issues here involve bad economics as well as bad theology, "Take these things out of here! Stop making my Father's house a marketplace!" What sends chills up and down the spine and challenges the mind is the realization that the marketplace mentality has, in our time, become a near god if not the only god. Many of us seem to have things backward here. Man is not made for the sabbath, but the sabbath is made for man. It has become common currency for many to imagine that there is nothing that the "free market" cannot fix. I am not against free markets, but when they become a god, as with any human creation being offered our undivided loyalty, then we are headed for trouble. What free-market incentive causes us to be brave enough to enter into marriages or trust enough to make churches? What calculation of self-interest lies behind those who found the best in themselves only by surrendering themselves to a love that was larger themselves? Are we saved by our calculations or our connections to one another?

When I encounter this scripture, I find myself wondering if my spiritual life has grown vapid. Is this when I have been most resistant to Jesus cleansing me by overturning the tables by which I calculate my life?

Application

One thing that has buffaloed me in life is table manners. It is not that if you sat next to me at a meal that you would have to endure a boatload of boorish behavior. However, you would find an anxious presence as I tried to sort out which fork and spoon goes in what order. It seems as of late that finer restaurants are adding all sorts of utensils to down a whole variety of new courses. The meals are prettier and there are whole new flavors and new cuisines from around the world that are making it onto my plate. Yet I feel discomfort and anxiety.

This is how I suspect a lot of lay people feel about much of the offerings of religious scholarship that are showing up in sermons, worship, and discussions. There are now feminist readings, liberation readings, gay/lesbian and transgender readings, and native aboriginal readings, to name a few. There is little doubt that we are all better off for these readings. Yet, they can be a heady mix for those who grew up with the only options being King James or Revised Standard Version.

Some advice on table manners from the lesson for this Sunday may be helpful if we are to enjoy the feast that God intends. Make sure you include both boards to expand the table so that it will include all. What does what we say about God say about people — not people in general, but specific people? When we make statements about people, how does that reflect our understanding of God? Furthermore, how does what we say of God relate to creation? It is not easy to hold these together. Then again, the clinical definition of death is the total absence of tension in the body.

When we come to the table, are we putting all our cards on the table so that God may transform what we bring? Some of us bring years of church experience, some of us bring the freshness of a recent conversion. All of us, "having come short of the glory of God" need the transformation of what we bring.

When you come to the table do not be surprised if things are turned or overturned. We might find ourselves ministered to by people we never suspected. We might find strengths for ministry that we never imagined.

There is a table prepared for us. Relax and enjoy the feast.

An Alternative Application

John 2:13-22. In my sermonizing, I know when I am most likely to have set myself up for a journey down a dead-end street. Interestingly enough, knowing this little gem rarely prevents me from often taking this unproductive journey. I think it has to do with the days when my belief in the resurrection is a little thin and a lot less open to understanding that Jesus is one that does walk and talk with me and tells me I am his own. Having been to college, seminary, and graduate school, I find myself all too often believing that I am dealing with texts to be examined more than a living presence to be encountered.

Paul writes, "Where is the one who is wise? Where is the scribe? Where is the debater of this age? Has not God made foolish the wisdom of the world?" I know the answer. I often want a text to be something that I can be wise about rather than be something that humbles me. I love being the scribe — the pastor of record. In such moments, scintillating phrases come out of my mouth such as, "In my day, we..." or "We have always done it this way," or "If you just had studied more, like I have, you would get it." I love it when a text enables me to make points and run up the score on my enemies. I appreciate it somewhat less when the text moves me, or helps me, as David Buttrick puts it, to make the helpful homiletical moves.

I suspect that there is a bridge here between lay people and clergy. Whether we are in the pulpit or the pew we may have more of the answers to Paul's questions than we realize. In sharing our answers I suspect that we discover the presence, in our midst, of the living Christ who has made foolish the wisdom of the world.

Lent 4
Numbers 21:4-9
Ephesians 2:1-10
John 3:14-21
David Kalas

Prescription on a pole

We have so many aisles of medications in our country today that home remedies may be a vanishing art. So many over-the-counter products boast that they can cure what ails us, not to mention the almost infinite number of prescription medicines that our doctors may commend to us for our good.

An older generation, however, remembers the homemade treatments and concoctions that were handed down from Grandma. It was hard to trace the science behind such traditional home remedies, but they had the credibility of years, experience, common sense, and love.

Sometimes our treatments — whether Grandma's or the pharmacist's — are quite distasteful. And, as children, we may have pursed our lips and turned up our noses, in need of persuasion that this curdled spoonful was really ultimately good. Likewise, as adults: the procedures and treatments we sometimes face bring both great pain and expense, and we may wonder if it's worth it all.

God looked out once upon a people who were dying. They needed some cures, and fast. And so he wrote out a prescription for Moses to fill: a bronze snake hung up on a pole for all to see. It was not an expensive remedy — at least not in its original incarnation — nor was it a painful procedure for the needy patients. And it was only at an intellectual level that this prescription was hard to swallow.

The Old Testament lesson this week tells us the story of this prescription on a pole. The gospel lesson invites us to rethink it, and the passage from Paul reminds us just how God's salvation works.

Numbers 21:4-9

The book of Numbers is seldom mentioned when folks talk about their favorite passages from scripture. Yet, while this obscure story, brief and tucked away in the rarely-read Old Testament, may seem initially unimportant to the people in our pews, the imagery of the episode is endlessly powerful for us as Christians.

First, there is the strange choice of remedy. In the twenty-first century, we think scientifically about our remedies — there is a traceable cause-and-effect relationship between our treatments and our cures. No such relationship can be detected here, however. There is no explaining how a look at a manufactured snake can heal a snakebite. In that sense, we might be inclined to give this remedy the label of "miracle." We might also label it an act of faith: to trust and obey God's inexplicable prescription.

Moreover, God's chosen remedy is a strange one not just in theory but also in detail. If we grant that the bitten Israelites can be healed by looking at some erected thing, what thing might we choose? What symbol would we guess or select? Not this one. We are surprised to find that the remedy recalls the malady.

Furthermore, we may also think God's remedy strange because it does not seem to strike at the root of the problem. The final line in our Old Testament lesson reports that "whenever a serpent bit someone, that person would look at the serpent of bronze and live." Isn't it odd that the Lord would provide a cure rather than simply removing the cause? Why should Israel settle for what a person could do "whenever a serpent bit someone"? Why didn't God remove the serpents altogether?

On this last point, of course, we find ourselves in the deep end of the pool. For now we are entertaining questions like "Why does God permit evil to exist?" and "Why didn't God just defeat the devil right away?" and even "Why did God allow the forbidden fruit and the serpent in Eden in the first place?"

Within the immediate context of this story, we observe that the poisonous serpents come into the camp as a result of the people's faithlessness and complaining. Interestingly, we see that God provides a remedy for the consequence of the people's sin, but he does not remove the consequence.

Also, we suggested above that God's remedy does not seem to strike at the root of the problem, but that statement presumes that the root of the problem is the poisonous snakes. Perhaps it is not. Perhaps Israel's real problem is faithlessness, and the serpents are only a symptom — or at least an effect — of that root cause. If so, then a remedy that requires a faithful response does, in fact, strike very much at the heart of the problem.

That faithful response brings us to the second compelling element of this story: the required participation of the afflicted. The human role is never static, never entirely passive, in God's saving acts. We are not necessarily instrumental to the deliverance, but still we must opt to participate in it. There is no sense in which the Israelites healed themselves, and yet they did have to make a choice to partake of the healing. They were not just suffering in their tents when, suddenly, they were healed. No, they were required to do something — to look at the serpent on the pole. In spite of the complete absence of empirical cause-and-effect, the people were called upon to respond to God's prescription, and that response was an act of faith.

That, finally, brings us to the third element: namely, the very limited nature of their participation. The Israelites were indeed required to do something to be healed, but not much. There was no act of heroism required, no expense to be paid, no meritorious deed to qualify for it. Therefore, just as there was no detectable medical or scientific cause-and-effect relationship between the remedy and their healing, likewise there was no real merit or effort figured into the calculation of God's healing. The people were not saved by their diligence, their money, or their righteousness. Instead, there was a simple act of faith, and then they were healed.

Ephesians 2:1-10

Good writing requires a good start. What will catch the reader's attention? What will make him or her bother to keep reading?

Paul catches our attention with the forceful way in which he starts this chapter of Ephesians. "You were dead," he declares, "through the trespasses and sins in which you once lived." To a novice, his language might seem hyperbolic, or at least metaphorical. Of course the Ephesians weren't actually dead; Paul is just trying to illustrate a point.

Taken with Jesus' use of verb tenses in our gospel lesson, however, we are confronted with a reality that is neither hyperbole nor metaphor. Jesus said, "Those who believe in him are not condemned; but those who do not believe are condemned already" (John 3:18). The condemnation, it seems, is not in the future; it has already occurred. Similarly, Jesus says, "Anyone who hears my word and believes him who sent me has eternal life, and does not come under judgment, but has passed from death to life" (John 5:24). We see that eternal life is not merely a promise waiting beyond the grave; it is a present reality. It's not that the person who believes will eventually pass from death to life; he already has.

Our human tendency is to draw the line of demarcation in the wrong place. We think of our physical death as the great pivotal moment, but the condemnation, the judgment, and the start of eternal life have all occurred long before that. There is some earlier point on our time line when we pass from death to life. That is the paradigm suggested by Jesus and the reality to which Paul refers when he tells the Ephesians that they "were dead through the trespasses and sins in which (they) once lived."

"Following the course of this world," at first blush, sounds innocuous enough. From a young age, we show our instinct to follow the crowd. It is an essential part of fitting in wherever we happen to be. And, similarly, Paul's later reference to being "like everyone else" seems like a harmless observation. After all, being "like everyone else" is, at times, precisely our aspiration.

But "this world" is never innocuous in the New Testament. And being "like everyone else" is a harsh condemnation when the paradigm says that "everyone else" is a child of wrath, a slave of sin, and dead in their trespasses. Indeed, even in matters of ordinary human goodness, Jesus questions the merit of being like everyone else (see Matthew 5:43-48).

In considering our Old Testament lesson, we observed the nature of our human participation in God's saving acts. On the one hand, we are not passive objects of his deliverance. On the other hand, we are not necessarily instrumental in our deliverance, either. Instead, in the case of the Israelites in the wilderness, they were required to participate, but their participation was more an act of faith than a cause-and-effect contribution to their healing.

In the light of Paul's explanation of the gospel here, we see that the Israelites' healing is an apt metaphor for our salvation. "By grace you have been saved through faith," Paul writes, "and this is not your own doing; it is the gift of God — not the result of works, so that no one may boast." The Israelites would have been hard-pressed to argue that their "works" had healed them — that is, that they had done anything to heal themselves. Likewise, we don't really do anything to save ourselves. But the Israelites around the pole — like Christians around the cross — access God's gracious remedy only through faith.

John 3:14-21

We may be accustomed to turning to Romans, Colossians, or Hebrews in order to explicate for our people the person and work of Christ. But here, in the familiar environs of John 3, we have Jesus' own explanation of who he is and what he came to do.

No single verse of scripture may be as familiar in our churches as John 3:16. Even in a day of such biblical illiteracy, a sizeable majority of the people in my congregation would be able to recite John 3:16. At the same time, however, I would be surprised if anyone in my congregation could recite John 3:14-15. One would think that such a bright spotlight on verse 16 would have cast at least a little light onto verses 14 and 15, but I suspect that Jesus' allusion to the serpent on the pole is largely unfamiliar to the people in our pews.

Nevertheless, that one reference by Jesus takes that obscure episode from the wilderness and elevates it to an event with enormous significance and meaning. It ceases to be just a strange little incident in the desert, and it becomes a grand foreshadowing of the grandest event of all. Now, as Jesus connects the dots for us in John 3, that peculiar pole becomes the cross. And, more remarkable still, Jesus becomes the bronze serpent.

The familiar passage moves beyond the reference to the serpent on a pole.

Verses 16 and 17 state marvelously the motive and purpose of God. It is surely an essential part of the proclamation of the gospel to report not only what God did but also to reveal what God wants. He does not want to condemn, but to save (see also Ezekiel 18:30-32). He is motivated by love, and that love prompts him to initiate. It is not merely that he responds mercifully when we come to him, but rather that he begins by coming to us (see also Romans 5:8). His love and salvation are not limited to an exclusive group, a covenant people, a worthy few, but for "everyone who believes" so that "the world might be saved."

The end of this gospel lesson makes abundant reference to "light," which is a large and significant theme in John's gospel. At the outset, John identifies "light" with the pre-existent Word. And just as God spoke light into the darkness and chaos "in the beginning," so now again his light "shines in the darkness, and the darkness did not overcome it" (1:5). John the Baptist, we read, came "as a witness to testify to the light" (1:6). And Jesus himself said, "I am the light of the world. Whoever follows me will never walk in darkness but will have the light of life" (8:12).

While the passage comes from a pre-scientific age, the imagery may feel reminiscent of a science experiment. A student in a lab will add a chemical to a solution and measure the change and reaction of that solution. Some chemical reactions are diagnostic in nature: That is, the application of a chemical reveals what the subject substance contains. And so it is here with light. The light suddenly shines into the world, and it elicits different reactions: some are drawn to it, while others resist and hide from it. Therein lies the judgment.

Jesus' observation here that "people loved darkness rather than light because their deeds were evil" recalls Luke's account of the Garden of Gethsemane. When the antagonists arrive in the garden to smuggle Jesus away, he notes that they had taken no action when he was with them "day after day in the temple." No, but rather they act at night, for "this is your hour, and the power of darkness!" (Luke 22:53).

Application

As we endeavored to illustrate above, the serpent on a pole episode in Numbers serves as its own microcosmic glimpse into how God works. The provision of a remedy, though the affliction is deserved and, in some respects, self-induced; is the required participation of people in God's deliverance, even while affirming that the deliverance is entirely God's doing; the strangeness of God's remedies; and the necessity of faith. These elements can, in their own right, be affirmed as characteristic of how God works.

Now that Jesus makes such a clear connection between that wilderness episode and his crucifixion, however, we are compelled to take it a step further. The serpent on a pole is no longer just a generic model of how God works. Now it is a very specific foreshadowing of God's saving work in Christ.

We rejoice in the truth that our salvation is not our own doing (see Ephesians 2:8-9), while at the same time affirming the necessity of faith (Romans 3:22-31) and our participation in our salvation (Acts 16:29-31). We are prompted to consider again the observation that the remedy recalls the malady. It was not some symbol of health hung on the pole, but a replica of the poisonous serpents. So, too, God "made him to be sin who knew no sin" (2 Corinthians 5:21). Beyond the notion of Jesus paying the price for sin on the cross, Paul goes a dramatic step further and says that he was made "to be sin." So, again, the remedy recalls the malady.

Alternative Applications

Numbers 21:4-9; Ephesians 2:1-10. "A Good, Healthy Appetite." "I just don't have much of an appetite." I have heard that lament countless times when visiting parishioners in the hospital. "I know that I need to eat," they say, "but I just don't feel like it."

That's a bad sign, for a good, healthy appetite is a sign of good health, and regaining an appetite is often an indication that someone who had been sick is getting better.

On the other hand, not all appetites are good and healthy.

The whole mess in the wilderness episode, you recall, began with the people's appetites. The problem did not begin with the poisonous serpents, but with the people's complaining. Their complaint was about food. "Why have you brought us up out of Egypt to die in the wilderness?" they whined. "There is no food and no water, and we detest this miserable food."

If, in fact, there had been no food, then perhaps their protest would have had some credibility, and their fear of dying would have been justified. But they had food. Daily and miraculously, God was providing food for them in the wilderness, so they allege that there is "no food" simply because they regard it as "miserable food."

Here, of course, is the hallmark of selfish ingratitude: We don't see what we do have simply because we would prefer to have something else.

In Paul's letter to the Ephesians, meanwhile, the apostle observes that "all of us once lived ... in the passions of our flesh, following the desires of flesh and senses." That is his way of characterizing our former condition, and it seems to be all about the flesh. Such a generalization is not uncommon to Paul (see also, for example, Romans 7 and 8; Galatians 5). Nor is a spirit vs. flesh paradigm unique to Paul (such as Mark 14:38; John 3:6; 1 Peter 2:11).

All of fallen humanity, it seems, needs to regain a good, healthy appetite. Not because we have lost our appetite, but rather because the appetites of our flesh are out of control. It's interesting that humankind's very first sin is represented in terms of a fleshly appetite. And ever since — like the Israelites in the wilderness, whose grumbling against God began with the grumbling of their stomachs — we have been "following the desires of flesh and senses."

Numbers 21:4-9. "Bound for the Promised Land." Israel's exodus experience has long been cherished as a meaningful metaphor for the Christian life. We begin as slaves, where God finds us and saves us. The Christian life is a journey, and we are dependent upon his guiding and providing throughout all of it. Some of the journey may feel like a wilderness, to be sure, but we press on with a hope rooted in God's promise.

Given the larger metaphor, one particular line from this wilderness episode is especially challenging to us: "The people became impatient on the way."

The people are on their way from the land of their bondage to the land of God's promise. They have witnessed his grace and his power. They enjoy his daily providence and constant guidance, yet they "became impatient on the way," and that led to trouble and to tragedy.

In spite of all that we have seen in our walk with God, we become anxious about what we do not see. The progress, the answer to prayer, some clarity about God's will, or victory over temptation — when we do not see these things, we may become impatient on the way.

Nineteenth-century Baptist pastor, Joseph Gilmore, wrote the words that the Israelites ought to have sung — and we ought also to sing — when becoming impatient on the way. "Lord, I would place my hand in thine, nor ever murmur nor repine; content whatever lot I see, since 'tis my God that leadeth me" ("He Leadeth Me: O Blessed Thought").

Starting over

A college professor presented his class syllabus on the first day of the new semester. He pointed out that there were three papers to be written during the term, and he showed on which days those assignments had to be handed in. He said that these dates were firmly fixed, and that no student should presume that the deadline did not apply to her or him. He asked if the students were clear about this, and all heads nodded.

When the first deadline arrived, all but one student turned in their papers. The one student went to the professor's office and pleaded for more time — just a single day! The student spoke of illness and hardships, which had prevented him from completing the assignment, but all the research was finished, and a few more hours would allow the paper to be ready. The professor relented, and granted a one-day extension without penalty. The student was extremely grateful, and sent a note thanking the professor profusely.

When the second deadline arrived, three papers were missing from the pile of student productions. The student who had previously asked for an extension was back, and so were two others with him. As before, all the reasons expressed for failure to complete the assignment were touching and moving and tear-jerking, and the professor again allowed some latitude. The deadline was set aside, and the papers were required by the end of the week. A veritable chorus of praise filled the professor's small office, and blessings were heaped upon him.

When the third due date arrived the professor was inundated with requests for extensions. Nearly a quarter of the class begged for more time — so many other assignments and tests were due, so many books still needed to be read, so much work was required this late in the semester. But this time the professor held firm. No extensions were to be given. Grades would be marked lower for tardiness. Stunned silence filled the classroom.

The large delegation that met the professor in the hallway near his office was very vocal in their anger. "You can't do this to us! It isn't fair!"

"What isn't fair?" asked the professor. "At the beginning of the term you knew the due date of each paper and you agreed to turn in your work at those times."

"But you let so-and-so have extensions. You can't tell us now that we can't have a few extra days."

"Maybe you are right," said the professor. He opened his grade book and made a rather public subtraction from the grades given to the four former late papers. Each of those students, now also in this group, protested loudly. "You can't do that, Professor! That's not fair!"

"What's not fair?" asked the professor. "Justice or mercy?" The question blanketed them heavily as each student silently slipped away. And the professor? When he reported the incident to others, he simply concluded (paraphrasing Henry Higgins from *My Fair Lady*), "They'd grown accustomed to my grace!"

We grow easily accustomed to God's grace. What will be most helpful for our congregations today is to become "wowed" again by the amazing thing that happens when God chooses to start over in love toward us, even after the Great Syllabus demands a divine reckoning.

Jeremiah 31:31-34

These are extremely powerful words. Jeremiah is living in desperate times; wimpy and changing leadership plays fast and loose with the powerful Babylonian overlords who are currently in control, thus bringing the small nation of Judah rather rapidly toward its certain demise. Most of the towns of the region have already been destroyed by siege and conquest, and the palace and temple treasuries have been pillaged by the Babylonian armies. Diseases stalk the overcrowded streets of Jerusalem where refugees congregate, and sanitation has long ago taken a holiday. Food is scarce, and God's glory doesn't seem to shine from the holy place.

With the other prophets, Jeremiah has been shouting about the impending "Day of the Lord." Soon, according to the gloomy school of apocalyptic voices, God will disrupt human history with a decisive incursion and bring judgment on the nations around, and also on the wickedness that clings like leeches to the people of the covenant themselves. The judgment on the nations will fall because of their great wickedness and violence; condemnation will rain on God's people for their failure to remain true to the Sinai covenant.

But all talk of the "Day of the Lord" by the prophets also included two other dimensions. That day would see God's mighty hand preserving and protecting a remnant of God's people as well. God had declared that God's initiatives were everlasting, so God would always have at least a faithful few who would not bow their knees to Baal or violate the stipulations of the Suzerain-Vassal covenant written on stone and sealed with blood at Mount Sinai (see Exodus 24).

Second, along with judgment and the spared remnant, the "Day of the Lord" would also inaugurate the Messianic Age in which righteousness would rule and blessings would abound. Isaiah saw it as a time when the exiles would come home, the roads to Jerusalem would be made more than passable, the greenery of earth would produce abundance beyond measure, the animals would be both tame and wild in appropriate ways, and the wealth of the nations would flow to Zion. Ezekiel would soon write of this age as the era when the temple would be rebuilt to greater glory and a refreshing stream would emerge from under God's throne (the Ark of the Covenant) to bring vegetation in desert places and healing for the nations. Hosea would tell of the renewal of marriage vows between God and Israel, and the lasting love that would permeate their relationship.

Jeremiah's take on these apocalyptic times is a direct mirror of the initial covenant making ceremony at Sinai. Through the battles with Pharaoh, God had won the right to determine the destiny of Israel. And in the "marriage ceremony" (think of Hosea's prophecy) at Mount Sinai, God had established an unbreakable partnership with Israel that included covenant stipulations.

While Israel was required by the oaths of the covenant to be faithful, Israel's human capacities were not up to the job. Israel had strayed, making inappropriate alliances with other nations. Israel had sinned, breaking the line-item requirements of the treaty. Israel had been pompous, forgetting that her strength was not in herself but in her relationship with God. Israel had become a prostitute, making love (or so it seemed) to other deities that promised much but gave little.

Here God, through Jeremiah, affirms that Israel has done wrong, but also admits that it was bound to happen. Israel cannot fulfill the demands of what it has perceived of as an externally dictated regimen. What is necessary is for a new form of relationship to begin, one in which Israel will love with the heart and know with the heart and experience intimacy with God from the heart. It will require that God take the initiative, and it will demand that mercy trump judgment in order to bring home the bride.

When will this all take place? On the "Day of the Lord," of course. Still, only from our New Testament perspective do we understand two things that Jeremiah could not see at the time. First, Jesus brought the "Day of the Lord" in his arrival as the incarnate deity, the Messiah of the nations. Second, Jesus split the "Day of the Lord" into two parts, inaugurating the blessings of the Messianic Age by way of his First Coming, and delaying the judgments of the day until his Second Coming.

Some, of course, might become accustomed to his grace. But those who feel the power and poetry of these verses in Jeremiah's prophecy will understand, and fall in love all over again.

Hebrews 5:5-10

Kenneth Schenck has authored a great introduction to the letter from which our epistle reading comes today. His study is called *Understanding the Book of Hebrews: The Story behind the Sermon* (Westminster John Knox, 2003). Schenck's view is that the letter was written to a mixed congregation of both Jewish and Gentile Christians in Rome who were in danger of dropping Jesus from their religion because of imminent persecution. Most prone to this move were those who had been Gentile pagans and then became Jewish proselytes before the message of Jesus was circulated. These people had already made a move to biblical religion because they found the society of their day too lax and immoral. A turning to Judaism brought them structure and meaning and godliness and moral rectitude. But when the message of the Jewish Messiah was preached, they like many other Jews were attracted to the excitement of knowing the Messiah and participating in his work. Now, however, with Jesus' delay in returning and the looming persecution, some of these Gentile Pagans-cum-Jewish Proselytes-cum-Jewish Christians were thinking that they should return to the safety of a moral code based Judaism, and in that way also disappear from the radar screen of official Roman maltreatment.

While the writer of this letter addresses many issues, in today's lectionary passage the focus is on Jesus as a fellow-traveler through times of suffering. If pain and punishment are part of the reason why some would wander from Christian testimony, they ought to learn from Jesus' own life how instead to endure suffering. Although Jesus had the capacity to claim his glory (v. 5) in a way that put him above and out of reach of suffering, he chose another way — the way through shared suffering — in order to accomplish his task and bring his people home. This choice, according to the writer, elevates Jesus into unique company; he is a priest like Melchizedek.

Melchizedek is a very interesting biblical character. He appears suddenly in Genesis 14 as a priest and king recognized by Abram for having deep spirituality and the ability to mediate between humans and God. Melchizedek then disappears until David refers to him in what we now know as Psalm 110. David uses Melchizedek as an example of a priest and king above and outside of the royal family systems in place in Israel, and therefore transcending ordinary human boundaries.

David's interpretation of Melchizedek's identity is picked up here by the writer of the letter. Jesus also surpasses human systems of priesthood and kingship by choosing to go through suffering in order to achieve the end of glory. In so doing he marked a different way for starting over — not through achievement or mere moral rectitude, but by way of submission.

For the first readers of this letter to the Hebrews, the implication was clear. Starting over in religious life was not to be had by going back to the good old days when people were more honest and ceremonies were clear cut; starting over takes place when we engage suffering as fellow travelers with the true suffering servant, Jesus Christ. There is no other way to find the throne of God (see Hebrews 10) or to absorb the essence of both Jewish and Christian religious identities.

John 12:20-33

This is the critical juncture in John's telling of Jesus' story. John is always careful to identify the characters that show up on the gospel stage. Nicodemus is a "Pharisee" in chapter 3; a woman is a "Samaritan" in chapter 4; here it is "Greeks" who come to see Jesus. Why?

The answer is found through an understanding of the literary development of the fourth gospel. In the prologue (1:1-18), God and the creative Word exist outside of the "world" (Greek *kosmos*) and bring it into being. The world falls under the spell of darkness until it is unable to see the light of God. Jesus (the Word) enters the darkness and begins to bring light. Not all are able to see or understand the light, but Jesus gives seven signs along the way to announce and display the beginnings of the light.

So the first half of this gospel has long been called "The Book of Signs." These heavenly billboards began with the "miraculous sign" at the wedding in Cana (ch. 2) where Jesus turned water into wine, and culminated in the raising of Lazarus (ch. 11). The seven signs did two things. First, they rehearsed major events from the Old Testament in which God gave profound testimony of his presence and power to Israel and the people of the ancient world. Second, these signs emerge through Jesus' unique revelatory activity and therefore identify him as the divine light penetrating earth's religious darkness with spiritual renewal.

Thus, for John, when all seven (notice the number of completeness, also used in a similar way in Revelation) signs have been displayed, it ought to be sufficient for people to know the full truth of Jesus. So, indeed, the news spreads (see the preceding verses), and even the Pharisees (who are blind to the signs) declare, "Look how the whole world (Greek *kosmos*) has gone after him!" (12:19).

Immediately after this declaration "some Greeks" come looking to "see" Jesus. For John, "Greeks" are the code word for those of the whole world. So Jesus has given the signs, the religious folk of Palestine have responded (or not), the leaders among them have declared that the whole world is going after him, and here come the Greeks! There is a marvelous unfolding of waves of impacts described in a few verses.

This helps us understand Jesus' seemingly cryptic response in verse 23. Rather than meet the Greeks, Jesus makes a declaration: "The hour has come for the Son of Man to be glorified." This is Jesus' way of confirming the literary development unfolding in John's gospel — the signs of God's glory have been displayed in a dark world; people have responded locally; now the world is coming out to look and understand. Hence, Jesus' mission has reached its point of culmination — the "world" was dark and did not see God's glory; now the "world" is coming to see God's glory through Jesus.

This transition ushers in the Passion, where Jesus will be glorified through his suffering. Using an illustration pulled from agriculture, Jesus offers a metaphor for the meaning of his death and the hope of the resurrection. The voice from heaven, however it is heard or interpreted by the people, is an affirmation that these things are true. John's picture is meant to remind us of the thundering of divine power and glory at Mount Sinai where, when God spoke, the people were terrified and did not necessarily understand what God said. A mediator (Moses) was necessary to complete the communication link.

In the theme of the day, this is the exact point at which God is starting over with the world. God's first creative work was virtually ruined by the dark mist of sinfulness that enveloped it; now, through the agency of the word/light/creator, the world is being remade and restored and renewed. Through Jesus, creation is starting over.

Application

Our experiences of starting over are often painful: bankruptcy, divorce, rehabilitation, renovation. So we must expect that the work of God in starting over with our world is a very painful process. Indeed, it will cost Jesus everything, including his life.

We are always tempted to make the restart as painless as possible. If a cake in the oven becomes a "burnt offering," we toss it and bake something else. If a dress is sewn badly or the fabric slashed inappropriately, all can be scrapped and a new pattern with different material brought in. If a career is cut short, we can move to a new city, a new state, or a new country.

But the problem for God is that God doesn't wish to toss us — God's image-bearing creature — on the cosmic junk heap of the universe. God will not destroy us, since we carry in our very essence the reflection God's own glory. So the way to start over is the way through suffering, through cleansing, through rebirth, through actual transformation of the existing stuff. This is a hard process, and Jesus' words remind us of the pain that shrieked from Calvary in order to make it happen.

We all want, at times, to start over, but we don't always want to pay the price or do what it takes. That's why God had to initiate the process of reconciliation. Still, even then, it was painful as hell.

Alternative Applications

We are only a week away from Palm Sunday or Passion Sunday and the events of Holy Week. So it would be very fitting to focus on either the epistle or gospel passages, and lead people in a commiseration with Jesus in his sufferings.

Hebrews 5:5-10. If focusing on the Hebrews, reading collateral verses from Hebrews 2:14-18 and Hebrews 4:14-16 might be helpful. These passages allow us to focus on the suffering of Jesus and walk with him through the dark valleys of our lives, but they also help us see the redemptive significance of Jesus' suffering. It is not merely that God suffers with us (*a la* Harold Kushner in *When Bad Things Happen to Good People*) but that God's suffering *with* us is also a suffering *for* us that cleanses and renews and restores.

John 12:20-33. If focusing on John 12, one might begin with the creative technology of farming, first developed thousands of years ago. Why should anyone take grain which could be used to feed the children, and instead throw it into the ground where it will rot and decay, and then somehow expect that something good will come of it? Well, farmers do that. And in the great theological agriculture of heaven, God had to plant living flesh to die in order that a bumper crop of living flesh might emerge.

Getting to a teachable moment

I spent part of a recent Sunday talking with a public school teacher who was quickly coming to the end of her rope. Talented, dedicated, one of the good people, she found herself with the class from hell and her life coming apart at the seams. We were well beyond being a non-anxious, fully individuated, differentiated presence. In short, we were at critical mess rather than critical mass. I have taught enough confirmation classes and have had experiences in the classroom in other forums to identify with the pain when you are in a non-teachable moment. On the other hand, in the church I currently serve, confirmation has become informative and fun — even inspiring. There is nothing sweeter for me than to see the pondering, the movement, the growing in wisdom and stature that comes with a rich learning experience.

In the Hebrew Testament lesson that Year B offers this Sunday, Isaiah ponders what it means to be given the tongue of a teacher. Paul pleads for the Philippians to have the same mind among them that was in Christ Jesus. In Mark's story of the passion there is a lesson to be had, which the Roman centurion gets, in the teachable moment we call the cross.

If you are in the education business in any sense when connections are made, hearts open and minds light up, you know you are in the presence of the miraculous. There can be so much that goes wrong and gets in the way. Rather than following in Isaiah's footsteps, the adversarial generational mood of the moment can hook people, causing the teacher to have a tongue that gives a lashing rather than the planned lesson. Crass cultural mindlessness can lead to folks being pretty far away from anything that looks like the mind of Christ. Context can cut out learning. Perhaps it is a Pilate moment: too much to prove, defend, or prosecute to have ears to listen to each other or eyes to see what is in front you.

One of the teaching tools that I use with our confirmation class is the movie *Twelve Angry Men.* It is the story of a trial in which one lone juror reverses the minds of the other eleven who are ready from the start to vote to convict the accused of murder. Made in 1954 and done in black and white we usually begin with moans, groans, and side comments about the quaint clothing styles, the incessant smoking, and the obvious fact that today there never would be a jury of twelve white men trying a Puerto Rican young man. That said, the students are soon captivated by how the one juror, the Christ figure, is able to lead the members of the jury through their fears, blind spots, self-doubts, emotional hang-ups, and closed-mindedness to a point where they doubt their original certainties.

The lone juror's relentless pursuit of meeting the others where they are, speaking what they are able to hear, risking rejection, and patiently waiting creates a powerful, teachable moment that turns things around. The jurors are saved from mindlessly acting on their prejudices, from a disastrous disconnect from their emotions, and a cowardly shamefulness that causes them to ignore what is right in front of them.

The saving moment comes from one who has the tongue of a teacher, the mind of one who puts himself in the place of others rather than puts them in their place, and who, in the selfless taking up of the cross of justice touches the hearts of others. The lessons for Passion Sunday affirm that this is what it takes if there will be a teachable moment.

Isaiah 50:4-9a

The prophet begins with the experience of being given the tongue of a teacher. Do you remember the voice of your teachers? No doubt some sounded like nails on a blackboard in their shrillness and demands.

There are teachers who find themselves with a voice hardened by the years of teaching. There are teachers who are battling to keep head and heart together; feeling that they are losing the fight to grade inflation, the surrounding culture, and a sea of societal expectations. Isaiah's description of the teacher has more truth to it than we care to admit: "I gave my back to those who struck me, and my cheeks to those who pulled out the beard; I did not hide my face from insult and spitting." It is not that these words readily conger up visions of flying spitballs in the midst of a blackboard jungle inhabited by smart-mouthed teenagers. It is the vulnerability of the teacher and the seeming inability of the teacher to make themselves understood that chills the soul.

As in our day, we might ask why anyone would undertake such a mission. What is at stake in enduring such exposure to endless demands, chronic self-doubt, and limited support? For Isaiah there is much more at stake than whether the next generation will be employable, or be able to make change without a calculator. Though Isaiah's people are living in Babylonian exile, tempted to pass into the surrounding culture, this is not the final word. Isaiah seeks to prepare his students not for the world that is, but for the age to come through God's activity. "So the ransomed of the Lord shall return, and come to Zion with singing; everlasting joy shall be upon their heads; they shall obtain joy and gladness, and sorrow and sighing shall flee away." God will act to free God's people and return them from exile.

As a matter of fact, in many ways the teachers whose voices still speak in my life had in their own way understood and preached the message of the prophet. As much as they prepared me for the world that was, they prepared me for the world to come. They radiated out a sense that I would be overcome by a joy that would lead me home. It could happen in a novel, a piece of music, a painting, in a moment of surpassing curiosity staring at the night sky. It might come in a moment when beyond all that divides I could discover all that unites people who share the human story. It might come in pushing hard to run six miles in under an hour at the age of 56. Or it could come in suddenly discovering that I could understand something of what Einstein was getting at. The amazing thing is that those who set their face "like a flint" on such a message and did not turn back turned out to be right. The marvelous thing about the commitment to such a message was that it affirmed me as a person. I was worthy of such experiences. I best be ready, lest I miss the opportunity.

The meaning of such experiences is that there is a God who is trying to lead us out of exile. Those who stick with this message will not be put to shame. They will be vindicated. I found myself in my educational experience most likely to listen to this voice when it came from the lips of those who were able to point in their own way to times and places in their lives when they too had made this discovery.

Philippians 2:5-11

Of course, we have to deal here with one of the most classic formulations of the Christian community's understanding of Christ. Approaching this text I do feel like I am back in school. The voices are saying, "Whatever you do, do not mess this one up!" This is important stuff here. After all, there are those that say this may be the earliest recorded expression of the faith community's understanding of Jesus. Paul writes from prison to the first church established on European soil. This is a job for commentaries and super study. With thirty years in ministry will my skills be up to it or have they atrophied? My home pastor, of sainted memory, studied with Dietrich Bonhoeffer as a classmate. I can't let him down. I hear a strange version of Professor Kingsfield from the movie, *Paper Chase*, the story of the rigors of Harvard Law School, "Here is a dime, call your mother, and tell her that you are not going to be a college professor or perhaps even a pastor." The recurring nightmare where I don't graduate from high school is occurring. I have a doctorate, for crying out loud, why am I afraid?

Having read the above you now have ample evidence of what it means to not have in you the mind which was in Christ Jesus. It just may be the mind of a country pastor who is a bit frightened that, as James Fowler has written, "It is unclear not only whether our children will have faith but whether our faith will have children." I find the general level of biblical illiteracy a bit nerve-racking as I ponder how we can implement the notion of having the mind of Jesus among teenagers. I find myself seriously calling into question my adequacy for the task.

While the commentaries intimidate, the text invites me to consider that my own life experience may actually make these words come alive. "But he emptied himself, taking the form of a slave, being born in human likeness. And being found in human form, he humbled himself...." So far so good, for in the face of this text I feel all too human. Perhaps that is the choice that I have not considered all along. Swept up in the culture I find it all too easy to pursue the super human rather than the fully human. I find it all too easy to evaluate myself in terms of my ability to be everywhere rather than fully there. I measure myself too often in terms of being able to fix things rather than be genuinely present even when I cannot fix things. I long to control people more than connect with them.

If I understand this text correctly, it seems that God surrenders the powers that I aspire to in order to save the world. Jesus chose specificity. He came in a specific place and among a particular people. He experienced the difficulty with trying to be two places at the same time — and it led to saving the world. He experienced the rich, young man who chose not to follow, yet he looked upon this man with love — and it helped to save the world. His encounters with the ambiguous responses shows one who connects but will not control — and it leads to the saving of the world.

I consider myself as one that is more than reasonably educated and master of my intellectual house. Yet, as I read this text it becomes clear that I am asked to give up something in order to hand on anything of the gospel.

In my congregational tradition, one is called as a pastor to a local congregation to be both pastor and teacher. Whatever the role as pastor, I know that a teacher is called to give up something in order to educate in the literal sense of "to lead out." Being a teacher involves entering into the world of the student and allowing some of one's preconceived notions to be challenged and to die. Being a teacher is like playing a perpetual away game on somebody else's home turf in order that they may feel at home. This passage reads to me less like theological certainty than practical reality.

Mark 15:1-39 (40-47)

We know where Mark is headed. He has telegraphed it right from the start. The lesson to be taught here is that Jesus is the Son of God. The heavens open at the baptism and the celestial voice proclaims it. Jesus' identity is once again proclaimed from out of the cloud surrounding the Transfiguration. Through conspicuous sparseness Mark is telling us where he is headed. Mark's teaching technique builds a sense of suspense as we move toward the events of Holy Week. According to Mark, Jesus' teaching maintains the suspense. When he was alone with the disciples "... he said to them, 'To you has been given the secret of the kingdom of God, but for those outside, everything comes in parables; in order that "they may indeed look, but not perceive, and may indeed listen, but not understand; so that they may not turn again and be forgiven." ' " It all feels a bit like the television series *Columbo*. It maintained the suspense not by keeping "who done it" a secret but by following how Columbo would figure out who done it. By the time the reader of Mark gets to Holy Week, we know that Jesus is God's Son and that it will remain a secret. Much to the frustration of the religiously learned pondering the parables does not solve the mystery of Jesus' full identity.

If anything, the mystery only deepens as one considers Jesus' actions and teachings. "They were astounded at his teaching, for he taught them as one having authority, and not as the scribes. They were all amazed, and they kept on asking one another, 'What is this? A new teaching — with authority! He commands even the unclean spirits, and they obey him.' "

Certainly, one would think that in the face of such obtuse behavior that Rome should be able to sort things out. That is what Rome does for a living and why it has developed a massive intelligence network.

Standing right in front of him, Pilate can still not get who Jesus is. Mark has spun his narrative over fifteen chapters and we find ourselves back at the same place as those who were unable to puzzle out Jesus in Capernaum. "But Jesus made no further reply, so that Pilate was amazed." Pilate comes up with a question that he thinks will be a closer, "Are you the king of the Jews?" The only thing to do is turn it over to the people when all else has failed. The Gentile who gets it is the Roman centurion. He has seen what Pilate could not and the rest of the world had not: the actual execution. Three things stand out, Jesus refused the myrrh, he cannot save himself, he cries out at the absence of God. The teachers who I have known that are most likely to have opened up a future, exposed themselves to the pain that comes with loving students, being moved by their students' lives, and open to their own growth in public contexts. The people whose authority I have accepted and who are most likely to cast out my demons are those who do not pull rank, deny their own pain or cover their needs with myrrh. Jesus is not able to save himself. Those who open something in me are those who do not save themselves from pain, embarrassment, tough choices, and places were they have to shake off the dust and move on. He cried out at the absence of God. No answers here, no rationalizations, the cry of pain at the mystery of life. The demonic is often given chase not by reason but the readiness to cry out that life is a mystery that we share. Who has not experienced the absence of God and our inability to fill the hole? Facing the hole opens us to the possibility that we will be made whole by something larger than us. As they say in the cancer business, "First you cry."

It is the irony of Mark that such human activity points to the divine identity of Jesus. Is it any wonder that Pilate as Rome's representative does not get it when Jesus is standing right in front of him?

Application

The Isaiah text tells us that the prophet has been given the tongue of a teacher. However, it seems that something more is required. The teacher sets about the task by setting his face as a flint as he prepares to endure insult and spitting. Four things come together to make a teachable moment: message, messenger, medium, and the moment or context. The story of Holy Week is that we come to understand how Jesus is the Son of God. The early church concluded that the activity of God was made known in a prototypical way in the life of this first-century Jew. The church reached this conclusion precisely because this life emptied itself of the usual attributes of God and took on human form in a way that revealed what being fully human means. For Mark, this is Jesus' source of power that enables him to authoritatively cast out the demonic. As with the excellent teachers that I have known, I am left amazed, but I am given significant understanding.

For Mark, the new understanding of God's activity and Jesus as God did not come easily. Neither healing, casting out the demonic, nor imperial inquisition is sufficient in and of itself to be an occasion when we get to the depth of understanding that Mark believes is necessary. Such understanding comes to one standing at the foot of the cross whom you would least expect to make significant testimony about the meaning of Jesus' life. This is a source of hope for all who have the tongue of a teacher. Standing at the foot of where life can get crossed up, shorted out by crossed wires, where people inappropriately cross over the line, where general crossness erupts; Jesus takes on significant meaning in a teachable moment.

An Alternative Application

Mark 15:1-39 (40-47). Why did the crowd go for Barabbas? There is scant evidence that there ever was such a custom as alluded to in the gospels. There is much evidence that neither Rome nor Pilate would be such generous souls that they would readily release a known political rebel in exchange for yet another religious leader with a seeming messiah complex. Neither calculation of the moment nor of the personalities involved suggests that we would head this way.

Yet, the gospels do us a favor by giving us this story, because when I am placed in the context of the crowd I find much evidence of who I am. I shout for quick answers. Jesus helps us come to terms with the unanswerable and the reality "of that day or hour nobody knows." I want solutions to problems. Jesus leads me to cherish the mystery that people are. I like to believe that most of what bedevils human experience can be handled by human inventiveness. I don't want to admit that I often meet failure in life because the most dangerous demons can only be cast out by a relationship with God that we call prayer.

Most often in the midst of a crowd I shout, "Give me Barabbas." Give me the stuff that will make me look good as much as do good. Give something that will make me feel good as much as give me a feel for the kingdom of God. Give me the stuff that keeps me on top of things rather than get to the bottom of things.

I know that on Palm Sunday I should be joining in the parade of palms, however, when I join with this crowd I get to the truth of me. In my shouting for what I want, I wind up crucifying the best that is in me, that surrounds me, and that is for me.

Maundy Thursday
Exodus 12:1-4 (5-10) 11-14
1 Corinthians 11:23-26
John 13:1-17, 31b-35
Wayne Brouwer

I'll never forget that night...

Years ago, a band called Lobo sang about an international memorable event. Describing the impoverished plights of a boy from Chicago's racial ghetto and a girl living among India's "Untouchables," the singers went on to shake their heads in wonder that both, on a "July afternoon," along with the entire population of planet earth, heard and saw Neil Armstrong "walk upon the moon."

Some incidents are so unusual or catastrophic or fraught with meaning that they cannot be forgotten, and all who were alive remember exactly what they were doing at the time. Pearl Harbor, Kennedy's assassination, the lunar landing, 9/11... we remember.

So, too, this night. This night, rooted in the exodus, shared in the intimacy of the upper room, and rehearsed by ancient formulary throughout the world. I'll never forget that night....

Exodus 12:1-4 (5-10) 11-14

Don't forget! Every year's rehearsal of the Israel's ancient exodus from Egypt is a re-presentation of the seminal event that determined her identity. Tonight, as we share the intimacy of Jesus' Last Supper with his disciples, it is important to recall what they, as deeply religious Jews, were thinking and feeling and experiencing. Passover was one of the highlights of the social and liturgical year, a time to gather with family and friends, and to draw all again into the drama of the initial sleepless night when all the world was turned upside down.

There are a number of things to keep in mind when reviewing the theological implications and literary location of this passage. First, it is the culmination of the last of the ten horrible plagues with which Yahweh assaulted Pharaoh and his Egypt. Exodus 7-11 describes a battle not between Israel and her oppressive national captors, but between Yahweh and Pharaoh. The plagues are the weapons of religious warfare wielded by Israel's divine protector and suitor. While these miracles of divine judgment make for great Hollywood screenplay, it is not always apparent as to the reason for this extended weird display of divine power, especially when it is interspersed with notes that Pharaoh's heart was hardened, sometimes, in fact, seemingly as an act of Yahweh. Could not Yahweh have provided a less destructive and deadly exit strategy for Israel?

The plagues begin to make sense when they are viewed in the context of Egypt's climate and culture. After the initial sparring with snakes to show magical skills, the stakes are raised far beyond human ability to merely manipulate the natural order. First the waters are turned to blood; then the marshes send out a massive, unwelcome pilgrimage of frogs; next the dust is beat into gnats, soon to be followed by even peskier flies; subsequently, the livestock gets sick from the dust, and this illness then spreads to human life in the form of boils and open sores; penultimately, the heavens send down mortar shells of hail, transport in a foreign army of locusts, and then withhold the light of the sun; finally, in an awful culmination, the firstborn of humans and animals across Egypt die suddenly.

Strange. But not quite as much when seen in three successive groupings. Among the many deities worshiped in ancient Egypt, none superceded a triumvirate composed by the Nile, the good earth, and the heavens which were the home of the sun. So it was that the initial plagues of bloody water and frogs both turned the Nile against the Egyptians, and showed the dominance of Yahweh over this critical source of national life.

The ante was then upped when Yahweh took on the farmland of Egypt, one of the great breadbaskets of the world. Instead of producing crops, Moses showed, by way of plagues three through six, how Yahweh could cause it to generate all manner of irritating and deadly pestilence, making it an enemy rather than a friend. Finally, in the third stage of plagues, the heavens themselves became menacing. Rather than providing the sheltering confidence of benign sameness, one day the heavens attacked with the hailstone mortar fire of an unseen enemy. Next these same heavens served as the highway of an invading army of locusts. Then old friend sun, the crowning deity of Egyptian religion, simply vanished for three days.

Finally, the link of life was severed when the firstborn died. The Egyptians believed that the firstborn carried the cultural significance of each family and species, so in a sudden and dramatic moment the very chain of life and being was severed. Furthermore, the pharaohs themselves were supposedly deity incarnate, descending directly from the sun by way of firstborn inheritance. Cutting this link eviscerated the life-potency of the Egyptian civilization not only for the present but also for the future. It was a true knockout punch.

Thus the plagues served not as gory illustration material for Sunday school papers, but rather as the divine initiatives in an escalating battle between Yahweh and the Pharaoh of Egypt over claims on the people of Israel. The plagues were a necessary prologue to the Sinai covenant because they showed the sovereignty of Yahweh as Suzerain not only over Israel but also over other contenders. Israel belongs to Yahweh both because of historic promises made to Abraham, and also by way of chivalrous combat in which Yahweh won back the prize of lover and human companion from the usurper who had stolen her away from the divine heart. Furthermore, Yahweh accomplished this act *without* the help of Israel's own resources (no armies, no resistance movements, no terrorist tactics, no great escape plans), and in a decisive way that announced the limitations of the Egyptian religious and cultural resources.

This is why the final plague is paired with the institution of the Passover festival (Exodus 12). It would become an ongoing reminder that Israel was bought back by way of a blood-price redemption and that the nation owed its very existence to the love and fighting jealousy of its divine champion.

All of this was gathered, year by year, into the annual Passover rites. More than just a polite religious pageant, Passover recalled the bloody battle in which a captor (Pharaoh) and a lover (Yahweh) fought for the right to claim Israel's hand. This event determined where Israel would live (so the instructions to make ready for hasty travel), who would provide for her needs, and to whom she would hold ultimate allegiance.

No Christian can fail to see the continuity between this Passover celebration and the remarkable Eucharist meal that Jesus turned it into. Whenever the story of Jesus' Last Supper is rehearsed, it is important to remember that it, too, along with the first Passover celebration, ended with a call to rise and go hence. To celebrate Maundy Thursday is to be dressed for the road and move off in haste into the night, following the *shekinah* glory light that leads to the promised land, Easter, and beyond.

1 Corinthians 11:23-26

It is evident from the manner in which Paul phrases his words in these verses that the formula for recalling Jesus' institution of the Lord's Supper was already a common and ritualized liturgical construct by 53 AD. Paul was in Ephesus on his third mission journey and was carrying on extended correspondence with his unruly former congregation in Corinth. Recently three leaders from that church (Stephanus, Fortunatus, and Achaicus) had carried to Paul a report of the divisions and moral problems in their home congregation, along with a list of theological and practical questions that apparently were causing a good deal of argument among the members. At this point in his letter of reply, Paul is explaining appropriate behaviors and liturgical acts when celebrating the Lord's Supper.

While these words need most to be spoken as a solemn call to those gathering to remember Jesus and his crucifixion on this night fraught with meaning, there are some interesting aspects of their instruction about which to reflect. First, why would Jesus use the bread rather than the lamb as one of the two elements around which to build a memorial meal? After all, the lamb was central to the Passover, and the bread seems to be only a peripheral nod to the travel haste that accompanied the ceremony. Moreover, Jesus himself would be the ultimate Passover lamb (see John 1:29; Hebrews 9-10; Revelation 5, 12), and it might seem that an ongoing memorial would best use the flesh of that animal as a tangible means by which to symbolically ingest Christ (see Jesus' own words in John 6).

Yet, there are good reasons for Jesus not to use the rack of lamb as a communion memorial. For one thing, underlying Jesus' ultimate sacrifice was its once-for-all character. If he were to call for repeated animal slaying after his own death had brought the need for bloodletting to an end (see Hebrews 10), animal sacrifices could have been misconstrued and misused. Symbols can take on strange lives of their own (see, for instance, what King Hezekiah had to do with the bronze snake of Moses that had traveled with the Israelites for several hundred years: 2 Kings 18:4) and must be chosen with care.

At the same time, the bread of the Passover was freighted with more theological significance than is betrayed by the mere instructions to prepare it in haste in anticipation of a quick flight from Egypt. Without refrigeration or preservatives, bread was baked fresh each day in ancient Israel. Moreover, there was no packaged dry yeast to throw into the dough in order to stimulate its rapid rise. Instead, the sourdough method of natural fermentation was employed to expand the loaf before baking. In order to accelerate this process, a small lump of one day's dough would be saved in a bowl to be added to the next day's new batch. Its fermentation, well underway, would quickly spread through the new loaf, rushing the rising.

But this meant, of course, that there was a clear link in each day's bread with those that had come before. Every fresh batch of dough was "contaminated" with a bit of fermenting stuff from yesterday's craft. So when the call came for the Israelites to prepare to leave Egypt behind, it was not only haste that kept the leaven from the new bread batter. It was also a theological and sociological determination that nothing of the life of Egypt was to travel with them into their new future. Even their daily bread was not to be contaminated by the dough of meals from their slave days.

Jesus would teach on this often in his public ministry, comparing sin to leavening or yeast, carried from the past into the present and contaminating our lives. We need to start over, with no lingering link to the past. In fact, Jesus himself, in the virgin birth, would be something of the same. Because of the miracle of Mary's divine insemination, Jesus was truly sinless, not linked biologically to the contamination of pollution that has been passed along from generation to generation of the human race.

So tonight, as some of the church's oldest words of instruction and institution are recited again, and the bread is broken and the cup is passed, call people's attention to the fact that they are part of the yeast-free fellowship. Just as their Lord was born pure, a herald of a new age, so they who share in his meal are leaving their sinful past behind, and are wedded by the Spirit to the bridegroom whose coming they anticipate this night above all nights.

John 13:1-17, 31b-35

The gospel of John is unlike any other biblical or extra-biblical writing. Certainly, it rightly forms part of the "gospel quartet" of the New Testament. But even a quick read will show significant differences from these other uniquely Christian writings. First, the fourth gospel has a global philosophic introduction, which places the story of Jesus in a comprehensive cosmological frame of reference. Second, it is often more cryptic in its conversational narratives than are the other gospels, making it harder to understand how or why some of these interlocutions could have taken place. Third, while it acknowledges that Jesus did many miracles, it reports only seven of these during his public ministry, and elevates the significance of these by attaching to them deeper and more complex secondary meanings. Fourth, there are extended monologues by Jesus scattered through the pages of John's gospel that are both mystical and doctrinal, and have no clear parallel to the manner of Jesus' teachings or conversations as recorded by the synoptics. In short, the fourth gospel is a wild ride in a theme park of its own.

Yet, it is also so homey and comfortable that elements of it are like old slacks and shirts worn easily. The Greek language, through which the text is communicated, is basic and simple, so that beginner students can quickly read it. Many of its teachings from the lips of Jesus have become the inextricable metaphors and motifs by which we know him and ourselves — the good shepherd, the light of the world, the resurrection and the life, the vine, and so on. Some of the conversations Jesus has with others are recorded in a manner that makes us feel we were the only ones they were penned for and we are always sitting next to Jesus again when we read them. Even our Christian theology and worldview has been so shaped by themes from this document over the centuries, that we cannot separate it from us, or imagine Christianity apart from these 21 chapters. The gospel according to John is a key element of biblical faith.

Although its literary development is markedly different from that of the synoptic gospels, there is a very clear pattern to John's rehearsal of thought and portrayal of Jesus' activities and teachings in this gospel. A significant transition in referential time takes place between chapters 12 and 13 (related to the coming of the "the hour" for Jesus; note 2:4; 4:23; 7:6; 12:23; 13:1; 17:1), and this change is further accentuated by the grouping of all of Jesus' "miraculous signs," as John calls them, into the first twelve chapters. For these reasons the first part of John's gospel is often called "The Book of Signs," while the last part wears well the name "The Book of Glory." A highly significant prologue opens the gospel (1:1-18), and an epilogue obviously written by another party and added after the initial gospel was completed (ch. 21) brings it to a close.

Following Mark's lead, the synoptic gospels clearly identify the final meal that Jesus shared with his disciples as a Passover celebration. Strangely, for all the other symbolism in the fourth gospel, John clearly steers away from that connection here in chapter 13. Why?

The answer appears to have several parts to it. First, John deliberately times the events of Jesus' final week so that Jesus is tried and sentenced to death on Friday morning (at the same time as the unblemished Passover lambs were being selected) and crucified during the precise hours when the Passover lambs were being slaughtered in the temple courtyard. In this way John accomplishes a purpose that he indicated at the beginning of his gospel, to portray Jesus as the "Lamb of God" (1:36). For this reason it was important to John *not* to identify the Last Supper as the Passover, since Jesus must die with the lambs that were being slaughtered prior to that meal.

Second, this does not immediately mean that either John or the synoptics are telling the story wrongly. Instead, there were actually several different calendars functioning among the Jews of the day, marking the celebration of the Passover with slight variations. These came into being due either to the chronological ordering of each new day (Roman: sunrise to sunrise, or Jewish: sundown to sundown), or the perceived occasion of the new moon that began the month (adjusted differently by Babylonian and Palestinian rabbis).

Thus, Jesus and his disciples probably ate a Passover meal together, as the synoptics identify it, but one that was tied to a different calendar than that used by the bulk of the Jerusalem population. In this way, John could leverage the different schedule to communicate a particular emphasis in his portrayal of Jesus' symbolic identity.

Two features of this short narrative are extremely important to note. First, even as Jesus is exploring and declaring his "glory," he cloaks himself as a servant. He kneels before those who are socially and theologically his inferiors, washing their feet and declaring to them the reversal of status in this kingdom of God that stretches by service, rather than pouncing with power.

Second, Jesus institutes the "new command" of the church on this night. It is not a different command, as he himself has noted elsewhere (see Matthew 22:39-40), but it is the activation and summation of what the Ten Commandments were all about. Love is to be the critical characteristic that defines the fellowship of the faith centered on Jesus' own acts of love and obedience. It is from this "new command," as expressed in the Latin language, that Maundy Thursday derives its name.

Application

A "Christ in the Passover" demonstration would be perfect for tonight. Perhaps someone from a messianic Jewish community or a local seminary or Bible school can help reenact the Hebrew Passover and show how Jesus transformed it into the church's celebration of Holy Communion. Don't preach too much tonight. Rehearse the story. Remind those gathered of its meaning. Then, in quietness, with reverence, sing the great hymns, feel the awful passion, and celebrate the meal.

An Alternative Application

John 13:1-17, 31b-35. Since it is Maundy ("New Command") Thursday, there must be words spoken about love: Jesus' love ("no one has greater love than this, that a man lay down his life for his friends") and ours ("see how they love!").

Good Friday
Isaiah 52:13—53:12
Hebrews 10:16-25
John 18:1—19:42
David Kalas

Personal history

A junior high school student sits down with his world history textbook, and he wonders what all this stuff has to do with him. Clearly, people like Alexander, Hannibal, Caesar, Charlemagne, and Napoleon had a great impact on the world in which they lived, but what do the Rubicon and Waterloo have to do with that thirteen-year-old American boy?

When he gets to senior high school, that same student may find a greater sense of relevance in his American history textbook. It is easier for him to see the connection between Jefferson, Lincoln, Roosevelt, and the contemporary world in which he lives.

Still, the history lacks a very personal quality. After all, the best that can be said is that those famous individuals and events helped to set the present stage, directly or indirectly. But they do not feel personal. The history textbooks are not the same as personal history.

Personal history is what happened to me. And what happened in the past that directly affects me. Personal history is the move we made when I was ten, my schools, my teachers, and my friends. Personal history is how my parents met and how my grandparents came over from Europe when they were teenagers. But Cleopatra's barge and Paul Revere's horse are not personal history.

Then we come to this event from ancient Palestine. In many respects, it may seem much less significant than any of the others we have referenced. After all, it was just a death. Not a battle, not an invasion, not a massacre of thousands; just the execution of an individual. And not even the death of a general or a king. Indeed, we'd be hard put to label this particular man with any sort of official title, at all.

Here is a poor man, without property, family, or office. He was unknown beyond the narrow confines of his own country — and an occupied country, at that. He won no battle, amassed no fortune, and generated no invention. He led a movement that was conspicuously small, mostly unarmed, and apparently not very courageous. Then he died, rather young.

It is a profile of insignificance.

And yet, the day of his death remains a holy day 2,000 years later around the entire globe. That death, though centuries before Charlemagne or Napoleon or Lincoln, somehow becomes personal history for you and me.

This day carries with it a definite and specific picture. The prophet Isaiah anticipates it. The gospel of John portrays it. The writer of Hebrews explains it. And you and I get to preach it today.

Isaiah 52:13—53:12

On the eve of his death, Jesus invoked this passage of scripture. At the conclusion of the Last Supper, just before departing for the Mount of Olives with his disciples, Jesus said to them, "For I tell you, this scripture must be fulfilled in me, 'And he was counted among the lawless'; and indeed what is written about me is being fulfilled" (Luke 22:37). Perhaps that brief reference to this suffering servant passage was meant to trigger in the disciples an understanding of what would follow. Perhaps with this seed planted, they could see him in a few hours on the cross and not be so entirely bewildered and frightened. There's little evidence, however, that they made the connection at the time.

123

Within a generation of Jesus' death, though, his followers had come to recognize that he was the subject of this prophetic passage. Peter quoted from it in referencing Christ's sufferings (2 Peter 2:22). And, still more pointedly, this passage became the pivotal text in the conversion of the Ethiopian eunuch (see Acts 8:26-39). Indeed, when the Ethiopian asked about whom the prophet was speaking in this passage, Philip did not hesitate to "proclaim to him the good news about Jesus" (v. 35).

You and I are called on to preach Philip's sermon on this day. Perhaps, again it should be followed by conversions and baptisms.

We do not have a record of all that Philip said to the eunuch. But we do have here what the prophet said about Jesus. We might summarize it in terms of the following five themes:

First, Jesus was innocent. It was "by a perversion of justice [that] he was taken away," Isaiah claims. "He had done no violence, and there was no deceit in his mouth." Surely this squares with what we see in the gospel accounts of Jesus' righteous life and unjust death.

Second, Jesus was unrecognized — and perhaps unrecognizable. Isaiah says that "he had no form or majesty that we should look at him, nothing in his appearance that we should desire him." From his lowly birth to his humble upbringing, he did not display that majesty that would make the people recognize who he was. We are reminded of John's early testimony that "He was in the world, and the world came into being through him; yet the world did not know him" (John 1:10). In our gospel lection for today, we see the ignorant soldier striking Jesus on the face, thinking that Jesus was not showing proper respect to the office of the high priest. So the soldier had a sense of propriety; but he had no idea whose face he struck. Likewise, we see the mocking crown and purple robe with which the suffering Christ was adorned: dramatic irony, as the scoffers did not recognize at all that he was, indeed, a king. King of kings and Lord of lords, no less.

Third, what happened to Jesus was the design and purpose of God. While the events of Maundy Thursday and Good Friday in the gospels appear to be entirely the orchestration of the jealous, conspiring Jewish leaders, Isaiah sees a different hand behind it all: "the Lord has laid on him the iniquity of us all." And then, more directly, "it was the will of the Lord to crush him with pain." So he suffers innocently, but he is not a standard martyr. No, there's something else at stake here.

Fourth, we are involved. We are exploring today the theme of "personal history." The prophet Isaiah helps to convey the personal quality of this event, for he makes constant use of first-person-plural pronouns. Unlike ordinary history, with its third-person characters, this passage keeps bringing us into the picture, with words like "we," "us," and "our."

Finally, at the intersection of points three and four comes the fifth theme: the doctrine of substitutionary atonement. I circled in this passage eight different phrases that all make the same basic claim: namely, that what happened to Jesus somehow benefits us. "He was wounded for our transgressions... upon him was the punishment that made us whole... he bore the sin of many" — this is the theology of substitutionary atonement. It is at precisely this point where Christ's death is not merely the result of a plot against him and not merely the death of a martyr. It is at this point where Good Friday becomes personal history for you and me.

Hebrews 10:16-25

An individual includes in his conversation and correspondence references to the things with which he is familiar. They may be pop culture references or mentions of sports. His conversation may feature traces of art and literature, allusions to music or theater, or the thinking of a scientist, a mathematician, or a philosopher. Whatever our area of special interest and exposure may be, it will reveal itself in our communication.

As we read Hebrews, we discover that this writer's particular expertise is the Old Testament Law, and, more specifically, the rites and images of the tabernacle. Because this field is likely to be unfamiliar territory to most of the people in our pews, however, the references will be lost and the allusions meaningless. So a bit of translation may be necessary.

Within these ten verses, we are presented with a half-dozen different allusions that may need to be glossed for our people: covenant, offering for sin, sanctuary, the curtain, priest, sprinkled clean and washed with pure water.

Such glossing, of course, could be tedious stuff. Merely defining the terms and explaining the background may be more the stuff of teaching a class than of preaching a Good Friday service. Our explanations of the passage should instead be woven into the larger narrative of the day.

Perhaps we might invite our people to see, first, in their mind's eye, the familiar Good Friday scene. There is the hill called "skull." Hear the grotesque, mocking mob. See the flanking thieves. And there, in the center, Christ: suffering, bleeding, thirsting, praying, caring, and forgiving.

Then, having established the familiar scene that is in the foreground, we invite our people next to squint to see the less familiar scene that is in the background.

It's a great, colorful tent in the midst of the wilderness. In the courtyard outside the tent stands an immense basin filled with pure water for washing. Nearby is a grand altar, with smoke from its offerings rising toward heaven. An ornately dressed priest presides over the altar, where the people come to make blood offerings for their sins.

Once a year, that priest takes the blood of an offering from that altar and goes into the great, colorful tent. He passes through the curtain that marks the entrance into God's presence. There, as the sole occupant of this most holy space, this sanctuary, is the Ark of the Covenant. It is a gold box, attended by golden cherubim and containing the stone tablets that articulate the covenant between God and his people. The priest sprinkles the blood of the sacrifice upon the top of that box — a part of the process of making atonement for a sinful, unclean people before their holy God.

The scene in the foreground at Golgotha is a familiar one. But a thousand years in the background stands a less familiar scene. It is against that backdrop of covenant and curtain, of priest and offering, of blood and water, that the writer of Hebrews sees the cross of Christ. And as you and I tell the story this Good Friday, we may tell it in light of that illuminating backdrop.

John 18:1—19:42

The gospel lection for this day is an immense passage — two entire chapters from the gospel of John. Unless our churches are in the habit of three-hour Good Friday services — and, specifically, three hours of preaching! — it is hopeless to think that we can cover thoroughly everything that is recorded in John for today.

The scope of the passage runs from late Thursday evening through late Friday afternoon: from the conclusion of Jesus' eventful meal with his disciples to his burial in the tomb. Interestingly, the entire passage is book-ended by gardens. At the beginning, we see Jesus going "out with his disciples across the Kidron valley to a place where there was a garden." And, at the end, we read that "there was a garden in the place where he was crucified, and in the garden there was a tomb... they laid Jesus there."

The two chapters cover fewer than a full 24 hours. It is already the dark of evening when Peter and his disciples are in the garden; and the next evening is coming on as Joseph and Nicodemus hurriedly take care of the corpse. Those few hours are eventful and painful. And the disciples' heads must have been spinning at how completely their world had changed in less than a full day.

As we watch the events of that day unfold — and, specifically, as we watch the people involved — we are impressed by several things.

First, there is the utter fearlessness of Jesus. He stands tall in the garden, knowing what's coming, yet never flinching. He is the one under arrest, yet one senses that he is also the one in control of the whole scene, maintaining an awareness and a poise that does not characterize either his opponents or his friends.

125

Likewise, as he stands before his judges, he does not cower or beg for mercy. He is calmly engaged in dialogue with both, even to the point of frustrating them, it seems. Even dying on the cross, John portrays Jesus as completely in control. The same caring one who healed Malchus' ear in the garden is now making arrangements for his grieving mother. And his final words have a triumphant ring, as he proclaims, "It is finished."

The fearlessness of Jesus makes him unique within the larger context of the story, for it seems that he is the only one who is not afraid. Peter is clearly unsettled, one moment flailing with his sword in defense of Jesus, and the next moment unwilling even to be identified with Jesus. The conspirators behind the whole process, the chief priests and Pharisees, were obviously operating out of fear, which is why they conducted the whole thing in the dark and in a hurry. Joseph and Nicodemus appear as timid characters: the former having been a disciple "in secret," and the latter having only "come to Jesus by night." Even Pilate, the nearest thing to a sovereign in the whole scene, is manifestly afraid.

The soldiers are perhaps the only other major players who do not exhibit fear, but that does not speak well for them. They do not come across as brave so much as obtuse. They mock Jesus as a king, unaware that he is, in fact, the King of kings. They then huddle around at the foot of the cross, contesting one another over the pathetic booty of their grim assignment, preoccupied with trivia, while the Son of God and Savior of the world dies just above them.

The whole scene ends with a hasty burial. The curtain is necessarily closed, as the sabbath is on the horizon. But then it would open again, early in the morning, on the first day of the week....

Application

We imagined a student, in both junior and senior high school, studying history in school. It may or may not be a subject of interest to him. In either case, though, he finds that there is a great distance between the people he is studying and himself — between those events and his own life.

That student then arrives at church, and he is presented with still more history. On this particular day, he is presented with a historical event that is many more years — and many more miles — removed from him than the Battle of Yorktown or the Gettysburg Address. Yet this distant episode from history is somehow presented to him as personal.

The old spiritual asks, "Were you there when they crucified my Lord?" That seems like a ridiculous question. No one asks, "Were you there at General Custer's last stand?"

But this is different. George Custer is not Jesus Christ, and their deaths are unequal in both importance and effect. Indeed, according to this day's texts, there is no other death like Jesus' death.

In our consideration of the texts above, we have laid out the case. We are involved in this death. The story of this suffering servant includes first-person pronouns. We discover that "our infirmities," "our transgressions," and "our iniquities" are all in play. And so we are different — our situation and our status are different — because of this death. For now "we have confidence to enter the sanctuary by the blood of Jesus."

"Were you there," the spiritual asks, "when they crucified my Lord?" Yes. It turns out that I was. For by that death, I was saved, healed, forgiven, and reconciled. It was 2,000 years ago, but it is part of my personal history.

An Alternative Application
Isaiah 52:13—53:12; John 18:1—19:42. "We Esteemed Him Not." For so many of us, the King James Version was the translation of scripture we first heard and where we learned some of the most familiar passages. In the case of Isaiah's suffering servant passage, I remain tied and drawn to the poetic language of the old King James.

One phrase in particular especially moves me: "We esteemed him not." The New Revised Standard Version renders it, "we held him of no account," which is fine and speaks the same truth. It lacks elegance, however. Still, of course, it is the truth, not the language, that we might well proclaim on this day.

As we observed earlier, this day carries with it a very specific picture. We have seen that picture so many times — perhaps thousands of times — in art, in movies, in passion plays, and on and on. And so when we read the detailed account in our long passage from John's gospel, we are not left without vivid images in our mind's eye.

Take those scenes from John and make them into a kind of slide show: one picture from each scene. The betrayal of Judas. The arrest of Jesus. The denials of Peter. The trials before Annas and Pilate. The mob's preference for Barabbas. The mocking cruelty of the soldiers. And the crucifixion.

And now put this caption from Isaiah under each picture: "We esteemed him not." It applies in every instance, doesn't it? Scene after scene, the people involved "esteemed him not." They did not recognize who they were dealing with, and so they treated him with epic impropriety.

But that grand failure is not limited to Good Friday. We saw it earlier in the story, as well. The cavalier scribes, who could direct the magi to the Messiah's birthplace, but who did not go themselves. The irritated people in the Nazareth synagogue. The unresponsive people of Capernaum and Chorazin. The would-be disciples. The antagonistic scribes and Pharisees. They all, in their own ways, esteemed him not.

And the tragedy continues.

In a myriad of ways today, people still esteem him not. As his name is misused, his words distorted, and his example ignored. When his opponents misunderstand him and his followers misrepresent him. Whenever you or I let our love grow cold, our allegiance becomes divided, or our priorities get out of order. Along with Isaiah and the circles of fools from Good Friday, we must reflect back on our own world and our own lives and confess that we, too, have "esteemed him not."

Easter Day
Acts 10:34-43
1 Corinthians 15:1-11
John 20:1-18
David Kalas

An annual reminder

In the opening verse of our passage from the epistles, the apostle Paul writes, "Now I would remind you, brothers and sisters, of the good news...."

That might well also be the opening line of our sermons this Sunday. After all, it is Easter. The calendar compels us to return to the foundation and the heart of the gospel message. And the people who will fill our pews this Sunday — some of them barely familiar to us since we last saw them on Christmas Eve — already know what we're going to tell them.

I sometimes wonder at the challenge faced by the first generations of Christian evangelists: Paul and others who traveled the Mediterranean world with the good news when it was still news. In our day, however, though heaven knows that the folks in our culture don't really know much about the gospel, the people who come out this Sunday will at least already know that Jesus rose from the dead. Or that we believe he did. And so our task, like Paul's in 1 Corinthians 15, is perhaps not to tell them something new, but to "remind (them) of the good news."

We must not minimize the importance of reminders. Human beings are so prone to forget things — even important and familiar things — that reminders are absolutely necessary.

I saw a friend of mine, while visiting a town from which he had moved 25 years earlier, unable to make the drive from the office where he had worked to the house where he had lived. It was a drive he had made virtually every day for ten years. And yet, with the passage of time, he had forgotten the once-familiar route.

In trying to help my daughter with her math homework, I find myself looking at problems and methods that are familiar from my own education. But so much time has passed since then, and the material in which I used to earn "A" grades has been so little employed in intervening years, that I have mostly forgotten how to solve these arithmetic problems.

Favorite song lyrics, names of people who were once among our closest circle of friends, details of monumental days in our lives or our children's lives — all these important and familiar things can slip away. And the things of God do not fare any better.

From the Israelites in the wilderness to the ye-of-little-faith disciples, we see in the pages of scripture, how often God's people forget: forget what he has said, what he has done, what he is like. And forgetting such matters is always a costly business.

So we may enter our pulpits this Easter Sunday and unapologetically "remind you, brothers and sisters, of the good news...."

Acts 10:34-43

We take some things so much for granted. Because a given thing has always been a part of our reality, we may find it hard to imagine a time without it. As I sit at my desk, for example, I am listening to a music CD. Now I remember well the days before CDs, to be sure, and my young daughters marvel at the musical oddities from my youth that they come across in the basement — 8-track tapes and record albums. Still, while I have witnessed the evolution from 8-tracks to iPods, I have never known a time without recorded music.

Whatever the medium, you and I probably have, for all our lives, taken for granted the phenomenon of recorded music. We have always been able to turn on some gadget and listen to the music of our choosing at the time of our choosing. And not only in our homes, but in our automobiles, on our bicycles, and wherever we care to go. But in the big scheme of things, this is a relatively recent phenomenon. For the lion's share of human history, people could only listen to music either by attending a live performance or by making the music themselves. It may be hard for us even to imagine that earlier time and experience.

Likewise, in our day, when the Christian church spans the globe, it may be hard for us even to imagine the circumstances and mindset of Peter and Cornelius' day. I remember a poster that hung in one of the Sunday school rooms from my childhood. It featured a picture of the Earth, with children representing virtually every racial and ethnic group holding hands around it. And the caption featured something very much like the words to "Jesus Loves The Little Children."

You and I grew up with that kind of picture of the church and of God's love. Peter and Cornelius did not.

In the days of Acts 10, there is something genuinely scandalous about Peter's words: that "God shows no partiality," and that "anyone" from "every nation" can be "acceptable to him." While not inconsistent with many hints of God's global embrace found throughout the Old Testament, Peter's words were surely in conflict with the prevailing paradigm of the time. What about a chosen, covenant people? What about circumcision and the law? What about the theology embodied in the temple architecture, with its symbolic representation of people's proximity to God: the court of the priests being nearest, then Jewish men, then Jewish women, and then Gentiles as the farthest away?

The message that Peter proclaims to Cornelius and the rest of his Gentile household has sometimes been cited as a kind of embryonic gospel. For if we were to expand on each of the several events and themes to which Peter makes quick reference — John the Baptist, Jesus going about "doing good and healing," "beginning in Galilee," followed by "all that he did both in Judea and in Jerusalem," including how the leaders "put him to death" and how "God raised him on the third day," followed by a record of those "who ate and drank with him after he rose from the dead" — we would have something very much like Matthew, Mark, or Luke. So it seems that the writing of the gospels was a natural outgrowth of the preaching of the gospel.

Peter includes himself among those "who were chosen by God as witnesses." It is notable that being a witness is not portrayed here as a voluntary thing. An individual does not sign up for the privilege; he or she is selected for it. The point is reinforced by Peter's statement that "he commanded us to preach to the people and to testify...." Peter and his companions are not mere volunteers; they have been called to the witness stand by God himself.

And that, in turn, reminds us that bearing witness is actually a secondary act. A person cannot witness until he has witnessed. I must experience something before I can bear witness to that something. There is no purpose in my climbing onto the witness stand unless I have first experienced something that is relevant to the case.

1 Corinthians 15:1-11

Twice in this passage, Paul uses the phrase "in accordance with the scriptures." In the first case, it is a reference to Christ's crucifixion; and in the second case, it is a reference to his resurrection. "The scriptures" for Paul, of course, were the writings that comprise our Old Testament. Ironically, the lectionary does not furnish us with any such Old Testament readings for this Sunday.

The significance of the phrase — "in accordance with the scriptures" — is threefold. At times, the biblical writers will make such a reference as a kind of argument from authority. The person and work of Christ are verified by the degree to which they fulfill the predictions and foreshadows of the scriptures. The way that Matthew cites the scriptures being "fulfilled" is a good example of this usage.

At other times, biblical writers will make such a reference as a teaching device. The person and work of Christ are explained in light of the scriptures that prefigured him. The letter to the Hebrews is a notable example.

And then, at other times, the biblical writers will make such a reference as a way of showing that God calls his shots. Like Babe Ruth's legendary gesture toward the wall in the 1932 World Series, time and again God tells what he is going to do before he does it. This is an especially crucial element in the Old Testament prophets: Let there be no mistake, when these things happen, that they were God's doing.

Paul affirms that both Christ's dying and rising were "in accordance with the scriptures." It is a truth echoed in the other two lections for this Sunday, as well. Peter assures Cornelius that "all the prophets testify about him," and the young man in the otherwise empty tomb explains to the startled women that they will see Jesus in Galilee, "just as he told you."

The irony of our lections this week is that this prominent theme of "in accordance with the scriptures" is unaccompanied by any of those scriptures. We have three New Testament passages this week; we should perhaps do our people the favor, however, of sharing with them some of the Old Testament texts in which God called his Good Friday and Easter Sunday shots.

As Paul recounts the resurrection of Jesus, he makes a careful point of Jesus' post-resurrection. This theme is paralleled in Peter's speech to Cornelius' household. Paul identifies himself as the "last of all." Our idiomatic phrase says "last, but not least." Paul, however, reckons himself both last and least of the apostles. He knows that he is "unfit." But, of course, that is always the testimony in the wake of God's grace.

Toward the end of this passage, Paul makes a statement that raises a sobering question. He makes the confident claim that God's "grace toward me has not been in vain." Are we able to make the same statement with the same confidence? To what extent has the investment of his grace enjoyed a good return in me, or to what extent has his grace toward me been in vain — like the seed that fell upon the path, or like the talent entrusted to the third servant?

"In vain" is something of a recurring concern for Paul. Perhaps it is a concern born of his natural pragmatism, or his competitiveness, or whatever regret he lived with for his pre-Damascus living. In any case, he uses the phrase twelve different times in his letters, including five times in this chapter alone. The people's believing (15:2), their faith (15:14), and the apostles' proclamation (15:14) could all possibly be in vain. But at the same time, he assures the people that God's grace (15:10) and their labor (15:58) have not been in vain.

Mark 16:1-8

One of my New Testament professors along the way once shared what he thought was the single greatest evidence of the resurrection. "Women were the first witnesses," he said. "If the early Christians were making up the story of Jesus rising from the dead, they would have used different witnesses in order to give the story greater credibility in that first-century world."

Likewise, at the end of this passage, Mark includes a detail that adds to my professor's method of verification. The women, according to Mark, were seized by "terror and amazement; and they said nothing to anyone, for they were afraid." Again, if you were making up this story, you wouldn't do it this way. It is the blemishes that make the photograph believable.

As a man, it's hard not to be embarrassed by the absentee disciples in this most important of events. It seems that they scattered from the Garden of Gethsemane on Thursday night, and they had been mostly laying low ever since. But it was these marvelous women, comparatively fearless and moved by their love, who were headed to the tomb at the first opportunity in order to care for their Lord, even in his death.

Perhaps there is a great truth here. The despairing, the fearful, and the self-absorbed are in hiding, and consequently they miss out on God's great work. It is those who boldly step out in love, if not in faith or understanding, who witness and share in what God is doing.

Mark adds a marvelously human touch to his Easter narrative. As he describes the women coming to the tomb, recites their wondering about the stone, and reports that it had already been rolled away, he inserts this descriptive phrase about the stone: "which was very large." It is a charming detail to include, as though the stone was the greatest obstacle to be overcome on Easter Sunday.

When the women arrive at the tomb, they are surprised to discover that the stone, which had covered the entrance, had already been rolled away. Naturally, they took the opportunity to step inside the tomb. After all, they had come for the purpose of anointing Jesus' body with spices. But they are astonished — alarmed — by what they find. Rather than the dead body of their Lord lying where it had been placed, they find a man, who is very much alive, sitting there instead.

The scene would be humorous, if it were not so initially horrifying. The analogy is imperfect, but imagine several grieving women arriving at a funeral home for the visitation. They walk over to the open casket, expecting to weep over the corpse of their loved one, only to discover that he's not there at all. Ah, but it's not that the casket is altogether empty. No, someone else is there, sitting up, alive, and apparently waiting to talk to them.

The "young man, dressed in a white robe" seems to be a kind of holy forwarding address. It turns out that the one they had come looking for was no longer there. He had moved on. This helpful young man waiting there was evidently waiting for precisely such visitors so that he could send them on to Galilee, where "he is going ahead of you" and where "you will see him, just as he told you."

The four gospels have slight variations in their accounts of Easter Sunday, including who sees the risen Christ, and when, and where, but there is this consistency: No one sees him in the tomb. Once he is raised, he is no longer there. Mark and Luke both have men in white waiting inside the tomb with the news of Jesus' resurrection, but it is not Jesus himself who waits inside the tomb. Indeed, Matthew's account seems to indicate that he was gone even before the stone was rolled away (28:1-6). He can be found by those who seek him, to be sure, but not there. He's not in the tomb.

Application

I mentioned earlier a friend of mine who forgot what had once been a familiar route, just as I have forgotten how to do certain mathematics. The result for my friend, of course, is that he got lost. The result for me is that I cannot solve the problems in my daughter's math book.

Perhaps we might consider, with our people, what variety of things we human beings forget — including some things we thought we would never forget! Next, we might consider the instances in scripture where God's people seemed to forget what he had said or done, identifying the consequences of their forgetfulness.

And then we might turn our attention to Easter. Is it possible that we could forget that? And, if so, what are the consequences?

My friend getting lost in what used to be his hometown proved that he had forgotten his way around. Perhaps, likewise, our occasional hopelessness, or gloom, or despair, or joylessness, or sense of defeat indicate that we have forgotten: forgotten the unparalleled, unmitigated, come-from-behind, once-and-for-all victory of our Lord.

That victory changes everything. It changes our death, and consequently it also changes our life. It changes how we mourn, how we hope, how we endure, and how we live. And so, it may be essential this Sunday to remind our brothers and sisters of the good news.

Meanwhile, the other part of the purpose of the reminder is the purpose of propagation.

Paul wrote to the Corinthians that "I handed on to you as of first importance what I in turn had received." The language suggests a relay race, and the baton is the gospel. It was handed to him, and he carefully and urgently handed it on to the Corinthians.

Of course, it is not meant to stop there. The baton should not end with any one person until the race has been won. Rather, "he commanded us to preach to the people and to testify that he is the one...."

With care and urgency, then, we hand the gospel baton to our people this Sunday. And we urge and remind them, in turn, to pass the good news along.

An Alternative Application

Mark 16:1-8. "The Very Large Stone." The stone, "which was very large," serves as a very useful metaphor for us. The women approached the tomb with apprehension about that stone. Who would move it for them? They were certainly unable to move it themselves.

Likewise, as the stone symbolizes the seal of death, we human beings indeed face something too massive for us to move ourselves. We continually invest the full strength of our technology and our own best efforts as individuals, yet we can barely budge that stone. Our little centimeters of achievement in this direction or that do not remotely change the immense reality: Namely, death is too big for us. We cannot escape it; we cannot conquer it; we cannot buy or learn or medicate our way out of it; and we cannot remove its seal from friends, loved ones, or ourselves.

Then comes the good news of Easter. The women arrive at the tomb and discover that the stone "had already been rolled back." What they could not do for themselves, God had already done for them, and in the same event, God also did for us what we cannot do for ourselves. So we will find, when we arrive at our tomb, that the great seal of death has already been rolled away for us, too.

Easter 2
Acts 4:32-35
1 John 1:1—2:2
John 20:19-31
Wayne Brouwer

Living on purpose

e. e. cummings' marvelous poem "i thank You God for most this amazing" gives us a hint as to what it means to live on purpose. The words to the poem are available online at, and it is worth your time to look them up.

cummings lifts purpose-filled living above the normal grind of repetitive day-to-day sameness. Theologically, this is what Rick Warren, in his best-selling books, has tried to do for pastors and church leaders (*The Purpose-Driven Church*) and also for Christians generally (*The Purpose-Driven Life*). To live on purpose is to have a well-developed sense of self, an ongoing assessment of life around oneself, a linear understanding of time and progress, a goal toward which one is moving, and a community of fellow pilgrims who nurture the mutual determination to keep going.

Often we lack purpose. One couple tells of sending their daughter to college. Instead of a degree, she came home with a boyfriend. When the younger folks expressed their desire to get married, the father thought a little heart-to-heart chat was in order. Taking his daughter's fiancé aside, he asked, "What do you hope to do with your life?"

"I'm not really certain, sir," came the reply, "but I have confidence that the Lord will provide."

"Do you have a place to live?" the father continued.

"No, sir," was the answer, "but the Lord will provide."

"What about an income? Do you have a job or some kind of career lined up? How will you take care of our daughter?"

"We are in love," said the young man, "and the Lord will provide."

Later, when the pair of young lovers was gone, the wife asked her husband how his talk with the would-be groom had gone. "Well," he said, "I have mixed feelings. On the one hand, I find him shiftless and ill-prepared for both life and marriage. Yet on the other hand, I get the feeling that he thinks I'm God!"

We are, at times, both — shiftless and trusting; life-blown and purpose-driven; meandering and marching under orders. This side of Easter, it is good to remember again some of the purposes that make life in the Spirit real *life*.

Acts 4:32-35

This is a powerful picture of Christianity lived on purpose. There are a number of qualities raised to prominence. First, there is unity of identity ("one in heart and mind"). This could never mean mechanistic robot-like spiritual cloning (think of Pink Floyd's powerful song "We Don't Need No Education" and the video that portrayed public schools as dehumanizing machines churning out cookie-cutter replicas, obediently civilized); rather, it means caught up together in a common purpose. The passionate unity displayed by early Communism as it coupled with the international workers' movement (summarized in John Reed's powerful description, *Ten Days That Shook the World*, and portrayed in the 1981 Warren Beatty film, *Reds*, based on it) carries something of the energy displayed in this first small Christian community.

Second, there is unity of possessions ("No one claimed that any of his possessions was his own, but they shared everything they had"). It is tempting to see in this early expression community a type of nascent communism. But, as the story of Ananias and Sapphira (which follows immediately in 5:1-11) shows, no communism of modern varieties can claim this scene as its own. The unity of possessions was not a collective ownership but a rich generosity. Private property was not excluded in this Jerusalem community; instead, there was a heightened sense of responsibility that placed every need in the public eye and challenged every resource to be used for the good of the group as a whole.

Third, there was unity of creed. The brief statement that "the apostles continued to testify to the resurrection of the Lord Jesus" carries great weight. The emphasis is on "resurrection." We are so used to people believing in the resurrection of Jesus on Easter that we cannot fully engage what it was like to live in a world where that idea was scandalous. Among the Jewish people Jesus' death proved he could not be divine, for God acts in power, and is not subject to crucifixion. But Jesus' resurrection confused things. How could a God powerful enough to turn back the universal authority of death still be subject to death as Jesus was? It was a theological conundrum. Similarly, in most of the rest of the Mediterranean, Hellenized world, the idea of deities actually taking on flesh and blood so that they become susceptible to death was ludicrous. The great thing that makes gods gods and not human was their general transcendence above physical reality and not being bound or consumed by it. Human spirits needed to be liberated from flesh; so why would God invest in flesh and blood, and become trapped and annihilated in it? Yet the Christian testimony of deity incarnate, deity mortified, and deity risen with human flesh and blood challenged all of this. Moreover, this testimony of the resurrection of Jesus was not a peripheral teaching; it was, in fact, the central element of Christian speech. It was the key declaration that bound these very diverse people together.

Fourth, there is unity of mission. Because possessions instantly became secondary to care for people, there was a great deal of energy released from this community. People mattered. People were cared for. People received attention.

Visitors came to a worship service I led years ago. They were vacationing with a family who belonged to our congregation. The visitors were not Christians and had never before been at a service of Christian worship. When I talked with them afterward, the thing that caught their attention most was the prayer for people who had special needs. They had never been in a public gathering where specific needs of people were highlighted, and a group consensus was developed to orchestrate care for these folks. They were very impressed.

Fifth, there is unity of submission. Gifts are brought and laid "at the apostles' feet." This is more than a reference to how collections are gathered. This has to do with recognition of the authority of the apostles within the community. Church government over the years has sometimes misshaped this in two directions. Where apostolic authority seeps into the organizational structures of the church, it often becomes a self-preserving authoritarian system. Oppositely, where apostolic authority defuses throughout the community it can easily become mere democracy, and lose direction with every shifting majority vote. The unity of submission in the early church reflected a broad recognition that Jesus continues to give shape and purpose to his people, and does so through wise and gifted leaders. There are no leaders without followers; there are no followers without leaders.

Where these five expressions of unity continue, the church is true to its origins. It also breathes with a great sense of purpose: relationships matter, generosity abounds, worldviews are challenged, neighborhoods are changed, and respect grows.

1 John 1:1—2:2

John wrote this letter late in his life. It may well have emerged after the book of Revelation, and around the same time as the gospel. Stories abound from early Christianity about John's elderly years as senior statesman of the church in Asia Minor, with primary pastoral responsibilities in Ephesus. He was brought on a litter to the front of the worship gathering week by week, infirm and wizened. When asked to speak a word from the Lord, John is reported to have said the same words again and again, "Little children, love one another."

"Brother John," they challenged him, "why do you always tell us the same thing?"

"Because that is all there is," he would reply. "Love is of God, and those who live in love, live in God."

Whether the tales are true or not, the ideas conveyed by them do emerge repeatedly throughout the first letter of John. The primary issue John was responding to appears to have been some early forms of gnostic Christianity.

The cosmogony described in gnosticism was quite specific. The good deity is pure spirit and cannot meddle in physical reality. Therefore there is a second deity, a lesser deity, a mean-spirited deity who created the world that we know. This is the God of the Old Testament, a God of vengeance and a God of harsh rules. Each of us human beings has a spark of divinity within us. It is trapped by our physical stuff, and often not recognized in our day-to-day interactions. Our greatest need is to have this divine spark released from its fleshly prison. Jesus is the one who showed us how this could happen. Jesus was an apparition, a manifestation of the good God who appeared to be human like us. Of course, Jesus could not be human, for that would mean that he was trapped in flesh like the rest of us. Jesus appeared among us as the great teacher who had the right wisdom (Greek *gnosis*) that would allow us to learn the method of escape from the physical into the spiritual. His teachings, if rightly understood and properly chanted, give some people the ability to transcend the flesh and escape from this existence to a higher expression of our divine core of being.

Because physical reality and flesh are inherently evil, it is important to ignore them, or to bother with them only because this is our lot for the time we are here. We have no responsibility to care for one another or to try to make life better for one another, since "life" and "flesh" are polar opposites. To try to help others here is, in fact, to promote the nasty lie that we are okay as fleshly creatures.

Furthermore, Jesus provides his secret knowledge only to those who practice mystery rituals developed among those "in the know." Therefore the gnostic Christians became a sort of secret society of those who were certainly better than anyone else. If these spiritual superstars played their words right they would be able to escape and no longer bother with life and others here.

With these ideas in mind it is clear to see why John writes as he does. First of all, he ties together the recent revelation of Jesus with the origins of the world in which we live. Jesus is both a revelation and a real human flesh-and-blood person. We saw him with our eyes. We touched him with our hands. John is promoting a teaching directly in contradiction to the tenets of gnosticism.

Second, the creator God and the human/divine Jesus are essentially the same, and they are essentially good. Gone is the gnostic idea that the creator God was a bad God that got us trapped in our difficulties. Instead, creation, creator, Jesus, and we are all essentially good. This is true even in our human physical form. Our physicality is not something to be escaped, but something to be affirmed. We are not divine sparks trapped in fleshly corpses; we are truly human and truly good, made to be the way we are.

Third, salvation through the work of Jesus is not a denial of our flesh, but an affirmation of our relationship with God. Rather than trying to win salvation by escaping our bodies, we need to recognize that we are saved (made perfect, walking in the light, living in the truth) in the context of our current existence. It is not merely a pie-in-the-sky-bye-and-bye that we are hoping for; we are made right and true and good within our current living circumstances.

Fourth, "perfection" is not to be understood as gnostic attainment of secret insight but rather in terms of a positive relational lifestyle. The gnostics could ignore the cries and needs of others because that was simply the unfortunate lot of all who are trapped in the flesh. To respond would be to mitigate the need to transcend the flesh, so the gnostics properly (in their own thinking) ignored the pain and suffering of others. What did it matter? Such was the inevitable end of all who lacked the secret wisdom (that they had) to escape. In contrast, John says that "perfection" is shown through good deeds and the help of others in need.

Looking at the Christian life in this way, John's emphasis on "not sinning" becomes meaningful. He is not proposing "perfectionism" in the way that some holiness theologies have put it forward. Rather, he is sharply contrasting the attitudes and lifestyles of those steeped in proto-gnostic thinking (perfection is only found through escape from this existence) from those who are deeply influenced by the true Jesus-in-the-flesh who encourages us to live here as Jesus himself did: with compassion and care for others, and affirming the life that we have, even if it is distorted by sin. This is what it means to "live on purpose."

John 20:19-31

On this Second Sunday of Easter we consider the only story in the Bible which is specifically identified with this day — the revelation of Jesus to his disciple Thomas. Thomas should not be seen as a bad guy. Too often he has gotten a bum rap because of his failure to quickly jump on the Easter bandwagon.

The truth of the gospel reveals more of deep substance about the man. For one thing, John tells us that Thomas was the one who was willing to go to Jerusalem during the worst threats against Jesus' life, and even die there with the master (John 11:16). Furthermore, it was Thomas who was honest enough to tell Jesus that he didn't understand the sometimes cryptic things Jesus would talk about (John 14:5). In other words, Thomas was a simple man in the best sense of the term. He was honest and good and loyal and true. You could count on Thomas. Thomas was well grounded. Thomas lived by convictions, and was even willing to die by them.

When Thomas refused to believe in the resurrection of Jesus because he was not with the others on the evening of that first Easter, it was not because he was ornery or cantankerous. It was simply because he had seen too many people go off on wild-goose chases when there was no goose to be had. The traumatic events of Passion Week ought to have made everyone a bit sober, and forced them to realize that wishful thinking is not enough to change reality.

But when Jesus physically appeared to Thomas along with the rest of the disciples a week later, Thomas was willing to change his mind and accept the reality of the resurrection. We are not even told that Thomas actually touched Jesus. The appearance may well have been enough.

Furthermore, Thomas becomes, in that moment, the patron saint of all who wrestle with doubt or disbelief. John concludes the scene with a call to belief, and indicates that Thomas' struggle is inherent in all who honestly investigate the signs offered by Jesus.

Application

How do we live "on purpose" this side of Easter? Rick Warren's five purposes are certainly instructive:

We live to worship God — we are not the center of life, but God is. We are not the authors of creation, but its recipients.

We live to be in community — there is no such thing as an "individual Christian." Historically, there have been many times when theologians declared that there was no salvation outside of the church. What they meant is that once one becomes part of Christ, one also becomes part of Christ's body. To live in symbiotic relationship with the rest of Christ's body and to engage in the compassionate acts of Christ brings us into community.

We live to grow — the alternative to growth is death. All living things grow. We grow in insight, we grow in understanding, we grow richer in spirit. This is a purpose that has many spiritual overtones.

We live to serve — Jesus continues to minister to others through our lives. The act of service is itself an expression of Christian character. A British doctor of a previous generation used to prescribe the "Service Cure" to his patients that were habitually depressed with no clear medical cause. These people were required to do at least one kindness per week to another human being for six weeks in a row. The doctor reported a near perfect healing rate for the ailments of mind and heart for these patients.

We live to witness — Jesus came to seek and save the lost. We cannot be Jesus, but we are certainly witnesses of Jesus. The church is a missionary enterprise, expressing the wonderful news that God lives, God cares, and God brings God's people into a renewed future through the work of Jesus.

Today would be a great day to remind people that they live on purpose and for great purposes. They are called to be God's people!

An Alternative Application

John 20:19-31. The gospel story of Thomas is one that fits particularly well today. Perhaps a review of the primary types of doubt (see, for instance, Os Guinness' great book *In Two Minds* or Wayne Brouwer's *Walking on Water: Faith and Doubt in the Christian Life*) might be in order. Then some encouragement to doubt well, but to doubt with the purpose of clarifying belief would be in order. Sermons on healthy doubt need to be preached often.

Learning from cancer

For the past seven years, cancer has been part of my journey. On the day before Christmas Eve, 1998, I was operated on for colon cancer. One more colon resection, two liver operations, experimental drugs, radiation, and somewhere close to a million dollars later and I am still here. Right now, I function in a near-normal region and the idea of renewing journal subscriptions or writing for them for at least the next two years is not an irresponsible act. We can even talk at a meaningful level of something that looks like a cure.

Part of the process involves the occasional surrender of privacy and any shred of dignity. I have been poked and probed and examined from every direction imaginable. Fundamentally, there have been three methods of determining where we are. The CAT scan is a very upscale x-ray, the PET scan uses a radioactive isotope, and the CEA blood level indicates what level of anti-cancer enzyme my body is producing. The x-ray scan gives us an anatomical picture; the PET scan shows the level of cancer cell activity. The CEA shows the level of my body's response to what is going on. The more my body responds, the more we know what is going on.

It seems the church could use something similar: a quick scan to give a big picture of what is there, a measure of activity, and a measure of responsiveness to what is going on in the world. In the three texts for this Sunday we are given some indicators of what we are to watch for, what activity is among us, and just how responsive we are to what is going on in the world. The passage in Acts gives an indication of how healing might be an indicator of faith. One of the things to remember in the cancer business is that this is only one indicator. I have had the experience of one scan showing something while the other measure indicated nothing. The passage from 1 John indicates somewhat of an anatomical measure. We have a snapshot of where things are today but no indicator of what will exactly happen or how we are responding. The pericope from Luke shows how the early community responded to the events of Holy Week, but it is far from clear as to what all this means or where it may be headed.

Of course, no single measure will give the complete picture that might lead to the desired outcome. Neither is any of this an exact science. Any of the diagnostic procedures have the potential to be set off by something else. This feels much like the challenge ahead for any reader of scripture; any piece of scripture taken in isolation can give a false lead. Indeed, some of scripture seems to have been set off by cultural considerations of their time in a way that might condone slavery, oppress women, and justify domestic violence. My oncologist often seems to intuitively weave things together based on his experience: even to the point of knowing what is going on before the high-tech machines can discover it.

On the other hand, as it is well known, the treatments for cancer can often feel worse than the disease. In my own case this has not been so. With modern medicine the side effects have been greatly diminished. However, there is often the curious bodily response. My current round of chemo includes a pill that has made me the hit of the youth group by giving me acne. No one knows why it does this. Sometimes, the side effects of being church can feel like having a prickly rash. The scientists have found that the more rash there is, the more the body is responding in a positive manner. The response of the body of Christ might be something like a rash when we face conflict, shaky nerves about the future, and theological challenges of the present. It could be a sign as well that we do have the big picture in focus as we scan the horizon.

Acts 3:12-19

As a cancer survivor, I approach any text involving healing with a great deal of fear and trepidation. So much harm can be done so easily. We can fall all too readily to inferring that people are not cured because of their lack of faith or that they are somehow, through their faithlessness, responsible for the illnesses that have befallen them. Even as one who I think has his theological head screwed on straight I can be swept up in such feelings. I suspect that this is because, if Elizabeth Kübler-Ross is right in her understanding of grief and loss, we are naturally swept toward such feelings. If we go through the stage of bargaining for our survival, what do we have to bargain with but the promise that we will do or be better? This pit of the metabolic activity is not picked up on the usual scans. Yet, as I scan this text I do find solace and wisdom. Peter asks, "You Israelites, why do you wonder at this, or why do you stare at us, as though by our own power or piety we had made him walk?" Well, this is good news. If there is any walking to take place here it is not the result of human effort. After proclaiming that God has glorified Jesus' name he says that, "And by faith in his name, his name itself has made this man strong, whom you see and know; and the faith that is through Jesus has given him this perfect health in the presence of all of you." We are told that the man has been lame from birth. Peter and John encounter him begging for alms at the entrance to the temple. He is confronted by the fact that Peter and John have neither gold nor silver but what they do have they will give in the name of Jesus. In a sense, he receives more than he bargained for and a life that will now glorify God.

As I scan my own cancer experience, I find myself being given more than I had bargained for. In the bargaining stage of things I would settle for some thing of gold or silver proportions. One bargains for more years to one's life rather than, as the television commercial has it, more life to whatever number of years one may have. I have received more than I bargained for. I am a better, wiser, and more prayerful pastor. I believe I am a more decent, loving human being. I build bridges more easily. Having done the cancer business for seven years I am a nonanxious presence in more places than I thought possible and have experienced more care and support than I could have ever imagined. I find myself wanting to join with the man lame from birth in leaping and praising God. In a sense, I am no longer such a lame human being. I can stride into more situations more confidently than I thought I ever could.

At this point in my life, the scans show little cancer activity. "And by faith in his name, his name itself has made this man strong, whom you see and know; and the faith that is through Jesus has given him this perfect health in the presence of all of you." As I scan my life, I find the activity of God.

Of course, the result is not always entirely unvarnished success. One of the themes of the book of Acts is that there are many who will want to use the power of God to advance their own aims. Demetrius, the silversmith, has an ongoing concern in making a profit out of religion. Simon Magus is willing to put out upfront money for the power offered in the Holy Spirit. Yes, I know what it is like to see people look on me with amazement. Having gone through this, folks don't quite know what to do with you, and listen to you with more attentiveness than you are used to or deserve. Often folks reject out of hand the holy and righteous one as the source of my level of health. Some do because out of ignorance they do not have a theology that can put such experiences into context. Many out of ignorance head for the exit at the thought of there being any faith/health connection. Some out of ignorance search for some rational explanation that they can apply to their lives. As I scan my life, all I can say is that if I am not limping through a lame life it is because it was a gift from a hand much larger than my own.

1 John 3:1-7

An MRI or a CAT scan can tell you something of how things are, but very little of how things might be. Occasionally, in my own experience, what will show up on a CAT scan will not show up on a PET scan. A CAT scan gives an anatomical picture but gives no indication of what kind of activity may be taking place. A surgeon who operates in the here-and-now needs more than a picture of how things are going to be. "Beloved, we are God's children now; what we will be has not yet been revealed." This is a truth that does require a deep scan to discover. The letter writer's community focuses on a realized eschatology that will enable them to operate in a very difficult present. It must not have been easy in John's community to make such a claim. We know that one of the themes of this community was the experience of being separated from the larger Jewish community. One wonders how many of John's people heard words like, "You are no son or daughter of mine as long as you fool with that stupid Jesus business. Do you hear me? If you go with them then you might as well keep on going for you have no home here." The promise in the gospel of John that the community would not be left orphaned must have meant a great deal to people who were facing angry family and friends. "See what love the Father has given us that we should be called children of God; and that is what we are. The reason the world does not know us is that it did not know him." Survey the situation and see that rejection and hostility abounds. However take a deeper scan and you will find a different reality.

The letter writer concludes that the root cause of the rejection of their true identity is not anything that the members of the faith community have done to bring this about. "The reason the world does not know us is that it did not know him." In the modern context the statement, "That in him there is no sin" is bound to raise the level of skepticism. Neither are people likely to be less dubious about claims that no one who abides in him sins. Such claims are likely to meet with rejection.

However, it seems today that it is not that we meet rejection because the world does not know Jesus. Indeed, the world often seems to be fascinated and longing for understanding about Jesus. For years the undergraduate course at Harvard University that had the highest registrations was an exploration of Jesus' life and teaching. It seems that today it is the other way around: that many do not want to know Jesus because of what they think they know of his church.

Indeed, how can they know him if we do not act like his children? How can they know him if we engage in red state/blue state bloodletting that leaves many of us wounded? How can they know him, if we play in a way that turns our interactions more into competition than collaboration? How will they know him if we think we do not believe that we should as children grow in wisdom and in stature? How can they know him if we seek worldly wisdom more than childlike faith? The words of verse 10, "The children of God and the children of the devil are revealed in this way: all who do not do what is right are not from God, nor are those who do not love their brothers and sisters" tie together the being a child of God with the ability to do right. How can we do right if we are more interested in doing battle?

The CAT scan may not reveal the way things will go, but it can reveal the way things are.

Luke 24:36b-48

The CEA blood level measures the response of the body to disease. As Luke scans the horizon, he gives an indication of how the post-Easter community was responding to the ministry, death, and resurrection of Jesus. Here we have the story of the gathering of the community in Jerusalem. Absent the presence of the risen Christ, the community is now gathered in fear. The reader is reminded of how the community is found in John's gospel with doors sealed for fear of what may happen next. Fear characterizes much of the initial response of the early church to its new situation. This is a natural response of the body when it feels itself under threat. The adrenalin begins to pump, the veins contract, the muscles stiffen, and the protective response kicks in. Interestingly enough, often this reaction turns out to be the least helpful to a challenge ahead. "They were startled and terrified, and thought that they were seeing a ghost. He said to them, 'Why are you frightened, and why do doubts arise in your hearts?'" They may not have fears because they have doubts but doubts because they have fears. When a burn patient is in recovery, the doctors must be careful that the protective tissue does not heal before the connective tissue that is at the deeper level. A person on crutches is told to relax if they begin to fall because if they tighten up and become rigid, they are likely to do serious damage. When a person has a heart attack, the initial panic response often causes the blood vessels to constrict in a way that will cause further damage.

Fear and flight come as a deep primal response to danger. However, our fear often puts us at greater risk. Jesus invites the disciples to take another reading of the situation. "Look at my hands and my feet; see that it is I myself. Touch me and see; for a ghost does not have flesh and bones as you see that I have." In a way, take a reading on your own wounds. Have they not also been opportunities for growth, bridges to others, and better self-understanding? How often have stumbling blocks become building blocks of the kingdom of God? God's purposes do not always seem to be contingent on our successfulness. My comfort zone and my capacity for compassion are not always concentric spheres. I take a scan of my life and there is much evidence of the pathology that leads to the primal primitive fear response. I have a quick response to Jesus' question, "Why are you afraid?" Yes, it often seems that we are more haunted by our past than helped by it. Yet, while the past cannot be forgotten, dismissed, or repressed it can be redeemed and made a tool of healing. Why do fear and doubts arise? Why do we allow a primitive response to get ahead of a more fully developed realization of what God is up to in our lives?

This text gives much evidence that the body of Christ began to give a more healthy response in light of the events of Holy Week and Easter morn. We find them gathered at a common meal. The breaking of bread together became a key to the breaking down of fear, estrangement, and hopelessness. The Emmaus pilgrims tell of how Jesus was made known in the breaking of the bread. The community found themselves having their minds open to understanding scripture in light of the Easter event. This new understanding will help their immune system to ward off the primitive fear response that leads to using scripture as a weapon to hurt and build barriers between people. The scriptures even recount a physical symptom to this immune response. They said to each other, "Were not our hearts burning within us while he was talking to us on the road, while he was opening the scriptures to us?"

Luke is interested in having the big picture. We are given a reading here that in table fellowship with Jesus, eating right, and with a burning sensation that indicates health, not infection, they are ready to journey to proclaim repentance and forgiveness of sins to all nations and to be witnesses of these things.

Application

The texts agree in taking as their focus not the well-being of the individual but the condition of the community. The health of the individual will be arrived at through the well-being of the community. The book of Acts tells the tale that for Luke the community shares all things in common and warns those who hold back from the commitment. When it comes to basic biology in an age when we are aware that potential pandemics could sweep the planet, we are more prone to accept this truth. However, it often seems that American religion is inordinately focused on individual fate. Having spent a good part of the last seven years waiting for various scans, I have found that much of the time spent waiting comes from the need to recalibrate the machines for the right organ study. These texts invite us to recalibrate our thinking in community terms. In our context and community can we name the activity of God in our midst? I doubt this can come without community conversation about our common life. I suspect that if we scanned any congregation we would find an immense amount of health that can only be attributed to the presence and power of God. In our day and age, what gets us through the tight spots of conflict and change?

I suspect that much of the road rage level of conflict that I find on internet forums and in the press comes from places of guilt, shame, and feelings of being abandoned that we have not scanned for. Such a scan might reveal that we are a lot closer together than we know or perhaps care to admit.

I wonder to what degree my church is driven by table fellowship with Jesus and a reading of scripture that is driven more by the mind of Christ and less by ideological mindlessness. We need to take a reading of our common life for the healthy levels of response to the events of Holy Week and Easter.

An Alternative Application

Acts 3:12-19. Ignorance! How dare anyone say that I operate out of ignorance? Who does Peter think he is that he should say such a thing? Repent of ignorance? Pardon me? I will not go there! While my first reaction is to feel offended, once my anger has blown out to sea, I begin to wonder how this applies to me and my church. Perhaps the real axis of evil is the combination of ignorance and arrogance that flows in its wake. When I begin to reflect, I realize how many images of people I carry around that bear little relationship to who they really are. I operate on first impressions too easily formed. No real human being could ever be reducible to the simple characterizations I have of them. I do crucify out of ignorance. Can any human being be as uncomplicated as my take on the motivations of red state and blue state people?

I don't take Saint Paul at his word when he wrote to the Romans, "behold I show you a mystery." I have found myself falling into the habit of experiencing people as something to be explained rather than as a mystery to be cherished, or honored, or cultivated. I come to believe people's reality actually does conform to all my psychological and theological theories. Too often, life becomes tactical rather than relational. Ignorance does not stop me from crucifying.

This is bad enough when it is done to people. I suspect that we become a one-person axis of evil when we think of God as something to be nailed down more than as something that opens us up.

Easter 4
Acts 4:5-12
1 John 3:16-24
John 10:11-18
David Davis

At least God is greater

A newly minted pastor heads out for a pastoral visit to the home of one the saints in the church. The pastor had come to enjoy the visits with this member more than most. The pastor learned so much about the congregation and ministry and faith there in that living room. The church member often kept a little list on a notepad of things she wanted to talk to the pastor about. Those afternoon conversations in the overly warmed house that smelled of heating oil covered all kinds of topics: current events, biblical texts, church politics, family stories. The pastor found herself scheduling such visits on a more regular basis because she came away encouraged and feeling loved. As many pastors fresh out of seminary find out, such visits are priceless.

Perhaps you can easily imagine such a fictional scene that plays out somewhere in the kingdom of God these days. One particular afternoon the conversation turns to world events and the fear of terrorism and war. The young pastor finds herself silent as the wise old saint talks a bit about living through World War II. She describes various church families and their experience during Vietnam. The more the church member talks, the more discouraged she sounds about all the news and she wonders in full voice about whether people will ever learn. As she reaches for the tissue tucked up the sleeve of her sweater, the saint heaves a big sigh and says, "Well, at least God is greater. God is greater than our hearts." And the church member so full of lament offers the wide-eyed pastor the reference of the verse from 1 John that she memorized in Sunday school some seventy years before.

"God is greater than our hearts." That's a striking promise found in the third chapter of 1 John. Sometimes the richest promises of our resurrection faith can be heard in the readings for the weeks after Easter. The Easter morning proclamation of "He is Risen" fades and the gathering crowds are less. However, amid the tension of the world stage and with hearts full of lament at the state of humankind, the church still gathers on the weeks after the celebration of the Resurrection. At least God is greater than our hearts. It is a promise that affirms the presence of the living God and that ultimate victory over sin and death.

Acts 4:5-12

The text from Acts 4 recounts Peter's address before the council of Jerusalem. Chapters 3 and 4 form something of a unit when read in light of the healing of the lame man at the Beautiful Gate (3:1-10). Last week's assignment includes Peter's sermon offered to the crowds who witnessed the miracle (3:11-26). That healing is still fresh in mind when, at the beginning of chapter 4, Peter and John are arrested and placed in prison. This text for the day represents Peter's defense when he appears before Annas and Caiaphas and the other high priests who made up the council. Peter responds to the reaction caused by the prior healing and the question as posed in 4:7. "By what power or by what name did you do this?"

Remembering that we are reading Pentecost narratives in the book of Acts on these Sundays of Easter, the reader will note Luke's affirmation that Peter was filled with the Holy Spirit (4:8). With the strongest of rhetorical style, Peter's address offers a direct answer. While some may question the good deed done to a sick man, let all now know that the healing occurred in the name of Jesus Christ of Nazareth. With title and place, Peter leaves no doubt that he refers to the one whose resurrection from the dead has given birth to the church. The rhetoric only intensifies as Peter defines the Lord's death and resurrection in terms of agency: this Jesus "whom *you* crucified, whom *God* raised from the dead" (4:10, italics added).

Peter follows up the clear setting of boundaries and responsibility with a quote from the book of Psalms. The quote from Psalm 118, one familiar to the council of Jerusalem, affirms the messianic role of this Jesus and suggests that his rejection at the hands of the rulers and high priests is simply a fulfillment of the sacred text. In rhetoric terms, Peter offers proof from that which is an authority in the world of his accusers.

At verse 12 Peter ends this address with a flourish. No doubt the affirmations related to "salvation in no one else" and no other name "by which we must be saved" become foundational statements in broader theological arguments about the uniqueness of Christ and the complexity of interfaith discussions. In the immediate context of these chapters in Acts that follow the healing of the lame man at the Beautiful Gate, the verse represents the exclamation point to two of Peter's sermons — sermons intended to witness to the power of the resurrection and respond to the accusers who have arrested them.

Peter and John's encounter with council of Jerusalem continues through the end of chapter 4. In addition, Luke's description of the formation of the church in response to the resurrection continues in the chapters that follow. Of course the broader theological questions then continue throughout church history. But for the purpose of one Sunday sermon, these two chapters affirm that this healing of the lame man came in no other way than through the name and in the power of the Risen Christ. Questions about the validity of the resurrection provide the subtext of this encounter with the rulers and high priests. Peter's rhetoric attempts to frame that healing as an Easter/Resurrection event.

1 John 3:16-24

This reading's opening verse, 1 John 3:16, is a fitting memory verse to accompany John 3:16, for it defines the God who so loved the world in terms of the love of the only Son. "We know love by this, that he laid down his life for us — and we ought to lay down our lives for one another." With such an ethic at its core, this scripture lesson from 1 John places our affirmations about the Resurrection within the framework of a commitment to and an understanding of community. According to 1 John, the message that has been entrusted to the church is not simply that of the resurrection of Jesus. It is a message of the Risen Christ that then results in a call to love one another.

The lectionary break here at the beginning of the pericope avoids the reference to Cain and Abel (3:11-15). It may be true that the church's celebration of the Great Fifty Days of Easter is dampened a bit by hearing of that piece of our sordid past. So the assigned text begins not with murder and sibling relationship but with reference to the atoning love of Christ. It is in that self-emptying love of Christ that we most clearly see the love of God. Thus, the author of 1 John calls for a faith that is lived out in deed and in action.

Even with the salutation, the author's plea is set within the context of the nurturing, loving relationship of community; "Little children, let us love, not in word or speech, but in truth and action" (3:18). It is in our love for one another that we find assurance even when the failure of our hearts reveals our own condemnation. God's love is greater than ours. God's love is stronger than our failures. God's omnipotence and perfect love creates community despite humanity's best efforts to tear it apart. A casual reading might see something of works righteousness here in 1 John. That as we love and obey, we shall receive anything we ask. However, even here within the frail nature of community, God's promise is first. The existence of a community where love thrives is indeed pleasing to God. That community, in turn, provides a witness to the love of God that is greater than the hearts of the faithful.

The author affirms this promise in the language of commandment. "We should believe in the name of the Son Jesus Christ and love one another" (v. 23). The promise is that the living Christ abides in us. We know that abiding presence, not because we obey his commandments but because God has given us the

Spirit (v. 24). Our life together in love is a response of joyful obedience to the promised presence of Christ made known to us in the power of the Holy Spirit.

John 10:11-18

The gospel lection for the day is the first Sunday reading in this Eastertide when the assigned text does not portray an appearance of the risen Christ. We have traveled from Easter morning to an encounter with Doubting Thomas to that Emmaus Road appearance. Now on this fourth Sunday of Easter, the lectionary takes us back to John's gospel and the image of Jesus as the Good Shepherd. This development of one of the "I am" statements of Jesus presents a challenge when pondering any direct connection to Easter.

The teaching of Jesus related to the metaphor of the shepherd comes throughout all of chapter 10. The teaching comes amid a larger section of John's gospel that is framed by the woman caught in adultery and the raising of Lazarus. An allegorical approach to the metaphor would want to notice the various themes Jesus develops: the voice of the shepherd, Jesus as the gate, the presence of a thief, and the comparison of the shepherd to a hired hand. At verse 11, Jesus begins that comparison by affirming that the shepherd is willing to lay down his life for the sheep.

In describing himself as the Good Shepherd, Jesus affirms both his love for and knowledge of the sheep. The love Christ has for those entrusted to him by God is analogous to the love and knowledge shared between God the Father and God the Son. Such intimate knowledge shared between Jesus and the sheep is balanced by the more inclusive theme of those other sheep that do not yet belong, those who do not yet know his voice (v. 16). Within the context of John's gospel, the other sheep are Gentiles. The work of Christ widens the understanding of those known to be the children of God still within the framework of one flock and one shepherd. Broadening the scope of those who receive the promise contributes to the heightening tension between Jesus and the Jewish leadership so aptly described in the second half of chapter 10.

In verse 17, Jesus again returns to the theme of laying down his life. The shepherd lays down his life "in order to take it up again." The work of Christ, understood here as death and resurrection, is a command of God. In the steadfast obedience rooted in that love and knowledge of God the Father, the command comes with the divine power to bring life out of death. We should not read the references to love, command and power in verses 17 and 18 as saying that God loves Jesus because of that willingness to lay down his life. Works righteousness — even assigned to Christ himself — rests at the top of a slippery slope. True, the language of verse 17 is challenging "for this reason" and "because." However, it would seem that the reason for the great love of God bestowed upon the Son is that the love stretches from the depth of suffering and death all the way to that promised resurrection. Rather than a simple equation of cause and effect, divine love rests at the foundation of the relationship of Father and Son and the promise of salvation.

Application

As the church gathers on the Fourth Sunday of Easter, these lectionary texts challenge the preacher to proclaim the presence of the risen Christ. Not surprisingly, the further we move away from Easter morning, the texts themselves point beyond those miraculous resurrection appearances. The texts from John's gospel and his first epistle share the theme of Christ's self-sacrificing love and the relationships within the community bound by that love. For the people of God, any proclamation of the message of the resurrection quickly turns to a proclamation of justice, righteousness and compassion.

The church that continues to celebrate the Great Fifty Days of Easter must affirm the miraculous presence of Christ there within the community. Beyond scarred hands and feet, the promised presence of Christ is revealed in acts of love and selfless compassion. The community itself, however, cannot sustain such a witness based on the quality of its life. As the church is moved to lament the state of the world, the church's life itself will inevitably cause heartache and hurt. History affirms the frailty of the church and the sinfulness of humanity's attempt at life together. The grace of resurrection hope and promise, however, is that God is greater than our hearts.

Within the sacramental life of the church, theology and tradition assert the presence of the Risen Christ in the Lord's Supper and in baptism. Of course, differences abound in how we understand that presence. The preacher's challenge in the weeks after Easter is to look into the community's life and name that promised presence of Christ. As young pastors learn from wise saints in the congregation, God is greater than the frailty of our hearts. In the brokenness of our life together, and despite the challenges facing the church and world, the darkness of evil and death shall not win. For the victory of abundant and eternal life belongs to God.

As we taste of the love of God and the love of another within the community of faith, we experience the risen Lord in our midst. It is the same divine power and presence that made that lame man rise and walk at the Beautiful Gate in the Acts of the Apostles. The exclamation point in our life together may match that of Peter in his own preaching. "There is salvation in no one else, for there is no other name under heaven given among mortals by which we must be saved."

An Alternative Applications

John 10:11-18. The context of John's gospel establishes the boundaries of Jew and Gentile in terms of the other sheep that do not currently belong to the fold. Jesus affirms that such sheep (the Gentiles) indeed belong to him and that he must bring them and they will listen to his voice. With the image of the Good Shepherd, John expands that notion of the gospel and its intended audience. In a post-Easter context, the preacher may affirm that widening gospel and the inclusive love of Christ. In this pluralistic, tense world, a reading of John 10 might reframe interfaith discussions. Rather than approaching the world with a conquering evangelism, the ethic here may just be a steadfast love and compassion, like that of a shepherd tending to sheep not yet belonging to this fold. All answers to the vast theological questions of the uniqueness of salvation in Christ may not be answered here in John 10, but as we continue to celebrate Christ's ultimate victory over sin and death, we may seek to cultivate that selfless compassion and shepherd's love in Christianity's ongoing encounter with the world.

1 John 3:16-24. The text from 1 John provides a clear vision statement for mission for the post-Easter church. The question about God's love abiding in anyone who refuses to help a brother or sister in need (3:17) ought to hang in the air. Similarly, the commandment from verse 23 that "we should believe in the name of God's Son Jesus Christ and love one another" may just be one of those sermonless texts. Years ago I observed a preacher walk into the pulpit, say this verse, and then turn and sit down. He did it a second time and then a third time. It may not be the best advice as a homiletical technique, but some commands of God are just that clear. By God's grace, may the church have ears to hear.

Acts 4:5-12. The two sermons offered by Peter in chapters 3 and 4 are ripe for analysis. The sermons have such different audiences. Right after the healing of the lame man in chapter 3, Peter preaches to the gathered crowds who are astonished at the miracle. The second sermon is intended specifically for the accusers and those who demand to know by what power and in what name this healing occurred. A preacher today may thus compare the content of the two sermons and then reflect upon how the Sunday morning audience influences our proclamation of the gospel message of the resurrected Christ.

Leveraging the family genome

Roman historian, Herodotus, told of the pride the Egyptians had in being the oldest civilization on earth. When Psammetichus became their ruler around 660 BC he decided to prove the antiquity of the Egyptian civilization through a scientific experiment.

Psammetichus ordered that two newborn children of ordinary parentage be taken from their mothers and placed under the care of a childless couple who lived in a very remote area. The shepherd and his wife were commanded to care for the children, but at no time were they to utter even a single word of speech within hearing of these babies. The children were to be raised in total linguistic silence. When, and if, they finally spoke, the language they used would obviously be the original human tongue.

One morning, when the youngsters were in their second year, they stretched out their arms in delight and cried out the word *bekos*. Knowing the gravity of the situation, the shepherd neither responded orally nor reported this incident until it had occurred several times. But then the news was conveyed to Psammetichus, and linguists were called in. After some deliberation, these scholars concluded that *bekos* was very similar to a term used by Phrygian peoples in referring to bread. Psammetichus was heart-broken.

The premise for Psammetichus' experiment is fascinating. What is our original language? What is the true speech of the human soul? Are we merely bits of biotic matter tossed against the cosmic winds or do we have internal wiring which reflects purpose for our existence that calls out a spiritual mother tongue no matter where we were born on earth?

The passages for today echo this quest. The Ethiopian eunuch travels thousands of miles in search of true religion, only to find himself already a child of God. John reminds his children that they are family of the one who made all things and infused them with divine character. Jesus teaches his disciples that in the loneliness of existence, home is found in spiritual reconnection with the family genome that is traced through Jesus' bloodline.

Acts 8:26-40

There are several helpful things to remember when preaching from the book of Acts. First, it is a two-part work that begins with the third gospel. Luke tells his readers at the beginning of each volume what his intent is — that "Theophilus" will understand more clearly the things he has been taught about Jesus and the spread of the Christian faith. But more than that, Luke develops the narrative of both books in a similar fashion: the power of God enters the human arena miraculously in each, lives are changed and the old guard is disrupted by this new revelation, and a great teacher is raised up with travel goals that lead in the direction of Jerusalem. After a farcical trial there, each is dispatched to other places — Jesus to heaven and Paul to Rome. There is a fascinating parallelism between these two volumes of Luke's documentation.

Second, the book of Acts has a rather well-defined internal structure of its own. Five times over (in 6:7; 9:31; 12:24; 16:5; 19:20) Luke gives us what might be termed "progress reports" that show how the gospel of Jesus has penetrated another broader circle of life in the first-century Mediterranean world. These phases of evangelistic engagement mirror Jesus' statement in 1:8 that power would come on his disciples when the Holy Spirit arrived, and they would be witnesses in Jerusalem, all Judea and Samaria, and to the ends of the earth. The first section after the introductory prologue (Acts 1) shows how the gospel came alive in Jerusalem (2:1—6:7). Then comes the section in which the message of Jesus broadens into regional impact (6:8—9:31). The reading for today comes from this section.

Reviewing that structure helps us understand the meaning of this story. When Luke explored the initial phase of gospel preaching in the first section of the book, the hearers and respondents were virtually all ethnic Jews. They may have emerged from various countries around the Hellenic Roman world, but they came to Jerusalem for the Jewish feast of Pentecost. In this next section, however, Luke is forcefully telling us that the time has come for the gospel to leap beyond the Jewish environment. Nowhere is that more clearly seen than in the story of the Ethiopian eunuch.

Think of these things: First, Philip is one of the newly appointed deacons of the Jerusalem congregation (see 6:5). Thus he was an early convert and a recognized leader within the Jerusalem church.

Second, the empowering of the Spirit, which was so noticeable among the disciples in that first Pentecost gospel presentation, is now similarly working powerfully in the life of this next-generation leader. Philip is visibly directed by an angel of God to make this journey (8:26), and along the way he is again instructed clearly by the Spirit of God (8:29).

Third, the gospel comes to this foreign diplomat through what we now call the Old Testament. There are at least five different ways in which Christians have used or relegated the Old Testament in their theological and missiological dealings: 1) treat it as outdated and inappropriate for this new age (cf. Marcion); 2) consider it the explanatory prologue to the real Bible, the New Testament; 3) think of it as the old version in a two-stage divine covenant development and thus largely anticipatory or typological; 4) understand it as the earlier pieces of one long salvation history story that is seamlessly continued in the New Testament; or 5) view it as the true scriptures of the church, with the New Testament added on as a footnote or appendix. While few of us opt for either the first or the last of these five interpretive options, the story of the Ethiopian eunuch must impress us as a realistic version of the last. Based solely upon the poetry of Isaiah 53, Philip is able to bring the eunuch to a profound conversion to Jesus.

Fourth, baptism happens quickly. There is no lengthy period of discipling or catechizing. While these are usually necessary in order to bring the mind and the will along with the heart into conformity with and love for Jesus, it is also true that God can work amazing wonders, and when the line is crossed, it is a done deal. The eunuch, though from a different culture and socio-political world than most of the Jerusalem Christians, is a member of the family and has found the missing link in his spiritual DNA. He has learned again for the first time the true language of his soul.

1 John 4:7-21

During the nineteenth century, Welsh manufacturer Robert Owen became increasingly discouraged with conditions in England's coal mines. He personally toured the collier districts and was appalled at the degradation of human life there. One evening, he stopped a twelve-year-old boy, coal-black, trudging off to a squalid rooming house after another day in the night below.

"Do you know God?" Owen asked him, concerned for his spiritual development.

"No," replied the boy pensively. "He must work in some other mine."

How unfortunate it is when God's own children (see 1 John 3:1-2) do not know God, and think that if God exists at all, he must be working in some other mine — ours is too dull and dirty and dreary and discouraging. John acknowledges that none of us can actually see God in the way that we are able to view one another (4:12), but he will not allow us quickly to set aside the reality that God exists within our sphere of reference.

John, of course, was responding to the specific heresy of early Gnosticism. According to that spreading secret society, deity is pure spirit and cannot meddle in physical reality. Furthermore, humans are the creative mistake of a lesser god, or even perhaps the cruel torture of a mad god who traps sparks of divinity in these wretched earthly bodies. Because we are sullied creatures, we do not have the capacity to love. Love is only available to those whose true selves, the spirits within, have been freed from material clutches. So imagined love directed toward other earthly beings is mistaken at best and false at worst.

In this way of thinking, Jesus could not be human, for that would mean that he was imprisoned in flesh like the rest of us. Therefore, according to those who were infiltrating the ranks of early Christianity with their Gnostic views, Jesus only *appeared* among us as the great teacher who had the right wisdom (Greek *gnosis*) that would allow us to learn the method of escape from the physical into the spiritual. Any visibility he might have had was a divine apparition wafted in our presence in order that we could catch some of his teachings. These, if rightly understood and properly chanted, gave some people the ability to transcend the flesh and escape from this existence to a higher expression of our divine core of being.

John writes with boldness to counter these false teachings. First, he declares that Jesus was and remains a real human flesh-and-blood person (4:14-15). Furthermore, this real flesh-and-blood person is also the revelation of God to us within this context. While Gnostics were trying to get their followers to escape the physical through chants and secret knowledge, John shows God inserting himself into our world. God cares for this world as it is, not in spite of what it is, and God shares our humanity in the person of Jesus.

Second, the testimony of faith is that we love others. Rather than being concerned about how we might escape the material existence that has us trapped, we can join God in spreading the love.

Frank Luther Mott, Pulitzer Prize-winning journalist, once published a short story called "The Man with the Good Face." It was about James Neal, a New York law clerk, who became discouraged by the sordid faces that peered at him day-by-day on his subway commute. Neal found himself becoming an expert in the state of the human heart by observing the descriptive lines that etched his fellow travelers' faces. So many showed sadness and suffering, emptiness and evil, lust and lechery, woe and weakness. Neal began to long for a face that shone with simplicity, transparent truth, and some kind of spiritual strength, which coupled meekness with gentle power. In fact, he became obsessed. He had to find such a face. He called it "the good face."

One day, as Neal sat in the 14th Street Station, he glanced at an express train across the open tracks. There, framed by a window, was the face of a man shining with all Neal had ever hoped faith and love to be. Jumping from his bench, Neal raced toward the man's rail coach, but the doors closed and the train fled without him.

Still, Neal thought he might be a better person for having seen that face. Indeed, it gave him hope that he would likely see it again sometime soon. More fascinating, though, was the strange thing that began to happen to Neal himself. Those who knew him best, saw him change. Once a loner, hovering at the fringes of society, he slowly began to reach out to others in friendliness and grace. Not only that, but his heart warmed to the suffering needs of his fellow travelers who had so long been the object of his study. James Neal was becoming a new man, all because he had seen "the good face."

So, Mr. Neal's death came as quite a shock. He was crossing the street at lunch hour when a car roared out of nowhere and struck him. An ambulance rushed him to a hospital and doctors performed emergency surgery, but to no avail. Mr. Neal died in post-op.

A doctor who was coming to check his vital signs, just as Neal died, asked the nurse on duty a strange question: "Who was that man standing over Mr. Neal?"

The nurse knew that no one had come to see her patient, so she was confused by the question. "That tall man," the doctor repeated, "the one with the good face; who was he and where did he go?"

Again the nurse assured the doctor that no one had been with Mr. Neal. "Oh yes," responded the doctor. "I saw a man bending over the bed — a very tall man with a remarkable face." Observing the peaceful smile that lingered on James Neal's face, the doctor continued, "He was very fortunate to have died with a face like that looking into his."

Mott's story is a wonderful allegory to John's teaching. Once we look into "the good face" of Jesus, our characters are changed and we become more good and loving. And when we finally pass out of this existence it will not be with a bang or a whimper; it will be with a smile in the face of God. For we are, in fact, truly the children of eternity, loved in this life and the next by the one who crafted the best lines on our faces.

John 15:1-8

These verses are at the heart of what we call Jesus' "Farewell Discourse" (John 13-17). One engaging study (see *The Literary Development of John 13-17: A Chiastic Reading* [SBLDS, 2000]), has shown how the discourse as a whole is wrapped around this passage in chiastic literary development. In outline the discourse is shaped as follows:

A Gathering Scene — Focus on unity with Jesus expressed in mutual love (13:1-35)
  B Prediction of the disciple's denial (13:36-38)
    C Jesus' departure tempered by assurance of the Father's power (14:1-14)
      D The promise of the Paraclete as a continuing link to Jesus (14:15-26)
        E Troubling encounter with the world (14:27-31)
          F The vine and branches teaching — "Abide in me!" (15:1-17)
        E' Troubling encounter with the world (15:18—16:4a)
      D' The promise of the Paraclete as a continuing link to Jesus (16:4b-15)
    C' Jesus' departure tempered by assurance of the Father's power (16:16-28)
  B' Prediction of the disciples' denial (16:29-33)
A' Gathering scene — Focus on unity with Jesus expressed in mutual love (17:1-26)

While this is not the only possible way to understand the literary structure of the "Farewell Discourse," it certainly makes plausible both the reason for the repetitions in the passage as a whole as well as the manner in which the themes resonate and circle around the idea of remaining in Jesus for light and life.

Indeed, there is a truly remarkable way in which the actions of Judas in chapter 13, coupled with Jesus' encounter with Nicodemus in chapter 3, help illustrate what Jesus is trying to say in these eight verses. Nicodemus came secretly ("by night") to Jesus to find out more about the teachings, which were troubling society in his day. Jesus talked with him about being born a second time (spiritually), but there is no indication in chapter 3 whether Nicodemus actually steps across the line and becomes a believer. We are led to assume it, however, because Jesus continues to talk in that passage about being in the light and walking in the light and living in the light. Furthermore, according to John's gospel, Nicodemus emerges from the shadows at Jesus' death in order to care for Jesus' body and provide it with an appropriate burial (19:39). One might say, from the witness of John 3, that Nicodemus comes to Jesus by night, and leaves in the light.

Keeping that in mind, it is striking to see the reverse movement taking place in Judas' life in chapter 13. Jesus announces that his hour has come, the hour in which the glory of God will be revealed. We know, from John 1, that this glory of God is the light of the world. So Jesus enters the room for the final meal, bringing his disciples with him surrounded by the glory (light) that is emerging through Jesus in this final revelatory event. Yet as they sit at table together, Jesus identifies the devious manipulations prancing about in Judas' heart and the disciple is caught cold. He leaves the table and the room, we are told, "and it was night" (13:30). In other words, Judas comes in the light, and leaves into night. Exactly the opposite of Nicodemus.

The interwrappings of the monologues and dialogues of the "Farewell Discourse" expound upon these themes: stay close to Jesus and you have life and light; leave Jesus and it is death and night. That's why Peter, along with the other disciples, needs to undergo the washing in chapter 13. Without this sacramental sign, he would be an outsider, and would be considered part of the night. Similarly, it is Jesus' departure, elaborated upon in chapters 14 and 16, that becomes the cause of concern for the disciples, for then they will feel the troubling of the world. Yet, Jesus will not leave them disconnected, for he will send the Paraclete, the Spirit, to reconnect them to him, and when the Paraclete comes, they will be reminded of all that Jesus taught.

With these things in mind, the vine and branches teaching seems like a summary exhortation. Our very spiritual genes are spliced into God through Jesus. We cannot be part of the family if we give up our birthright. But when we remain connected to the source of our existence, the RNA of his Spirit ensures that life flows through out mortal veins. And when it does, whatever our lives are about will bear the fruit of his grace.

Application

It may seem silly and trite to the sophisticated among us, but Myra Brooks Welch got it right in her poem "The Touch of the Master's Hand" (http://www.cs.rice.edu/~ssiyer/minstrels/poems/1199.html).

An Alternative Application

Acts 8:26-40. The story of Philip and the Ethiopian eunuch would make a fine message for bringing new believers into the fellowship, especially if your church had a massive evangelistic campaign for Easter.

Prisoners for love

In a scene from the hit Broadway show, *The Producers*, a chorus of convicts sings about being prisoners of love and how even when locked up that their hearts are always free when they are in love. The refrain expressing this is sung by the jailhouse chorus in hopes that it will catapult the lead characters, Leo Bloom and Max Bialystock, back to the legitimate theater. This speaks of Christian experience. It seems that Christianity is all about love, love, love, but it seems that the love that Christians practice has a way of getting folks into inescapable tangles.

The three texts for this Sunday show how complicated love can be. The passage from Acts is the crowning conclusion of the entire tenth chapter. While Leo and Max sing about blue skies above that comes with being a prisoner for love, in this chapter from Acts, the sheet that falls from the sky in Peter's dream contains a variety of creatures that we will inescapably meet up with in life and that we are obliged to call clean; though many of our friends, family, and neighbors have their doubts. What is worse, not only are we to treat them as a part of us but it seems that God wants these creatures to be a part of the church on an equal par with us. "Can anyone withhold the water for baptizing these people who have received the Holy Spirit just as we have?" (Acts 10:47). It is one thing to accept "them" whoever they might be and quite another to see God legitimately at work in the lives of others who are quite different from us. The circumcised believers, astounded at this turn of events, must have wondered just what kind of situation they had cast themselves into. Is the Holy Spirit really leading us to loving people that eat like that, raise their children like that, and bring so little respect for the niceties? If the Holy Spirit, to top the whole thing off, then expects folks to sit down to common meals with that lot then we have some issues. "Hearts in love are always free!" according to Leo and Max. Perhaps this is why Christians found that prison cells have never been a complete hindrance to the spread of the gospel. As Thoreau's and Martin Luther King's lives witness to, some of God's best work is done in a prison cell. Christians early on found themselves freed when they were engaged by the inescapable clear direction in which the Holy Spirit was going. Christians have found true freedom when they have found themselves bedding down with bunkmates not of their own choosing: prisoners for love.

The gospel lesson for this day also suggests how people might feel more incarcerated than liberated by love. Perhaps it is not without significance here that a common derogative term for a spouse is "the ball and chain." "If you keep my commandments, you will abide in my love, just as I have kept my Father's commandments and abide in his love" (John 15:10). Here Jesus says that as a result of obeying his commandments you will abide or dwell in a place of his love. It is ironic that the people of John's church were finding it increasingly difficult to dwell in a house of love. John's people are living out the separation of Christianity from Judaism that was dividing families, friends, coworkers, and, if they had them, chess clubs, soccer teams, and the gardening club. Folks must have found their dinners imprisoned in stony silence, their emotions caged, and their conversations confined to the safe and familiar: prisoners for love.

Now you would think that John's people would, after an experience like that, create a veritable love feast of a church once they had gone through the difficult work of accepting the distance that would now be between them and many of the people with whom they had shared their lives — a distance they would have to live with for the rest of their lives. That is not exactly what happened. The letter of John addresses yet another split that John's community is facing in its own ranks. We seem to have here a church community that, like many families, is imprisoned in a dysfunctional pattern that it cannot help but repeat. "We know that we have passed from death to life because we love one another. Whoever does not love abides in death" (1 John 3:14). When you read a thing like that you expect that some of your folks are not on board with the program and that there has been a very big elephant in the room.

Love, love, love — it is never as easy or as smooth as you expect or hope for. Where the Holy Spirit takes folks seems to be the very places where people commonly say, "Don't go there." Unlike the board game, we do not receive a "get-out-of-jail-free card." If anything we seem headed toward a place where we will be bunking down with some interesting mates who are not of our own choosing, dwelling in places where you might find yourself with a case of lockjaw if you do not know how to speak the truth in love. I like to think of myself as a free spirit. A good way to get me to do what is not good for me is to command me to do what is good for me. I find it too confining, too suffocating, and too imprisoning: none of this prisoner-for-love business for me. Yet, like Leo and Max, the producers are on to more than they realize: locked up, keys lost, but knowing freedom lies in a heart full of love.

Perhaps the prison metaphor seems a bit over the top, yet on the street it seems that there are a lot of serious parallels. In prison you do not get to choose your roommate, most prisoners deny they are guilty, and why they are in is usually not a topic of dinner conversation. Sounds like church to me. In their own way, each of these texts deals with these dynamics. All of them hold out that these prisoners of love will, as the first letter of John has it, conquer the world through the faith that believes that such prisoners are truly free.

Acts 10:44-48

You don't get to choose whom your roomies are in prison and neither do church folks get to choose who it is that will be a part of the faith community. Often we like to think that we choose. We often believe that the creeds, dogmas, social stance, political activity, and neighborhood will do a sufficient job of doing the sorting and sifting needed to establish a comfort zone of uniformity. However, in my ministry, I am continually, hugely, impressed by the level of diversity I find in my congregation. Perhaps it is attributable to being a lifelong member of a mainline church, but on a Sunday morning the sheet that falls from heaven is stretched by the push and pull of card-carrying Unitarians rubbing shoulders with former High Church Episcopalians who, in turn, often outdo their Roman Catholic brothers and sisters in seeking to have their liturgical needs met.

On any given Sunday, congregational shoulders that believe in the high biblical notion of once-a-quarter communion bump up against folks who, though they have made the move into a new tradition, still feel that they have not had church if they have not partaken in the heavenly banquet. On most Sundays, we are a combination of people who swoon to white, northern European, dead composers and those who find praise music the only musical expression worthy of their deepest feelings. Now I know that in such moments, the author of Acts reports "for they heard them speaking in tongues and extolling God." Well, that is not exactly how these diverse communities characterize each other's liturgical and musical approaches. While they do not always hear fighting words in each other's prayers and music, they still don't understand each other as extolling God in their approaches to worship. As the gospel of John has it, "You did not choose me but I chose you" (John 15:16). Such choices might not amount to the ones that we would make to "conquer the world." Most who have taken a shot at conquering the world have done so through a disciplined, uniform army that marches in lock step. I suspect that your congregation does not look that way.

Indeed, as I look out on my congregation I see a community of people that is composed of those who have issues, those who have children and raising them is priority one, those have grandchildren and are facing mid-life issues, and those who have great-grandchildren and are dealing with end-of-life concerns. This continuum of folks often finds its members speaking in strange tongues to one another.

Any preacher to this congregation runs the danger of finding themselves tongue-tied as they try to speak to this broad spectrum. As a matter of fact, there are days that we would not choose this assembly and in which we might find ourselves fighting the notion that we are chosen for this ministry of potential mayhem. From the very earliest, the church has struggled with how this will all hold together. Though this might not be our choice, Peter and the rest of the church must face the hands-on physical evidence that a choice has been made by the Holy Spirit in bestowing its gifts upon the Gentiles. I suspect that what was now obvious is something that had not been entirely obvious before. I do not believe that Peter is saying the Gentiles are talented, competent professionals that will make great committee members because they really know how to run a business. Who could deny that? Remember these events take place in Caesarea. This was Caesar's town and who could disallow that you were in the fast lane of talented, gifted people in such a place? Yet, precisely in the midst of such a town and after Peter had preached, the Spirit comes and people are touched. At one of the centers of the empire, people were reachable.

Perhaps the ties that bind are woven around the notion that we are all reachable. This changes how I look at myself and at others. In what regard we hold others goes a long way toward determining how things will hold together in the church. That we are all reachable by the same Lord ought to cause us to reach out to each other in ways that might give new meaning to conquering the world.

1 John 5:1-6

Often the church, as it has faced its diversity, has chosen the easier path of sectarian splits. Frequently in our struggles, we seem to find ourselves dominated by the secular model of how we can keep it all together. Some suggest a sort of commercial, entrepreneurial model in which we provide different services for various constituencies. Others rely on a political model of vote taking and *Robert's Rules of Order*. Paul in his New Testament letters chooses an organic model where the parts are named as part of the body of Christ.

I have watched enough prison movies and viewed enough episodes of television's *Law and Order* to know that the conventional take on prison life is that almost all prisoners deny they have committed their crimes. Perhaps more than denial is at work here. If they have any chance at cutting their sentence or beating the rap it will come through dogged determination in maintaining innocence and finding a loophole somewhere in the system through which they can escape.

The letter of John takes a pretty dim view of this approach for the prisoners of love that we call the church. "If we say that we have no sin, we deceive ourselves, and the truth is not in us. If we confess our sins, he who is faithful and just will forgive us our sins and cleanse us from all unrighteousness. If we say that we have not sinned, we make him a liar, and his word is not in us" (1 John 1:8). Busted: There is no jailhouse, "Philadelphia" lawyer that is going to get us out of this one.

So what is the sin of your church? This can invite more venting on the part of the preacher than is desirable. Yet, if our starting point is wrong, we are going to miss the opportunity to clean up our act. All churches have their sins. I am persuaded that our sins as churches are most often centered on our models of what holds things together. We often hold too tightly to the past, hold out too much for the latest programming fad, hold out for the idealized candidate for pastor, and hold up the preacher to the standards that we have seen in the latest mega-church we have heard about.

I think that most churches would recognize the sin of John's church. "Those who say, 'I love God,' and hate their brothers or sisters, are liars; for those who do not love a brother or sister whom they have seen, cannot love God whom they have not seen" (John 4:20). This sin was expressed in the theological understanding that misread the meaning of the incarnation. "By this you know the Spirit of God: every spirit that confesses that Jesus Christ has come in the flesh is from God, and every spirit that does not confess Jesus is not from God. And this is the spirit of the antichrist, of which you have heard that it is coming; and now it is already in the world" (John 4:2-3). John's people seem to have failed in loving folks in their fleshiness. Often our flesh crawls at differences rather than loving those who in the flesh have issues, are shaped by generational differences, or who are living out in the flesh a different stage in life. The text from this letter for the sixth Sunday of Easter reminds us that Jesus "came by the water and the blood." In other words, he came in the flesh. When we rub shoulders we may generate more heat than light if we do not love people in the context of their flesh: flesh that jumps with the enthusiasm of youth, flesh that sees the world through the lens of certain issues, flesh that crawls at all the changes it has had to endure, flesh that needs to be soothed from the ravages of age. Love seeks to know the other, risks being known by the other. Love appreciates the gifts that folk bring with them in the flesh and sympathizes with the weaknesses of the flesh. This conquers the world. It conquers distance, despair, and resistance. "For whatever is born of God conquers the world. And this is the victory that conquers the world, our faith. Who is it that conquers the world but the one who believes that Jesus is the Son of God?" (1 John 5:4).

John 15:9-17

Time and time again in the movies and on television, I have seen one prisoner ask another, "What are you in for?" only to be greeted by an icy stare. I don't know to what extent this conforms to actual prison practice. I do know that a counter theme of the prison saga is that no one's personal history remains a mystery for long. How else could they beat to death the child molesters? I do know that where the "prisoners for love" gather, that when asking what you are in for is also greeted with an icy stare. It is a look that conveys and asks right back, "Who wants to know?" or "What is it to you?" Given that American religion tends to be such a private matter, talking about "what you are in for" does not come easily in all the dwelling places where we can abide in his love.

The gospel lesson comes clean as to what Jesus is in for. "I have said these things to you so that my joy may be in you, and that your joy may be complete." In the fourteenth chapter of John, Jesus says, "Do not let your hearts be troubled. Believe in God, believe also in me. In my Father's house there are many dwelling places. If it were not so, would I have told you that I go to prepare a place for you? And if I go and prepare a place for you, I will come again and will take you to myself, so that where I am, there you may be also" (v. 2). We don't like being in a place where what counts is less our choice than the one who has chosen us to dwell with roomies not of our own choosing. We are put off by being in a place where everyone is guilty, us included, and where we might find our place on the continuum of human imperfections and limitations. For the most part our culture does not relish being caught dead or alive in such places. We think we can find our freedom by being in other places. However, Jesus is saying that if we are in it for the joy, then it will be found in the place of limited choice and recognition of our limits. We can be locked up, we can lose the key, but our hearts, in love, stay always free. In the place prepared for us where we abide in his love we know the joy of being truly free.

Application

I suspect that many will resist the prison imagery as, shall we say, too confining. By and large, our society is driven to define joy in terms of unlimited choice. The gospel bumps up against the cultural norm when it claims that true freedom comes not in making choices but in being chosen. Others may object that most of the folks who read these words have no more than a passing acquaintance with prison. Yet the Christian testament makes clear that the end result of Christians being labeled "disturbers of the peace" would be that much Christian ministry would be prison ministry from the inside out. The place prepared for us has been a Birmingham Jail; a Concord, Massachusetts, prison cell; and an offshore island prison in South Africa among others. From such places have come love, joy, hope, and the kind of presence that makes us truly free: prisoners for love that make us truly free. Can we in good conscience avoid the places that Jesus has prepared for us where we might abide in his love?

Some will find it difficult to admit to the fleshiness of the church in all its diversity. Yet seeing such diversity does not lead to division. Rather, masking the diversity behind pleasantries and denial lead to miscommunication and a failure to fully love one another. Such a failure means that we have not responded with faith in Jesus when he says, "This is my commandment, that you love one another as I have loved you" (John 13:34).

An Alternative Application

Acts 10:44-48. I often begin the work of preaching by asking myself what words in the text set me off. Like Mark Twain, it is often the parts of the Bible I do understand that bother me more than the parts I do not understand. Often it is the clearest words or phrases that set me off, not because I do not understand them but because I cannot stomach them. In the Acts passage, it says that Peter ordered the Gentiles to be baptized in the name of Jesus Christ. I do not feel comfortable with military images and chain-of-command thinking. Yet can I completely throw overboard the warrior archetype? I must ask of myself if my ministry is impoverished because I have not been fully honest about those places, some good and some not so good, where I do expect alignment and people to get in line. If I am going to abide in God's love and dwell in the place prepared for me I need to consider what orders I have given, what orders need to be rescinded, what sense of orderliness I have counted on in my life.

Ascension of Our Lord
Acts 1:1-11
Ephesians 1:15-23
Luke 24:44-53
David Kalas

What goes up

"What goes up must come down." So goes the old saying, in an axiomatic testament to the gravitational reality in which we human beings live. But what of something — or someone — not bound by gravity?

This Sunday is Ascension Sunday, and all three of our texts this week invite consideration of that event. Both the Luke and Acts selections tell the actual story of Jesus' ascension, and the passage from Paul alludes to it (God "seated him at his right hand in the heavenly places").

In many churches, Ascension Sunday would pass unnoticed if the preacher did not make a point of it. A few Christian holy days have risen to the surface of our cultural consciousness, but this Sunday's commemoration does not rate much attention.

It's not surprising that the world around us pays little attention to Jesus' ascension since the church itself doesn't seem to make much of it. We faithfully echo the good tidings first told to the shepherds at Jesus' birth each Advent and Christmas season. All through the year, the life, ministry, example, and teachings of Jesus inform our preaching and our living. And, even beyond his birth and his life, we find that the real good news is found in Jesus' death and resurrection.

But what do we make of his ascension?

In the churches I've served through the years, folks have had a sense of the importance of Christ's coming. They have cherished the stories of his life. They have embraced his cross and celebrated his empty tomb. However, most church folks do not have a sense of the importance of Christ's ascension.

That, then, becomes our task this Sunday. To a people who likely know the good news of his coming, living, dying, and rising, we now preach the good news of his leaving.

Acts 1:1-11

Carpenters know that the poorest way to join two pieces of wood is simply to butt one up against the other. The connection is much stronger when the two pieces of wood overlap or intersect one another. Luke, as a storyteller, shows his craftsmanship by the way he joins the end and the beginning of his two pieces.

The book of Acts follows and continues the story that he had begun to tell in his gospel. But the two books do not merely abut end-to-end. Rather, Luke has crafted the beginning of Acts to overlap and intersect with the end of Luke.

Both our gospel lesson and this passage tell the same story (the ascension), and by the same author (Luke). The accounts are not identical, though their differences may be owed only to the fact that Luke is a good writer. They are naturally similar, and together they form the miter joint that joins Luke's two works.

This first passage from Acts presages several themes that are recurring and significant throughout the rest of the book: the Holy Spirit, "convincing proofs," and the spread of the gospel.

Three different times in just eleven verses, Luke makes explicit reference to the Holy Spirit. The prominence of the Spirit in just this introductory section reflects Luke's view and understanding of the events he is recording. The Holy Spirit is more expressly prominent in Luke's gospel than any of the other three, and the Spirit is arguably the central character in the book of Acts. Some have rightly observed that, while we call the book "the Acts of the Apostles," the real title ought to be, "The Acts of the Holy Spirit."

Closely related to that theme of the Holy Spirit is the importance to Luke of "convincing proofs." The word Luke uses (*tekmerion*) suggests evidence that is irrefutable, indubitable. Indeed, the King James and New King James Versions translate the word "infallible proofs." And while the word itself appears nowhere else in Acts — or in the entire New Testament, for that matter — Luke has given an early indication of an issue that is important to him.

A concern for convincing proofs surely lies behind Luke's interest in signs and wonders. Eight different times in the book of Acts (2:22; 4:23; 4:30; 5:12; 6:8; 7:36; 14:3; and 15:12), Luke makes pointed reference to signs and wonders. He understands these as evidence of God's work and, by extension, of God's authentic and empowered workers.

Luke also demonstrates his interest in convincing proofs by his portrayals of Stephen, Apollos, and Paul. Not only does Luke point to flashy miracles as the proof of God's work, he also embraces the less-spectacular proof of wisdom and irrefutable logic. We read that Stephen was opposed by men "who stood up and argued with (him). But they could not withstand the wisdom and the Spirit with which he spoke" (6:9-10). Similarly, Luke reports that the newly converted Saul "became increasingly more powerful and confounded the Jews who lived in Damascus by proving that Jesus was the Messiah" (9:22). Likewise, Apollos was "an eloquent man, well-versed in the scriptures" who "powerfully refuted the Jews in public, showing by the scriptures that the Messiah is Jesus" (18:24, 28).

Interestingly, the theme of what the apostles were able to prove about Jesus is set in contrast to the malicious things that the apostles' opponents could not prove about them (see 24:13; 25:7).

Finally, the third great theme introduced by our first paragraphs from Acts is the spread of the gospel. This is the very essence and content of Acts. Luke introduces that theme right away with Jesus' "you will be my witnesses" instruction, as well as the spread implicit in "Jerusalem, in all Judea and Samaria, and to the ends of the earth." As the story unfolds, the book of Acts follows that general outline. The story focuses initially on Jerusalem in chapters 2-7. It turns to the more regional gospel activity in and around Judea and Samaria in chapters 8-12. Then, beginning in chapter 13, the reader follows Paul to "the ends of the earth" — throughout the Mediterranean world and Rome, where the book concludes.

Ephesians 1:15-23

Paul's reference to having heard of the Ephesians' "faith in the Lord Jesus" and their "love toward all the saints" is the sort of line that raises basic, critical questions about authorship and audience. Paul spent more time in Ephesus than in any other single place during his missionary journeys (apart from two lengthy imprisonments, that is). Acts 19:10 indicates that Paul was in Ephesus for a full two years, and yet this "I have heard" line sounds more distant and not so personally familiar as we might expect from his relationship to the Ephesians, given his tenure there.

Leaving aside the critical questions raised by it, the line contains a beautiful and challenging truth. "I have heard," Paul writes, "of your faith in the Lord Jesus and your love toward all the saints." What a tribute to the Ephesian Christians. How easy it would be for a church to be known for lesser things, or not to be known at all. Yet the church in Ephesus had carved out the grandest possible reputation.

As a congregation, perhaps we will want to consider the question: What have folks heard about us? For what, if anything, are we known?

The good report and reputation of the Ephesians inspires and informs Paul's prayers for them. And, as is so often the case in the early verses of Paul's letters, the occasion of giving thanks and praying for the people turns the attention from the people to the Lord. The Ephesians begin as the subject; but by the end of the passage, Christ is the subject.

The transition is marvelous to behold. We can almost picture Paul's eyes gradually rising — much like the disciples' eyes did at the ascension. He begins with a horizontal gaze, focusing on the Ephesians. He prays for them, which draws his attention upward to their "hope" and their "glorious inheritance." Now Paul is focused on the "great power" of God's work, which turns his attention to Christ. Once his eyes are set on Christ, the scene rapidly escalates beyond the clouds. He begins with Christ being "raised." He is in "the heavenly places," "far above," and "all things (are) under his feet."

The passage is a magnificent doxology, as well as a great Christological declaration. It also unfolds a pattern emblematic of the disciples' own experience at Christ's ascension, as they see him eye-to-eye at the beginning and are craning their necks upward at the end. Finally, as Paul moves seamlessly from talking about the Ephesians to marveling at Christ in glory, the passage serves as a metaphor for a larger truth in Paul and in the New Testament: namely, that all things point to Christ.

Luke 24:44-53

We associate with Matthew a concern for the Old Testament, yet Luke's post-resurrection accounts highlight the revelatory importance of those scriptures. In the Emmaus road conversation found earlier in this chapter, as well as in our selected passage, Luke records Jesus' deliberate statements about "the law of Moses, the prophets, and the psalms." He pointedly explains to the Emmaus road travelers — and references to the disciples here — all that was written about himself in those Old Testament writings.

That material might come as news to some of the people in our pews. Even before the prevailing biblical illiteracy of our present generation, there was a dismissive attitude in much of American Christianity concerning the Old Testament. It had second-class status, at best; or, at worst, the Old Testament was rejected as something bad or wrong. It's a neo-Marcion attitude, often exemplified by the discounting phrase, "Yes, but that's Old Testament," as though referring to stale milk or Beta VCRs.

In contrast to all of that, Luke reflects here what the early church understood and preached: that the Old Testament scriptures point to Christ. They are even, as Paul later wrote, "able to instruct you for salvation through faith in Christ Jesus" (2 Timothy 3:15).

Among the Old Testament explication that Jesus offered the disciples on this occasion was this core statement: "Thus it is written, that the Messiah is to suffer and to rise from the dead on the third day." That, of course, is essentially the same thing that he had told them deliberately three times before (for example, Luke 8:21-22; 9:44; 18:31-33; and counterparts found in Matthew and Mark). On those prior occasions, the disciples had responded with confusion, misunderstanding, and even outright objection. When the predicted events began to unfold in Jerusalem, the disciples seemed genuinely stupefied by them.

We see the same thing at work in the Old Testament. God sent the prophets to warn the people of Israel and Judah about what was going to happen.

The important and marvelous pattern is that God tells his people in advance. Lest we think that events are random or that the world is spinning out of control, God's prior warning should give us peace, and even understanding. Yet here, on the other side of Gethsemane, Golgotha, and the garden tomb, Jesus still needs to go back and explain to his disciples what had happened. Of course, it was essential that Jesus explain to them what they had seen, for now the time had almost come for them to serve as "witnesses of these things."

Taken all together, we are presented with a marvelous time line under the plan and providence of God. At the center stand the death and resurrection of Christ. To the left, back in the days of Moses and the prophets, God had declared in advance what the Messiah would be and would do. Closer to the moment, Jesus himself had alerted his disciples to what was to come. And now, on the right side of the time line, just beyond that death and resurrection, comes the Holy Spirit and the empowered apostles proclaiming "repentance and forgiveness of sins... in his name to all nations."

159

Finally, while Luke would not have a native reason to cherish the temple in Jerusalem, it appears favorably again and again in both Luke and Acts. In spite of the architectural design that would have set him, as a Gentile, at a greater distance from God, Luke seems to embrace the importance, beauty, and significance of the place.

In his gospel, Luke includes two temple events that none of the other gospel writers do. Shortly after Jesus' birth, Mary and Joseph bring him to the temple, where they are met by Simeon and Anna. Likewise, in the sole canonical episode from Jesus' childhood, Luke tells the story of the boy Jesus sitting in the temple with the teachers. It is, as Jesus sees it, the natural place for him to be, for it is "my Father's house" (2:49).

As in the other gospels, the temple figures prominently in Luke's holy week account, but he is the only one of the four evangelists who places the post-ascension disciples so deliberately back in the temple. "They were continually in the temple blessing God," Luke concludes. It is a line reminiscent of Anna, to whom Luke introduces us at the other end of his gospel. He says she "never left the temple but worshiped there with fasting and prayer night and day" (2:37). The image of the disciples with which Luke closes his gospel is revisited early in Acts, where he reports that "they spent much time together in the temple" (2:46).

Application

We had a friend some years ago who had a reputation for falling asleep in certain group settings. (Truth be told, it was an exaggerated and unfair reputation, but it was good fodder for teasing among her good friends.) Our observation was that, when she was at or near the center of attention, she was the most animated person in the group. When we weren't all talking about her or things that involved her, however, she would fall asleep.

That sounds quite self-absorbed, of course, which she was actually not. Her pattern may serve as a kind of metaphor for much of American Christianity. We may be quite interested as long as it's all about us, but we become indifferent when the subject is something or someone else. This is perhaps most evident in our doctrine.

I wonder if our relative disinterest in Jesus' ascension traces back to the fact that we can't see that it has anything to do with us. We have a sense for the personal relevance of his coming, his living, his dying, and his rising, but what about his leaving? We have a doctrinal understanding of these other matters, and their importance to us may derive from their relevance to us.

The old J. Wilbur Chapman song says, "Living, he loved me; dying, he saved me; buried, he carried my sins far away; rising, he justified, freely forever; one day he's coming — O glorious day!" I love the hymn, but I recognize that it articulates a certain anthropocentricity that may characterize our doctrine: that is, what Jesus has to do with me. Better that the story of Jesus should become personal than remain impersonal, and yet, when it comes to his ascension, I am reminded that it's not about me. It's about him.

Paul declares that "God... seated [Christ] at his right hand in the heavenly places, far above all rule, authority, power, and dominion, and above every name that is named, not only in this age but also in the age to come." It is a magnificent picture of ascended Christ in glory. But I am not in that picture.

The Acts account of the ascension concludes with the disciples "gazing up toward heaven," while the gospel account reports that "he was carried up into heaven" and "they worshiped him." This, then, is the appropriate posture for Ascension Sunday. And for every Sunday since his ascension. We gaze upward, and we worship him. He is glorified, with all power and authority for all time. And we do well to remind ourselves that it's all about him.

An Alternative Application

Acts 1:1-11. "Are We There Yet?" Some expressions are so universal among children that one wonders if they have undertaken some formal training in order to learn the lingo. "It's not fair," "But Johnny's parents let him," "I promise I'll take care of it and clean up after it" are all among the common idioms of childhood.

Then there is the dreaded refrain of a long, family car trip: "Are we there yet?" Almost any parent who has made a long trip with a child has dealt with this query. The first time, it can be amusing. My five-year-old daughter once asked the question before we had even gotten on the highway. As the trip wears on and patience wears thin, however, the question can become an irritant.

I see that childish question in the disciples. "Lord, is this the time when you will restore the kingdom to Israel?" They have a notion about what God's destination is, and they want to know if they're there yet. Or almost there.

While parents joke — or perhaps complain — about the impatience of young travelers, we should note that there is a certain virtue in it. After all, that expressed impatience for the destination means that they want to get there!

I remember asking my parents, "Are we there yet?" on certain occasions; but not on every occasion. I don't recall using that phrase when I was being taken somewhere I didn't want to go. I never impatiently asked, "Are we at the dentist's yet?" or "Are we to the piano teacher's house yet?" The fact that the children are impatient to arrive at the restaurant, the motel, the relative's house, the vacation destination, or wherever, means that they feel a commendable eagerness for what lies ahead.

I may preach a sermon in which I cast the disciples in the familiar role of children in the back seat — fidgety and impatient. They want to know if we're there yet. And just about the time I have my congregation bemused by the disciples, I will remind them of the virtue. Better to be impatient for God's destination than to be indifferent about it.

A prayer we can help answer

Have you ever been to a committee or board meeting maybe even in the church and have this happen to you? You speak up and ask for something or suggest that something needs to be done. When the meeting is over, you found that somehow you were made chair of the new committee to see that it would happen! I have run into many sneaky moderators of meetings who could do that! I think this is one reason why there are so many people in committee meetings who never say a word!

It seems to me that God does the same thing to us sometimes in our prayers. We tend to think that prayer is us asking God for something. We are the askers. God is supposed to be the giver. But God does not always respond that way or fit into the nice little boxes in which we would place God. Sometimes God says when we pray, "Okay, let's just see how badly you want this prayer answered. You are going to have to do something more than merely ask. I'm going to use you to help answer it."

I find this especially true in praying for others. You pray for someone. You pray that God would give them peace, comfort, strength, love, help. If you pray that enough, you just might find yourself on their door step or sitting beside their hospital bed, giving them comfort, strength, love, and help yourself! God uses you to answer your own prayers for that person! God's sneaky.

God quite often uses others to answer our prayers. Think about it. I imagine that all of us if we took time to think have had times when we were really praying about something and God's answer came to us through another person or persons. God enjoys using us to answers our own prayers and the prayers of others!

John 17 is often called the "high priestly prayer of Jesus." It's very close to the time when he will be arrested, tried, and killed. In this prayer to God we see Jesus baring his soul, showing what's really on his heart. You know what we see and hear at least four times in it? "That they might be one." He was praying for his disciples, for you and me. He was asking God to make us unified, to keep us and hold us together. The unity of the church was on the heart and mind of Jesus the very night he was arrested.

We have it within our prayer to help answer one of the last prayers of the Son of God — that we might be one! With our words, our actions, our attitudes we can help answer this prayer!

We can help answer it right here and now within our own church. The unity of the church should be a very high priority for us. We need to be careful that our words, actions, and attitudes always build up our church and not tear it down.

We can help answer the prayer of Jesus "that they might be one" by lifting up our church, by looking for the good and upholding that, by praying for one another and always speaking and acting with its best interest in mind.

The church is like an orchestra. It has one conductor, various instrumental sections — brass, strings, percussion... And numerous musicians. Each has a different part to play. Many of us are beginning to realize that we need each other. We are stopping to listen to each other. We are discovering that, though we may play different instruments, the symphony we are playing is the very same one! And that playing it together makes it so glorious, so moving that it can touch and transform this world.

I think this is why Jesus prayed so fervently that we might be one. For it is our unity, our coming together, our working together to share the love of God in Christ that this broken world can find wholeness and healing. For if we who call ourselves Christians cannot find in the love of God the power to overcome our differences, to knock down the walls between us, then what do we really have to offer this broken, shattered world?

Acts 1:15-17, 21-26

One of the things you really notice about today's passage is that there are lots more people associated with Jesus than we knew, that is, other than the apostles like Peter and the others. Here we are told there were well over a hundred of them (and perhaps more). About them we know nothing.

It's also interesting that Peter comes to the leadership here, in spite of his denials of even knowing Jesus when Jesus was arrested and tried. In fact, Peter has a key if not main role in the early part of Acts. We know, too, that James, presumably the brother of Jesus, would soon become the head of the church in Jerusalem. Then Paul takes the spotlight in much of the rest of Acts. Of course, the true hero or main character in Acts is the Holy Spirit.

Where this group met isn't told. It's probably Jerusalem. Tradition says that they continued to meet in the upper room but it's not likely so many people could have met there. Also, so many people would have drawn attention. Were they all together or was this number the total amount of believers at this time?

Peter's speech is really a kind of state of the believers address. They are together and much has happened, wondrous things, but there's some housekeeping things to take care of — replacing Judas.

Now Peter gives the standard line here about Judas — that Judas was, so it seems, destined to do what he did — that is — betray Jesus. In other words, it was a fulfillment of scripture, of prophecy. The scripture in mind seems to be a very free reading of Psalms 69:25; 109:28. This was an attempt to help explain why Judas did what he did and to show that everything that happened was really in accord with the will or plan of God laid out for some time. Even in the prayer of Jesus for today we are told of Judas that he was "destined to be lost" (17:12).

What do you think about that? Did Judas have no choice? Was it his destiny? If so, then can he really be held responsible? If it was already determined anyway, how can anyone blame him? In fact, should he not be praised for doing his part, detestable as it was, in this great and grand scheme?

Here we see again that there were a number of other people who had been present since the beginning of the ministry of Jesus. The apostles themselves were just one group, albeit a special kind of inner circle, but there were others. From those who had been there from the beginning, who had witnessed all the apostles had witnessed, the replacement of Judas must be found (vv. 21-27).

The thing that stands out to me is that they looked for one primary thing — not the oratory gifts or anything else about this person — but the kind of relationship, communion, fellowship that person had with Jesus. That was the top and determining requirement.

Two such people are set forth or nominated here. Is it Peter who makes the nomination or others? Joseph called Barsabbas is probably identified this way to distinguish him from Judas Barsabbas (see Acts 15:22). We know little about him. Eusebius numbers him, like Matthias, among the seventy, while Papias mentions a tradition that he drank poison (like in Mark 16:18) and was unharmed.

Matthias means "gift of Yahweh." It's surely related to the popular name "Matthew." About him there are only traditions. One, because the name confuses him with the apostle Matthew. Another identifies him with Zacchaeus and yet another sees him as being Barnabas.

The simple truth is that just who these men were has been lost in the sands of time. Only God knows them. Indeed, only God knows the names of all these unknown men and women who followed Jesus so faithfully. They are lost to us but not to God.

Then they prayed. To whom is this prayer addressed — God or Jesus or both? It's interesting that the word for "chosen" here is the same as the one used in Luke 6:13 where Jesus originally chooses the apostles. So this may be an indication that they are asking Jesus now to choose another one to replace Judas.

Then they cast lots and it fell on Matthias. The practice of casting lots was an old one. It was often done by having the names of persons on stones, put in a jar, then the one that fell out was considered the chosen one. But the Greek word here for casting lots might also mean that they simply "cast their votes." However it was done, they believed that the Lord was guiding the process.

1 John 5:9-13

One of the chief points made in this whole chapter is that the heart of our faith is the belief that Jesus is indeed the one who God sent to overcome sin and bring abundant and eternal life. It is not just an intellectual consent to a set of doctrines. "Belief" here also means a personal trust in a living Lord. It is a faith that comes out of a personal relationship with Christ. Faith is the acceptance of all that God gives us through Christ. It is believing that all God has done for us in Christ is in fact a reality.

Verses 9-11 give us three great testimonies to the truth of what God has done for us in Christ. The first is the human witness. John probably has in mind those who had witnessed the life of Jesus and who could give eyewitness accounts. But he also has in mind all those who have experienced Christ and received life from him.

Think about your own life. How have the testimonies and lives of other Christians influenced your own Christian life?

The second great witness is a divine one — God. Throughout the life of Jesus, God bore witness to him. Through the promises of the Messiah in the Old Testament, through the miracle of his birth, through the announcement at his baptism, through his resurrection, through countless signs and miracles, and through the continuing presence and work of Christ, God bears witness to him. In other words, we have God's own word that all he says he's done for us in Christ he has done. If we can't accept God's word, whose can we believe?

The third testimony is an inner one (first part of v. 10). We know that Jesus is God's Son and that God has given us life through him because we have experienced these things. Indeed, Christ, through the Holy Spirit, lives in us. The Spirit gives us the inner assurance that Jesus is Savior and Lord and that it's right to give ourselves to him.

John tells his readers to keep on believing in what they know to be true. Jesus is God's Son. He died for them. Only through faith in and fellowship with him can they have abundant and eternal life (vv. 12-13).

John 17:6-19

This "high priestly prayer" of Jesus falls into three parts:
1. Jesus prays for himself and his work (vv. 1-5).
2. Jesus prays for his disciples (vv. 6-19).
3. Jesus prays for us or the church universal (vv. 20-26).
Some call it "Jesus' Farewell Prayer."
The setting is still the upper room.

To me, anyway, it is an example of the kind of intercession Jesus makes for us as the ascended and glorified Lord. This ties it to the Acts ascension story for today. Imagine this: Jesus, the Son of God, sitting beside God, the one who has God's ear, prays for us! If we truly believe that, then we can be his witnesses, we can do anything, for what would God deny the Son? What good thing would the Son hold back from us that we needed to be his servants and witnesses?

It also connects with the Acts passage as the disciples devoted themselves to prayer. Jesus is often depicted as praying. If Jesus felt this need, how much more do we need it?

Many see the Lord's Prayer as a model for us. It is but so is this one. It provides a kind of guideline for us, as well as the kind of attitude we should have in prayer. It's okay and right in all our prayers to pray for ourselves, for one another, and for the whole church everywhere. If we pray as Jesus does, it will also be for unity among God's people. The marvelous thing about praying for unity is that this act itself moves us toward unity. I have found in my own life that anytime I truly pray about anything, I find myself being drawn to that very thing in my words and actions, so that God might better use me to help answer that prayer.

One of the keys to the unity of the early church that we see in Acts is their prayers. They even attended the daily prayer times/hours in the temple and certainly prayer was a natural and constant part of their lives when together or apart.

Would that prayer were as natural to us as breathing.

One interesting theological note is that the work of Jesus us about to be completed. He will suffer and die but arise! He will also ascend as the glorified Christ to sit by God's side, interceding for us as we bear witness to the saving work God has done through him. All that is needed will be accomplished. All that remains is for us to be faithful, Spirit empowered witnesses to him and that work. Part of our most powerful witness to him is our unity, which is a very important part of this prayer of Jesus.

An important theme that is stressed more in John's gospel than anywhere else is that what Jesus brings, this salvation, is "eternal life." Eternal life is described as knowing God through the one who reveals God — Christ. It is a relationship and not so much another kind of existence on streets of gold that is emphasized. I have heard others say that heaven is being eternally in fellowship with God that we have but a taste of here. And hell? That is being perpetually in a state of sensing only God's absence. That is our choice and not God's. Such is the quality and power of this relationship with God through Christ that not even death can take us away from God.

Application

Acts 1:15-17, 21-26. "And the Lot Fell Upon Matthias." This passage is a good one to talk about calling, leadership.

Part of the leadership had failed — Judas had failed to be the apostle he was called to be. Other leadership had to be found.

The church went through a process of prayer and discernment.

They looked for those who had firsthand experience with the risen Lord to fill the place of Judas. For how can one give testimony that he or she has not had? How can they bear witness to something they have not experienced? The first and foremost requirement, the one qualification they looked for was this one of companionship with Jesus himself.

They found such a person in Matthias. The lot fell upon him. That sounds, at least to me, kind of painful — to have something fall on you. It certainly was a heavy responsibility. As far as we know, he accepted it and served well.

Now, many years later, the call still goes out for leadership in the life and work of the church. The lot falls upon us. Will we accept it?

An Alternative Application

Acts 1:15-17, 21-26; John 17:6-19. "The Call." Many denominations are experiencing a shortage of clergy these days. Today's passages provide an opportunity to talk about this particular calling, of setting it forth as a possible way that God might be calling some of the people from your own church (not just younger ones). Perhaps a good and effective way to do this is for you to share your own call story. It seems to me we do not talk about this enough. You might also wish to talk about the calling of every Christian as Jesus says in the gospel lesson, we are all sent, we all have a calling, too, each and every one of us.

Spiritual chinook

In northern parts of the United States winter weather reports include phrases like "cold Canadian air" sweeping down, "the Alberta clipper" driving storms in from the northwest, or an "arctic system" whistling through the upper midwest or New England states. But those who live in Alberta know that the strongest winds are not the coldest. The most powerful winds of Alberta are the chinooks.

One account of a chinook wind appeared in *Christian Courier* some years ago (11/27/87):

It was one of those deceptively bone-chilling Alberta mornings when the sun shines so brightly in a cloudless sky that you think the warmth of heaven has swallowed up winter in its fire. But the first step out of the door crunches snow like gravel, and the biting claws of minus-forty-degree air tears at your nose and lungs. Your face even shrivels up into a grimace as your muscles pull back, each retreating behind others for protection.

The engine in my pickup truck groaned in agony, trying to lubricate itself with oil as thick as tar. And the vinyl seat was a cold stone throne, stoutly protesting the pastoral visits its young master was called to make. But driving westward near Picture Butte a strange and wonderful thing happened.

Something like a wall of air was moving toward me, a captivating sight that words can't really describe. There had been no wind at all when I left Iron Springs, but suddenly now my truck shuddered, slapped in the face by a violent blast. All of the chrome and metal parts of the vehicle clouded over with a frosty mist, and the windshield fogged dangerously. I pulled to the side of the road and stepped out — only to find that the temperature was warm, already trying to push above the freezing mark! The chinook had arrived!

According to weather records, chinook winds rival hurricanes in speed, and rapidly raise temperatures. Calgary, Alberta, reported a 51-degree warm-up in four hours on February 7, 1964, and a 43% drop in humidity at the same time. While the name for the North American blast is derived from a tribe of Indians who lived in the area, similar winds are found in mountainous areas around the world. Sweeping down from the Andes, Argentinians call them *zonda*. In Switzerland the term is *schneefresser*, which translates as "snow eater."

Although any analogy is limited, the idea of a chinook wind or a "snow eater" seems a marvelous hook on which to hang today's teachings. In a world frozen over by sin's winter, the Pentecost wind blows in with the warmth of heaven and fans a spiritual passion that is still burning around the world. (Think of C.S. Lewis' *Chronicles Of Narnia*, and how, in *The Lion, the Witch and the Wardrobe*, Mr. Beaver laments that in his country it is "always winter but never Christmas," although things might be changing because there are reports that Aslan is on the move.) Luke's report in Acts 2 describes the incidents as they unfolded that first Pentecost Sunday. Paul breathes pastoral warmth as he talks about the power growing within when the Spirit takes root in our hearts. And the words of Jesus in the fourth gospel remind us that the Spirit is our only true link to the departed, ascended Jesus.

Acts 2:1-21

John Wesley once tried to explain why the crowds amassed when he stood to preach. He said, "God has set me on fire and people come out to watch me burn."

Something of that sort has been true ever since the first Pentecost Sunday when a sign of the Holy Spirit's presence was the consuming fire that distributed itself among the disciples. Years earlier, when John the Baptist preached his hellfire and damnation sermons on the banks of the Jordan River, he announced this day. He said to the gathering throngs, "I baptize you with water for repentance. But after me will come one who is more powerful than I, whose sandals I am not fit to carry. He will baptize you with the Holy Spirit and with fire" (Matthew 3:11).

The symbolism of fire was particularly fitting for this occasion. God met Moses in the burning bush in the wilderness (Exodus 3). God led Israel through the deserts by means of a fiery cloud, and when God took up residence in the camp, it was heaven's *shekinah* glory light that enveloped the tabernacle. Fire had long proclaimed the living presence of God on earth.

But the peculiar actions of this particular flame, recorded by Luke, declared another important theological message. The fire was one, yet it divided itself into identical replicas above each individual in the place. The God whose unique fiery presence had stood over the tabernacle and temple now moved into the apartment complex of the church. God's single will invaded each room, each heart, and joined it with the others through a vast network of consuming love.

Furthermore, both the Hebrew (*ruach*) and Greek (*pneuma*) languages each have a single word that captures the ideas of "wind," "breath," and "spirit." Certainly, in reflection, the disciples couldn't help but recognize the parallels between themselves and young Adam in Genesis 2. He was only an inert blob of clay and water until the warm wind of God's breath gave him the life of the Spirit.

The sound of wind was a thrilling announcement of the powerful, loving, and life-giving Spirit of God. Sailors in ancient days sometimes got stuck in the quiet death of the doldrums near earth's equator. Nothing was more welcome, after weeks of listless apathy, than the mighty roar of heaven's unseen hand against their sails. In fact, in the 1800s, when a ship carrying missionary, Hudson Taylor, was becalmed near an island known for its cannibal residents, the crew grew fearful as the vessel drifted toward shore. Knowing Mr. Taylor's occupation and the strength of his convictions, the captain pleaded with him to pray to the almighty for wind. Taylor agreed, but only on the condition that the captain unfurl the sails. This seemed foolish, for not a breath of air stirred. Still, Taylor was adamant and the captain, in fear, complied. Taylor went to his small room to pray. Soon a knock came at the door. It was the captain. "Are you still praying for wind?" he cried.

When Taylor affirmed that he was still wrestling with God, the captain said, "Well, you'd better stop now; we've got more wind than we can manage!" Wouldn't that be an amazing thing to hear in our worship gatherings today?

In quoting words from the prophet Joel, Peter links the coming of the Spirit to the great "Day of the Lord." As the life of Israel was chipped away in Old Testament times, ripped away by invaders, and tipped away by internal failures, the prophets increasingly looked forward to a time when God would once again directly intervene in human history to do three things: destroy the power of evil both in the nations around and within the people of Israel themselves; preserve a remnant of the chosen people as a testimony of God's goodness; and usher in the times of the messianic kingdom in which life would resonate with goodness and all creation would celebrate the return of its original goodness.

In a very real way, the wind of Pentecost Spirit signals the return of spring to Narnia. Aslan [Jesus] is on the move wherever the wind blows.

Romans 8:22-27

Paul gives a full history overview in his letter to the Romans. He talks about creation and the intrinsic connection between creator and creature, as well as the fall into sin and how it disrupted this bond. In chapter 4, Paul reviews the days of the patriarchs, showing God's growing relationship with Abraham, the father of Israel. Chapter 5 pulls the story up to Jesus, outlining how his work provides the redemption that reinvigorates the old family tree of Adam that was wilting from the roots up. Then Paul makes things personal in chapters 6-7 as the struggles of spiritual warfare wrangle in every human heart. In chapter 8, the promise of a great outcome is given, as consummation is inferred.

Whatever it is that will happen to us and for us, however, has begun to take shape already through the inner presence of God's Spirit. Paul acknowledges the weaknesses, challenges, and ravages that have become part of our existence because of sin, but he doesn't stop there. The God who shaped our world in its beginnings is doing a powerful work of re-creation that has already sprouted wherever the Spirit roams. In a sense, it is Babel undone.

In Genesis 11, the whole human race, in the years after the great flood, adopts atheistic humanism as its working philosophy. "We don't need the God of the heavens!" is the rallying cry. "There is only one god, and he is us!"

The people begin to build their brave new world around themselves. A single skyscraper will house them all. The flagpole at the top will float the banner of freedom: a huge yellow smiling face with the words underneath, "I'm okay; you're okay!" All residents of earth are part of the city, but the God of heaven is confined to a hidden slum because he speaks a different language.

According to the Genesis story, God visits the construction site and makes a few alterations. At coffee time the next day, as the crews are reaching for their thermoses, the friendly bantering turns into verbal abuse. No one can make sense of the strange "babel" of others. Tempers flare as tensions slice through the community. Ethnic groupings form and people back away from one another with weapons drawn, isolating themselves behind military fences and in panic rooms.

Then, across the centuries and through 1,000 ethnic wars, as the bigoted minds of humans shun a child for the strange twist of a tongue, God steps out of heaven again. While the splintered world shakes its many heads in the "babel" of disbelief, a single voice pierces the fog of the divided mind. A single Word speaks love, and a single Spirit creates a new humanity, not based on the evils of human ingenuity but rather on the grace of divine forgiveness.

The God who once defused the power of evil by turning it into a cacophony of many dissonant voices at ancient Babel now binds the many into a single new humanity with the delightful miracle of tongues at Pentecost: "We hear them declaring the wonders of God in our own tongues!"

With these ideas in mind it is clear to see why Paul writes as he does. First, he brings the pastoral comfort of one who understands suffering. While Paul is more logically precise in his letter to the Roman Christians than in many of his other more rambling epistles, he is also very empathetic throughout. In chapter 8 and in the agonizing introspections of the previous chapter, Paul writes like someone who has known much of personal suffering and interior reflection.

Second, Paul ties together in quick order the creation-fall-redemption-consummation links he forged into an extended chain in the earlier chapters. Paul identifies the goodness of original creation, the agony experienced in a fallen world, the provisions of redemption, and the anticipation of the restoration in the coming age.

Third, the idea of creation suffering is a powerful motif. This perspective is unique to biblical literature. In other religions, the world around us is a trap which seeks to prevent us from full self-actualization, or a neutral territory which is mostly unaffected by human morality, or, at best, the natural order of things, which is basically good. And the best of human expression comes when societies give up civilization and return to innocence. Only in the theology of the Bible does the world emerge as a good creation of God, which suffers along with humankind for the sins introduced through the disobedience of God's first human partners.

Fourth, there is incredible comfort found in the idea of God's active investment on behalf of us. Even when we do not know what to ask of God or how to communicate with God, God is already, by way of the Spirit, reaching within us in kindness and empathizing with our mystifying need. We have an ally — a divine ally. We have a divine ally who proactively reaches out to us like a mother anticipating the needs of her child. Reflecting again on the wind of Pentecost, our ship is pushed along through rough seas by the wind of God's grace, even when we lack the fuel to run the engines of our own making.

John 15:26-27; 16:4b-15

The Spirit functions in a unique way in the theology of John. Within the "Farewell Discourse" of Jesus (John 13-17; for a thoughtful and accessible reflection on its structure and themes see *The Literary Development of John 13-17: A Chiastic Reading* [SBLDS, 2000]) the Spirit provides the link between the disciples and the soon-to-be-absent Jesus that allows the "Abide in me!" instructions of the vine and branches teaching in 15:1-8 to make sense. When Jesus ascends to glory after his death and resurrection, it will be the Spirit who will function as Paraclete (advocate, counselor, and teacher are all various attempts at conveying the meaning of this Greek term), ever renewing the disciples' relationship with their master and friend.

This instruction on the night before Jesus' death helps us understand why Jesus would wait for ten days after his ascension before sending the promised Spirit (see Acts 1). Pentecost was one of the three high holidays of the Hebrew people, a yearly event during which every observant Jew would focus thoughts on the providential care of God and the constant need for God's blessing. Its importance can be seen in a legend first spoken by Rabbi El'azar ben Pedath: "Pentecost is the day on which Torah was given." In other words, God first spoke to his people Israel at Mount Sinai on the day now commemorated by Pentecost.

This complemented the significance infused into Pentecost by Old Testament commands for the celebration. It was supposed to be a special sabbath — not the normal weekly event but a second sabbath day on which no work was to be done. All adherents were to assemble in the temple and bring with them the first sheaf from the fields, produced when the sickle was first put to the standing grain. This was to be waved before the Lord as an offering (Leviticus 23:11). From the realm of animal husbandry, two male lambs were to be offered (Leviticus 23:12). During these presentations all the men danced around the altar singing Psalms 113-118.

The theological edge came with this instruction: No further harvesting could take place until these first fruits were offered up to God. When the people had acknowledged that the harvest belonged to God, and that only God could bring in the rest of the harvest, were they free to begin roaming the fields for the thrill of reaping.

Suddenly, John's description of the Paraclete's place in helping the disciples serve as ambassadors of Jesus becomes clearer. Furthermore, the reason why Jesus delayed sending the Spirit until the visible expressions of theological meaning were portrayed in the Pentecost celebrations is fully understandable. God powerfully brings in the first of the mission harvest in Jerusalem and then the workers are dispatched worldwide to the rest of the fields.

Application

Today is a great day to speak of the fresh wind of God. The devastating power of storm winds (such as Hurricane Katrina) has been in the news. But through the church come tales of great winds of grace. One might do well to quote a number of the great hymns of faith, or have them sung within the worship celebrations of the day:

Breathe on me, breath of God,
till I am wholly thine;
till all this earthly part of me
glows with thy fire divine.

— Hatch

Teach me to love thee as thine angels love
one holy passion filling all my frame
The baptism of the heaven-descended dove
my heart an altar and thy love the flame.

— Croly

Or, as the apostle Paul wrote to young pastor Timothy in Ephesus, "Fan into flame the gift of God which is in you!" (2 Timothy 1:6).

An Alternative Application

Romans 8:22-27. While it is always beneficial to read the biblical story of Pentecost on this day, it is sometimes helpful to preach from a different passage. The Romans text is particularly engaging for every congregation. There is no person who has not been touched by pain and suffering. In fact, an old Chinese legend tells of a woman who was deeply despondent because of the untimely death of her son, and went to a priest for comfort. Unable to console her, the priest offered this remedy: Her agony of spirit would abate when she was able to bring to him a mustard seed from a home that had never known suffering.

In great hope, the woman set out on a quest to find relief from her heart's hurt. But traveling far and wide, she soon discovered that there was no home untouched by bereavement and no dwelling distant from pain. In the end, the woman found empathy rather than release, and devoted her life to helping others who suffered.

Paul's words about our hurting world and aching selves mirror universal need. On this Pentecost Sunday his teachings about God's caring Spirit are a message that connects quickly with hungry ears.

Holy Trinity Sunday
Isaiah 6:1-8
Romans 8:12-17
John 3:1-17
Bass Mitchell

It's a mystery!

One of the most delightful movies I have seen in awhile was *Shakespeare in Love*, which won the Oscar for the best movie of 1999. One of the favorite lines throughout the movie was, "I don't know. It's a mystery."

That's what I feel like saying every time Trinity Sunday comes around: "I don't know. It's a mystery."

Isn't that, in a way, what even Jesus is saying when he speaks of the wind or Spirit in the gospel reading today? The wind, like the Spirit, is a mystery. You cannot comprehend the wind or control it. The wind goes where it will. So does the Spirit.

The doctrine of the Trinity is an attempt to explain a mystery that is, in the final analysis, unexplainable. "I don't know. It's a mystery." And that's not such a bad thing to admit, to accept, and even celebrate.

Isaiah 6:1-8

Isaiah 6:1 through at least 8:18 forms a memoir Isaiah shared with the whole world. It's really his call to ministry. So what he is sharing is deeply personal but something that made him who he was, determined his identity and place and work in the world.

But his calling was within the scope of what was going on in his nation and world. Isaiah was called at a critical time in the history of his people — during the events leading to the Syro-Ephraimite War (when Syria and the northern kingdom of Israel banded together against Judah) and the pressure being placed on King Ahaz. These two kingdoms wanted Judah to join them in rebellion against Assyria but Judah was reluctant to do so. Isaiah will tell Ahaz not to listen to this plea as the two kingdoms will not last very long. There is nothing to fear, Isaiah says, but Ahaz doesn't listen. Isaiah's task, in other words, would not be an easy one (see v. 9ff, which is not in today's reading). He would speak judgment on a wayward nation and government. Many would oppose him. Prophets are not without honor except in their own countries. They are not the most popular of people.

The setting for Isaiah's call is most likely the temple in Jerusalem. From the description of the setting, it appears that Isaiah is looking through the entranceway into the inner sanctum of the temple. Why is he there? By what right? Perhaps he is already a priest serving there, as many scholars think. Or maybe he was a court official of some kind.

Why is he there? Perhaps getting ready to carry out his priestly duties or maybe he was there for prayer and worship. Perhaps he was there praying for his people as it was a time of crisis. Uzziah, their king, had died (this was probably 736/735 BC). We know from 2 Kings 15:5 that Uzziah had leprosy, while his son, Jotham, was acting as king until both he and Uzziah died, leaving Jotham's son, Ahaz, to take the throne.

Isaiah has a vision. The temple had become the throne room for God. God was high and lifted up on a throne and the train of God's robe filled the whole room. What a vision! Isaiah felt himself in the presence of God.

Earthly kings always had servants and bodyguards standing by. Likewise, Isaiah sees "seraphs," God's servants or attendants. They seem to be serpent-like creatures with three pair of wings but human hands and feet. They fly and they sing. Such creatures were often seen or used in Egyptian royal symbolism as the bodyguards of the king (some in the form of a winged cobra). But as far as we know there were no actual images of seraphim in the temple itself.

The seraphim are singing a song of praise to God: "Holy, holy, holy." Many scholars believe what Isaiah is hearing, if he is indeed having this vision in a worship service, is a choral antiphon or song used in the temple. The song sings of the majestic, mystery, power, and worthiness of God. Indeed, God's glory is such that it fills the earth. God's greatness can be seen everywhere if we look.

The voices from the choir and the seraphim and the incense all combined to make the prophet feel the temple or whole earth shake and tremble, perhaps as a way of also praising God. So it's no wonder that the prophet begins to shake and tremble as well! The prophet has an intense fear that he is a sinner and not worthy to be in the presence of God. This might well spell his doom! Perhaps he had sensed for some time this call from God but had felt that his lips were unworthy of such a task as being God's messenger. He is certainly aware that he's not alone in his unworthiness and sin — the entire nation is sinful. None are worthy of being God's people, God's servants.

Then Isaiah hears God's voice asking who can God send to these sinful people. Without hesitation Isaiah says, like so many before and after him, "Here I am; send me."

Romans 8:12-17

The Christian has been given a life on another level — the level of the Spirit — and must seek to live on that level. It's explained here as living as God's children. Because the Spirit dwells within us, we are God's own children. So we can call upon God as our heavenly parent and look forward to a share in a great inheritance.

Verses 12-13 sum up and build on what has gone before this. Paul addresses the Roman Christians in more friendly, intimate terms as "friends" or "brothers and sisters." They are free now from the domination of sin, the lower nature, and even from death. But they can fall back into it and that would mean death to them. What Paul seems to have in mind is going back to living in the flesh, *sarx*, following the way of the lower nature, the way that does not follow Christ and the leading of the Spirit. Such actions or lifestyles are named in Galatians 5:19-20. All of these must be put to death. Refusing to go back to that way of life, with the help of the Spirit, then results in true life, life as God intended it to be.

Verses 14-17 explain the nature of this new life given in and by the Spirit. We are sons and daughters of God. The Spirit makes us thus. The Spirit creates a whole new relationship with God.

This idea of the Spirit living in us and making us God's children is interesting. I can feel that something of the "spirit" of my parents lives in me. This is a mystery that is hard to explain or demonstrate but it is true nonetheless. There is this unexplainable connection I have with them. They live within me. Perhaps this is also what Paul has in mind. The Spirit lives within us, too, it is our connection to our heavenly parent. The Spirit assures us that we are God's children.

Paul fears, however, that they might forget their new and exalted status and that they might go back to dependence on the law for their justification and that would be slavery, he says, and to doom themselves to a life of fear, never really knowing for certain if they were right with God. But that is not their birthright. The Spirit gives them an assurance of being loved and accepted by God as children, not based on who they are or what they have done or not done, but based solely on the free grace and love of God.

Knowing such love and having the presence of the Spirit, we are able to call upon God as "Abba," or "Father." It is the word a child would use for her dad. It's an intimate word, a word that shows a close and loving relationship with God. This is what Christ desires for us to have with God. It is our birthright. We were created for such a relationship but sin broke it. Christ restores it through the power of the Spirit. The Spirit then, working in us, enables us to call upon God as a heavenly parent, really knowing and feeling that God loves us like a parent, and even more so, like the most loving parent we could ever have. The Spirit keeps working to assure us that we are children of God.

Because we are God's children, we are heirs and joint heirs with Christ. We stand to inherit all the things one might receive being an heir of God. This does not include only material things but more spiritual things, I think. The greatest inheritance is the presence of God, that is, knowing God each and every day. What greater thing can God give us than God's own self? Yet, this inheritance also includes eternal life — life always in the presence of God. A taste or foretaste of this is seen already in the resurrection of Christ, who himself lives within us. No earthly inheritance even begins to compare to this one!

John 3:1-17

John 3:1-21 is a series of dialogues between Jesus and a Pharisee named Nicodemus who perhaps witnessed some of the signs/miracles Jesus had been doing (ch. 2) and came to Jesus at night curious about just who this man was.

In this encounter with Nicodemus, we see the new confronting the old. Nicodemus is a teacher of Israel, a theologian, an expert in the laws and traditions of Judaism. He is a member of the Jewish Sanhedrin — their supreme court. If ever there was an expert in the Jewish faith, it was Nicodemus.

But he is curious about Jesus. Here is a whole new movement. Nicodemus had heard things, seen things, but now wants to meet Jesus personally and see for himself what Jesus was all about.

Nicodemus is a learned man but Jesus in essence tells him that he needs to make a whole new beginning. What's needed now is not new information, new laws to follow, but a whole new birth, a new start, a new orientation to God. It can only be compared to a whole new birth.

Impossible! Nicodemus says, thinking only in physical terms. Jesus is thinking of spiritual rebirth or regeneration — coming to a whole new understanding and experience of how God relates to us and works in our lives. This would be the way of grace and love, not works and law. All of this was what God was bringing about in the life and teaching of Jesus. This would be as difficult for Nicodemus to experience and understand as labor pains. He could not grasp it.

This wondrous new work of God was already happening as John the Baptist was preaching repentance and then giving baptism. But more than water was needed. One also had to be awash in the Spirit or born of the Spirit (v. 5). This gift is only given by John's successor — Jesus (who John said of himself, "I wash or baptize you with water, but the one coming after me will baptize you in the Holy Spirit). Christ is the one who reconnects us with God. Christ restores our fellowship with God so that God's own Spirit lives within us (as Paul says in the epistle reading for today).

Then perhaps a night breeze blows through the place they are that evening and Jesus uses that to further explain what he means. This is a mystery. "I know it is hard to understand. So is the wind that we feel right now. It comes and goes as it wishes. We cannot see it but we feel its presence and see its power. Likewise, this new thing God is doing, which you need so much, is the work of God's Spirit. You may not see the Spirit, but if you open your heart and mind, you will feel the presence and power of the Spirit moving in your life, making you a new person." Nicodemus still does not get it. Maybe he could not at this point nor could any of us until that time when Christ was "lifted up." Only as they came to look up at the Christ on the cross would they begin to see, to feel the Spirit blowing away the old and bringing the new.

The heart of this passage is found in verses 14-16. Jesus makes reference to the Numbers account of the bronze serpent, how it was lifted up and those who looked up in faith to the God who had commanded it be made were then healed, given life. Likewise, when Christ is lifted up (the Greek word here for "lifted up" is *hupsoun*, which means both lifted up on the cross and lifted up to glory — ascension). Those who also look up in faith or who "believe in him" will receive not just life but eternal life.

God's gift of love in Christ also brings judgment, though this is not why Jesus came (v. 17). Jesus came to bring life, salvation, light, and truth. But how one reacts to Jesus brings condemnation or salvation. In Jesus, the love and grace of God comes into our world. That presents us with a choice, a decision. Will we believe God loves us? Will we accept it? Will we then let that love flow through us and in everything we do?

To believe is to live. To not choose or to reject is to close ourselves off from the life and love God gives in Christ.

Application

To affirm that there are things we don't understand and that God is in many ways a mystery to us is an expression of faith and sound theology. For how can we ever fully explain God? If we could, would God be God? There is always a hiddenness about God, a mystery. That is part of what's wonderful about God and our relationship with God.

And isn't this true with our other relationships?

I have been married to my wife for 27 years. I know her well. But quite often when relating to her I find myself wondering, "I don't know. It's a mystery." I do not mean that in a negative sense at all. There is still a wondrous part of who she is that I am still getting to know. There is depth and mystery there that keeps our relationship fresh and renewing. Of course, I'm not sure she would say the same about me!

I think we need the mystery! We need to not know it all. We should accept that and celebrate it.

Lynn Anderson is the author of *If I Really Believe, Why Do I Have These Doubts?* Anderson makes a strong case for the mystery of God. We should affirm it. He writes:

There is nothing wrong with trying to understand our faith. But many of us try too hard. We attempt to explain the unexplainable, find out the indefinable, ponder over the imponderable, and unscrew the inscrutable. A life of real meaningful faith can't be treated that way. Trying to do so only leaves people with swollen heads and shrunken hearts. ([Howard Publishing, 2000], 36)

Anderson goes on to relate how one astronaut who walked on the moon found the experience disillusioning. James Irwin was on a European tour after his *Apollo 15* moon mission. Spanish journalist and Christian Juan Monroy asked him,

"What did you feel when you stepped out of that capsule and your feet touched the surface of the moon?" To everyone's surprise Irwin answered, "It was one of the most profoundly disillusioning moments of my life... All of my life I have been enchanted by the romance and the mystery of the moon. I sang love songs under the moon. I read poems by moonstruck poets. I embraced my lover in the moonlight. I looked up in wonder at the lunar sphere. But that day I stepped from the capsule onto the lunar surface and reached down at my feet, I came up with nothing but two handfuls of gray dirt. I cannot describe the loss I felt as the romance and mystery were stripped away. There will be no more moon in the sky!" (Ibid., 37)

Stripping away the mystery, even if we could, would leave us with a lot of doctrine as meaningless as a handful of gray dirt. It makes our faith empty, passionless. "I don't know. It's a mystery," is a great affirmation of faith and one that keeps us ever hungry for God and for growing in our knowledge of God.

"I don't know. It's a mystery." That's not a bad thing for us to affirm this Trinity Sunday and each day.

Alternative Applications

Isaiah 6:1-8. Many of us find ourselves wondering who we are, why we are in this world. Michael W. Smith wrote a popular song that's even been on the secular charts called, "My Place in This World." It's about finding your place, your calling in the world.

Do you ever wonder about that? Have you found your place in this world? It's not just a question for young people. We can find ourselves at most any time in our lives wondering about our calling — just what should we do with our lives?

I think Isaiah was going through that as well. He was seeking to know his calling, his place in this world. From Isaiah's call, we can gain some insights into discovering our own call. For example, Isaiah goes to the right source — God. He is worshiping God when he discovers his calling; his call also involved others — that is, the needs of others — so does our call.

John 3:1-17. Nicodemus just did not get it, did he? Christ tried to explain new spiritual things to him but he was still thinking the old way. He could not understand the need for a new spiritual birth.

But do we get it? Is our understanding any better? This Trinity Sunday, do we get it? Is our understanding any clearer? This wonderful passage of scripture seeks to help us "get it," to deepen our spiritual understanding.

* Get this: Christ the Son died for you (vv. 13-15).
* Get this: God the Father/Parent loves you (vv. 16-17).
* Get this: God the Holy Spirit re-creates you, gives you new life (vv. 5-8; and epistle lesson).

The Spirit is the one who conveys God's loves to us, who helps us experience the salvation of God; who assures us that we are the children of God.

Proper 5 / Pentecost 2 / Ordinary Time 10
1 Samuel 8:4-11 (12-15) 16-20
2 Corinthians 4:13—5:1
Mark 3:20-35
Bass Mitchell

Who do you trust?

We are in the midst of an election year. Candidates from the office of president all the way to local board members are here, there, and everywhere basically asking us to place our trust in them because they have the skills, experience, desire, and wisdom to lead. So, in a way, it all comes down to, "Who do you trust?"

Such trust, some say, with good reason, is in short supply these days and not easily given. We have seen the good, the bad, and the ugly of elected leaders, especially in those who betray the public trust. It is easy to become cynical about all leaders, isn't it? It's so tempting to throw our hands up, curse them all, and never vote again! Or vote for, "None of the Above!" None of them are trustworthy is a very popular sentiment these days.

Our scriptures today provide us some insights into leadership and trust. The first one gives us some very blunt and realistic perspectives on the frailties that all leaders have and how they can all let us down sometimes. It concedes the need for leaders, for joining together, for sacrifice for the good of all. But it bids us not place our ultimate trust in mortals, in kings and leaders, but in God.

The second and third lessons paint us different portraits of leaders. In Paul we see someone who is willing to suffer, even losing his life, for the goal, the good of others, even to the point of being rejected himself. And in Jesus, we see a leader confronted by evil, by opposition, but who still seeks to do the right and good things — to bring greater wholeness and healing everywhere he goes.

1 Samuel 8:4-11 (12-15) 16-20 (11:14-15)

There are very few people in Israel's history greater than Samuel. He did so much for his people. He was a priest, a prophet, and a reluctant king-maker.

Samuel was getting on in years. The leaders were getting anxious. Samuel had no sons who were following in his footsteps to take over after him and provide leadership. What would become of the people when they were left leaderless? So they come to Samuel and ask him to find them a king, for they had taken notice of how other countries around them did things, that is, had kings. So why shouldn't they? They wanted to be like other nations. They were afraid. They were feeling very insecure. They were placing their trust, their future in human hands (vv. 4-5).

Samuel wasn't happy with this request. No one likes to be called "old" and of no longer much use. He took this very personally. He was hurt and angry. How could they say such a thing to him after all his years of selfless service and sacrifice (v. 6)?

Knowing the leaders would not hear his complaints, Samuel goes to the Lord with his wounded ego. In essence he prays, "Lord, just look at how these people are treating me! How ungrateful can they be? They have rejected me after a lifetime of giving to them. How could they do such a thing?" (vv. 7-9).

God listens patiently and understands. God's reply basically is, "Well, Samuel, welcome to my world! They have been doing the same thing to me since I brought them out of Egypt. You know all I have done. Yet, they do not remember or give thanks. But what hurts most is that they do not trust me — though look at all I have done for them. Have I not proved my trustworthiness? They would replace me with a mortal king. Do they not know I am the only king they need? No, Samuel. They have not really rejected you. They have rejected me. But what's new?"

God tells Samuel to listen to the request of the people, to first give them a very good idea of just what they are asking for, and if they still want a king, Samuel is to find them one. Apparently, the leaders are so afraid that nothing Samuel says to them about what life will be life under a king held any sway for them. He goes on at some length to tell them exactly the burdens a king will place on every part of their lives — from taxes, to taking and using their land and the fruits of their toil, as well as their own sons and daughters. Samuel sees them one day crying out to the Lord, wishing they had never asked for or even thought about having a king like every other nation. It's as if Samuel is warning them, "Be very careful what you ask for." But under the present circumstances, they would not heed his dire warning (vv. 10-20).

Much happens between these verses and the ones above. Samuel, for example, dejectedly goes king hunting. He's really not in any state of mind to be doing that but he does and he makes mistakes. He falls into, in a way, the same trap as the people. If they must have a king, then who among the tribes looks the most kingly? He chooses Saul, who stands head and shoulders above most everyone else. He looks like a king but Samuel only looks on the outward appearance. He does not take the time, apparently, to peer into the heart and mind of Saul, who, we know, has some frailties that will greatly hinder him fulfilling the role of a king. Knowing nothing of this yet, Samuel calls the people together at the sacred site of Gilgal and anoints Saul their first king (vv. 14-15).

2 Corinthians 4:13—5:1

It is clear from these letters to the Corinthians that Paul as an apostle was constantly under attack. There were those in Corinth who had sought to undermine him. They had accused him of many things — not the least of trying to enrich himself or promote his own authority, get his own way. So he feels forced to respond, to defend himself and the whole role of apostles (apostle means one sent out on a mission, and this is very much how Paul saw himself, based on his encounter with Christ on the road to Damascus). Paul's basic points he makes over and over in different ways is that there are only three things of concern to him and any true apostle. One, serving Christ. Two, serving the body of Christ — the church. Three, seeing others come to the knowledge of God given through Christ. To these ends apostles often suffered even death. To the contrary, then, Paul says, a true apostle's last concern is for himself but always for God and others. Paul knew he was a true apostle and that God knew this, even if some did not. Nonetheless, suffering was something he knew that he would face. So would the Corinthians themselves. Followers of someone who has been crucified should not expect a bed of roses with no thorns.

If they share in the suffering of Christ, they must remember this joyous truth — they will also share in the resurrection of Christ! The cross was not the end for Christ but a glorious beginning. Those who follow him to the cross will also share in this new life that is given (vv. 13-14).

So, all the suffering of this life is set in the context of the new, resurrected life God gives in Christ. This suffering is but "slight" and temporary. His eye was on a distant prize, just as a runner looks only to the crown at the end of the race, gaining endurance for the trials and suffering of the race by remembering what awaits at the finish line. His knowledge of the risen Lord and what awaits him and all believers enabled him to face whatever hardships came his way. Even they could be used to shed the light of the knowledge of God in Christ into the lives of others (vv. 16-18).

Paul has a wonderful way with words. His images are often striking and difficult to forget. None more so than those he shares here. He compares this life or this present body as being a "tent." A tent is a temporary thing. You take it with you. You move it around but it's not something in which you will always live. Hopefully you will have a more permanent house. Here Paul says that such a house, such a body will be constructed by God and that it will be "eternal in the heavens," that is, a body, a house that will never breakdown, never need repairs, but last forever. Paul has already written in some detail about this (see 1 Corinthians ch. 15, especially vv. 35ff) (v. 1).

Mark 3:20-35

One of the points Paul makes in our reading today is that as an apostle of Christ, he, like Christ, had experienced suffering. Today's gospel lesson begins to show some of the suffering that Christ began to endure, even very early in his ministry.

In the first part of this chapter, we see that Jesus has been out and about, mostly healing people, casting out "unclean spirits," making people whole. He healed a man with a withered hand one sabbath right there in a synagogue. That ticked off many as such an act was thought to be work, something you were not supposed to do on the sabbath.

Next Jesus goes to the lakeside and spends a great deal of time healing the sick and curing many of diseases and unclean spirits. Many from all around were flocking to him there. His reputation was growing, something that would not have been welcomed by many of the leaders.

Then he selects his disciples, the ones who he will give special training to and send out to do the same kind of things he has been doing. Even Jesus could not be everywhere. This, too, would not have made many of the religious leaders very happy.

Next he comes home (today' reading) — to Nazareth. Perhaps he expects a little warmer welcome there, a respite from the suspicion and growing opposition. Alas, it was not to be. Folks again flocked to him, seeking, no doubt, to see him out of curiosity or need. For many, he was not welcome there anymore. They had heard things about him, things he had supposedly been saying and doing. He was, you might say in their eyes, an embarrassment. So, a delegation goes to his family there — presumably his mother, brothers, and sisters (no mention of Joseph, who perhaps had died). Their message to the family was basically: "You better go and get your son. He's lost his mind. He's going to bring shame on you and us all if he keeps on like this." And his family comes to do just that — take him away from the public and, no doubt, to try to get him under control.

Among the people there that day were scribes or teachers of the law all the way from Jerusalem. Isn't that interesting? They were following Jesus. They were keeping a close eye on him, which tells us just how concerned they were about what he was doing and the impact it was having. No doubt they were the ones whispering in the ears of others and even speaking out loud, accusing Jesus of being possessed himself by a demon or being the devil himself!

Jesus, no doubt more than a little hurt by this rejection and outright attack, nonetheless begins to try to show them how irrational they are being. It's as if he is saying, "Well, if I am the devil, I am certainly pretty stupid, because I am working against my own agenda. I mean, you have been following me. You know what I have been doing. I've been casting out demons and unclean spirits. I've been healing people. Don't you think that a strange thing for the devil to do? If this is true, then the devil's house is divided and a house divided will surely fall. Indeed, it is falling. The devil, like a strong man, has been overcome, tied up and I am plundering his house! I am taking back what he thought was his, for the kingdom of God is at hand. Why can't you see this?"

Then Jesus makes a dire announcement. Some there had become so lost, so hard-hearted and closed-minded that they were attributing good (him and his works) to evil. They could not or would not see that God was working through him. Instead, they were so afraid, or jealous, or mindful of their own position and power that they could actually attribute his deeds to the devil! To do so is to make oneself beyond being able to receive forgiveness, as they are so utterly lost and self-deceived. This is what sometimes has been called "the unpardonable sin." It is not so much one act or sin but a state of being so opposed and blind to the work of God that their hearts are not open to seeing the truth, to repentance and forgiveness. It is not that God does not seek to forgive, it's that they are so utterly beyond even seeing their need for it.

As hurt as Jesus surely must have felt by their rejection and accusations, surely he also felt pity for them.

What must have hurt even more, however, was that even his own family did not understand him and was being persuaded by the views of others. So it is that when he is told that they are there, he, I think somewhat sadly, asks, "Well, who is my family?" Without waiting for an answer, he looks upon his new disciples and others who saw and accepted him for who he was, and says, "Here is my family — those who know and do the will of God," which is what he was seeking to do with all his heart.

Application

Wounded Healers. I have never known anyone who has suffered more than a friend of mine. She had had numerous physical ailments, as well as mental challenges. Several times she has been close to death, with even family members being called in, only to be brought back to life. Still to this day she has to live with chronic pain and her family has known great suffering as well from many causes. I have often prayed for and with her.

What amazes me is her faith. There is a joy that radiates from her. I cannot really explain or adequately describe it. Had I endured just one or two of the things that have fallen upon her, I think I would have become embittered, depressed, and perhaps even given up my faith. But not her. When you hear her talk, when you see her face, she is aglow. Being in her presence is like standing in warm sunshine on a cold winter day. For in spite of her suffering, which is immense, she talks of her joy, her gratitude, her faith, and how God has seen her through so much. She says over and over that she is not afraid of suffering and death anymore. She knows she is in the hands of God and that nothing can take her away. So no wonder others who are suffering often ask for her to visit and pray for them. She is a walking witness, a glowing example of how the living Christ can move us from suffering to triumph.

In today's passage from 2 Corinthians, we see another example of this — Paul. There is very little suffering that Paul did not endure. Quite often he was at death's door. He was shipwrecked, stoned, hungry, sick, snakebitten, and persecuted by enemies and so-called friends alike. But through it all, he learned that God's grace was sufficient to see him through anything. In fact, he learned that his suffering was but a reflection of the suffering of Christ, and that God could even use that to shed light onto the love and grace of God given in Christ.

We need examples like Paul's and my friend's, for we, too, will face trials and suffering. We are truly like clay pots — easily cracked and broken. We are fragile. Christians are not known for avoiding suffering. Some seem to preach and teach otherwise — that somehow we can avoid it. Not if you ask Paul. What distinguishes Christians is not that we avoid it but how we see it, what we do with it. We face suffering and even death not as those without hope, for ours is a risen Lord! Our faith is such that God can even use our suffering to bear witness to the light and love of Christ. So we can face it with confidence, knowing that Christ is with us and that nothing can take us away from the love of God which is ours in Christ.

An Alternative Application

Mark 3:20-35. "The Unpardonable Sin." This is a good opportunity to cover a passage and teaching that has caused a great deal of misunderstanding and even pain, as there are more people than you think who, for many reasons, have convinced themselves that they are beyond forgiveness and that they have in fact committed the unpardonable sin. A sound sermon will go into some detail about what this isn't. It is not one sin that dooms. Think of all the people in the Bible — from Moses to David and even the disciples themselves who committed some very serious sins. Yet, they experienced forgiveness. Even the thief on the cross who had probably committed many heinous acts, perhaps even murder, receives a word of freeing grace from Jesus.

What Jesus is referring to here is a persistent state of denying what is good, of thinking of it as evil, and evil as good. It is to become so twisted in heart and mind that one no longer even sees the need for or seeks the truth or forgiveness. Isaiah says it this way, "Woe to those who call evil good and good evil, who put darkness for light and light for darkness, who put bitter for sweet and sweet for bitter" (Isaiah 5:20). Those in today's gospel reading who are actually attributing the life-giving works of Jesus to the devil are an example of this very state. What he was doing was by the power of the Holy Spirit. It was good. It was making people whole. To be in such a state that you could not see or acknowledge that, or think that it was in fact the work of the devil, is to be in a place where you are not able or open to receiving forgiveness. Although you may wish with all your heart to forgive someone, and even do forgive them in your heart, if they see no need for it or aren't open to receiving it, then they have placed themselves in an unpardonable state. Indeed, one of the sure signs that one is not in such a state is concern about it! If you are worried that you have committed it, good news! That in and of itself shows you have not.

Do you see what I see?

Sellers will sometimes advertise with the initials "WYSIWYG" — What you see is what you get. It is an endorsement that reflects our dependence upon our eyes, our reliance upon what we see.

Toothpaste makers boast that "four out of five dentists surveyed..." — an endorsement that reflects our trust in experts and professionals. Book jackets feature an assortment of endorsements, as the publisher assumes that you and I will find there the name of someone whose judgment we admire or whose taste we trust.

But, there's nothing that human beings believe as much as *seeing*. More than anything, advertisers will rely on a "see for yourself" approach. They do not just tell us about the automobile — they show it to us, doing the things that we need or want our vehicles to do. The restaurant menu includes pictures of featured items, knowing that we will be attracted to what we see. Everyone from cereal makers to law firms pay close attention to "packaging," knowing that we make so many of our judgments based on appearances.

The good folks of Missouri express this truth in their motto — the "show me" state. When we want something proven to us — when we need to be convinced — we have to see it for ourselves. "Seeing is believing," we say.

Except that it's not. It turns out that seeing and believing are quite different and separate matters, as we will discover in this week's readings.

1 Samuel 15:34—16:13

This is a marvelous episode, a watershed day in Israel's history. The flag that waves over the modern state of Israel still bears the star of that nearly forgotten youngest son whom Samuel anointed that day. While he seemed least important among his brothers, the angels a thousand years later would refer to his family's hometown as "the city of David." And decades after that, the great affirmation of the Palm Sunday crowd was that Jesus was "the son of David."

It must be noted, however, that this dramatically important moment was born out of a moment of sadness. The story of Saul is an unutterably tragic one. He is, at the start, God's chosen man, full of promise and potential, and yet he ends in such sorrow and disgrace. The final verses of 1 Samuel 15 make for a grim — and early — epitaph on the life and reign of this tragic son of Kish.

We should note in the next breath, however, that sorrow and disgrace never get the last word with God. He does not wave the white flag and walk away when things do not go as they should. Saul's end may be tragic, but God has a good plan — and man — in store for his people.

God's regrets about Saul prompt him to send Samuel on a mission. He is to go to Bethlehem to anoint one of the sons of Jesse to be the next king of Israel.

Samuel, who has been notably bold in earlier episodes (see, for example, 1 Samuel 3:18; 7:3; 12:1-25; 13:10-14; 15:12-33), is uncharacteristically fearful about his assignment here. "How can I go? If Saul hears of it, he will kill me," Samuel worries aloud.

While Samuel had been fearless in face-to-face confrontations with Saul, he was reluctant to go behind Saul's back. Perhaps Samuel was intimidated by the prospect of defying protocol in this blatant way. Perhaps he sensed the murderous paranoia in Saul that would later manifest itself in his treatment of David.

Meanwhile, the apprehension of the elders of Bethlehem at Samuel's arrival seems strange to us. Certainly this unarmed old man could not have seemed threatening in any conventional sense. The elders' trepidation, therefore, must be read as an indication of the reputation Samuel had gained in Israel (see 3:21) as a man of God and a spiritual force.

On the other hand, while the mood of the Bethlehem elders may be a kind of tribute to Samuel, it reflects badly on the elders themselves. After all, if Samuel is a powerful man of God, shouldn't we welcome him rather than dread him? These men of Bethlehem are reminiscent of the later residents of the Gerasenes, who chose to evict Jesus (Luke 8:35-37) rather than welcoming his presence and his power.

For all of Samuel's credentials as a man of God, however, he is still a man, and he demonstrates his humanity in the superficiality of his response to Jesse's oldest son, Eliab. We talk about the phenomenon of "love at first sight." Samuel bordered on an even more dangerous venture: anointing at first sight. He took one look at the apparently impressive Eliab and concluded, "Surely the Lord's anointed is now before the Lord."

We are forever, it seems, judging books by their covers. We continually need the reminder that God first gave to Samuel: "The Lord does not see as mortals see; they look on the outward appearance, but the Lord looks on the heart." The familiar Christmas song asks the question, "Do you see what I see?" Perhaps the question for us to consider is of a still higher order: Do we see what God sees?

We would do well, swimming upstream against both our nature and our culture, to make sure that our churches focus on what our Lord focuses on. And, on a personal level, we do well to remind ourselves about what God looks at and sees in us. It's an easy thing to pose habitually for a world that is impressed by externals, only to disappoint in the end the audience of one, for whom we promised to live.

Finally, David is brought before Samuel, and the Lord instructs Samuel to anoint him. At that moment, and from that time, "the spirit of the Lord came mightily upon David," and so we are presented with a bit of sacramental theology in story form: a beautiful and mysterious recipe of the ordinary and the holy, of the physical and the spiritual, of the human and the divine.

It is God who does the choosing, but it is a human who does the anointing. And it is a common element that Samuel pours on David, yet it is the Lord's Spirit that came upon him.

2 Corinthians 5:6-10 (11-13) 14-17

We have three young daughters at home, one in elementary school, one is a preschooler, and the youngest is still in diapers. As every parent knows, the needs of young children sometimes get you up in the middle of the night.

How many nights have I stumbled blindly in the dark, trying to find my way to meet the need? And if, on our way to bed, we had been too tired to pick up the kids' toys that might be in the hallway or the bedrooms, the midnight walk can be a mildly treacherous one. One hesitates to turn on the lights, lest the others might be awakened, and so I gingerly feel my way down the dark hall and into the dark bedroom, hoping not to step on something that will hurt me, or make a noise, or be broken under my foot.

Paul's early words in our selected text juxtapose an unlikely pair of images: confidence and sightlessness. "We are always confident," Paul asserts, only to follow with the observation that "we walk by faith, not by sight."

Well, as the television commercial says, "That's just not natural." When we human beings can't see where we're going, we don't look and act confident at all. Instead, we are slow, hesitant, tentative. We feel vulnerable and uncertain. And yet Paul claims and exudes great confidence, even though he walks "not by sight."

It isn't natural, to be sure, but it is sensible, for it simply reflects a transfer. As one might transfer funds from one account to another, so we transfer our confidence. What comes naturally to us is to have confidence in ourselves, our abilities, our senses, and such. Paul, however, had made the switch from confidence in himself to confidence in the Lord — his love, his grace, his providence. He walked, therefore, by faith, not by sight, and he did so with an unnatural but understandable confidence.

The struggle that Paul does articulate is reminiscent of the one he shares in his letter to the Philippians (1:21-24). We might call it a life-or-death struggle, although it is not the conventional sort. For the average mortal, a life-or-death struggle suggests a life-threatening situation, and the natural struggle to cling to this life and preserve this body. Not so for Paul, however. For him, the body represents being away from home; to die, for Paul, is to go home, for that will mean being with the Lord. In either case, however, Paul understands that he — and we — operate with the same, single modus operandi: "We make it our aim to please him."

Meanwhile, we all find ourselves marveling from time to time at someone who manages to keep going in spite of difficult circumstances. The athlete who turns in a heroic performance for his team in spite of his injury. The mother who keeps the home and family going in spite of the death of her spouse and financial hardship. The saintly soul who keeps caring for others and brightening their lives in spite of his or her own personal burdens. We marvel at such people, and we wonder how they keep going.

Or, in the midst of our own difficulties, we lie in bed and wonder how we ourselves will keep going.

The apostle Paul, who was no stranger to difficulties and hardship, offers an insight and key: "The love of Christ urges us on."

It is worth asking ourselves what it is that urges us on. For some folks, it is ambition — often a selfish or unwholesome ambition — that drives them. Some are urged on by their appetites, some by pride, some by fear.

At our human best, of course, we are urged on by love. I think of a woman I knew who had a severely handicapped child. He was not expected to live much beyond infancy, but he did. He lived into his teenage years, which meant that he had grown quite big, even though he still could do almost nothing for himself. His mother was an average-sized woman, and she remained his primary caregiver. Every meal, every stairway, every bathroom need, every car trip, every bedtime and awakening was an immense chore for her. How did she have the strength to do it each day, all day, day after day? She was urged on by love. It was, as we say, a labor of love.

But now see how altogether lovely this motivation of Paul's is: It is the love of Christ that urges him on. Not Paul's love, but Christ's love.

It is a noble thing if I am animated and motivated by my love. It is still more full of beauty and joy, however, when it is his love that urges me on.

Mark 4:26-34

I led a Bible study series in my church on the parables of Jesus. At the first session, I wanted to get a sense for what the folks already knew about the parables. I asked them to define the word "parable." And I asked them to guess how many parables of Jesus we had recorded in the Bible.

Next, I asked the participants to draw two columns on a piece of paper, and I invited them to write down the first seven parables that came to their minds. In the left-hand column, they were to write whichever parables came immediately to mind; and, if that didn't amount to seven, put in the right-hand column the parables they had to think about in order to remember.

Even though most folks guessed that Jesus told twenty or more parables, they had a hard time coming up with seven. And the ones that did come to mind immediately for most folks, not surprisingly, were the longer stories — the good Samaritan, the prodigal son, the sower.

Several people in the class said that the parable of the mustard seed was one of the first that came to mind. When I read them the passage found in this week's gospel lesson, however, they didn't much recognize it. They were thinking, instead, of Jesus' teaching about having faith the size of a mustard seed (see Luke 17:5-6).

Here we are presented with two of Jesus' parables, but they are short, and probably not on the radar for most of our members. Furthermore, the theme of both parables is the kingdom of God. This is an undeniably prominent theme in the synoptic gospels, and yet it may not have garnered proportionate attention and interest in our churches. While it is manifestly important to John the Baptist and to Jesus, it may not rank as being very important to us.

The two selected parables present us with some similarities, which we in turn may consider as larger principles.

First, as we have already noted, they are both expressly parables of the kingdom.

Second, they are both organic parables. One wonders where Jesus would turn for his illustrations if he were embarking on his earthly ministry in this time and place. Would he use the contemporary realities of email and iPods, of cyberspace and outer space? Or would he stay still with the timeless realities of planting and harvest, of nature and relationships? In this passage, Jesus' illustrations are typically organic: samples taken from the field and the garden.

Third, there is process. One of the depicted realities of the kingdom is that it is not a static thing, but rather it is in process. And a very particular sort of process at that: growth and reproduction. In this respect, the parables are doubly revealing. For they not only serve as metaphor, analogy, or allegory for some spiritual truth, the organic ones also reveal that certain realities always characterize God's work. Whether that work is the natural world we see around us, or whether it is in the invisible stuff of the kingdom, it is God's work. And three of the hallmarks of God's work are growth, reproduction, and abundance. The process is growth, which includes reproduction, and leads to plenty.

The kingdom's growth is particularly central to the parable of the mustard seed. Jesus illustrates the truth that the kingdom starts small — so small that it might seem fragile and insignificant. But that small start will grow, and in the end it will be large and encompassing.

Charles Wesley captures this truth beautifully in a hymn, "See How Great A Flame Aspies" from 1749:

When he first the work begun,
small and feeble was his day;
now the Word doth swiftly run,
now it wins its widening way;
more and more it spreads and grows,
ever mighty to prevail;
sin's strongholds it now o'erthrows,
shakes the trembling gates of hell.

Application

Samuel was impressed by what he saw when he looked at Eliab. But human beings are not a "what you see is what you get" proposition. What is visible is only a tiny fraction — and a sometimes misleading fraction, at that — of what you get with a human being.

And just as there is more than meets the eye with human beings, so, too, with the rest of life and the things of God. So it is, for example, with the kingdom of God.

There is surely more than meets the eye with the mustard seed. By Jesus' own description, the mustard seed is such a tiny thing that it seems the height of improbability to hope that it should become anything substantial. Indeed, that it should become anything at all. And, likewise, the seed that the man scatters on the ground disappears into an invisible process. And although the man who scattered it is not privy to what happens or how, he plants the seeds with the faith that they will generate a harvest.

We sometimes use the phrase "the eyes of faith." The idiom acknowledges a truth that faith sees things that our ordinary vision is not in touch with. So it was that by faith Abraham "looked forward to the city...

whose architect and builder is God" (Hebrews 11:10). And so, just as the farmer's planting is by faith, not by sight, so is all of life under God.

Alternative Applications

2 Corinthians 5:6-10 (11-13) 14-17. "We Aim to Please." The resolution Paul comes to is, on the surface, a simple one. Yet it is a profound point, and it offers clarity and wisdom to all of us. "Whether we are at home or away," he writes, "we make it our aim to please him."

"We aim to please" would be a worthy subject for a sermon. And we might broaden Paul's struggle in order to apply his wisdom more broadly. That is, rather than saying merely "at home or away," we might go further. Let us say, "Whether we are where we want to be or not; whether our circumstances are ideal or disappointing; whether we are in tumult or in calm; whether we are being praised or persecuted; we aim to please him." That would be a good policy and perspective for the man or woman of God in every situation.

Mark 4:26-34. "God's Tree House." The Lord says to a bird, "I am preparing a place that you can call home — a shelter and a shade where you can build your nest." The bird replies, "Great! Let me see it!" And so the Lord reaches into his pocket, and pulls out a mustard seed. "There it is," he says.

It's only because the bird's eyes are designed to be able to see such tiny things that it doesn't require a second look. Still, the bird is bewildered. "I thought you were going to provide a place to build my nest. This looks more like board than room."

"No, this is what I have in store for you."

"A tiny seed that I could eat and not even be satisfied is where you want me to make my home?"

We are the birds. God is always preparing and providing for us. Yet we are so often bewildered by his plans. He wants Moses to appear before Pharaoh with only a shepherd's staff. He wants Gideon to go into battle with just a few dozen questionably qualified soldiers. He wants to feed the multitude with a little boy's bag lunch. He wants to make disciples of all nations with just a handful of heretofore unreliable and under-educated men.

He is the God of the mustard seed.

Looking for heroes

The year was 1934. Times were difficult around the world. Times were especially difficult in the repressed economic and political climate of post-World War Germany. But recovery was in sight. A group of theologians at Württemberg saw a rising star of hope and together penned a declaration of faith that would be signed by 600 pastors of churches and fourteen theology professors at seminaries.

The promising statement of this group included these words: "We are full of thanks to God that he, as Lord of history, has given us Adolf Hitler, our leader and savior from our difficult lot. We acknowledge that we, with body and soul, are bound and dedicated to the German state and to its Fuhrer."

This is quite astounding, isn't it? In retrospect, we can only shudder at the horrific and demonic twists of history that could produce such unqualified devotion to a man who would later rip God's world apart and destroy, insofar as he was able, both the church and the children of God.

That same year, 1934, Hitler summoned a group of church leaders to his office. Martin Niemöller was among this group of leaders. Niemöller had been a great hero in the German Navy during the previous war, commanding a submarine that caused massive destruction to the Allied fleet. He had been ordained in 1929 and became the beloved pastor of the Church of Jesus Christ at Dahlem, yet he remained an ardent supporter of Hitler, often speaking out in favor of the Fuhrer.

Hitler's meeting began cordially enough. But suddenly, Hermann Goering burst into the room with a charge of treason against Niemöller. Hitler raged in an angry tirade. Finally, he regained his composure and told Niemöller, "You confine yourself to the church. I'll take care of the German people."

But Niemöller stood and quietly replied, "Herr Reichskanzler, you said just now, 'I will take care of the German people.' But we, too, as Christians and churchmen, have a responsibility toward the German people. That responsibility was entrusted to us by God, and neither you nor anyone in this world has the power to take it from us."

Hitler knew a showdown when he saw it. Niemöller went to trial and was convicted of misusing his pulpit for political reasons. Hitler cowardly refused to pardon him, declaring, "It is Niemöller or me."

We need heroes who are willing to stand up to the bullying powers of our world. We need examples of strength and commitment that will steel our nerves, quicken our resolve, and reinforce the godly values that drive us. In today's lectionary passages we have several examples of heroes who can build our courage to live for God.

1 Samuel 17:(1a, 4-11, 19-23) 32-49

The story of David and Goliath is almost too familiar to preach well. Perhaps a fresh entry point would be the idea of boasting which pervades the battle line scene.

Boasting can be an invigorating sport. Two lads found a stray puppy and both wanted to take it home. They finally decided to hold a contest of skills; they would tell fantastic stories, and the bigger liar would get to keep the dog. As they swapped tales, the local pastor walked by and asked what they were up to. When they told him, the pastor said, "Boys, boys! You shouldn't do that! Why, when I was your age, I never told a lie!"

The youngsters looked at each other regretfully. Then the oldest said to the minister, "Well, that's got to be the biggest fib of all. Here's your puppy."

Some people boast out of pride. In his story, "How the Camel Got Its Hump," Rudyard Kipling took a potshot at prideful boasters like Goliath. According to Kipling, when God first created earth and the animals, each was given a unique job. The camel, however, refused to work, and whenever any of the other animals asked for his help, he just said, "Humph!" and walked away.

God saw and began to collect all of the camel's "Humphs" and then dumped them back onto the camel. That, according to Kipling, is how the camel got its hump.

Prideful people are like that, humphing their way through life. Last century people used to say of Mussolini "He could strut sitting down," and "He was a solemn procession of one." The Philistine Goliath was probably a distant relative.

The problem with pride is that it is a deceptive measure. One young boy wanted to know how high he had grown, so he made a ruler and measured himself. He was nine feet tall! When you measure yourself by tools you craft for yourself, you are likely bigger in your own eyes than when seen by those who use an outside standard.

On the other hand, there can also be a good pride, like the pride David showed. He measured himself and others by both the infinity and the love of God (see Psalm 8). And when he assessed the situation with Goliath, he knew who had the power. Certainly not Goliath.

In her novel, *Out of Africa*, Isak Dineson wrote, "Pride is faith in the idea that God had when he made us. A proud man is conscious of the idea and aspires to it." That may well describe young David on the battlefield while all others were measuring armor. Certainly Phillips Brooks had it right when he said that the way to be humble "is not to stoop until you are smaller than yourself, but to stand at your real height against some higher nature that will show you what the real smallness of your greatness is."

2 Corinthians 6:1-13

The ancient rabbis said that God made Adam out of the dust of the ground so that he would always love the earth and feel the wonder of it in his fingers. Then, because Adam was incomplete by himself, God made Eve to complement him as an equal. God didn't make Eve from his head, said the rabbis, for then she would rule over him. Nor did God make Eve from Adam's feet, because then he would be tempted to always walk over her. Instead God made Eve from one of Adam's ribs, at his side, close to his heart, so that they would know the joy of friendship and partnership.

Certainly that reflects what we know from our own lives. We all need friendship. We need companionship. We need another to stand with us through the struggles of life, to be close to us, to love us and to support us. These are ideas that flow from Paul's pen as he writes this letter to the Corinthian church. It is at least the fourth letter he has written (we only have his second and fourth in our New Testaments as 1 and 2 Corinthians), and each one was forged out of pain and love.

In the lectionary passage for today, Paul rehearses both his love for the church and also his suffering on behalf of the church. He is their hero, in a real sense. He is one who sticks by when all others leave, and who has tried to absorb into his own body the pain that might otherwise come by attacks directed at the church.

It is interesting that Paul begins with this theme in chapter 1 of the letter. Nine times in five verses (1 Corinthians 1:3-7) Paul expresses the idea of "comfort" received and given. Always it is in the context of hardship, and always, as here, it is expression derived first from God. The whole of 2 Corinthians breathes with that idea. In fact, the letter closes with one of the most pointed expressions of the trinity anywhere in the Bible: "May the grace of the Lord Jesus Christ, and the love of God, and the fellowship of the Holy Spirit be with you all" (2 Corinthians 13:14). It may well be said that Paul's idea of companionship and mutual care is derived from the doctrine of the Trinity.

There have been two major schools of thought on the Trinity over the years of Christian theology. The first uses the psychological analogy to talk about how one person can exist in different expressions — a man who is a son to parents, husband to spouse, and father to children, all in complete ways, all originating from the same personal identity, yet all unique in interaction. The other way of thinking about the Trinity uses sociological analogies and talks about a single deity that exists as three unique persons (much like we talk of one humanity and many persons, each of whom is fully human). This second way of looking at the Trinity is very enlightening when brought alongside Paul's expressions of care here. If the value and existence at the center of the universe is community, then the fullest expression of human identity, made in the image of God, is care and commitment.

Years ago, a reporter had a happenstance encounter with Henry Ford. Not wanting to miss an opportunity he introduced himself, spoke with admiration, and sought some advice from Ford. In response, Ford asked him a question: "Who is your best friend?"

The reporter wasn't sure how to answer, but Henry Ford was certain. He reached into his pocket, pulled out a scrap of paper and a pencil, and wrote a note, which that reporter kept until his death a few years ago. The note said: "Your best friend is he who brings out the best in you."

This is certainly what Paul had in mind when he told the stories of his suffering on behalf of the Corinthian congregation. He was not merely boasting, but seeking instead to bring out the best in them.

Furthermore, Paul's understanding of how a friend brought out the best in his friend was crafted in the spiritual exercises of faith. For it was Jesus who had first brought out the best in him. The words of Ben E. King, from his song, "Stand By Me," come to mind — won't be afraid.

Mark 4:35-41

Psychiatrist, Viktor Frankl, often wrote about the meaninglessness of his patients' lives. He was able to sympathize with them in powerful ways because he had spent part of the WWII in a concentration camp. He remembered the dark weeks of 1944 vividly: the numbness of the gray days, the cold sameness of every dreary morning.

Then, like a bolt of bright colors came the stunning whisper that the Allies had landed at Normandy. The push was on. The Germans were running. The tide of the war had turned. "By Christmas we'll be released!" they told each other.

Frankl recalled the changes that took place in the camp: every day the workers went out to their same jobs, but their hearts were lighter and the work seemed a bit easier. Each meal time they peered into the same cauldron of slop, but somehow it seemed less difficult to swallow since every bite was a countdown to freedom. The stress in each barracks community was the same: people fighting for a little privacy, jealousies and dislikes aired in spicy retorts; yet forgiveness came a little easier those days, for the ups and downs of the present dimmed as the promising future came closer.

It was interesting, said Frankl, that fewer people died during those months. Even the weakest ones began to cling tenaciously to life.

But Christmas 1944 passed and the Allied troops never came. There were setbacks and defeats, and the bits of news smuggled into the camp made no more promises. Then, said Frankl, people began to die. No new diseases came into the camp. Rations remained the same. There was no change in working conditions. But people began to die as if some terrible plague had struck. Indeed, it had. It was the plague of hopelessness, the epidemic of despair.

Studies show that we can live forty to sixty days without food, eight to twelve days without water, and maybe three minutes without oxygen. But without hope, we cannot survive even a moment. Without hope, we die. Without hope, there is no reason to wake up in the morning. Without hope, we are like the disciples nearly swamped on the Sea of Galilee — frightened and overwhelmed by death.

But then comes Jesus! Like the Allied troops that eventually broke open the death camps, Jesus emerges from the clouds and storms of life and breathes into the hearts of his disciples new hope and new courage. Jesus calms the storms, and a true hero is born.

Years ago, when Dr. Arthur Gossip lost his wife and the overwhelming threat of death closed in on him, he recalled Jesus calming the waters of Galilee and he preached a sermon that echoed the themes of Christian's trek toward the Celestial City in Bunyan's *The Pilgrim's Progress*. Said Dr. Gossip: "Our hearts are very frail, and there are places where the road is very steep and very lonely. Standing in the roaring Jordan, cold with its dreadful chill and very conscious of its terror, of its rushing, I... call back to you who one day will have your turn to cross it, 'Be of good cheer, my brother, for I feel the bottom and it is sound.' "

That sound bottom, in the surging terrors of life, is found wherever the footprints of Jesus fall.

Application

"Screw your courage to the sticking-place," says Lady Macbeth to her doomed husband in Shakespeare's tragedy, "and we'll not fail." But fail they do, and no amount of courage in the world can save them or turn them into heroes.

Courage is a funny thing. It's a bit like happiness: the more you seek it, the more you demand it, the more you try to call it up, the less it shows its face.

Words can stir us to courage. Who would not rally around the "I have a dream..." speech delivered by Martin Luther King Jr., in 1963? Who would not feel stronger listening to the dogged determination of Winston Churchill in the dark days of 1940: "Let us... brace ourselves to our duty, and so bear ourselves that if the British Empire and its Commonwealth last for a thousand years, men will still say, 'This was their finest hour!' "

Courage thrives best in the company of heroes. David said, in one of his Psalms, "In God I trust; I will not be afraid!" (Psalm 56:10). That was the thought in Dorthea Day's mind when she changed the wording of William Henley's self-centered poem "Invictus" and brought about a testimony for Christian heroes who follow their great hero, Jesus:

Out of the light that dazzles me,
Bright as the sun from pole to pole,
I thank the God I know to be
For Christ, the conqueror of my soul.

Beyond this place of sin and tears
That life with Him! And His the aid,
That, spite the menace of the years,
Keeps, and shall keep, me unafraid.

Since His the sway of circumstance
I will not wince nor cry aloud.
Under the rule which men call chance
My head, with joy, is humbly bowed.

I have no fear though strait the gate;
He cleared from punishment the scroll.
Christ is the Master of my fate;
Christ is the Captain of my soul.

An Alternative Application
1 Samuel 17:(1a, 4-11, 19-23) 32-49. The story of David and Goliath may make a great theme for today's worship. Even though the idea of killing enemies is politically incorrect, there are many more facets of the larger biblical story that make great handles to grasp in communicating this message. First, there is the idea of questioning where God's power is to be found. Is it in the army with the biggest stick (guns, armaments, and the like)? Certainly that was a theme in the world of ancient Israel's day. And it is often found in our own settings. Might makes right. We do because we can.

Second, there is a theme of honor. Can someone boast crudely and not be held to account? It is not only Israel's army that hears the insults of Goliath, but also the nation and God. There must be some form of redressing that honors fairness and the true expression of values in society.

Third, there is salvation history. While the single battle between the Philistines and the Israelites has its consequences, the more important focus ought to be on the purpose for Israel's existence in the land of Canaan. Why should God's people be there? What is the larger witness to be given, and how does that witness become fleshed out in the life of the nation?

These ideas have ready application to nations today, and to the life of the church.

Proper 8 / Pentecost 5 / Ordinary Time 13
2 Samuel 1:1, 17-27
2 Corinthians 8:7-15
Mark 5:21-43
Timothy Cargal

Even apostles hate passing the hat

If you are like most pastors, then you probably dread preaching the annual stewardship sermon or (gasp!) stewardship sermon series. One of the widespread cultural stereotypes about ministers is that preachers are always asking for money, and mainline pastors are usually so afraid of falling into the stereotype that they hardly ever preach about money. Our concerns about stewardship sermons are legendary. Several years ago a television show was producing a segment on the training of preachers (imagine that!), and in interviewing one of the leaders in the field of homiletic continuing education it came out that preachers dreaded preaching stewardship sermons more than any other topic. We all have to do it ("The stewardship committee chair made me!"), and we all hate it.

For most pastors, stewardship season comes in the fall. It is a happy coincidence that the autumn is traditionally harvest time, when society is full of reminders of our great bounty and thanksgiving. Not a bad time to choose to promote stewardship as a faithful response to God's blessing, but if we were honest we would admit that it is just a coincidence. What really drives most of those fall stewardship sermons is the work on the annual church budget that must be approved before the start of the year. We keep telling our congregations (and ourselves) that stewardship is about thankfulness and faithfulness, but the timing betrays the unfortunate truth.

So if we hate preaching stewardship sermons so much — and some of our congregants make no bones about expressing their hatred for listening to them — and if we have managed to relegate them to the autumn stewardship campaign, then why am I bringing it up now? For many families school is just letting out, and almost everyone's mind is focused on getting away on vacation. Wouldn't a stewardship sermon now just reinforce the stereotype that preachers are always asking for money?

Well, one reason for preaching on stewardship now is to break that connection with annual church budget planning (unless, of course, your fiscal year begins July 1). It is the beginning of Pentecost season (or "Ordinary Time," depending on your tradition) when the liturgical emphasis is on growth in the Christian life. Another reason is that a group of church funding specialists gives as the number one way "to raise less money for your church" is to "preach stewardship once a year in the fall." But most importantly, now is the time because the lectionary presents us with one of the prime New Testament texts on stewardship. And take some comfort from this: the text suggests that even the apostle Paul hated passing the hat!

2 Samuel 1:1, 17-27

The psalm of lamentation contained in the Old Testament lesson is different in form and purpose than the laments found in the psalter. There the lament psalms take the form of petitions for assistance during times of extreme distress. This lament is a mourning song, a funeral dirge if you will, that expresses both the national and personal sense of loss that David felt on the death of Saul and Jonathan in battle against the Philistines. It is one of two psalms in the Deuteronomic History drawn from a collection called the "Book of Jasher" (or, "Book of the Upright"; see Joshua 10:12-13). Many scholars believe that it may be an authentic psalm by David himself.

The note in verse 18 that David "ordered that The Song of the Bow be taught to the people of Judah" has been the subject of much scholarly debate. The Hebrew Masoretic text does not have the words "the song of," which translators have added because of the lament that follows. (The Greek version of the Old Testament reads simply, "he ordered [it] to be taught," omitting any reference to "the Bow.") Although it is possible that David might have ordered military training in the use of the bow in response to the renewed threat from the Philistines, the context makes it more likely that "the Bow" is either the title or musical genre of the lament itself.

Scholars also are divided on the connotation that is to be drawn from the references to Israel's "high places" as the location where Saul and Jonathan fell (vv. 19, 25). Clearly in the view of the Deuteronomistic Historian, the "high places" as the sites of worship of foreign deities were a major reason for the judgments on Israel and Judah. But since there is no reference to religious activity within the lament, the direct reference here is probably to "the heights" of Mount Gilboa (vv. 6, 21). That the "high places" lacked any cultic references in the original context of the Book of Jasher does not, however, rule out the possibility of a subtle sense of foreboding here in 2 Samuel. Just as Israel's first king fell on the heights of Gilboa, so the nation itself would ultimately fall on its high places for having turned away from God.

The lament divides into two stanzas. The first (vv. 19-24) is directed toward the people of Israel calling for them to mourn the loss of the king and crown prince. It is framed by references to improper and proper responses to this news. For the "daughters of the Philistines," word of their defeat and deaths would have been an occasion for exultation (v. 20); for the "daughters of Israel," it was a summons to weeping and mourning (v. 24). The psalm suggests two reasons for why Saul and Jonathan's deaths are to be mourned: first, because they had shown themselves to be valiant and effective warriors (vv. 22-23), and second, because Saul's reign had brought a measure of economic prosperity and political advancement to Israel (v. 24b). Given the protracted animosity that Saul demonstrated toward David (1 Samuel 18:6—28:25), what is amazing is the sincere respect that David held for Saul as "the Lord's anointed" through the time of his death (see especially 2 Samuel 1:2-16).

The second stanza of the lament (vv. 25-27) is much more personal, and directed to David's fallen comrade rather than to the surviving people. He refers to Jonathan as "my brother," and extols the love they shared for one another, "passing the love of women" (v. 26). Given all the concern with homosexuality and the church in recent decades, it is not surprising that some have seized on this description to suggest a sexual relationship between David and Jonathan. Bruce Birch (New Interpreter's Bible, 2:1208) has correctly observed, however, that the phrase probably reveals far more about the status of women in the society than about David and Jonathan's relationship. Love was not the basis for marriage in that culture; marriage was fundamentally about economic interests, most notably the supplying of heirs. "Love of women in such limited contexts might indeed pale in comparison to the deep and personal commitment" between men who had formed personal and political covenants between them (see 1 Samuel 18:1-5).

2 Corinthians 8:7-15

The composition history of 2 Corinthians is complex and difficult to reconstruct from the available evidence. Space does not permit even an overview of the issues here, but any recent critical commentary can familiarize you with the literary problems and proposed solutions. What is important to note from a homiletical standpoint is that this lectionary reading is part of a note written by Paul to the Corinthian church to encourage them to bring to completion a collection for Christians in Jerusalem (see 1 Corinthians 16:1-4). It is often asserted that this collection was specifically for famine relief (cf. Acts 11:27-30), but that connection is historically dubious. More likely the collection was conceived as a way of consolidating the relationship between the Gentile churches of the Pauline mission and the ethnically Jewish, apostolic congregations in Jerusalem (cf. Galatians 2:1-10, especially v. 10). That Paul respectively plays the churches in Macedonia and Achaia off against each other in 2 Corinthians 8 and 9 (compare 8:1-6 with 9:1-5) suggests that these chapters may have originated in separate letters dealing with the collection.

The correspondence in 2 Corinthians 8 serves specifically to commission Titus with the task of finalizing the collection (vv. 16-24). Paul is especially thankful that Titus is eager and willing to accept this responsibility, and he himself seems eager to have the matter completed by others before he arrives. Given the contentious relationship between Paul and the Corinthians at times (see for example 7:6-12) it is perhaps not hard to understand why.

The portion of the note giving Paul's reasons for urging the Corinthians to participate in the collection sets the limits of the lectionary reading. It is a prime example of Pauline rhetoric. He begins with the explicit statement, "I do not say this as a command" (v. 8a), but then proceeds to offer what is in essence a command because he himself characterizes it as a "test" (v. 8b; cf. Philemon 8-9, 21) of their love over against the generosity of Christians in Macedonia (see 2 Corinthians 8:1-6). The ultimate standard, however, has been set by Christ who gave up everything he had for their benefit (v. 9; cf. Philippians 2:6-8).

Having brought such a daunting challenge to bear, Paul again assumes a more modest stance; he will give his "advice" regarding what is "appropriate" (2 Corinthians 8:10). Nothing is to be gained by great intentions to give at the beginning if those intentions are not followed up with actions. The proper guide for measuring one's generosity is proportionality, a "fair balance between your present abundance and their need" (v. 13b). Paul even envisions the possibility that some future time there may arise circumstances when the Jerusalem Christians will need to reciprocate the process in order to maintain that "fair balance" during a time of need for the Corinthian Christians (v. 14).

The stewardship of material goods involves viewing them as resources rather than possessions. Just as Christ transferred spiritual "riches" to those who were spiritually "poor," so we are called to view our "abundance" as the means by which we meet both our own needs and the needs of others. Paul's proof text in verse 15 is drawn from Exodus 16:18, part of the report of the provisioning with manna in the Sinai. Like that "bread from heaven," our abundance is strictly the result of God's provision, and any attempt to hoard it will end in ruin.

Mark 5:21-43

One of Mark's characteristic literary devices is the intercalation of one story in the midst of another story. Other examples include the mission of the twelve that frames the story of the Baptist's beheading (6:7-13, 14-29, 30) and the cursing of the fig tree that frames the temple cleansing (11:12-14, 15-19, 20-25). One function of the technique can be to create time for events to unfold without slowing the rapid pace of Mark's narrative. Yet these inserted stories are not chosen haphazardly. There are clear connections between the paired stories (the end of John's ministry and the beginning of the disciples'; the fig tree as a symbol of Israel). The connection between the two stories in the lectionary text is forged by the two female characters who confront death apart from Jesus' healing touch.

A woman who had been hemorrhaging for more than a dozen years came looking for Jesus. She found him walking with a look of studied determination on his face, surrounded by a crowd of disciples, followers, and hangers-on. She needed to be healed, but she didn't want to draw attention to herself. You see, her physical problem was bad enough, but it was its communal implications that no doubt were causing the greatest strain on her having survived for twelve years. People who were continually bleeding were ritually considered no different than the dead. The presence of life was in the blood (Leviticus 17:11), so those who were shedding blood were shedding life. No doubt weakened physically by the anemia, she had been drained in every other way as well by having been denied physical contact and life in the community.

She needed to be in contact with Jesus so she could be in contact with her community and whole in her body. She would not — could not — allow the mob to deter her. In the anonymity of the crowd she made her way through the tussle, came up behind Jesus, and managed to make contact with his cloak. Even in the midst of such jostling, Jesus "was aware that power had gone forth from him" and asked, "Who touched my clothes?" It was a stupid question given the circumstances. Who hadn't brushed up next to him? But the woman had felt the power as well, and "in fear and trembling" told Jesus what she had done. As Jesus told her, "Daughter, your faith has made you well," she could feel in her body, in her emotions, even in her mind, that Jesus was right. She was alive to her community once more.

Jairus, a leader of the local synagogue, had come looking for Jesus. His daughter was "at the point of death." He had to make a choice. He could either go to the undertaker and begin to make arrangements for her burial, or he could go in search of Jesus and make arrangements for her life. It was a "no-brainer" as far as he was concerned. With faith driven as surely by shear desperation as anything that he may have heard or seen of Jesus' miracles, this father asked Jesus to come and touch her so that she would live.

But Jairus and Jesus were detained, and so by the time they approached the house word came that she was already dead. It was still a "no-brainer" to this devastated father. He needed God to restore life to her, and through her to his home. But the decision to continue to impose himself on Jesus was a "no-brainer" to those who were crowding the house as well, playing dirges and ululating their cries of grief. The child had died, and the only way to get on with living themselves was through the catharsis of the rituals of mourning. Jesus tried to dismiss the crowd by telling them, "The child is not dead but sleeping." But to the mourners those words were a "no-brainer," but in a completely different sense. "Look, Jesus, we all know the common euphemism about 'sleep.' We too have shielded ourselves from the harsh realities of death by saying our loved one was only asleep. But, Jesus, you and this father have confused a figure of speech with reality," and they laughed.

Jesus, however, would not be deterred. Touching her now, as Jairus had requested from the beginning, would render Jesus ritually impure. Holiness demanded that the worlds of the living and the dead be kept separated. But the demand of a father that his daughter's need for life be heeded was the only demand that concerned Jesus. So he took her by the hand and told her to get up. And she did.

Application

It is interesting to compare the reasons Paul presents for giving in 2 Corinthians 8 with his argument for giving in chapter 9. In the earlier chapter Paul based his theology of stewardship on proportionality and balance. We are to use our abundance to meet both our needs and the needs of others. Paul's concern in chapter 9 is that the collection be prepared "as a voluntary gift and not as an extortion" (v. 5c, perhaps evidence that his earlier "test" [8:8] had not been well received?). In order to promote their will to give, then, Paul proposes a new "test" (9:13).

Paul challenges us to see our giving as akin to planting seeds. Those who are more generous with seeds reap a more bountiful harvest than those who are stingy. Because of some abuse that has been made of this analogy, it is important to stress that Paul is not arguing that God engages in a quid pro quo relative to our gifts; we cannot manipulate God into giving us even more by our generosity. Rather, since God is the source of whatever abundance we have in the first place, Paul asks why should we conclude that God will stop providing for us if we further God's generosity in the world (v. 8). Thus, in his planting analogy, Paul is suggesting that God is the one planting the seeds, not us (v. 9). Our abundance is proof that God "sows bountifully [and] will also reap bountifully," and our gifts for others are indeed a means by which God is doing this sowing. The new "test," then, is whether we will have the faith to share in this process, or whether by our unwillingness to give we will restrict the harvest by having restricted the sowing.

So why does the apostle hate passing the hat? Because he shouldn't have to in the first place. Paul did not want to issue commands, but he nevertheless felt compelled to because the Corinthians had not followed through on what they had started. If only they could see that their stewardship was the means by which God was bringing provision to everyone in this wilderness, was in reality God sowing seeds to assure an abundant harvest, then there would be no need to play Macedonians against Achaians, and Achaians against Macedonians. Sure, passing the hat can feel like extortion. The answer, however, is not to stop the collection but for people to give voluntarily and cheerfully as Christ has freely and graciously given to us. For the Corinthians it had been a year or more (8:10; 9:2). For your congregation maybe it's been six to nine months since pledges were made in the fall stewardship campaign. To both Paul's advice is "now finish doing it, so that your eagerness may be matched by completing it" (8:11).

An Alternative Application

2 Samuel 1:17-27; Mark 5:21-43. Like David who chose to sing a dirge rather than to compose a lament of petition, our first response to the presence of death in the midst of life is simply to cry out in our grief and mourning. But the message of the gospel is that God can restore life to those whose families have experienced death. God can make whole bodies that need healing and bring restoration to the life of the community. God does not fear being in contact with death and is able to restore life if we move past our grief and ask for God's touch.

The tragic agnostic

One of the most profoundly beautiful pictures in the gospels is the moment when Jesus, suffering on the cross, prays for the forgiveness of those who were responsible for this unparalleled error. He observes about them: "They know not what they do" (Luke 23:34 KJV).

I wonder how many of those people for whom he interceded overheard his prayer. And if they did, what did they think of it? Were they even momentarily flummoxed by the sublime love of this man who, while a victim of their cruel plots, still prayed for them? Or were they offended by the suggestion that they needed to be forgiven? Indignant at the implication that they — who had been so clever, so calculating, so effective — were actually clueless?

From Jesus' point of view, his was a generous evaluation of his persecutors. He could have attributed to them all sorts of malevolence, injustice, spiritual blindness, and hard-heartedness. It was a charitable conclusion to say that they simply did not know.

We have a word for someone who doesn't know. Technically, the word for such a person is "agnostic" — someone, literally, without knowledge.

That is not how the word is commonly used today, however. Rather, individuals will rather proudly claim the term for themselves. It has become a kind of theological version of being a "moderate" politically. The self-acclaimed agnostic is not claiming ignorance as much as he is saying that he is thus far unconvinced, undecided, open-minded. But our three lections for this Sunday suggest a different, more tragic picture of agnosticism — the terrible tragedy of not knowing.

2 Samuel 5:1-5, 9-10

In the wake of the deaths of Saul and Jonathan, the nation of Israel faced a leadership crisis. Not since the death of Joshua had Israel been so uncertain about whom to follow.

For most of their history, Israel's leadership had been clear. Prior to their years in Egypt, they were a large family, and so their leadership was patriarchal (Abraham, Isaac, and Jacob). During their centuries of slavery, their undesirable leaders were Egypt's pharaohs. During the exodus experience and wilderness wandering, their leader, Moses, had been chosen and appointed by God. And a generation later, Moses' clear successor for the next phase of Israel's history was Joshua.

After Joshua, however, Israel suffered through a period of very loosely defined leadership. The judges were ad hoc heroes, but they did not represent a centralized government, and they did not present a clear line of succession.

The last of the judges, Samuel, was arguably the strongest and most godly leader Israel had had since Joshua. But when his time was clearly waning, the people came asking for a king. While Samuel initially balked at the suggestion, the people no doubt assumed that a throne and a royal line would provide the kind of strength and stability that the nation had lacked before Samuel's day.

Saul was the first king, chosen by God and anointed by Samuel. When he and his oldest son had died in battle with the Philistines, Israel faced a kind of constitutional crisis. The crisis created a crack in the confederation of tribes, and Judah decided to go its own way. They regarded their favorite son, David, as the obvious choice for next king, and they turned to him immediately. David ruled this southern subset of

196

Israel for seven-and-a-half years from Hebron. And then, finally, in our selected passage, the rest of the nation came calling.

After much unrest, civil war, and a failed attempt to continue the royal line of Saul in the north, the remainder of Israel came to David to make him their king, too. The people came with three expressed reasons: 1) We are your kin, your flesh and blood. 2) You've already been our *de facto* leader for some time, even during Saul's reign. 3) The Lord has already chosen you for the job.

It was a face-saving presentation on the part of the Israelites. They did not, for example, include among their expressed reasons the fact that the Ishbosheth experiment had failed miserably. Or the fact that David and Judah had effectively prevailed in the civil strife. And, truth be told, all three of the reasons that the people did articulate for making David their king were also true seven-and-a-half years earlier, when the tribe of Judah made the same self-evident decision.

This episode may be one more among several dozen examples in scripture of people discovering the truth that there is no point in fighting against God's plan. As the wise writer of Proverbs observed, "The human mind may devise many plans, but it is the purpose of the Lord that will be established" (Proverbs 19:21). God had already chosen David to be king: The people's alternative plans, therefore, were bound to fail.

It is perhaps noteworthy that "they anointed David king over Israel." Reminiscent of denominational debates over the issue of re-baptism, the people were doing something that had apparently already been done some years before (see 1 Samuel 16:1-13). It occurs without comment, leaving us to wonder and come to our own conclusions. Did they do an appropriately symbolic thing? Or did they presume to take upon themselves a prerogative of God, thereby failing to recognize properly what he had already done?

David solidifies his new position as king by a cleverly unifying act. Rather than remaining in Hebron, where he had been enthroned during the civil strife, he gives his administration a fresh start by conquering and relocating to a new city: Jerusalem. He builds there, and the passage ends on a note of great promise and hope. Not too long before, Israel was in a leadership crisis. Now they are entering into their golden age.

2 Corinthians 12:2-10

I've often wondered how the people in the churches I've served would fare on a sort of true/false test of biblical passages. That is, if we were to read aloud a number of unidentified quotes, would our people be able to recognize which ones came from the pages of scripture and which ones did not? I suspect, for example, that a good many church folks would say that "cleanliness is next to godliness," "actions speak louder than words," and "the Lord helps those who help themselves" are all quotes from the Bible. Meanwhile, I doubt that many would recognize the first three verses of this passage from 2 Corinthians. This is not the stuff of children's Sunday school lessons or church parlor needlepoint. It's strange and mysterious, and so it is likely unfamiliar.

The larger context is a strange disharmony between Paul and the Christians in Corinth. They have apparently become quite enamored with other leaders — sometimes glibly referred to as "super apostles" — and their admiration reflects a certain shallowness on their part. What we admire is always revealing, and the Corinthians' admiration apparently revealed their preoccupation with a kind, flashy spirituality and the bold claims these super apostles made about themselves.

Paul does not share their priorities. Indeed, he seeks to correct them. At the same time, he knows he can beat the super apostles at their own game, and so, reluctantly, he lays out his own credentials. Uneasy with catering to that sort of nonsense, however, he distances himself a bit by making his claims in the third person.

Paul refers to having "heard things that are not to be told, that no mortal is permitted to repeat." He does not give us any insight into the content of what he heard, but we are reminded of other instances in scripture that reflect similar experiences. Daniel, for example, was urged to keep secret the meaning of a vision that had been revealed to him (8:26), to keep the words of the book secret (12:4), and he later heard secret things that he did not understand (12:9). Likewise in the book of Revelation, John is prevented from revealing something that he had overheard (10:4). Even people who had contact with Jesus' ministry were instructed to tell no one what they had witnessed (see Mark 9:9; Luke 5:14; 8:56).

I heard two young teenage girls playfully teasing each other recently. The one had rather obviously fibbed to the other about some matter, and the second girl was calling her on it. Once she had proven the untruth, she joked, "You were lying through your little yellow teeth!"

The friend turned suddenly cool. Her feelings had been hurt. But not because she was accused of lying; rather, because her friend suggested that her teeth were yellow.

I was at once both amused and disturbed by the episode. Is it perhaps a reflection of a hopelessly superficial culture that a young woman should be more bothered by yellow teeth than by lying?

I'm suspicious that the Corinthians were similarly superficial. I wonder, as they heard this part of Paul's letter read, if they missed the point. I wonder if they became so distracted by the marvels of verses 2-4 that they missed the wisdom of verses 5-6.

One senses from both of the Corinthian epistles that the people there struggled with a flash-over-substance preoccupation. They might feel right at home, therefore, in our culture — and perhaps also in our churches.

We remember that Paul, in the midst of his corrective discourse concerning the gifts of the Spirit in 1 Corinthians, pointed the people to the "greater gifts" and the "still more excellent way" (12:31) of love. And now, here in 2 Corinthians, he must again retrieve their attention from the fantastic to the fundamental.

Paul does not want his reputation to be based on his résumé. He is more pragmatic than that. He knows that the Spirit's influence in a person's life should yield certain apparent fruit (see Galatians 5:22-23), and so what people think of him should be the result of their own experience with him. What a magnificent perspective: that he should be judged, not based on what he has seen, but based on "what is seen in me." Not based on what mysteries he has heard, but on what has been "heard from me."

And then, following the lead of the one "who, though he was in the form of God... emptied himself, taking the form of a slave... (and) humbled himself" (from Philippians 2:6-8), Paul masterfully reorients the entire discussion. Having trumped the hand of those who were inordinately impressed by flashy strength, he introduces a new suit: weakness.

Let others boast of their strengths; Paul will boast of his weakness. Why? Because, as with Gideon's army so long before (see Judges 7:2), then the strength and the glory belong entirely to the Lord. And while the "super apostles" may care to draw attention to themselves, Paul's mission is to direct all attention and devotion to Christ.

Mark 6:1-13

As I drove along a little country road in Kentucky, I came into a little town that had a big welcome sign, which read: "Welcome to" (followed by the name of the town) and "Home of" (followed by the name of a certain professional basketball player). I don't know how often this hometown hero gets back to visit the people and places that knew him when, but the sign suggests to me that he gets a warm welcome when he's there.

The town of Nazareth did not take such pride in their most famous son. The local high school band didn't play, nor did the citizens plan a party or parade, when Jesus came back to his hometown. On the contrary, "they took offense at him."

Clearly, the people of first-century Nazareth did not realize who he was. The great irony of that, of course, is that they were so very certain of who he was: "Is not this the carpenter, the son of Mary and brother of James and Joses and Judas and Simon, and are not his sisters here with us?"

Perhaps that is why "prophets are not without honor, except in their hometown, and among their own kin, and in their own house." In a strange place, the prophet is unknown, and so the jury is still out. The people to whom he is unknown are wide open to who or what he could be, for he could be anyone or anything.

Back home, however, the prophet is known. The jury is in. They know all about him already. Or so they think.

Here is a common mistake — we see it repeatedly in scripture in individuals' encounters with the Lord. People do not recognize who they're dealing with. Egypt's Pharaoh refused to recognize him (Exodus 5:2). The people about whom Isaiah prophesied did not recognize him (Isaiah 53:2-3). The "builders" in the psalm did not recognize him (Psalm 118:22-23; Luke 20:17). And Jesus said to the woman at the well, "If you knew... who it is that is saying to you, 'Give me a drink,' you would have asked him, and he would have given you living water" (John 4:10). But she didn't know with whom she was dealing. And neither did the people of Nazareth.

Accordingly, Mark reports that "he could do no deed of power there." What a tragic epitaph to scrawl across the memory of Nazareth. To think that the one and only was there in their midst, and they didn't know it. And because they didn't recognize and believe, they limited what he could do in their midst.

We have seen that phenomenon before. The original generation of liberated slaves coming out of Egypt did not receive all that God had intended for them because of their lack of faith. And so, instead of living in the land of his promise, they died in the wilderness of wandering.

Mark tells us that Jesus "was amazed at their unbelief." What a sad distinction: that a people should be so altogether faithless as to be an amazement. And while Jesus was oppositely amazed by the faith of two Gentiles along the way (Matthew 15:21-28; Luke 7:1-10), the people of his own hometown amazed him for their lack of faith. We are reminded of John's grim assessment: "He came unto his own, and his own received him not" (John 1:11 KJV).

Of course, it doesn't pay for us to tsk-tsk about the people in the Bible who failed if all of our head-shaking keeps us from seeing ourselves clearly. If we have been incredulous; if we have underestimated him; if we have failed to receive him; then let the familiar failures of our predecessors awaken and correct us.

The gospel reading concludes with a notable contrast. While the faithless citizens of Nazareth could hamper God's work in their own community, they could not ultimately hamper God's work. After that hometown disappointment, Jesus and his disciples set out with power and purpose to do the work of the kingdom far and wide. And they do so with a conspicuous lack of tolerance for people and places that are unreceptive.

Application

In each of our three readings this week, we witness a group of people who didn't know — people who didn't realize with whom they were dealing.

In Corinth, the people apparently did not fully recognize all that Paul was. They had become quite enamored with the self-promoting "super apostles," and in the process they had lost sight of the true greatness of Paul.

In ancient Israel, the northern tribes were latecomers to the recognition about David. For seven years, they had resisted and fought him — either forgetting or deliberately ignoring the facts of who he had been, what he had done, and that the Lord had anointed him to be king.

And, in the most devastating instance, the people of Nazareth did not really know who Jesus was. They thought they did, to be sure, but they were altogether agnostic.

While the obtuseness of the people of first-century Corinth and post-Saul Israel hardly compares in significance to the people of Nazareth rejecting Jesus, there remains a common and troublesome theme: namely, the people of God not recognizing — and therefore not accepting — the work of God.

David was God's chosen man. Paul was his uniquely special instrument. And Jesus was his Son. Yet in every case, people — God's people — didn't seem to know or recognize.

Their sad stories serve as sober warning and exhortation to us: to set aside our misguided loyalties (such as Ishbosheth); to rise above our worldly preoccupations (such as flashy strengths); and not to limit God by what we think we already know (such as "Is not this the carpenter...?"); so that we might know the work of God among us.

An Alternative Application

2 Samuel 5:1-5, 9-10. "The Stuff of Bestsellers." At the very end of this passage, we come across a word that is of immense interest to our culture — "for." The Old Testament writer concludes that "David became greater and greater for...."

That word, "for," you see, introduces the answer to the questions we want to ask. How did David become greater and greater? What was his secret?

We have books, articles, interviews, profiles, and infomercials devoted to precisely this word: "for." We want to discover and understand the why and the how that lie behind people who become "greater and greater." Whether the success story is a coach or an executive, a celebrity or an entrepreneur, a parent of happy and healthy children, or the pastor of a growing and active church, we want to know the secret of their success.

The matter is no mystery to the biblical writer. David became greater and greater for a single reason: "The Lord, the God of hosts, was with him."

As we noted above, the human plans and endeavors that do not coincide with God's purposes are destined to fail. And, by contrast, the great heroes of faith (such as Joshua and Caleb, David facing Goliath, Elisha at Dothan) have operated with the confidence that, because God was with them, they were destined to succeed.

"With" was the great word of reassurance to an uncertain Moses (Exodus 3:12). "With" was the difference-maker for the psalmist in "the darkest valley" (Psalm 23:4). "With" was the significant name of the baby born to a virgin (Isaiah 7:14; Matthew 1:23). And "with" was the ultimate promise of Jesus to his followers (Matthew 28:20).

The world wants to know the key to success — to becoming "greater and greater." It's all in who is with us.

Shall we dance?

In both its original Japanese and later American versions the movie, *Shall We Dance?* was a big hit. A lonely businessman, trapped in the repetitions of unfulfilling work, notices a young woman gazing with forlorn sadness from a second floor dance studio. Desperate for some change in his routine and intrigued by her wistful solitude, the man uncharacteristically bounds out of his predetermined path and hesitantly climbs the stairs to the school.

Although he intends merely a one-stop curiosity visit, he ends up joining a class and sneaking time away from work and home to become proficient in the craft. Along the way he has to choose: who is he — a businessman or a dancer? Committed to his wife or a free spirit who can tickle other attractions? Firmed by the schedule or freed by the steps?

In the end, the man proves himself a marvelous dancer, and brings his wife into his stunning and passionate success. He has been liberated and transformed by the dance.

Today's lectionary passages are all about dancing. David invents new steps as he leaps before the Ark of the Lord in its journey to Jerusalem. Paul is caught up in worship of the Lord of the Dance as he plays the music of ecstasy for his Ephesian readers. And Salome wins the weirdest prize ever awarded in a dance contest.

Dancing remolds ordinary steps into graceful works of art. It also releases passions that can bring life or death.

2 Samuel 6:1-5, 12b-19

David is in the groove. His winning streak is several seasons long now. After the initial media splash when he defeated Goliath, there were quite a few rocky bumps —Saul made things desperate and hellish. But now David is back on track. The scrapper has consolidated Israel and defeated the perennial Philistine pestilence. Now David reinforces his stake in Israel's game by bringing Yahweh on board as Chief of Staff.

The Ark of God was the portable throne designed to travel with Israel from its Sinai encounter with Yahweh. Exodus 20-24 is shaped as a Hittite Suzerain-Vassal treaty document, with all six parts of preamble, historical prologue, stipulations, curses and blessings, witnesses, and ratification and renewal clause. The Hittites always created two copies of their covenant documents, leaving one with the subject people and carrying the other back to the Hittite capital city. Two copies were made of the essential Sinai covenant as well, but in this case both were kept in the same location: the base of the Ark, which functioned as the foundation upon which God's throne, the "Mercy Seat," was positioned. Symbolically, this represented Yahweh's plan to live with his people, allowing both copies of the treaty document to be kept in the same location. The tabernacle was essentially the portable palace of the true ruler of Israel.

David's desire to bring the Ark into Jerusalem may have been a ploy to manipulate the Yahweh cult and make it a vassal to his own kingdom (the worst speculations on David's intents usually peg it this way). Or, on the other hand, the report in 1 Samuel 6 may in fact truly reflect David's desire to align himself with the God of the Sinai covenant and the true Ruler of Israel. Certainly the psalms that are identified with David point in this direction.

If 1 Samuel 6 is read at face value it exudes with straightforward praise about God's symbiotic relationship with Israel. God is the creator of all things, and the one who brought Israel into being and freed Israel from slavery to be established as a settled people in this land. Israel, on the other hand, is the human contingent of God's cosmic rule and the servants through whom God extends the divine kingdom into the nations of this world.

So the leaping of David has a twofold purpose. First, it announces to the people of Israel who hold him as their leader that he, in fact, is subservient to this greater ruler, the God of the Sinai Covenant who rides into Jerusalem on his portable throne, the Ark. Second, it calls Israel into a celebration that exudes the triumph of Yahweh over the powers that have enslaved Israel. Long ago, of course, it was Pharaoh and the Egyptians. More recently, it was the pesky Philistines. Today, however, is liberation celebration, and Yahweh marches into the capital city surrounded by his victorious human armies and his adoring subjects.

Michal's sour reaction to the scene provides appropriate counterpoint confirmation. Michal does not wish her husband to be subservient to anyone; after all, just like her father Saul, he is the king and must not bow to anyone. Furthermore, celebrations like this detract from David's victories because they are now Yahweh's victories. Michal despises David and cannot dance.

A Peace Corps volunteer in Ghana recently made a marvelous report about the Presbyterian church in her village. It was established through the efforts of the Scottish Presbyterian Church nearly a century ago, and carries in its religious DNA some of the staid and rational precision of that heritage. Most songs are sung in European cadence, and the sermon is delivered with logical precision. Even the elements of worship parade in military rigor.

Except for the offering. The offering was always seen as a time for the community to bring its own expressions of worship. So, during the time allotted, people dance down the aisles with baskets of food on their heads. Children jump and laugh and sing, carrying coins in their chubby fists. Men leading goats do a double step toward the front of the meeting space, chiding their clumsy partners into a comical dance of sacrifice. Most striking, according to this eyewitness testimony, were the faces of all the people. While most of the worship services proceed with subdued and minimalist expressions, all are laughing and smiling while the offering time rolls on. Here is worship in its purest expression, wedding passions of the heart to movements of the body.

Ephesians 1:3-14

When 93 short newspaper articles of Canada's famed literary genius, Robertson Davies, were gathered and bound, the collection was called *The Enthusiasms of Robertson Davies*. It was a fitting title, for Robertson Davies seemed always to exude energy through his passionate reflections on life and events.

The first chapter of Paul's letter to the Ephesians might well be called *The Enthusiasms of Paul*. The words nearly dance off the page. The modifiers tangle till there is sometimes no clear way to separate them and point them in neat directions. The entire passage for today's consideration is actually a single serpentine sentence in the Greek language, twisting and flapping and wriggling and writhing until it looks like a cache of garter snakes uncovered among the dull mess of fall foliage.

If one were to depict Paul at the helm of an orchestra, striking the right passion among the church players, he would look far more like Leonard Bernstein than Eugene Ormandy. Bernstein actually dislocated a shoulder once or twice in the exuberance of his conducting, while Ormandy would never be accused of over emoting. Paul is emotionally wrapped up in this thing called grace and salvation and the love of God and the divine purposes.

It may be of interest to reflect on the fact that the designation "in Ephesus" in verse 1 is not found in the earliest manuscripts. It may well be that this is the letter Paul referred to in Colossians 4:16 as having landed first in the hands of the Laodicean congregation. This would make Ephesians a circular letter that was intended to be passed around the various congregations of the Lycus River valley, and it would explain why there are virtually no personal references among its pages.

Biblical scholarship continues to debate Pauline authorship, but that need not detract from the essential message of these verses as being in full harmony with the rest of scripture. The classic view of the letter is that it was written by Paul from Rome while he was under house arrest as described at the close of the Acts of the Apostles. He had been arrested in Jerusalem because a mob had caused a commotion around him and the temple precincts and the Roman authorities assumed he was the ringleader or the cause. Political uncertainties kept Paul imprisoned in Jerusalem, then Caesarea, and finally transported to Rome as he went through his appeal process. While in Rome, a runaway slave named Onesimus found him and became his fast friend. But Onesimus belonged to Paul's good acquaintance, Philemon, who lived near Colossae in Asia Minor. To ensure propriety, Paul sent Onesimus back to Philemon accompanied by Tychicus. These two carried a personal letter to Onesimus' master (Paul's epistle to Philemon), a letter of warning and encouragement to the Colossian congregation reflecting on a growing heresy in that church (Paul's epistle to the Colossians), and this circular letter that appears to have ended up in the custody of the Ephesian church.

If, indeed, this history is true, there are some striking implications for understanding today's text. First, the close parallels between Ephesians and Colossians are natural, since they were both written by Paul within a few hours or minutes of one another in preparation for Onesimus' journey home. Since the theological problem plaguing the Colossian congregation had to do with understanding, manipulating, and serving the great spiritual powers, Paul's words here in Ephesians 1 have an uncanny ring of resonance to Colossians 2. It would be well to read Colossians 2 alongside Ephesians 1 in order to increase the depth perception.

Second, these letters were written in light of the pressing implications of a master-slave relationship that was being affirmed and restored. These illumine the way in which Paul talks both about the subservience of God's people to the huge rule of the powerful One, but also about the marvelous development in that relationship in which we are "adopted as his sons through Jesus Christ" (v. 3). This is exactly the language and insight Paul uses in his letter to Philemon as slave Onesimus is to be received back as a brother because both are sons of God in Jesus Christ.

Paul's enthusiasms are stacked on top of each other in this passage. Note these things, at minimum. First, God becomes closer to us through the filial relationship of Jesus (v. 3). Second, in spite of the ruin of sin splattered all around us, there is an eternal plan of grace which trumps it at every turn (vv. 4-5). Third, salvation is a dance, not a duty (v. 6). Fourth, the cross is the turning point of history (v. 7). Fifth, forgiveness brings new vistas of experience and enjoyment (v. 8). Sixth, we can see the eternal plans of God already, even though they still need to be worked out in their finality (vv. 9-10). Seventh, salvation is a great dance with powerful music and a wonderful band leader: the Holy Spirit (vv. 11-14).

Joni Eareckson-Tada, the well-known paralytic messenger of grace, expressed well where Paul ends up in this passage. She said, "I have hope in the future. The Bible speaks about bodies being glorified. I know the meaning of that now. It's the time after my death here when I, the quadriplegic, will be on my feet dancing."

Perhaps some of the dance could begin this week in our worship services. Maybe even we should sing, as one of our testimonial hymns, Leanne Womack's hit, "I Hope You Dance."

Mark 6:14-29

A Hassidic story tells of the triumph described in Exodus where the Israelites are saved by the miracle of the parting Red Sea and the armies of Pharaoh are drowned. As the Israelites strike up a party and sing the songs written by Moses, Miriam, and others (see Exodus 15), a wild day of dance erupts among the angels of heaven as well. Everyone is cheering.

Everyone, that is, except God. During the height of the celebration one angel notices God's unusual absence. He sidles up to archangel Michael to check things out. "Where is God?" he asks. "This is his party; he should be in the middle of it!"

But Michael demurs. "Carry on," he urges the angels. "This is indeed a day of victory and celebration. But don't look for God around here. He has gone off by himself for a little while to mourn. You see, although God's special people Israel were saved, many of God's other children tonight are mourning, and God shares their tears."

There are truly mixed signals in the gospel reading for today. Amid the high frivolity of a royal party flows the red streak of John's blood. Herod was intrigued by John, the last of the prophets in the great Old Testament tradition. Yet, he feared John because John spoke judgment against Herod's own family. Herod had killed his own brother in order to marry Philip's wife. John never minced words when it came to pointing out sin.

Herod seems to have been a somewhat timid soul, afraid of John, but even more afraid of the God John seemed so convinced about. He had John arrested as a sign of his displeasure in John's accusatory words. But he did not go so far as to have John executed. Perhaps the people would rebel, for many of them saw in John a divine messenger. Perhaps the God of John would exact a pound of vengeance if his servant was harmed.

But that all changed on the day of this festival. Herodias, former wife of Philip and current wife of Herod, did not appreciate John's intimidating haranguing. So, when the wine flowed and her daughter danced to please the men, and Herod stupidly shouted out a promise to give the pretty young twirler anything she asked, Herodias was right on the spot. Through her daughter she demanded the death of John. Foolishly, Herod complied in order to save face — his, and in quite a different way, John's.

Notice that Mark tells this story as a sort of flashback interjection. The story of Jesus is entering a new and more public phase in chapter 6, with Jesus expanding his ministry of healing through the mission of the twelve. Verse 30 follows immediately on verse 13, with verses 14-29 thrown in between as an aside (telling of Herod's superstitious reaction) and an interpretive recapitulation (explaining how Herod's fear of Jesus had evolved through the awful events of John's death).

The dance in Mark 6:14-29 is the dance of death. But surrounding it, in the stories of healing emitting from Jesus' miraculous ministry, are the dances of delight and life.

Application

Calvin Miller created a trilogy of poems years ago called *The Singer*, *The Song*, and *The Finale*. *The Singer* gave a marvelous reflection on God creating the world. Most striking was its use of the metaphor of song as the creative energy that produced all living things in a harmonious chorus. Sin, of course, was a dissonant counterpoint, messing up the good chords and creating squeaks and squawks that irritated. *The Song* was Miller's way of telling the life of Jesus. When the music of creating had been too far muted, the Singer sent the Song into the world to revive the right melodies. *The Finale*, of course, was a crescendo of conflict that depicted scenes from the book of Revelation. While the Song was strong, so, too, were its competitive recitatives. In the end, to be sure, the Song won the day, and any dissonance was banished to whimper in eternal night.

Miller's theme emerged from some reflections on Sydney Carter's famous song, "Lord Of The Dance." Jesus is the great musician, in Carter's hymn, who leaps and dances from creation through consummation. He is the one who dances with the monkey of legalism on his back. He is the victorious ballet artist who erupts from Easter's tomb. And he is the choreographer of the great dance of creation that is winding up for its never-ending finale.

Today, it might be good to infuse into worship some of the dancing motifs that brought David to leap before the Lord and caused Paul to rise in ecstasy. Perhaps the morning of worship could end with a grand rendition of "Love Divine, All Love's Excelling."

An Alternative Application

Ephesians 1:3-14. The themes of Ephesians 1:3-14 almost cry out for extended treatment. It might be well, today, to build a message that had a kind of energizing repetition to it. Perhaps something along the lines of Tony Campolo's wonderful tale, "It's Friday, But Sunday's a-Comin'" might do it.

Care should be taken not to dwell on the arguments of biblical scholars about whether or not Ephesians is an authentic letter of Paul. This is not necessary. The letter is part of the scriptures received by the church for edification, and its themes are consistent with the larger message of the whole.

Proper 11 / Pentecost 8 / Ordinary Time 16
2 Samuel 7:1-14a
Ephesians 2:11-22
Mark 6:30-34, 53-56
Craig MacCreary

That's a plan

The best laid plans of mice, men, and ministers often go astray. We seem to have fallen somewhat short of the scientific expectation of my youth. Not every home has a heliport, all food has not been reduced to a once-a-day nutrition pill, we are not using the medical wand from *Star Trek* for diagnoses quite yet. On the other hand, I do not recall anyone anticipating anything along the lines of the impact that the internet would make or the role that the personal computer would have in our lives. Who would have ever thought that as a result of global warming we could anticipate that beach front property would extend so far inland? I was not raised with the hope there would ever be an end to the international communist menace. Neither was there anything in my upbringing that anticipated that in the minds of many, the Arabic people would become a replacement for our former nemesis.

Certainly there was little that prepared me for how human sexuality would become a source of such deep divisions in the faith community. None anticipated the extent to which the culture of the evangelical movement would come out of the closet of American thought into such prominence. Few foresaw the degree to which the mainline would be sidelined, or the development of megachurches that mimic shopping malls, and I have not even mentioned the impact in the change in the role of women and the degree to which America would become a multicultural feast.

You get the pattern. I have limited enthusiasm for presidential state of the union messages: not being able to remember what was prominently featured last year, or unanticipated in the coming year.

The lectionary readings for this Sunday deal with the never-ending cycle of plans made and lives rearranged when plans must be altered because of unintended consequences. Each, in their own way, reminds us that the source of difficulty here may be that *we* are not the only authors of a plan. God has a habit of becoming a player in human history in surprising ways and in whatever the schemes are of human beings. Of course, one can feel the theological ground shaking and potential chasms of controversy opening up. One should not make this claim lightly or easily. The texts do not do so, but they clearly point to the divine intention that, anticipated or not, human beings will have to wrestle with this change.

David's attempt to centralize worship through consolidating liturgical activity at a national center runs up against God's "not yet." The Ephesians are clear as to the foundation but seem to be reminded that the superstructure will contain more rooms than they had anticipated. Diversity, manifest at meals, and in the smells emanating from the kitchen, and in the way "they" raise their kids, can be the source of some mighty interesting moments in church life. In many congregations it remains to be seen what will be the cement that holds up the edifice of church life. What lies behind Mark's account of the ministry of Jesus and the disciples is an unanticipated success. How could one find that problematic? Most churches I know would be more than ready to handle the scenes that Mark describes. It is just not paranoid fear that leads New Englanders to look up at a perfectly clear blue sky and remark. "That is good storm-brewing weather." Often the unintended consequences of success can bring churches to the brink as power shifts and agendas change.

In all these reversals and advances there might be less "gospel" than we had hoped. Sitting at the counselor's table in David's court, pulling up to the table at an Ephesian potluck, or tabling the motion on the new additions in Mark's church must have been quite an eye opening, daunting experience. However, there is a plan that in all these things we might grow in wisdom and stature, enter into the fullness of life, and find our joy complete. We recognize then that there is room for some hope. From time to time, my experience in church life has shown that there is a sign of a larger plan than my own and a greater planner than any of us can envision.

2 Samuel 7:1-14a

David does what good kings and responsible executives do. Looking to the long term needs and the stability of the nation, it is a good thing that worship be centered at the national capital. It is not a good thing that the king be living in a well-appointed detached home of cedar while God camps out in a tent. Not only is this a bit embarrassing but it also has the potential of being a threat. A God in a tent has the mobility to up and do holy things in any old place imaginable. What happens if the people find this God making holy places that would lend credence to sources of authority outside the royal line? What happens if people begin to believe that the power of God could show up anytime, anywhere, in an unregulated fashion? A God that could do that could do just about anything and anything might prove a problem to the royal realm. Is it a good thing to have a constant reminder that there is an alternative history to the current national direction?

Do the people need a graphic reminder that the national ethos was defined in the camps and under the tents of those who have been set free by the hand that defeated and deflated the Egyptian monarchy? Monarchs tend to be supportive of the monarchial system in general. None of this can be good for the crown. Smart politics suggest that it is the wise thing to have everybody under the same tent, to paraphrase Lyndon Johnson, facing out rather than any one soiling the tent from the outside. Since David is not about to live in a tent, it is time to bring God in from the cold.

The inclusion of Nathan in the story perhaps indicates how the religious community thought of all this. "Nathan said to the king, 'Go, do all that you have in mind; for the Lord is with you.' " It is evident that this insight is not the product of any conversation with or word from the Lord. I suspect that the thinking process here has much to do with the awareness that this will bring the religious community to the table in a very formal and significant way. Here comes a new day: jobs, careers, national prominence. Now how could the almighty be against anything like that? The Lord must be with the king on this one. Not only will everyone be under the same tent but there is going to be significant upgrade in status and housing. This could be a very good thing.

Of course there is one flaw to the plan. God will have none of it: not now and not this way. It is time for some history here. This idea of a king is not client driven — the client being God. This has come up in this context not by divine imperative but human impetuousness. Nathan's role as a religious leader is to go over some national history with David: "Now therefore thus you shall say to my servant David: Thus says the Lord of hosts: I took you from the pasture, from following the sheep to be prince over my people Israel; and I have been with you wherever you went, and have cut off all your enemies from before you; and I will make for you a great name, like the name of the great ones of the earth. And I will appoint a place for my people Israel and will plant them, so that they may live in their own place, and be disturbed no more; and evildoers shall afflict them no more, as formerly, from the time that I appointed judges over my people Israel; and I will give you rest from all your enemies. Moreover the Lord declares to you that the Lord will make you a house."

Leadership has come not from centralized bureaucracy but from the people of the pasture. God has had a significant role in foreign policy cutting off enemies. God has appointed judges and therefore is the source of justice. This is a bit unnerving for kings, presidents, and prime ministers.

Committed advocates of democracy that we are, we cannot be entirely comfortable with God's plan to create a dynasty. However, with which part of that are we most uncomfortable — the dynasty part or that it is God's choice that we must come to terms with as basis of national leadership? Of course, we know

207

that eventually there will be a temple and a centralized religious bureaucracy. Of course, it does not turn out quite the way that God wanted, at least according to Jesus' observations and experience. It was not in David's plan or anyone else's to have this in the corporate memory as a source of reflection.

Ephesians 2:11-22

The text proclaims the fulfillment of God's plan. "He has abolished the law with its commandments and ordinances, that he might create in himself one new humanity in place of the two, thus making peace, and might reconcile both groups to God in one body through the cross, thus putting to death that hostility through it. So he came and proclaimed peace to you who were far off and peace to those who were near." No doubt, in the end, this is good news. Who could not want and long for an end to the kind of fractured living that we experience in a "red state, blue state, Generation X, self-fulfillment vs. self-sacrifice, neo-liberal neo-con, and Clear channel vs. Air America world? A little sense that we are all on the same page as human beings would not hurt.

However, I wonder if we are quite ready to have the kind of unity that passage is talking about. "But now in Christ Jesus you who once were far off have been brought near by the blood of Christ." Often I am hoping in the scheme of things that those who are different from me will either be brought around to my way of thinking or be brought down from places of authority, or brought to their knees so that they will be seen to be innocuous and infective. Brought near me, however, I am not so comfortable with. Does this mean that they will be brought into the fold? Lord knows what ideas, habits of being, eating, and raising their children they will bring along with them.

"Being brought near" without being brought around to my way means that they might bring down my settled way of living. If we allow them to bring this off, Lord knows what is going to happen. They just might find themselves being made deacons or elders without having observed the usual ten-year apprenticeship of membership that many of our churches seem to wisely require. Brought near? Do you have any idea of what some of them think is a suitable candidate for ordination?

I just interviewed a candidate for licensed ministry in my denomination. Do you know that he couldn't even name the first president of our denomination and had never read a word of any of the Niebuhrs? He has been a whole year in seminary for God's sake and never heard of the fundamentalist modernist controversy. And another thing, get this; he didn't even begin his religious life as a Christian. How reliable can that possibly be?

All right, I am feeling a little better now. I bet you have heard versions of those words. Maybe even you have had the kinds of feelings that generate such outspokenness. Bringing folks near will bring no quarantines of what might be brought off here: changing standards of ordination, changing conversation in the hallways, changing the kitchen accommodations so that vegetarian meals can be served (vegan and non-vegan). Does it never end? Well, yes, that is the point — the risk and the challenge. This being brought near by the blood of Christ never ends and there are no guarantees as to where this might go. Despite our plans to live a more settled existence it seems that in the scheme of things we will have to enter into the experience without any guarantees. We enter in only with the reminder that if we have not love we are going to sound like a noisy gong as our fears reverberate through the household that God is creating.

When we start talking blood as the binder that keeps us together, moderns are bound to be put off. It seems that too much blood has been spilled in our world already. Blood ties and blood oaths have led to mayhem. If anything it seems that too many in too many places are ready to sacrifice their own and others' blood. Yet here we are talking of the blood of Christ, "But now in Christ Jesus you who once were far off have been brought near by the blood of Christ. For he is our peace; in his flesh he has made both groups into one and has broken down the dividing wall, that is, the hostility between us." Yet the hope here is that where things cross there can be redemption and healing. Crossed wires, crossness, cross-ups can be places where growth takes place, peace that passes all understanding but that brings understanding may come, and new life might open up. Sometimes it happens in the "sweating of blood" through the growth of a marriage relationship. It can come in the bleeding out of heart and soul of a school teacher trying to breathe life into a troubled child. It can come in the actual shedding of blood.

The late civil rights leader, James Farmer, has written that he knew the struggle would achieve many of its goals following the Sunday school bombing that killed four black girls. The hate in America could no longer bear that kind of burden after Americans were brought together in that horror and the sorrow. If nothing else the "blood of Christ" runs in ways that will surprise those who seek to build walls and maintain barriers to human unity!

Mark 6:30-34, 53-56

Mark recounts an aspect of church life that for many of us has proven elusive — massive, undeniable success. "For many were coming and going, and they had no leisure even to eat." Now, is that not the epitome of the kind of church that earns kudos and plaudits? Too many to do business as usual, too busy to eat. There is a congregation that is not letting any grass grow under its feet. Many of us in the mainline do not anticipate such success in our life times. It is not that we plan to fail, or even that we fail to plan. It is just given the way things seem to be trending — we should plan on giving some thought to the theology of failure. Who would have ever thought that this would happen? As it has some of us are not quite ready to deal with it or trust it.

So, Jesus calls for a time out. "He said to them, 'Come away to a deserted place all by yourselves and rest a while.' For many were coming and going, and they had no leisure even to eat." Mark's gospel in particular is wary of such unbridled, successful, feel-good moments. Well, some people, I suppose, can't give it a rest even when things are going well. We want to say to the Marks among us, "Chill out and enjoy the ride."

Yet, Mark is on to something here. He is not just being a downer spoilsport. His entire gospel is a reminder that God's plan for us, to quote Calvin, is "not just success but faithfulness." We often experience faithfulness as something less than a feel good moment. The gospel calls us to gain a feeling for what the kingdom of God is like even in the midst of something less than a feel good moment — even failure. The gospel of Mark builds to the moment when the Roman centurion pronounces the words, "Truly this man was God's Son." The cross certainly does not feel like a plan for us but it is the place where we can gain a feel for what is God's plan. Here is God's love and power to bring life out of death.

Application

Well, what can we plan on? All of these texts point in the direction that human beings can plan on — having their own plans and calculations challenged and interrupted by the incalculable power of God. God has a way of limiting royal pretensions. It seems that when these pretensions are carried out in the name of God they are particularly liable to being upset. Walking the line in church/state conversations becomes very important in light of a God whose ways are not our ways.

We can try and build walls to manage just who is in and out of our church life. However, the plan seems to be, as the book of Revelation testifies, that the gate to the heavenly city is never closed. Plan on people showing up who will challenge and both stretch your wineskins and get under your skin. In welcoming others into your shared common life you will be welcoming in change. The others having been brought near but not entirely brought around to your way of thinking: You can count on being brought to your knees in prayer. However, from such a posture people have a way of rising up to more life than they had thought possible.

Count on success not being the only measure of kingdom centeredness. Indeed some successes can divide and ruin churches, separating those who have experienced the golden years from those who come after. Success wears grooves that make it difficult to respond when "New occasions teach new duties, time makes ancient good uncouth." When churches can stand at the crossroads and say, "Truly Jesus was the Son of God," then they are most open to God's plan for them.

An Alternate Application
Mark 6:30-34, 53-56. "And wherever he went, into villages or cities or farms, they laid the sick in the marketplaces, and begged him that they might touch even the fringe of his cloak; and all who touched it were healed." Mark's rhetorical reflection intrigues me. Villages, cities, farms, and the sick laid in the marketplaces. I walk slowly here, considering what this might mean. Jesus invites people to bring the wounded and hurting into a public setting of the market. Jesus' healing power invited and makes possible a gathering and awareness of the wounded and hurt that otherwise would not happen. Could there have been buying and selling in the marketplace that day in the face of all the sick laid out in the center of commerce? Certainly it could not be business as usual. Can it ever be business as usual in the face of those usually kept out of sight?

Mark is fairly specific about where the sick come from. There seems to be no place where the ills of the world are escaped; rural bucolic, urban hip, industrial, or farm — Jesus seems to have had the power to address the ills that came from all these places. The people did not get to the place of healing by themselves. The begging seems to have been done not by the people themselves but by their advocates. Reading this text, I find myself wondering how avid my faith community is in making public the sickness and the hurting that comes from these places. To what degree have we permitted our marketplace to be disrupted so that it cannot be business as usual when there are so many from so many places that are hurting?

Proper 12 / Pentecost 9 / Ordinary Time 17
2 Samuel 11:1-15
Ephesians 3:14-21
John 6:1-21
David Kalas

Serving an underestimated God

From time to time in the car, especially during football season, I listen to sports talk radio. The talk, for the most part, falls into one of two categories. First, there are discussions about what has happened (last week's games, a recent trade, great dynasties, and so on). And, second, there is conjecturing about what will happen (next week's games, possible trades, which coaches might get fired or hired, and the like).

When the talk to turns to what will happen in an upcoming game, I am exposed to a whole new world: the rather sophisticated world of odds-making. I do not gamble, and I do not condone gambling. But I have come to appreciate the science developed by the people who make picks for a living.

As a fan, I can hardly see past my own personal preferences and prejudices when guessing which team might win a certain game. But these professional pickers carefully weigh and deliberately consider all sorts of data and factors. Home or away. Natural grass or artificial turf. A team's record coming off a bye week. A team's past performance when playing early or late. West coast or east coast. And on and on.

The bottom line, of course, is that the gambler wants to place a very well-educated bet. And I have been impressed by how dispassionate those picks and bets are. As a fan, I'm rooting for my team. But as a gambler, this other guy is making a hard-nosed calculation about probabilities. And his conclusion about what will happen in any given game is largely an extrapolation of the teams' past performances.

I wonder if, perhaps, a gambler might be an example to the believers. I wonder if a typical gambler might have more faith in God than God's own people sometimes do. After all, if a gambler's expectation for the future is based on past performance, he would have rather high expectations about the Lord. God's own people, however, so often do not.

As we explore this week's lections, we'll ponder God's past performance, and our tendency to serve an underestimated God.

2 Samuel 11:1-15

My wife has a saying. It's not original with her, but it embodies both her principle and her goal: "A place for everything, and everything in its place." That phrase, for many people, is the ultimate expression of order, of everything being "just so."

Conversely, there is a disorder when things are out-of-place: when they are not where they belong. And, in some circumstances, that out-of-place item could become a serious problem. If, for example, you have small children in the house and certain chemicals, medicines, or hazardous tools are not put away where they belong, there's trouble on the horizon.

People, too, can be dangerously out-of-place. The person who crosses the street against the light. The hunter who has moved from the spot where his fellow hunters understood he would be. The small child who leaves the yard. The driver who is in the wrong lane. Being somewhere other than where you belong in any of these instances can end in tragedy.

So it is in this terrible episode from David's life. He is not where he belongs, and it ends in tragedy. The biblical writer subtly offers two details that suggest David is not where he belongs.

First, it was "the time when kings go out to battle," but David was back home in his palace in Jerusalem. The idea of a "war season" may offend our sensibilities, but the fact remains that David was not where he ought to have been. His responsibility as king was to be "with his officers and all Israel." But he was not.

Second, it was "late one afternoon, when David rose from his couch." Here is a portrait of the proverbial "idle hands." In stark contrast to more wholesome examples in scripture — Jesus stealing away to pray; the Proverbs' model of diligence and hard work; the psalmist who meditates on the law of the Lord day and night — here is a picture of a man who has been lying around in the afternoon.

As the foreboding music warns the movie-going audience that trouble is ahead, so, too, the terse observations of the biblical author. Everything is not in its place. The king is not where he belongs. And we sense that trouble is on the horizon.

In the New Testament, John summarizes the things of this world in three categories: "the lust of the flesh, the lust of the eyes, and the pride of life" (1 John 2:16 NKJV). Perhaps we see all three issues at work in David in this episode. Perhaps it was pride that made him feel exempt from his responsibilities to be on the battlefield, and pride again that permitted him to exercise his sovereignty in such a reckless way in fetching Bathsheba and dispatching Uriah. Surely it was the temptations of sight that lured him to inquire about the bathing woman. And the lusts of his flesh trumped the fact that she was identified to him as "the wife of Uriah the Hittite."

When David's sin finds him out, he shifts into cover-up mode. We've been responding to our sin that way since Eden. And our passage reveals three unfolding parts to David's devious plan.

Step one is to bring Uriah home from battle on leave. Uriah is instructed to "go down to your house, and wash your feet," with the assumption that nature will take its course from there. Some months later, then, when Bathsheba's pregnancy becomes a public matter, everyone will recall Uriah's visit home.

The great irony of this episode is that Uriah stands in such stark contrast to David himself. Uriah senses that it would not be right for him to enjoy the comforts of home while his compatriots are on the battlefield. It is exactly the compunction David apparently did not feel as he lounged on his couch in the middle of the afternoon while the officers and soldiers of Israel were doing his bidding in battle.

Plan B was David's choice to detain Uriah and to try to get him drunk (vv. 12-13). When nature did not naturally take its course, David applied man's favorite lubricant. But Uriah proved, still, to be too noble, too principled to accommodate David's plot. And so, when the Plan B failed, David resorted to Plan C: a barely disguised murder plot.

Ephesians 3:14-21

We use a phrase, "strong language," to describe remarks filled with profanity. The phrase is misapplied, of course, since profanities and obscenities actually reflect a weakness of language and limitation of expression. But to this passage from the apostle Paul we can rightly apply the descriptive phrase, for he uses strong language, indeed.

Consider the power-packed vocabulary of these verses: "riches," "glory," "surpasses," "fullness," "abundantly," and "power" three times. Plus, see the extremes: "in heaven and on earth," "rooted and grounded," "the breadth and length and height and depth," and "forever and ever." And in the midst of all this strong language, Paul acknowledges that our human efforts are still too limited to cover the subject — we do not naturally have "the power to comprehend" — and so he points beyond our own very limited boundaries: "far more than all we can ask or imagine."

We see this same phenomenon a few places in the corpus of Paul's epistles. The apostle becomes so caught up in his subject matter — usually the love, glory, and grace of God — that his language becomes grandiose, even doxological. Here, still in the midst of his letter, his prose reaches such heights that it can only be rightly concluded by an "amen"!

Paul's compelling language in this passage is seen also in his turn of a phrase. He prays, for example, that the Ephesians would come to "know the love of Christ which surpasses knowledge." At first blush, it seems a non-sequitur: to know what surpasses knowledge. He might as well pray that they would reach what is unreachable, or measure what is immeasurable. Yet, that may be precisely what Paul desires for the people. For it is only when we take our poor yardstick to the unfathomable love of God that we begin to marvel properly. And so, too, it is when I begin to know it that I discover how mind-boggling it is.

We products of the twentieth and twenty-first centuries may have a better perspective for understanding Paul's oxymoron than the ancients did. We have discovered, in areas of our exploration and exploding knowledge, how much we do not know. We have traveled and seen into outer space, and we know more about it than previous generations could have imagined. Yet, for all of our telescopes, satellites, textbooks, and planetariums, we have only come to demonstrate more fully how vast and beyond our knowing the universe is. By coming to know it better, we have found that it surpasses our knowledge.

Our modern generation does not have an advantage over the ancients in exploring and knowing the love of God. But for both Paul's first-century congregations and our twenty-first-century congregations, the more we come to know that love, the more we find that it surpasses our knowledge.

The Greek word behind "surpasses" in this text is the verb *huperballow*. We find the word five times in the thirteen letters traditionally attributed to Paul, and three of those five occurrences are here in Ephesians (1:9; 2:7; 3:19).

One of the influences of social sciences on our theology is that an important directional sign has often been turned around. We have come to regard the human characteristics and titles attributed to God as anthropomorphisms — as though any similarity between him and us is something we have projected onto him. The revelation of scripture, however, suggests that the flow goes in the other direction: that the ways in which he and we are similar begin with him. We are imitations of him, not the other way around.

Paul weighs in on this truth in the matter of family. He is "the Father, from whom every family... takes its name." Family is not a human institution that we have projected onto God to recreate him in our image. Rather, before we and our kind ever existed, he was already a Father. And all of our human experience of family is just a poor and pale imitation of a reality that begins with him: the Father of us all.

Finally, God's people should be encouraged by the location of God's wonders. If he was far off on some cosmic stage doing his marvelous works, we could admire from afar. We could praise. We could be in awe. But we would not necessarily be involved. And yet, see where Paul locates God's wondrous work: "Now to him who by the power at work within us is able to accomplish...."

In the splendor of creation, in the miracles of Exodus, in the providence of Esther, in the ministry of Jesus, we see that he is "able to accomplish abundantly far more than all we can ask or imagine." But Paul brings it close to home: "at work within us (he) is able...." That is good news, and a right reminder for people who may affirm what God can do elsewhere, but discount what he can do in and through them.

John 6:1-21

Somewhere in our early education, we all learned about the difference between the union of sets and the intersection of sets. The union of two sets, you recall, contained everything within both sets, while the intersection of two sets contained only those items common to both.

The intersection of the four gospels contains relatively little material. The elements that are common to them all include John the Baptist, the key events of Holy Week, and this particular miracle. The familiar story of the feeding of the 5,000 is the only miracle of Jesus — and the only story from his ministry outside of Jerusalem — to appear in all four of the gospels.

John's account of the event is distinctive in several ways.

First, John introduces early the word "signs" (v. 2) and repeats it later (v. 14). This is a characteristic concern of the fourth gospel, as Jesus' miracles are referred to as "signs" and often deliberately connected to what they signify about Jesus. In this instance, the significance is unfolded later in the chapter as Jesus is revealed to be the "bread of life."

Second, John's version of the feeding of the 5,000 is the only one that has Jesus initiating the action. In the synoptic gospels, the disciples come to him with the problem of the hungry crowd; but in John, Jesus presents the problem, and specifically to Philip.

Third, John's account is more personal and individualized. While Matthew, Mark, and Luke refer to the disciples en masse, John identifies three individuals in the episode: Philip, Andrew, and the boy with the bread.

That brings us to the fourth distinctive element: John is the only one of the four gospel writers to trace the source of the food. The other three all make reference to the five loaves and the two fish, but only John mentions the boy who provides them.

Fifth, all four gospels report the twelve baskets of leftovers. Only John portrays Jesus as initiating that collection: "Gather up the fragments left over, so that nothing may be lost." His expressed concern poignantly anticipates his other, later reference in the fourth gospel to what was and was not lost: "While I was with them, I protected them in your name that you have given me. I guarded them, and not one of them was lost except the one destined to be lost, so that the scripture might be fulfilled" (17:12).

Sixth, John's version of this episode comes to a more troubled conclusion. The sign seems to get out of hand, as the crowd speculates about Jesus and he finds it necessary to escape lest they "come and take him by force to make him king."

Finally, Luke is the only gospel writer who does not follow the feeding episode with the event on the lake. And, among the three that tell the story, John's account is again distinctive. The occasion of Peter walking on the water is not mentioned. And the miracle — beyond his walking on the water itself — seems to be that "immediately the boat reached the land toward which they were going" rather than the fact that the wind ceased (cf. Matthew 14:32; Mark 6:51).

Application

If Team A has beaten Team B the last 25 times they've played; and if Team A has routinely outscored Team B by fifteen points; and if Team A and Team B are scheduled to play again this weekend; don't you think my money is safe if I bet on Team A to win?

And if God has proven himself to be unparalleled in glory, in power, in generosity, and in love, then am I not safe to count on him to win? To rescue? To heal? To provide?

The problem is not explicit within the boundaries of our Old Testament text, but it is part of the larger story. When God sends Nathan to rebuke David, he reminds David of what he had done and would further do: "I anointed you king over Israel, and I rescued you from the hand of Saul; I gave you your master's house, and your master's wives into your bosom, and gave you the house of Israel and of Judah; and if that had been too little, I would have added as much more" (2 Samuel 12:7b-8). David's sinful behavior indicated that he had forgotten all that the Lord had done and could do for him. Thus he had underestimated God.

The two miracle stories from John's gospel, too, reflect the disciples' tendency to underestimate Jesus. Philip cannot imagine how the multitude could be fed without a half-a-year's wages. And the disciples responded with surprise and horror rather than with relief and delight when they saw Jesus come walking to them on the water.

In our Ephesians passage, meanwhile, Paul sets a magnificent context for our faith and perspective. A people who keep in clear view the truths Paul enthusiastically proclaims will not fall into the trap of underestimating God.

An Alternative Application

John 6:1-21. "Growing Up Like a Child." Some years ago, I heard a provocative twist on a familiar teaching of Jesus. Jesus said, "Truly I tell you, whoever does not receive the kingdom of God as a little child will never enter it" (Mark 10:15). The paraphrase I heard someone offer said, simply, "There will be no grown-ups in heaven."

On several occasions during his ministry, Jesus held up children as an example, and this episode from John's gospel gives us a striking example of what we sometimes refer to as "childlike faith." For we are presented here with a classic juxtaposition: adult calculation and childlike trust.

Philip provides us with the typically adult approach to things. Jesus points out a need — "Where are we to buy bread for these people to eat?" — and Philip responds with a calculation — "Six months' wages would not buy enough bread for each of them to get a little."

It is important to note that Philip isn't wrong. His position is reasonable and entirely realistic. His failure is not in his math. Indeed, he is very likely correct; and yet still he is not the commendable character in this episode. Instead, it is the anonymous little boy who steals the show.

Some little boy in the crowd was innocent enough to contribute his laughably disproportionate resources to the multitude's need. By the time Jesus had finished his work, there were more leftovers than there had been provisions to begin with. And so, while Philip's calculation was technically correct, it proved to be inaccurate in the end, for it had not factored in faith or the power of God.

As a little boy, I had such an admiration for my father that I regarded his abilities as unlimited. I didn't think there was anyone taller, smarter, or more capable. I boyishly assumed that, out there in that grown-up world where he lived, there was nothing my dad couldn't understand or do.

Such childish assumptions about my earthly father, of course, were quite inaccurate. But the reason childlike faith is so essential for us as Christians is that, with our heavenly Father, such grand assumptions are right on target.

Proper 13 / Pentecost 10 / Ordinary Time 18
2 Samuel 11:26—12:13a
Ephesians 4:1-16
John 6:24-35
Wayne Brouwer

Know thyself

While this famous Greek maxim is attributed to any number of ancient Greek philosophers, including the great Socrates, according to the ancient historian Plutarch, "Know Thyself" was originally the admonition inscribed on the sun god Apollo's Oracle of Delphi temple in ancient Greece. Plutarch should know, since he was once one of its caretakers.

Located on the slopes of Mount Parnassus, the Oracle of Delphi stood at the crossroads of the ancient world. Greek legends said that Zeus, the chief Olympian god, released two eagles, one in the east and the other in the west, and where they met he threw a sacred stone marking the center of Earth. This happened to be Delphi.

For thousands of years, according to this legend, the Sacred Stone of Delphi was zealously guarded by a fearsome snake named Python. But Apollo killed Python and made Delphi the home of the Muses — creatures who inspired artists and writers. These Muses informed the priestess of Apollo (called Pythia in honor of the great Python) who was then able to respond to the specific questions brought to her by mere mortals.

Most oracles given by way of the swooning Pythia could be interpreted in several ways. King Croessus wanted to do battle with Persia, but consulted first the Oracle at Delphi. "If Croessus makes war against the Persians," he was told, "he will destroy a great empire." Confident that he was blessed by the gods, Croessus went to war, and was resoundingly defeated; the "great empire" he destroyed was his own.

In Plato's biography of his master Socrates, the *Apology*, a man named Chaerephon goes to the Delphic Oracle to ask if any man is wiser than Socrates, and is answered in the negative. No one, not even Socrates himself, believes this. And that's why the most famous remembrance related to the Oracle is the inscription over the temple's entrance: "Know Thyself."

In the ancient world and now, this seems nearly impossible. The inner world of the self is not easily penetrated. We lie to others and are deceptive with ourselves. The story of David in today's lectionary readings reminds us of the truth of Jeremiah's invective, "The heart is deceitful above all things and beyond cure" (Jeremiah 17:9). The epistle and gospel readings remind us that insight, stability, and focus can return to our lives only when we become connected to Jesus. His perspective mirrored back at us helps shape how we live.

2 Samuel 11:26—12:13a

Why was David so obtuse? Why could he not see the evil in his own heart, while remaining righteously indignant about the failings of others? This story plumbs the depth of the human mystery. We are not what we seem. We cannot be what we hope. We have beams in our eyes, as Jesus put it, and yet do not realize that we are blind, even as we look for the specks of dust in others' vision equipment.

C.S. Lewis captured the tension of Truth and Lie, of Light and Darkness in spiritual combat in his space trilogy about Venus. The planet Mars, in his tale, is populated by an ancient race of God's creatures who never gave in to the lure of evil, and remain holy and just. Earth, as we know, has fallen under the domain of the dark shadows, and the great creator has posted warning signs around it in space. It is off limits to other races, quarantined until the end of time.

Venus, though, is a neophyte planet with a more recent "paradise" story of creaturely development. A newly formed pair similar to Earth's Adam and Eve dance about in innocent delight.

The evil power in the universe will not leave any divine masterpiece long unmarred though, and he sends a vicious Earth scientist named Weston to introduce sin on Venus by way of attempting to corrupt its Lord and Lady. In a countermove the great creator sends an ambassador of his own to Venus. The universe holds its breath as the future of this bright world hangs in the balance.

In these novels, Lewis pictured the tension in every human heart. We are surrounded by dark powers, yet long for the light of redemption and love. One man grew up in a "religious" home and was forced to go to church all the time. Yet, the message of religion was dark and foreboding. His father ruled with a heavy hand, and the righteousness of the church was ugly, demeaning, and joyless. As soon as he was able he left home, got married, started a career, and raised children.

Now, however, he goes to worship services only because his wife thinks that it is important for their children. Yet, he is full of anger at his father, and that rage is vented at the church that demanded, scolded, forced, and twisted him when he was younger. He shakes his head and his fist at the vengeful and mean-spirited god of his parents' religion. It has become a problem of identity for my friend. He can never serve the god who dwells in the shadows and cruelly vents meanness and pain. Yet, he will never find the truth of his religion until deception's shadow has been sent packing by the illuminating glow of grace "coming down from the Father of heavenly lights, who does not change like shifting shadows," as James puts it in his New Testament letter.

Most of our lives we struggle to see more clearly. Like David, life gets lost for us, often, in the shadows. Grace breaks through, now and again, when prophets like Nathan become windows of insight and illumination. And those are the moments we have to hang onto in order to regain our sense of self. Knowing ourselves is often painful. But there is no truth without full truth, and this truth will reveal in us many lies, little and big.

Ephesians 4:1-16

This passage begins with a kind of literary stutter. Paul had actually begun these ideas at 3:1, and then got sidetracked in his thinking as he felt the need to affirm his apostolic authority and mission. Now he starts over with one of the most concise and powerful statements of ecclesiology in the New Testament.

The big themes are these: Jesus is Lord of the church and we all participate in it through him by way of baptism, community, and lifestyle. At his coronation Jesus began distributing gifts to citizens of his realm, members of his ecclesiastical body. These gifts equip all to serve in an interdependent missional community, but we function best when responding to those who possess leadership gifts.

The entire passage is dense with theological implications, and rich with homiletic metaphors. Since Paul wrote this letter and the one to the Colossian church at the same time, it might be helpful to read Colossians 3 as a complimentary background when exploring the richness of the church's link with the ascended Christ.

Moreover, this would be a great Sunday to sing "The Church's One Foundation." No other hymn captures so well the actual words of this passage and also so much of its theology.

John 6:24-35

Food is a very big part of our lives. Hunger can be a time clock ticking inside, regulating the hours of our days with calculated passion. Or it can be a biologic need, demanding fuel stops on our restless race. Even more, hunger functions as a psychological drive, forcing us to crave chocolate when we lack love, or driving us to drink, drugs, and sex. But deeper than all of these things is our search for meaning beyond the drudgery and repetition of our daily activities. It is the spiritual need each person has to know that she is not alone in this gigantic and sometimes unkind maze of life.

Hunger is what the writer of Ecclesiastes means when he said that God has "set eternity in the hearts of men" (3:11). Hunger is the pilgrimage of the soul. In other words, the old adage is true: "You are what you eat."

Life beckons us to follow the latest fad, to search for the newest fulfillment, to seek the richest treasure. We consume and devour until we are fed up with life, so to speak. And still we want more.

Then a word comes to us from heaven. In part it is a word of judgment against us: Since you are what you eat, take a look at what it is that you are consuming. If you eat garbage you become garbage. If you feast on pornography, as Ted Bundy said in his dying confessions to James Dobson, you become filthy. If you think that wealth can satisfy the cravings of your soul you will become a calculator and a penny-pincher. If the adoration of the community feeds the hunger of your psyche you refashion yourself into a code of law and ethics, toeing the line without compassion. If another high is what it takes to get you through the stomach cramps of another day you will shoot up or smoke up or pop some more or tease yourself with illicit sex, and end up becoming a bag of used chemicals and a bottle of cheap thrills.

You are hungry and you are what you eat. The cravings of your soul will not be stilled. A meal will reset the alarm of your biological clock. Food will keep your hungry body going. Potato chips and a soda will stop the munchies for a while. But what are you eating for your soul?

John remembers the beauty and simplicity of what Jesus told people one day: "I am the bread of life. He who comes to me will never go hungry, and he who believes in me will never be thirsty" (John 6:35). Through the symbolic nourishment of spiritual depth and richness, something satisfying begins to grow inside. Tasting the things that make heaven shine and earth blossom we begin to find the values and goals and visions and dreams of God giving shape to our lives.

Augustine knew this as he reflected on the spiritual character of our race. "Man is one of your creatures, Lord," he said, "and his instinct is to praise you. The thought of you stirs him so deeply that he cannot be content unless he praises you, because you made us for yourself and our hearts find no peace until they rest in you."

What are you eating today? Tomorrow and next week those who are close to you will know whether there was any eternal nourishment in your diet. Know thyself!

Application

Some years ago, a major research firm conducted a survey to determine what people would be willing to do for $10 million. The results were astounding. Three percent would put their children up for adoption. Seven percent would kill a stranger. Ten percent would lie in court to set a murderer free. Sixteen percent would divorce their spouses. Twenty-three percent said they would become prostitutes for a week or longer.

Most astonishing was the category at the top of the list. One fourth of all surveyed said that they would leave their families for $10 million.

Everyone has a selling price at which he or she will step over a line of conduct and allow someone else to dictate the terms of behavior. It might be $10 million or it might only be one more bottle of wine. It might be a night in the spotlight or a night in bed. In Shusaku Endo's powerful novel, *Silence*, the missionary priest Rodriguez steps over the line when torture exceeds what his soul can bear, and he desecrates an image of Jesus. We all have our selling price.

Our selling price is linked to our identity. But do we really know who we are? The stronger our sense of who we are the higher our selling price and the deeper our character. There are, however, several identities that each of us wears.

The first is the identity we receive from others. We get our looks and temperament from our parents. We garner our tastes and styles from our culture. There is even something mystical about us that we receive as a gift from God, unique to our personalities. Paul talks at length about these spiritual gifts in 1 Corinthians 12-14.

Poet John Masefield understood that when he reflected on how it was that he started writing and rhyming. One day he picked up a volume of Geoffrey Chaucer's works and was gripped by the art of the lines. Masefield couldn't put the book down. That night, he read until a whole new world opened for him. By the time morning broke, said Masefield, he had finished the entire book, set it down, looked at the dawning day and quietly said, "I, too, am a poet." And so he was.

A second identity we have in life is the one we make. In the drama, *The Rainmaker*, the main character is a con artist who calls himself Starbuck. He travels from town to town during the Dirty '30s scheming to get people to pay him to bring the rains for their parched fields.

Young Lizzie Curry catches his eye and they spar with building passion. But Lizzie is no fool and she challenges him to come clean with her about his true name. It can't really be Starbuck, she knows.

Starbuck admits that he was born a "Smith," but asks, "What kind of name is that for a fellow like me? I needed a name that had the whole sky in it! And the power of a man! Starbuck! Now there's a name — and it's mine!"

Lizzie tries to contradict him, telling him he has no right choosing his own name and giving up his family heritage. Yet he will not capitulate quickly. "You're wrong, Lizzie," he says. "The name you choose for yourself is more your own name than the name you were born with!"

Starbuck is on to something. Much of what we see in people around us has to do with what they have made of themselves. When an English nobleman named Roberts was having his portrait painted, the artist asked him if he would like the lines and creases in his face smoothed over.

"Certainly not!" he objected. "Make sure you put them all in. I earned every single wrinkle on my face!"

He was a man who knew the identity he had made.

There is also a third and deeper human identity. It is the identity that transforms us from what we were to what we are becoming. The poet saw a friend clearly when he wrote:

And there were three men went down the road
As down the road went he:
The man they saw, the man he was,
And the man he wanted to be.

The person we each want to be when we find our truest selves in God is larger than either the identity we have received from others or the one we try to create. So we must truly know ourselves. Anything that sullies us by trying to define us on terms less than God's grace limits our best self.

Someone has suggested a powerfully illuminating analogy. When a ship is built, he said, each part has a little voice of its own. As seamen walk the passageways on her maiden voyage they can hear the creaking whispers of separate identities: "I'm a rivet!" "I'm a sheet of steel!" "I'm a propeller!" "I'm a beam!" For a while these little voices sing their individual songs, proudly independent and fiercely self-protective.

But then a storm blows in on the high seas and the waves toss, the gales hurl, and the rain beat. If the parts of the ship try to withstand the pummeling independent from one another each would be lost. On the bridge, however, stands the captain. He issues orders that take all of the little voices and bring them together for a larger purpose. By the time the vessel has weathered the storm sailors hear a new and deeper song echoing from stem to stern: "I am a ship!"

It is the captain's call that creates the deeper identity. So, too, in our lives: minor stars in a world of glamour try to sing Siren songs pulling bits and pieces of us from the voyage of our lives. Those who hear the captain's call are able to sail true and straight.

An Alternative Application

While any of the three passages for today are extraordinarily "preachable" in and of themselves, few pericopes compare with 2 Samuel 12 in terms of narrative punch and homiletic application. It might be unpacked by itself through several homiletic moves (a la Buttrick):

* How would a "successful" middle-aged businessman like David get himself caught in this trap?
* Why does he think he can get away with it?
* How can David be so blind to his own moral failure?
* What are our possible responses to challenge?
* What happens to us when the prophetic word breaks through?
* How does repentance change us?
* Where is God's grace in this whole episode?

While care should be taken not to dwell overmuch on sexual improprieties to the exclusion of other sins in dealing with this passage, it is also important to be open and frank about the insidious and pervasive character of sexual sinfulness in our culture. Men try to recapture waning youth through sexual encounters; women fantasize about lost loves when husbands are overly occupied by business and careers; porn is extremely accessible and a shortcut quick fix to our emotional desires. We do not know ourselves. We need friends and mentors and religious leaders like Nathan who can love us with prophetic sternness in order to recover something of what God intended our best selves to be.

Proper 14 / Pentecost 11 / Ordinary Time 19
2 Samuel 18:5-9, 15, 31-33
Ephesians 4:25—5:2
John 6:34, 41-51
Craig MacCreary

Maker of heaven and earth

Okay, sooner or later, and more likely sooner than later, if you engage in the homiletical enterprise you are going to have a gut-wrenching moment of, "Oh, my God, what I am going to do with this?" We are presented with such a stellar moment as we consider the interesting richness of the texts given for, in my part of the world, a warm Sunday morning. Sometimes it is too much potential, other times it is too little possibility in the texts. Often, as on this Sunday, one is plunged into pondering just how these texts hold together in providing a course we can chart. Deep breaths: We are given "David, be angry but do not sin," and "the bread of life." Deeper breaths, heart in mouth now: "Absalom hanging from a tree, a fragrant offering sacrifice, and smell of the bread of life." That's it: smell of corpse, fragrance, bread rising. That's it, whew!

An alarm goes off in head, "Attention, attention, this is not a drill!" You are about to crash and burn. You have just entered preaching purgatory. The oxygen masks will deploy. Please wait for instructions to proceed to the emergency exits located over the wings and in the forward areas of the cabin.

I begin to feel like Absalom suspended in the forest caught hanging between heaven and earth. Struggling for breath, swinging above the texts, and feeling totally vulnerable: If things don't come together soon, this column may be shorter than anyone imagined or desired. Between heaven and earth, is in some sense where I live all the time trying to make the tradeoffs between one and the other. Of course the vulnerable, exposed, desperate, "My God, my God, why hast thou forsaken me?" moment is not the place I want to go to write. However, between heaven and earth is the place that becomes the source of life for that is where I find myself falling into the hands of God. More often it is where I come alive. In the wee hours of the morning caught between slumber and alertness, in the place between nightmares of the way the world often is and daydreams of the way things might be: these are often the places from which sermons do come.

"Attention, attention, we have the situation under control. Please return to your seats and fasten your belts and remain seated until we have arrived at the gate. Thank you for flying Pneumatic Airways."

The three texts invite us to spend some time flying between heaven and earth to consider what should rise to heaven and what comes down from heaven and how it should be handled. David as well as Absalom is caught between heaven and earth. The letter to the Ephesians defines Christ as a sacrifice that produces a fragrant offering to God. The gospel speaks of rising to eternal life through the one who has come down.

Language seems here to burst the bounds of the human mind. The words seem to race ahead of our ability to absorb the thoughts. However, isn't that what we are called to do — maintain the tension between heaven and earth: at a funeral, with a youth pondering a career that provides big ticket vacations, or a vocation from God; a congregation considering how to think globally and act locally, or a church facing financial crisis? Resolving the tension leaves the gospel flat and bereft of energy. Somehow our lives must have both the positive and negative polls for any energy to flow. In a way those who were saying, "Is not this Jesus, the son of Joseph, whose father and mother we know? How can he now say, 'I have come down from heaven'?" were so earthbound that they flattened out heavenly realities. The letter to the Ephesians brings us down to earthly realities, "Be angry but do not sin; do not let the sun go down on your anger, and do not make room for the devil." The reading from the Hebrew Testament makes clear that not even kings escape the tension between heaven and earth. Kings cannot escape this reality, then are we likely to do any better?

2 Samuel 18:5-9, 15, 31-33

"Deal gently for my sake with the young man Absalom. And all the people heard when the king gave orders to all the commanders concerning Absalom." From the moment that we read these words, we know that the stage has been set for ominous events. Knowing David as one does by this time in the story this cannot be good. That his son is in rebellion can only set the stage for tragedy of biblical proportions.

Yet, David's life, while of biblical magnitude, is a story that has very human dimensions. While few of us will find ourselves caught in midair like Absalom, all of us deal with the tension of living midway between heavenly possibilities and earthly responsibilities. David finds himself caught between loving his child and the difficult tasks of living out the family script. In many ways this son of his is living out David's own story, for he, too, was a tribal leader who found that he was at odds with the central authority. Unfortunately, this struggle must be acted out and lived out in a family context. Of course, in some sense it is always lived out in a family context. Where do we not find our strength but by testing it out in the relatively safe confines of parent-child relationships? David counsels his commanders to deal gently with the young man Absalom, not even mentioning that the young man in question is the king's son. In the midst of family scripts and living out family struggles, we do turn our children over to the world and hope that they will be dealt with gently.

The tragedy arises, as it does in our lives, from the naive expectation that the world will be able to accommodate our expectations for an easy transition into adult roles. As in our world, "The battle spread over the face of all the country; and the forest claimed more victims that day than the sword." The battles stretch from what our children will watch and listen, to the wars they will fight, to the commercialism they are exposed to, and the commoditization of the human soul that they will be expected to participate in. In the ensuing fog that envelops all as the battle spread over the whole country no one will escape for the forest will take as many as the actual physical killing. It will take the child who is eating breakfast watching the morning news and hearing war characterized as "shock and awe." It will take young imaginations as they are taught to believe in something like surgical air strikes and smart bombs as the answer to human fears. In the darkness of the forest, and the inability to see the forest for the trees, it will take time from the development of young minds to do civil defense and bomb drills as was routine in my elementary school days. By the time I had gotten to high school, it seemed that someone had figured out that these drills had little to do with our surviving a nuclear attack and had much do with our accepting the notion that victory was a meaningful term in a nuclear conflict.

Samuel warned the Hebrews this would happen in their pursuit of a monarchical solution to their polity problems. He said, "These will be the ways of the king who will reign over you: he will take your sons and appoint them to his chariots and to be his horsemen, and to run before his chariots... He will take your daughters to be perfumers and cooks and bakers. He will take the best of your fields and vineyards and olive orchards and give them to his courtiers." Here David finds that not even the king's son is immune from being "taken."

David is caught between public role and private life: public life that will give power and privilege, but that will take much of what he cherishes. Can we avoid this struggle? Can we afford to be oblivious to what the forest can take? Somehow we must live in the tension and look for openings in the forest that might provide some opportunity for coming through unscathed. To deny how we will be taken is to limit our ability to respond when we are taken to places that take our youth and threaten our future. This is a dilemma that human beings live in and with. Walter Brueggemann reminds us that there was even an opening in the forest for Richard Nixon in his going to China when others could not politically afford the journey. On the other hand, the Advent carol pleads for the coming one to ransom captive Israel from having been taken.

Ephesians 4:25—5:2

Here is life's problem and life's opportunity: caught between two legitimate polls that have potential to short out or provide significant energy flow. Daily I know the near magical capacity that computers provide by enabling me to seemingly be everywhere at the same time. On the other hand, I also experience their demonic facility to rob me of the ability to be fully there at any one time. I struggle with law and love, justice and mercy, zigzagging my way through life. My path often leaves me and others dizzy and feeling that life can be quite a roller coaster.

I feel all contact with the ground slipping away from me as I ride the roller coaster called the letter to the Ephesians. As I scan today's reading, I find myself on the going up side of the roller coaster experience. "Thieves must give up stealing; rather let them labor and work honestly with their own hands, so as to have something to share with the needy." Yes, yes: it is about time. Thieves at the garage that services my car, thieves at the cable company that charge so much to be entertained, thieves that hold me hostage when I go looking for a parking space to watch a live Red Sox game, thieves that charge the entrance fee at the national park that my tax dollars paid for, or thieves that rob me of my sanity as I try to figure out Medicare Part D. These people need to be brought into line. I exult when the letter goes after those who have a mouth. It is time, in my opinion, for a lot of people to shut up. "Let no evil talk come out of your mouths, but only what is useful for building up, as there is need, so that your words may give grace to those who hear." It's about time that those people get with the program. How am I expected to function if they are not uttering words that make it possible for me to operate gracefully? "Put away from you all bitterness and wrath and anger and wrangling and slander, together with all malice." Yes, it is time for those people to lose the attitude. Does anyone doubt that such smarminess has been the downfall of many congregations? Gee, I never knew what impact and power the letter to the Ephesians could have!

There is a bit that does put me off. "Be angry but do not sin; do not let the sun go down on your anger." That is not all that helpful. It is one of those places that I do not wish to be caught between two truths that have the potential to grind me into spiritual pulp. I have no trouble speaking the truth in a rage. Speaking any truth in a rage has a way of coming out much less than the truth. On the other hand, the truths that I speak in well-modulated, carefully crafted sentences, often come out less than the truth because they are disconnected from what I am really angry about. Being angry, but not sinning, does not come easily. Either I overshoot the mark with an anger that does outlast many sunsets or the sun comes up and I so cushion my anger that what I am really feeling never sees the light of day.

I am struck by the closing image of this lesson. "And live in love, as Christ loved us and gave himself up for us, a fragrant offering and sacrifice to God." While it leaves me in the same place suspended between heaven and earth, attempting to stay connected to my anger without sinning, it affords me a way of faithfully living positioned between these two polls. If it is the fragrance offered to heaven then it must be fueled by something earthly. The image suggests that I must pay attention to both — where I am coming from and where my anger is going. In a jumble of metaphors that nevertheless straightens me out, does the anger lead to as much light as heat? I suspect that the test here is not the temperature, but the fragrance and just to whom it is the most pleasing.

John 6:35, 41-51

"No one can come to me unless drawn by the Father who sent me; and I will raise that person up on the last day." Once again, I hear the alarm bells going off and I have a sinking sensation that I am headed for a spiritual crash. What scares me is that these words evoke another passage that reverses the equation. "No one comes to the Father except through me." Such a passage has a way of throwing the modern

223

multicultural understanding completely off balance. Can we live with a text that might leave us with the only permissible position being aggressive attempts to convert one another? Not only does this leave me uncomfortable, it seems less likely to win people to a more excellent way than aggressive efforts at conversion. This world already suffers from too many people who claim to be the sole possessors of the truth.

However the lections today suggest maintaining balance between the heavenly hope and earthly reality. These texts must be read together. No one comes to Jesus except through the Father. Elsewhere Jesus says, "You did not choose me but I chose you." This is a bit humbling. We do not come because of our own insights or traditions but because of God's gift and our openness to receiving the gift. This is something that cannot be forced. "The Spirit blows where it blows." If folks somehow manage to find themselves being Christian, it is because of a mystery, that though we cannot fully explain it, it has embraced us.

This has a wonderful way of toning down the moral intensity that leads to insensitivity, which comes from exclusive reading of "no one comes to the Father except through me." On the other hand we must admit that what has made Christianity a driving force is not just intellectual acuity but a missionary vibrancy. Christianity must somehow generate both ends of the equation. It is a place where we are caught. In such places we find ourselves working out our salvation in fear and trembling.

Jesus' auditors seem to have a problem with this balancing act. They were saying, "Is not this Jesus, the son of Joseph, whose father and mother we know? How can he now say, 'I have come down from heaven'?" If he comes from heaven it cannot be from families that we know. If it is a working out of the family dynamics that we are acquainted with, then it cannot be from heaven. Yet, it is often in the facing and working out of the family dynamics and the human relationships that we are familiar with that we can experience the more excellent way that can draw us to Jesus. On the other hand, does not Jesus' teaching about family say that those who do the will of God become part of his family?

Once again we find ourselves caught between two polls as we seek to respond to Jesus' words: living out and learning from the families of our origins as we move in the direction of the kind of human relations that God intends for us. In one sense, we find that we must use all the strength that we can muster to live between these two polar opposites. On the other hand, in living in this space we find all the strength that God has to offer us. It is when we ignore the opposite poll and the dynamics of "living in, but not of, the world" that we find ourselves in trouble.

Application

I began with a sense of panic at the thought of trying to find a unity of purpose in these texts. I found myself in one of the states of suspended animation where I stare at the texts and ponder how close I am to retirement. Often I find that texts drive me to such places of desperation. Indeed, not until I am willing to go to such places, finding myself stripped of all my images of competence and self-sufficiency, that I am ready to be vulnerable enough to let the texts speak to me. More often than not, I find the clue to shaping a sermon lies in a thought or image that was cast away too early in the process.

In the process that led to my reflections on these texts I found meaning in the notion of "being in suspended animation." When you think about it, that phrase is a bit of an oxymoron. Something of biblical proportions begins to take shape here. After all, we Christian folk believe that life comes from one who is suspended on the cross midway between heaven and earth. My thought begins to move in the direction of asking, "Is there any other kind of animation than the suspended kind?" In, but not of, the world, keeping food on the table and keeping human, think globally — act locally, add years to your life and life to your years: life seems to come at us in pairs, if not opposites, and at least requires us to do the work of living in the tension between the two. The clinical definition of death is the total absence of tension in the body. The definition of life is finding what it means to live faithfully between the polls of tension that life presents us with. It is there that life moves beyond stiltedness to a lively animation. As the letter to the Ephesians puts it, this pattern of life leads to something that begins to replicate the kingdom of God: Therefore be imitators of God, as beloved children, and live in love, as Christ loved us and gave himself up for us, a fragrant offering and sacrifice to God.

An Alternate Application

Ephesians 4:25—5:2. "Thieves must give up stealing; rather let them labor and work honestly with their own hands, so as to have something to share with the needy." To whom is this actually addressed? Do you visualize some kid on the run with a pocketful of candy from a local all-night store? Do you see a home invasion with the attendant sense of violation so that going home never quite means the same thing?

Do you see a corporate board room?

It is interesting that the end result is to share something with the needy. Is it just something to give the needy? Or, if we expand our understanding of robbery, do we discover that what we have to share with the needy is their sense of exposure, powerlessness, and marginalization? We might find that we have victimized ourselves by engaging in robbing others of their dignity and pride. If you have tried figuring out Medicare Part D you might feel that you have been robbed of your sanity. Perhaps what we need to discover is that we have been among those that have been the robbers and who need to hear this text in another way. On the other hand, it is often hard for us to admit that we were not smart enough to avoid having fallen in among robbers let alone fallen in with robbers. We do not like admitting that we have been had. Our anger might be projected on those who have fallen among robbers, leaving us more prone to blame victims that change the system that we otherwise benefit from. One wonders how our children and grandchildren will hear this text in light of global warming and the level of national debt that we are carrying.

Much of how we act in faith now will depend on how we hear this text.

Sober counsel

It's hard to talk seriously to people who are in the midst of frivolity. It's difficult to give advice about the future to people who are naturally shortsighted. And it's nearly impossible to go deep with people who are superficial.

In my work as a pastor, I have found it generally easier to do marital counseling than pre-marital counseling. For even though the engaged couple comes to me full of love and hope, while the married couple may come with considerable baggage and bitterness, at least the married couple has the capacity to understand what I say to them. The two young people who are embarking for the first time on life together — who think they know each other so well because they've been together for an entire three years — cannot possibly understand some of what I tell them about marriage.

This is also, of course, one of the constant challenges of parenting. Our children need to be taught some of the things that we know, and yet they don't begin with the wherewithal to understand what it is we would say to them.

In our selected passages for this week, we encounter three different instances of people who may be unprepared to hear what they need to learn.

1 Kings 2:10-12; 3:3-14

The author of 1 and 2 Kings is subtle in his portraits. He does not draw caricatures of evil people, with enlarged and distorted features. Nor does he airbrush the pictures of good and heroic people, artificially hiding their blemishes. Instead, he presents the reader with a skillfully rendered depiction of people as they are: which is, typically, mixed.

So it is with Solomon. This episode from early in Solomon's reign is an unmistakably good one. It shows a young man of humility, gratitude, and wisdom. It is the blueprint for a good start. And it anticipates the golden age that is to come under his leadership.

At the same time, however, the author gives us a hint of trouble right from the start. Like a prelude that includes motifs from all the scenes that will follow, this early passage from Solomon's reign does not only anticipate the rise, but also the fall.

"Solomon loved the Lord, walking in the statutes of his father David," the writer cheerfully reports. Then comes this ominous reservation: "only, he sacrificed and offered incense at the high places."

By the time we have reached the end of Solomon's story — well beyond the borders of this lesson — we see a tragic figure. This one, who had started so well, ends so badly, prostrating himself before all sorts of gods and altars. The one who builds the one place of worship for the one true God, in the end, worships promiscuously. And his spiritual demise spells also the demise of Israel as a united kingdom.

God's offer to the young, promising Solomon — "Ask what I should give you" — is a marvelous symbol of his generosity. When I take one of my young children on errands with me, I invariably find myself having a talk with them in the parking lot of stores. Dreading the constant begging — "Daddy, can we get this?" "Daddy, can I have that?" — I try to head it off at the pass before we even get into the store.

In stark contrast, though, stands our heavenly Father. "Ask what I should give you," he says generously to Solomon. And not just Solomon. "Ask, and it will be given you," Jesus promises (Matthew 7:7).

226

And, likewise, he assures his disciples at the Last Supper, "Ask and you will receive, so that your joy may be complete" (John 16:24). He reasons that "if you then, who are evil, know how to give good gifts to your children, how much more will your Father in heaven give good things to those who ask him!" (Matthew 7:11). Paul offers a similar logic about the generosity of God: "He who did not withhold his own Son, but gave him up for all of us, will he not with him also give us everything else?" (Romans 8:32). And so James concludes, simply, "You do not have, because you do not ask" (James 4:2b).

Solomon's request for wisdom, of course, reflects considerable wisdom in the first place. And God's response to Solomon's request is reminiscent of Jesus' promise in Matthew 6:33. In that case, Jesus' recommended priority is "the kingdom of God and his righteousness." But the assurance is that, when we make those our goal, "all these things (referring to matters of food, drink, and clothing) will be given to you as well." So, likewise, Solomon has sought first a proper thing, and God has promised to accompany it with a great many fringe benefits.

And yet, at the end of the passage, a question mark remains on Solomon's future. For all of his God-given wisdom and blessings, for all the promise and hope of his strong start, there is still a life to be lived. It can be a life of faithfulness and obedience, but that is not inevitable. He has to live it that way. "If you will walk in my ways," God exhorts Solomon, "keeping my statutes and my commandments, as your father David walked, then I will lengthen your life." But we discover that, in the end, and in spite of his strong start, Solomon did not walk in God's ways. And so his end is dismal and his legacy mixed.

Ephesians 5:15-20

Paul begins his counsel in this lesson with a compelling image: "Be careful how you live." The idea of living carefully is so foreign to our culture. We are much more encouraged to be carefree, and even careless. And yet Paul's word to the Christians at Ephesus calls to mind the ancient advice of Moses to the Israelites at Nebo. The call to be careful and to observe carefully God's commands is a recurring theme in Deuteronomy.

It would be a worthwhile exercise to consider just what things we are in the habit of doing carefully. Some people, for example, drive carefully, while others, frankly, do not. Some people spend and save carefully; but not everyone does. Some people are careful with their furniture, while others are rough and casual with theirs. If we begin by identifying some thing we are in the habit of doing or treating carefully, then we can use our own example as a standard by which to ask the question: Do I live carefully? Do I live my life before God with the same sense of caution as I drive; or the same emphasis on value and potential as I spend and save; or the same cherishing stewardship as I handle my possessions?

The initial phrases of Paul's guidance are set in balanced phrases of contrasting options. His style seems to reflect the influence of Hebrew poetry, "with its echoing second line to answer and enrich the first" (Derek Kidner). More specifically, his form resembles what James Wood calls the "antithetic parallelism" of certain Proverbs, which are "based on the difference between the first and second part of the proverb." Paul's counsel presents us with three sets of options: 1) not to live as unwise people but as wise people; 2) not to be foolish but to understand what is the will of the Lord; and 3) not to get drunk with wine but to be filled with the Spirit.

These sets of options, of course, imply opposites. In the first case, the antithetical relationship is obvious: wise vs. unwise. If we asked our people what is the opposite of "unwise," they would generally answer, "wise." But what if we were to ask them what is the opposite of "foolish"? Paul's suggestion that the antithesis of foolishness is to "understand what the will of the Lord is" is a provocative notion. We are thus reminded again that God's view of wisdom and foolishness will not often coincide with the world's (see also 1 Corinthians 1:18-25). We are challenged by the prospect that, by Paul's standard, there must be a very great deal of foolishness.

The juxtaposition of wine and the Spirit is reminiscent of the day of Pentecost. On that occasion, you recall, the effervescent disciples were misunderstood by some as being drunk (Acts 2:13-15). Even in our language today, we have a similar association, for we sometimes refer to alcoholic beverages as "spirits." We will explore below the useful application of this biblical and cultural association.

Paul's reference to singing is not typical for him. Only five times in his thirteen letters does he make reference to singing or songs, and two of those come in the context of quoting Old Testament passages (Romans 15:9; Galatians 4:27). In 1 Corinthians 14:15, he makes reference to singing, but only as a passing image to illustrate a point he is making about tongues.

The other two references to singing, meanwhile, are nearly identical. Here in Ephesians, he writes, "... as you sing psalms and hymns and spiritual songs among yourselves, singing and making melody to the Lord in your hearts" (5:19). And in Colossians, he writes, "with gratitude in your hearts sing psalms, hymns, and spiritual songs to God" (3:16).

In contrast to the "debauchery" that characterizes the world's drunken gatherings, the Christian gathering is marked by glad singing and gratitude. And, implicitly, that Christian fellowship is marked also then by unity and harmony.

John 6:51-58

In his gospel, John makes a more deliberate effort than the other three gospel writers to connect the dots between what Jesus does and who Jesus is. Accordingly, he makes a great point of referring to Jesus' miracles as "signs," for he understands that they do in fact signify something about Jesus, and that is at work here in the larger context of this passage.

Shortly before this teaching section in John's gospel, Jesus fed the 5,000 with a few loaves of bread and a couple of fish. Then the crowds, who "ate your fill of the loaves" (v. 26), came seeking him out in Capernaum. He urged them not to be preoccupied with "food that perishes" (v. 27), but to work for "the food that endures for eternal life, which the Son of Man will give you." The episode is reminiscent of the earlier (ch. 4) encounter with the woman at the well. Jesus uses ordinary water and ordinary bread to beckon folks beyond to eternal food and drink, which he himself provides.

The conversation moves next to a manna allusion. That is the "bread from heaven" that their ancestors ate. But Jesus then identifies himself as "the true bread from heaven" (vv. 32-33) and "the bread of life" (vv. 35, 48). And then, at the beginning of our gospel lesson, he really begins to expand on the image.

Jesus refers to himself as "the living bread," promises that whoever eats the bread will live forever (a central theme in John), and then identifies the bread with his flesh. These remarks generate a predictable murmur. But Jesus does not back off; rather, he chooses to intensify the whole matter by insisting, "Those who eat my flesh and drink my blood have eternal life... for my flesh is true food and my blood is true drink."

We addressed earlier what comes before this passage. Meanwhile, what comes after is an understandable uproar, with the result that "many of his disciples turned back and no longer went about with him" (v. 66).

One school of thought quite naturally attributes these words to the later author rather than to Jesus himself. Surely, the thinking goes, it would have been quite anachronistic and senseless for Jesus to say such things prior to and apart from the Last Supper, and so it was a later insertion by a church in which the sacrament was already well-established and understood.

On the other hand, the gospel accounts suggest to us in more than a few places that Jesus did not shy away from saying things that did not make immediate sense to his hearers: things that his disciples came later to remember and understand in retrospect.

At first blush, Jesus' words seem offensive to us, as they apparently also did to those original hearers. The imagery, taken literally, is grotesque and cannibalistic.

On the other hand, William Barclay points out that "these ideas would be quite normal to anyone brought up in ancient sacrifice. The animal was very seldom burned entire... Part of the flesh was given to the priests as their perquisite; and part to the worshiper...."

Eating part of a sacrifice was standard fare for the people in Jesus' audience. What they could not have known or understood at that moment, however, was that Jesus himself was going to be that sacrifice. Like so many other of his sayings, the full meaning could not be grasped by Jesus' followers until they (and we) were on this side of the cross and the empty tomb.

Application

We don't know the names, the faces, and the stories of the people to whom Paul wrote our selected passage from Ephesians 5. But we may discern certain things about them based upon what Paul said to them. Among his counsel to them are these admonitions: Be careful how you live; do not live as unwise people; do not be foolish; do not get drunk with wine.

That is all good advice, to be sure, but it is not necessary advice in every setting, with every audience. I can think of some folks I have known along the way for whom this would be appropriate instruction. But for the vast majority of the people among whom I have ministered in the churches I have served, this would be unnecessary. Not that they are perfect, of course. But carelessness, foolishness, and drunkenness are not their Achilles' heels.

I suspect, therefore, that Paul's audience was a bit immature and untamed. And they lived in a world where rowdiness and foolishness were the strong prevailing winds. In the midst of that context, Paul had to offer them sober counsel about the choices they had.

Were those people prepared to receive what Paul had to say? We don't know.

Solomon seemed ready for what God had to say to him. He started out so strong and earnest. And even before he was granted unparalleled wisdom from God, he displayed considerable wisdom and judgment in knowing what he needed and seeking that above all. Still, at the end of the passage, God offers his exhortation: "If you will walk in my ways, keeping my statutes and my commandments ... then I will lengthen your life," with the implicit and sobering alternatives. And, when we see the rest of Solomon's life and reign played out, we recognize that he was not, in fact, ready to receive God's exhortation, for he detoured dramatically from God's ways.

The bulk of the audience around Jesus in John 6 was manifestly not ready to receive the word he had for them. They were offended, and many of them reportedly chose to walk away from him at that moment.

In every setting of life, the person who is not prepared to hear and receive a word of wisdom and truth both misses out on blessing and sets himself up for trouble and disappointment. It would be better for the children simply to trust their parents, even when they don't — can't — understand. And it would have been better for the abandon-ship crowd to stay with Jesus and receive what he had to give them than to walk away because they didn't understand it.

The sober truth is that we, as God's people, will not always be prepared to hear, understand, and welcome everything that God has for us in his word. Sometimes we are even sufficiently troubled to want to walk away. But we may be encouraged to trust our Father, even when we don't — or can't — understand.

Alternative Application

Ephesians 5:15-20. "Living Under the Influence." We noted above the association of the Spirit with strong drink. Paul's specific exhortation, of course, is twofold, as he at once discourages drunkenness and encourages a spiritual filling up.

Perhaps it would be interesting to set aside, for a few moments this Sunday, the deliberate condemnation of drunkenness and use that worldly phenomenon as a kind of parable. In short, the question we might consider is this: If I were so enthralled by alcohol that I wanted to live with a constant buzz, how would I do it? Within the context of my own daily life, how would I implement such a dubious goal?

I would not preach this sermon if I were new to a congregation, but only in a place where I had been long enough that I would not be easily misunderstood. Also, I would not take this tactic in a congregation or community where some alcohol-related tragedy was prominent in the minds of the people or recent in their experience.

Still, without minimizing the personal calamity of it, it would be instructive to consider the strategy of a drunk. And so, in the first-person, I would articulate my own endeavor to live under the influence. Drinking would be early on my day's agenda. I would no doubt make a constant supply and availability of liquor a personal priority. I would probably seek and sneak opportunities to imbibe throughout the day. I might seek out friends with whom I could drink at lunch, after work, and on weekends. I would be sure to stop at a bar on my way home each day. I would faithfully observe "happy hour." I would have a drink or two with dinner. And I wouldn't go to bed without a nightcap.

Admittedly, such a life revolving around alcohol is profoundly troubled. And yet, for our purposes, it is also exemplary. For if I am not to be drunk with alcohol, but instead filled with the Holy Spirit, then my imaginary alcoholic has blazed my trail. If I am to live my life under the influence of the Spirit of God, then I should let each day be ordered — using scripture, prayer, and fellowship — along the same lines described above. Let these things of the Spirit be in constant supply; let them be first and last each day; let me turn to them repeatedly throughout the day and the week; and let me seek out people with whom I can enjoy them together.

Proper 16 / Pentecost 13 / Ordinary Time 21
1 Kings 8:(1, 6, 10-11) 22-30, 41-43
Ephesians 6:10-20
John 6:56-69
Bass Mitchell

A great, big, wonderful God

One of the songs I learned as a child in Sunday school was that God is a "great, big, wonderful God." I found myself humming that as I read the passages today, especially the one from 1 Kings where Solomon is leading the people in the dedication of the new temple, the place where this great, big wonderful God would be worshiped.

But what most stood out to me this time was that Solomon realizes that God's too great, too big, and wonderful even for this temple! No place can truly "house" God and we get into all kinds of trouble thinking otherwise or forgetting that God is bigger than all we can conceive. I think of that wonderful book by J.B. Phillips, *Your God Is Too Small*. And that is the warning I hear so clearly in this first passage and even that of Jesus talking about the mysterious act of communion, of feasting on him.

Perhaps you recall years ago when a movie called *Godzilla 2000* came out?

The commercial for it featured the little dog from Taco Bell. He sets up a taco under a box that's held up with a stick and a string tied to it. He going to trap Godzilla. When Godzilla comes around the corner, the little dog looks up and says, "I think I'm going to need a bigger box!" Today's first and last readings remind us that no matter how large and ornate our "box," God is always bigger.

1 Kings 8:(1, 6, 10-11) 22-30, 41-43

For the last three years, the people in our church here have planned, worked, given money, raised funds, and done lots of praying — all for a new and much needed fellowship building. It started as a dream, a vision, and slowly it has become a reality. It was completed about three weeks ago. On one Sunday afternoon very soon we will dedicate it to the Lord. We are already feeling the excitement. It will be a historical and inspirational day that will affect the life and work of this church for years to come. So, I understand the kind of joy and excitement expressed in this reading. This grand and glorious dream, this vision that David first had but could not do and was left to his son, Solomon, had now come true. It began about 960 BC and was complete seven years later. It would be the center of Israel's worship for over three centuries.

I like how the Bible talks about such a place. For Solomon, the place he built and was dedicating was called "the house of God." This magnificent temple replaced the "Tabernacle" or "Tent of Meeting" that went back to Moses and days in the wilderness. It was called the "Tent of Meeting" because that's where the Ark of the Covenant was kept and where Moses went to meet with God. There are accounts of Moses going into the Tent of Meeting and it filled with clouds as God's presence was manifested there.

In our text today, we see the same experience. God has a new house. The house is ready. God's moving in! With great reverence and joy, they bring the Ark of the Covenant into the temple. The Ark was a chest, a portable throne for God. It was a symbol of the presence of God and as soon as they took it into the holy of holies, the innermost part of the temple, something happened. The room filled with a cloud and dazzling light. In other words, the story is telling is that the very presence of God filled the place! God moved in!

Yet. Solomon acknowledges that no house, no one place of worship, however magnificent, can truly confine or contain God. That was important to remember and perhaps one of the fears that some of the religious leaders had. Once this is seen as "the dwelling place of God," then it is not too long before people could begin thinking that they had God trapped or controlled and that as long as the house stood, God would be with them. This is precisely the attitude of Jeremiah's day. Worship in a centralized place can quickly lead to manipulation and control but only if the mystery, power, and majesty of God are lost sight of.

Solomon prays that his prayers and the prayers of his people will be heard by God in this place. But he goes on to do something else quite striking — asking that the prayers of foreigners also be heard there! Yes, Solomon is opening the doors of the house of God to outsiders, to those in the present and future who would come to this place in trust and prayer. His prayer, his attitude was one of inclusion, not exclusion. Centuries later when this temple was long gone and a new one built by another king (Herod), Jesus comes one day and chases out the money changers, proclaiming that it had been turned into a "den of thieves" instead of being "a house of prayer for all people."

Ephesians 6:10-20

Many people have a job that requires them to wear certain clothing like a hard hat or steel-toed shoes, or other protective equipment. Think of all the gear police officers and soldiers have to wear. Because they have a pretty good idea that they will be facing some things out there that could do real harm to them.

In this passage, Paul is thinking the same thing for Christians. The world can be a most unfriendly place. It's important to be prepared and not to go out without being sure you are geared up in what he calls "the whole armor of God." Perhaps this image comes to mind because he was under house arrest during this time and maybe even chained to a Roman solider. Looking at all the armor that solider wore, got him to thinking about the armor a Christian is provided.

He began by talking about strength. A soldier had to have it. Stamina. Living a Christ-like life requires great power but our power does not come from ourselves. It does not come from lifting weights. Paul says to be "strong in the Lord" (v. 10). God is our strength!

Next Paul points out how no soldier goes out wearing only part of his armor. Likewise, Paul tells us to wear the "whole armor of God" (v. 11), to make use of all the protective resources God provides. In verse 12, Paul says we must do this because evil is alive and well... the darkness will fight against the light... the One after whom we are named faced this evil and it crucified him, as it did many of his followers.

Soldiers who are well prepared, strong, and fully equipped, have a good chance of being victorious. Likewise, when we depend on God's strength and we are fully equipped, we can hope to be able to stand firm and go on to victory (v. 13).

In verses 14-20, Paul names the pieces of armor God provides for our protection but the pieces of equipment Paul describes here are more internal than external. They are traits, values, and beliefs that mold and shape our lives each day.

Buckle the Belt. Roman soldiers wore a belt or girdle made of leather that protected their lower stomach and thighs. Later it also held their sword. Paul says we have the "belt of truth" (v. 14). We buckle on truth, for we know what is right, what is good, what is true in life, and we know the one who is the way, the truth, and the life.

Protection for the Heart. Roman soldiers often wore a breastplate made of metal. Sometimes they were molded as if they had rippling muscles beneath them, making the soldier seem even more fierce. Of course, all of this is to protect vital organs like the heart, ribs, and lungs. To protect our heart, Paul says we need the "breastplate of righteousness" (v. 14). I think this means that we know the truth, what is right and good, and we live by the truth. In other words, our protection also comes from living right.

Foot Fashions. Roman soldiers also wore boots made of leather straps that went up to their knees. What kind of shoes does a Christian wear? Shoes of "the gospel of peace" (v. 15). I think two things are meant here. First, that we live with the peace of God in our hearts, the peace that comes from knowing the love and forgiveness of God in Jesus Christ. This is peace that passes understanding, that stays with us and sees us through every circumstance. Second, shoes made of the "gospel of peace" are ones that help us move quickly to share this peace with others, to help us be peacemakers wherever we go.

Shield. Roman soldiers had two kinds of shields. One was small and round, often used in hand-to-hand combat. They also used oblong shields about four feet high and two feet wide that covered their whole body. They were made out of a special kind of wood and leather, so that when arrows that had been dipped in tar and set on fire were shot at them, they would hit the shield, sink into it, and thereby be put out. This is the kind of shield Paul is referring to here but he calls it "the shield of faith" (v. 16). Life has a way of throwing some pretty scary fiery arrows our way. We can and do face things that seemingly could consume us or take from us all we cherish. At such times, our faith helps us stand up to them, absorb them and keep on going.

Head Gear. Roman soldiers also wore metal helmets, for the head was a favorite target. Paul says that ours is the "helmet of salvation" (v. 17). We go out each day in the assurance that we are saved, we are now and always in the loving hands of God.

Word Power. A Roman soldier also carried weapons — a spear and sword. Some swords were very long while others were shorter and two-edged for close fighting. This is the one Paul refers to here. God has also provided us with a very powerful sword — "the word of God" (v. 17). The words of a general are powerful. How much more so those of God!

Time Out. Soldiers could not march all the time. Sometimes they need R&R. Paul says our R&R time is "prayer" (vv. 18-20). With all the protective equipment God gives, there is still this one piece of powerful armor. Wherever we are, whatever the situation, we can always call upon God, knowing that God hears and will act for our good. I think this is such powerful armor because it serves to remind us that we are not alone and that God is right there at our side.

One of the most impressive, powerful scenes in the ancient world was the Roman soldier. Disciplined. Powerful. Well trained. His helmet, breastplate, shield, and sword glimmering in the sun. Just the sight of a soldier sent shivers in the hearts of their enemies. But no soldier has ever had the gear you and I have been given as Christians — the whole armor of God!

John 6:56-69

It seems Jesus had a fixation with bread, doesn't it? We have been hearing him use this image over and over but with some subtle differences. Bread is a metaphor for him, for his life, for who he is, and why he came. Bread was such a part of their culture (as it is ours) that using it this way was to give them and us an image we could not escape.

Bread is the "staff of life," that which gives life. It is not just a food made from grain but a symbol for all food, for all that gives and sustains life. But Christ uses it spiritually. What bread/food is to our physical lives, Christ is to our spiritual lives. What water is to our lives, Christ is to our lives. We cannot live without bread and water, neither can we truly live abundant and eternal lives without partaking of the living bread and the living water.

I think at its most fundamental level Jesus is talking about our relationship with God. We cannot leave God out of our lives and expect to truly have life. We cannot leave bread and water out of our lives and expect to live very long. We were created for a relationship with God, with the divine, one of love, intimacy and of service. This is what God offers us and the whole world in Christ — bread, water, a whole new relationship with God.

Jesus goes on to talk about eating his flesh and drinking his blood. Jesus is using these words to get his message across in a striking way. You have been offered bread and water, plenty of it, but if you just sit there and never eat or drink, they do you no good. You will die. You have to eat and drink them before they are any good to you. Jesus is saying that if we are to have the spiritual and eternal life he offers as the living water and bread, then we must eat his flesh and drink his blood, that is, take him into our lives through faith, worship, service, holy communion.

Those listening (even the disciples) did not really understand what Jesus was saying. So maybe we should not feel too bad about it either. There is a mystery here. There is something here beyond full understanding or explanation. I believe it was John Wesley who said of holy communion, "It is something we experience far better than we can explain."

Application

1 Kings 8:1, 6, 10-11, 22-30, 41-43. "Guess Who's Here?" I can remember a little game my parents played with us sometimes when we were young. We would come home from school or from playing somewhere in the neighborhood and, with a smile on their faces my parents would say, "Guess who's here?" We all would take turns trying to guess who it was. The excitement built until one of us came up with the right answer. And then we would enjoy a weekend with a favorite aunt and uncle, cousins, or grandparents who would then come out of hiding to surprise us.

Guess who's here?

The one who created you; the one who loves you more than anyone. God is here! Right now in this sacred place!

A minister in a church in England was told by an excited member of the congregation one Sunday morning, "You'll never guess who's here today." And before the minister could guess, the answer came, "The King of England! Aren't you nervous?" The minister replied, "Yes, but only because I know that every Sunday the King of kings is here!"

Guess who's here?

The King of kings! The Lord God has come to meet us here!

God IS here. And this is the reason we are here.

We come together in this place each Sunday to seek God. We know God is here and what we need more than anything is to be with God, to be reminded that God is with us.

I can't explain this. I can only point to my experience and that of countless people down through the centuries all the way back to Solomon. When God's people consecrate a place like this to God and gather to worship, God is with them. We experience the presence of God in a deep, profound way when we are together in this holy place.

Yes, I have known God's presence outside these walls... many times and in meaningful ways. God is truly with us always and everywhere. But I tell you that there are no substitutes for the powerful and enriching experiences of God when we gather together in this place to worship and praise God. In fact, my sense is that if we "neglect the assembling of ourselves together as is the custom of so many," that our awareness of God's presence in our daily lives will diminish.

I have a calendar I take most places with me. Most of us do. Some even have Blackberry's and other electronic gadgets to help us keep up with our busy schedules. Well, here's an appointment I'd recommend you write down or type in there for each week. This is the place and the time. It's an appointment you really don't want to miss, for guess who's is going a be here?

An Alternative Application

John 6:56-69. "Flesh and Blood." Throughout chapter 6 of John, Jesus talks about eating his flesh and drinking his blood. This sounds like something Stephen King would write or maybe something from a modern-day horror picture. It's revolting. What in the world is Jesus saying?

The people in the crowd that day and even his own disciples did not understand what he meant. Was he telling them they had to become cannibals? (This is a charge made against Christians throughout history as they came together to eat the flesh and drink the blood of Christ.)

As I thought of this, I began to remember the meals we had at home when I was growing up. Even as a child I remember having this strange thought sitting at such a meal. I remember watching my family consuming this bounty-laid table. My eyes first came upon father. He looked tired but happy. He had just gotten home from his work — a carpenter — and there were bits of sawdust in his hair and on his clothes. And then I looked at my mom, also tired, some flour on her cheek, her hair a bit frazzled, but she was also looking around at her family. She smiled when her eyes met mine. It was then that I had this strange feeling that the food we were eating was no longer food at all but had become my parents. We were feasting on them! The food that we were eating had cost them their life, their time, their energy. It was their love we were consuming, their love and their very lives.

Is it, then, so strange that the Son of God could tell us to eat his flesh and drink his blood? For he gave his life for us. This bread is his broken body, for us; this cup, his shed blood, for us. In them is his life, his love. He gave all he had in order to bring us to God, to give us God's grace, forgiveness, and a whole new abundant and eternal life.

Proper 17 / Pentecost 14 / Ordinary Time 22
Song of Solomon 2:8-13
James 1:17-27
Mark 7:1-8, 14-15, 21-23
Craig MacCreary

What's carved above your church door?

There is a certain irony here as we approach the Sunday before Labor Day and the unofficial end of summer. The lesson from the Hebrew scriptures proclaims that, "winter is now past, the rain is now over and gone. The flowers appear on earth...." This Sunday seems to be the last gasp before we return to the more familiar prosaic pace of life that governs us most of the year. Vacation is over, the pictures we have taken go back into the closet, here in New England, reality will set as we settle in to the Red Sox not quite making it again. We hear the letter of James loudly and clearly that playtime is over, it is time to be doers of the word not merely hearers of the word. It is time to put into play all those ideas that you have picked up at the summer conferences of your choice. The inventiveness of vacation Bible school will soon be a dim memory. The novelty of new music combinations made necessary by the absence of the regular choir will soon fade from memory. The permission granted in summer time to attempt the new and novel on a regular basis will soon be withdrawn. As we get back to the more familiar routines, we will soon struggle with the guilt inducing words of Jesus, "In vain do they worship me, teaching human precepts as doctrines. You abandon the commandment of God and hold to human tradition." Many of us will find our Christian education efforts stymied by the pedagogical design of classrooms built in the 1950s. Some of us will long for more intimate worship space and liturgy but find ourselves and our congregations abandoning the commandment of God and holding fast to the tradition of men, stymied in our efforts to bring about a more vital worship. Others of us will endure the lecture from one of our members as to why we cannot have the kind of simple praise music that they have at the growing church down the street.

For many of us, the sense of anticipation and joyful tension that is found in the Song of Solomon seems painfully absent in churches. I do sympathize with the letter of James. Unlike Martin Luther who thought it a straw epistle worthy of being dropped from the canon, for me the emphasis on doing well and James' take on the consequences of not doing is well worth our consideration. However, I wonder if Martin Luther was not on to something. A child of the '60s, I have often been haunted by the fear of not doing the gospel. I am apprehensive about the fate of any church that remains only sanctuary from the world rather than being a launching pad into the world. I fear for the church and the world in that circumstance. Yet, I have often found among the doers of the word a reliance on taking votes at church meetings that do not help people hear each other. I find mantras of guilt among some doers of the word that leave folks feeling more ashamed than hopeful. I am bothered by litanies of political left or right that seem to reflect as much human traditions as the promise of the kingdom of God. I am sometimes more than mildly irritated by the sense I get from many of the doers of the word in our time that they have not come short of the glory of God like the rest of us.

I believe it was the television commentator, Andy Rooney, who pointed out that Labor Day more than January first marks the turning point toward a new year. More is at stake here on this Sunday than the sin of wearing white after Labor Day. If in some sense the vitality and vigor and irrational exuberance of the Song of Solomon are normative, then the letter of James and the gospel passage for this Sunday remind us of what may be getting between us and the kingdom of God.

I have seen many different passages of scripture carved above the doors of churches and painted on sanctuary walls. I have yet to ever see these words from the Song of Solomon, "The fig tree puts forth its figs, and the vines are in blossom; they give forth fragrance. Arise, my love, my fair one, and come away." I suspect that would be quite an eye opener if not a heart healer.

Song of Solomon 2:8-13

Just say the words, "Song of Solomon," and you can unleash a dash toward the exits and cries of, "Check, please" as folks want to bring the conversation to a quick close. The kind of sensuality let alone sexuality that comes to the surface of this book is not usually heard in the sermons of the churches of most of the pastors who read this publication. These words lightly considered or facilely expressed from the pulpit have the potential for the career ending moment. Let's face it; this is not on your top hit parade of the most favored texts to preach on. Dietrich Bonhoeffer once said that just about every piece of scripture has been used for a salvific purpose at one time or another. If on a Saturday night all you have is this text and a sermon that you suddenly discover you are not ready to preach because it might push the outside of the envelope with your congregation a bit too far, then you might find Bonhoeffer's words a bit hard to swallow.

However, perhaps the words from the Nike Corporation's advertising campaign, "Just Do It" might have something to say here. What if on a Sunday we approached morning worship in anticipation of seeing the beloved red state or blue state member, fill in the blank, come leaping up the mountain and bounding up the hill? Can we imagine a church that proclaims winter is over because we dwell in a unity that is larger than democratic agreement on all issues? Can you imagine a church community that would have carved over its main entrance to the church, "Arise, my love, my fair one, and come away"? Imagine the church advertisement in the local newspaper, "Arise, come together with us and come away from the things that divide people, belittle their efforts, and that devalues their experience. It is time to blossom and sing for the voice of the turtledove is heard in our land." That kind of advertising would be some pretty hot copy — certainly worthy of the fire of Pentecost. With all due respect to those churches who advertise in the newspaper, from my experience the usual run of those advertisements don't give much reason to mop your brow from inordinate titillation.

If I understand the major themes of the Song of Solomon it comes down to the notion that I cannot be me without loving you. I cannot be me without loving that character on the board of deacons who keeps frustrating my efforts, even delighting in his presence. There is sensuality in the Song of Solomon that might cause us to yell, "Check, please" as we head for the door. Yet, if we longed for the completion that can only come from embracing the other, not tolerance of the other, as essential to our wholeness, then we have something that looks like the flowers blooming and the time of singing arriving.

I know that the Great Reformation understanding of the church hovers around the idea of, "The word rightly proclaimed and the sacraments rightly performed." This text asks of us as well, "Does it smell right?" "The fig tree puts forth its figs, and the vines are in blossom; they give forth fragrance. Arise, my love, my fair one, and come away." My home church had a room where much of the Christian education program took place called the Pine Room. To this day the smell of pine carries me back to the first time I understood through UNICEF films that the world was more complicated than I thought. The Pine Room would fill, at Christmas time, with the musty smell of old costumes pulled out once again to tell the old, old story that has the potential to make all things new. At Easter, it filled with the smell of flowers that proclaimed God's intention that we really live in a garden that the kids in the UNICEF films never seemed to share in. I even still associate the Word with the smell of all those mimeographed bulletins. This text just might have it right — that the test of being true church is whether it smells right.

If it is all doing, knowing, and not smelling then something is wrong. The sensual turns out to be a very genuine path into the ways of the Lord. A recent credit card commercial asks, "What's in your wallet?" Perhaps, we should also ask just what text is carved over your door or in your heart.

James 1:17-27

James struggles with a church community that has things out of order and in doing so has invited disaster into their midst. "You must understand this, my beloved: let everyone be quick to listen, slow to speak, slow to anger; for your anger does not produce God's righteousness." Now you would think that this sad situation was the result of a people who were overly passionate and committed to too heavy an agenda. Isn't that what propels Christian folk to step over the line in their relationship with the world and each other? When you are heavily invested in engaging the world in the name of faith, you find yourself facing disappointments with others and many defeats along the way. It is natural to want from our religious life a sanctuary that will provide serenity in the midst of a world that will surely let you down and dole out its share of frustrations.

Amazingly, James takes the opposite view on the source of our error. It is disengagement from the world that begins to bankrupt our faith. "Religion that is pure and undefiled before God, the Father, is this: to care for orphans and widows in their distress, and to keep oneself unstained by the world." When we are disengaged from the world we become overdrawn. It is all too easy to draw conclusions about the world and others that are reflections of our own gaze into the mirror of our lives, but that does not reflect our entry into the experience of others. We often gravitate to conversations and discussions with friends that will reflect and support our own points of view. At the coffee shop, the hairdresser, and the local pub we can be assured of the kind of conversation that will leave us reassured that we are right in our assessment of who is to blame for the downfall of the world. In such contexts, we gain fame and prominence by speaking in a way that confirms other's fears and hostilities. We can wind up deceiving our hearts and rendering our religion worthless for the sake of acceptance and approval by others. We can walk away forgetting what the conversation was really about — not so much the truth that makes us free but the words that make us comfortable. You can leave such conversations dead certain that you are justified in your anger at whomever you have named as public enemy number one. When we do so, we are in a precarious position, "... for your anger does not produce God's righteousness."

James invites us to engagement with the world that will not be stained by the monophonic conversation that does not take in all the voices, perspectives, and experiences through which God speaks. God always speaks in stereo and probably quadraphonic. At least we have not heard God until we have taken in the variety of human experience. A trip to Palestine and Jerusalem a few years ago proved the truth of this to me. It is quite easy to have some very pronounced idea about the Middle East and the Israeli/Palestinian conflict if you don't live there and your information is confined to the American media. Go there and hear the stories of folks living with terror and under occupation and you find that you cannot rely on the simple-minded platitudes that come all too easily out of your mouth. A deep hearing that comes from being really engaged with people is required. My journey through the Holy Land was guided by Palestinian Christians who are committed to engaging in the kind of bridge building and listening that comes from seeking to do the word by making a place where all can come together and hear each other. Doing the word means hearing each other.

The people I spoke with had an irrational exuberance and excited anticipation that conversation with the other could lead to peace. They looked to others not as enemies but as those who needed to be heard and to speak. From such doing of the word as the Song of Solomon puts it, "The flowers appear on the earth; the time of singing has come, and the voice of the turtledove is heard in our land."

Mark 7:1-8, 14-15, 21-23

They smell, they are dirty, they are angry; they are cynical about authority and suspicious about offers of help. Welcome to the world of street people. Welcome to the reality of many if not most of the people in the world. It is fascinating what the Pharisees and some of the scribes noticed about Jesus' disciples — that they were eating without having gone through the appropriate ritual washing. The question here was not "Why do you not observe the minimal standards of cleanliness?" but, "Why do your disciples not live according to the tradition of the elders, but eat with defiled hands?" How did they come to make such an observation and why did they not notice in a way that might validate what Jesus was doing — that the smelly ones, the unclean ones, felt that at Jesus' table they were the beloved — that Jesus himself might proclaim, "Look they come leaping upon the mountains, and bounding over the hills"? When you feel love like that it can do a lot to put some serious spring into your step. The kingdom of God just might look like the smelly ones, whether from living on the street or wearing cologne that is part of the uniform of working on the street, dancing and leaping for they are accepted regardless of the smell.

When it is about who has clean hands more than Jesus' call for all hands to be on deck and join together in feasting together, then we are at the level of keeping up with the human traditions that keep at bay those who bother us rather than welcoming God's beloved into our midst in a way that would cause them to leap for joy.

What was it that caused the Pharisees and some of the scribes to rivet their attention on the small detail of ritual washing? What was it that caused them to cling to the human traditions and precepts that would cause them to be very far away from God? Can we attribute this to a sort of Freudian obsessive compulsiveness that overwhelmed them? Before we get them on the couch we ought to see them in a larger context. People often obsess when they are deeply afraid of what is or might happen to them. When the order of things is breaking down, then you attack at any place where you can stick your finger in the dike of changing times. Clearly, the purity system that gave place, position, and authority to some folks was losing force. The kingdom of God was breaking in through Jesus' teaching and the old certainties were breaking down. If the sanctity of a shared meal is about whether folks are feeling that they are so beloved that they leap for joy more than whether they can leap through the hoops that the scribes have set up, then the times they are a changing.

It certainly happens in churches when suddenly we find ourselves clinging to human precepts as doctrine about what color the church bathrooms should be painted. Suddenly, we find ourselves dealing with a host of surface issues as if they are the source of our problems when underneath it are the oceans of change in every other part of our lives that cause us to want to cling to at least one place where we can fend off the rapidly changing order of things.

Certainly, Jesus points out that our downfall is more about our stance in life than our circumstance. The Pharisees' obsession has left them unable to see the dinner table as a place where people may be cleansed of their fears, that they do not belong, or that they are not worthy, or that they do not matter.

Application

There is a deep irony here in these lessons that is summed up in Jesus' words from the gospel, "You abandon the commandment of God and hold fast to human tradition." It seems that in the name of the human we often wind up denying and frustrating the human. Religion in Jesus' world had become preoccupied with its all too human tradition which prevented many from feeling they were accepted. James' letter reminds us of the danger of looking in the mirror and seeing only the reflection of our own humanity in a way that causes us to miss seeing the humanity of others. The Song of Solomon is ready to exult in the full depth of our humanity, yet we tread lightly. None of us would be too comfortable with having, "We teach human precepts as doctrines" carved above our church doors. Our humanity must be rooted in something more than human if we are going to avoid the inhuman. Perhaps we should carve the words, "We will never allow human traditions to get in the way of our humanity," or, "We will never let unclean hands prevent us from holding each other's hands." Or we could try, "We will leap for joy when we see you coming." Imagining the essence of what we are about carved above the church door might help us in opening those doors to all.

An Alternative Application

Song of Solomon 2:8-13. Occasionally, I find myself wanting to take on a piece of scripture. Perhaps that comes across as somewhat blasphemous. Perhaps it is. On the other hand, one of the central Hebrew heroes is Jacob who takes on God in a wrestling match in which he finds himself in a no-holds-barred match. Of course, he leaves with more than a bit of a limp. I suspect that this is not the kind of thing that should be tried by a nonprofessional. However, I believe that wrestling with God is very much a part of the strength of the Hebrew's story. Jesus found himself wrestling with God as he faced the reality of his own crucifixion. He did not get to, "Nevertheless not my will but thine be done" without serious blood, sweat, and tears.

I wish to take on the author of the Song of Solomon as he celebrates the passing of winter and the arrival of spring. Hold on here. The season of growth is not all that it is cracked up to be. Often our infatuation with growth has caused the church to resort to gimmicks and come-ons that fall short of the gospel. It often seems that, like the song writer, we have an easier time building up to highs in the church year without being quite as adept at helping people come down from the highs of Christmas and Easter. Certainly, winter is the time of hibernation for much of the animal kingdom. It might not be fashionable but the church often seems unable to give it a rest. In our business we often imitate the worst in the surrounding frenetic culture. Yes, winter in New Hampshire where I live is the season of delayed and rearranged plans. However, the season has a way of reminding me that God's plan for me is to grow up no matter how many times my plans go awry.

Saying good-bye to the summer on Labor Day is hard to do. However it might be an opportunity to think through what God might plan for us in the seasons to come.

Proper 18 / Pentecost 15 / Ordinary Time 23
Proverbs 22:1-2, 8-9, 22-23
James 2:1-10 (11-13) 14-17
Mark 7:24-37
David Kalas

Practically Christian

I parked next to a car yesterday that looked like a bit of a junker. It was pretty banged up and featured several significant rust spots. As I got out of my own car to go into the store, I walked next to the junky car, and I noticed that it wasn't a thing of beauty on the inside, either.

Now the car I drive does not clear, by much, the bar of "basic transportation," so I don't have any sort of superiority attitude about cars. And yet, I was struck by how shabby this particular car was. Apparently the owner of the car knew how bad it looked, for he had a bumper sticker to answer people who thought what I was thinking. The bumper sticker said, "At least it runs."

I laughed to myself as I walked into the store, for I thought how right the bumper sticker was. At a couple of points in my life, I have found myself in a car that stopped running, for one reason or another. I know that, when push comes to shove, that is the most important issue with a car: Does it run?

This jalopy in the parking lot was not sporty or stylish, but it got its owner where he needed to go. And if I, by contrast, had a very sporty car, with a plush interior, state-of-the-art navigational equipment, and a top-of-the-line sound system, but my car didn't run, then the guy with the junker would still be ahead of me.

The law, the wisdom writings, the prophets, the epistles, and the teachings of Jesus all call us back to such practicality. Religion that is shiny on the surface — superficially attractive and seemingly sound — but doesn't actually "run" isn't worth much. That was a problem for the people of Judah (Isaiah 58:4-7), the people of Israel (Amos 5:21-24), and the Pharisees (Matthew 23:23-28). It is a concern we see in our selected passages for this Sunday, as well, as we hear the call to be "practically" Christian.

Proverbs 22:1-2, 8-9, 22-23

One hallmark of the wisdom literature is its balanced perspective on wealth. The writers of Proverbs, Job, and Ecclesiastes do not rush to some indefensible extreme: either that prosperity is an unqualified good and a proof of God's blessing, on the one hand, or that all wealth is always bad, on the other. Instead, we discover in these wisdom books, in general — and in Proverbs, in particular — a nuanced view of wealth.

On the one hand, the writer of Proverbs offers plenty of counsel on how to succeed and prosper. His are not the questionable get-rich-quick schemes of certain email offers or late-night infomercials. Rather, he is an advocate of basic virtues: discipline, prudence, careful planning, and hard work, and he warns against all sorts of imprudent behavior and choices. Prosperity, therefore, is seen as the predictable cause-and-effect result of wise living.

Yet, as we see in our brief selected passage, wealth is not satisfactory as a highest goal. The bumper sticker jokes, "The one who dies with the most toys wins." But the writer of Proverbs knows better. The mere accumulation of things is not the final measure of success, and such accumulation does not, according to our lesson, rank as high as these three significant matters: 1) a good reputation, 2) generosity, and 3) justice.

I suppose it would be easy target practice for a preacher to cite certain individuals from the headlines or notorious characters from history to illustrate each point.

We have certainly become acquainted in the not-so-distant past with executives who risked, and eventually lost, their reputation because of their greed. They may read with sad appreciation the proverbial wisdom that "a good name is to be chosen rather than great riches." And every adult in our congregations knows — some, perhaps, from painful personal experience — that a reputation is a difficult thing to change or to repair.

Your reputation is what the rest of the community knows about you and thinks of you. And so it becomes both the community's conclusion about you and the basis for what they will or will not believe about you at once. When an allegation is whispered about the man whose reputation is already sullied, the hearers nod and say, "Well, I'm not surprised." But when such gossip is spread about the man whose life has been impeccable, the hearers shake their heads, saying, "Oh, no, that can't be right. I just don't believe it!" Such is the power and protection of a good name.

The wise author also implicitly ranks wealth lower than generosity. While the pursuit of a good name may sometimes clash with the pursuit of wealth, generosity always seems to clash with the pursuit of wealth. On paper, they are competing interests. Giving vs. getting — sharing vs. hoarding. These are the seeming contradictions that Proverbs invites us to suspend as we live with an interest broader than our own. And we do so with a faith that says there is more to be calculated than mere credits and debits, for we live before a God who made us all, and whose jurisdiction it is both to bless and to despoil.

At the other end of the spectrum from generosity, meanwhile, is perhaps a surprising vice. It is not mere stinginess that opposes generosity, but something still more diabolically selfish. Injustice. The stingy person merely keeps what he has acquired. The unjust and oppressive person, however, acquires what he has at the expense of others. That person sets himself up to be judged by the one who pleads the cause of the poor and the oppressed.

Almost every soul who hears us preach this Sunday will know or know of someone who sacrificed a good name for greed, who is more miser than benefactor, or whose wealth came through either subtly or blatantly unjust treatment of others. The trick is that they will know or know of someone else. The challenge for us in the pulpit, of course, is to help our folks see the application to their own lives.

Most of the people in our pews do not regard themselves as wealthy — a debatable point in the larger context of the world and of history — and so the potential virtues and vices outlined in this passage may seem to apply only to others. We blithely assume that these matters are the province of only the high stakes players in life, but not us. We are challenged this week to hear the wisdom of Proverbs for ourselves, not just for others.

James 2:1-10 (11-13) 14-17

The wizened writer of Ecclesiastes insisted, "There is nothing new under the sun" (1:9b). You can't prove a negative, but the juxtaposition of our experience within churches in twenty-first-century America and James' critique of first-century churches in the Near East may lend support to Ecclesiastes' claim. There's nothing new. What was a problem then is still a problem here and now.

Have you seen, as I have, an embarrassing difference in how various visitors to our churches are treated? The young, white-collar couple with two children is fawned over. Enthusiastic church members line up to greet them, to answer their questions, to find out their interests, and to extol the virtues of the church's children and youth ministries. Meanwhile, the gentleman who wandered in late, who looks and smells not recently bathed, is not warmly and frequently greeted. Instead, he is monitored cautiously from a distance. "What do you suppose he wants? Is he looking for a handout? Do you suppose he'll make trouble?"

The stunning element of this passage, of course, is the whole premise with which James begins the discussion. Without pussyfooting, James challenges the people with this almost insulting question: "Do you... really believe in our glorious Lord Jesus Christ?"

Some of our congregations have the tradition of reciting one of the great creeds of the church during each Sunday morning worship service. Perhaps a gutsy preacher might take James' tack, following the creed with a sermon that begins, "Do you really believe?" And not "believe" in the sense of some theoretical and detached doctrinal adherence, but rather "believe" in the sense of something practical and manifest. James does not ask, "Do you with your words — your memorized creeds and recited confessions — really believe?" No, but rather, "Do you with your *acts*... really believe?"

It is, of course, characteristic of James to emphasize works. It is not, as some mistakenly assume, a case of works-righteousness. Rather, James is a pragmatist who knows that a tree is supposed to bear fruit (as in Psalm 1:3; Luke 6:43-44). If a sign in front of the tree says "Apple Tree," but the tree is growing oranges on its branches, we will dismiss the sign and believe the fruit. And, likewise, James contends that a "believer-in-Jesus" tree ought to produce some "believer-in-Jesus" fruit. If it does not, then it must not be what it claims to be.

While we observed earlier that the Old Testament wisdom books take a nuanced position on wealth and the wealthy, James is more polemical. The poor, he asserts, are especially chosen and favored by God. The rich, meanwhile, are the ones who oppress and blaspheme.

Interestingly, James' remarks suggest that the congregation to whom he writes are not themselves among the rich. Rather, he reminds them that they are victims of the rich. The church's problem is not merely a homogeneity issue — we just want our own kind here. But these Christians of apparently more limited means are showing deference to the wealthy ones who come their way.

Apart from James' dualistic paradigm concerning the rich and the poor, the two underlying issues of this challenging passage are partiality and faith. Throughout scripture, showing partiality is portrayed as a form of injustice. In the Old Testament law, for example, the issue is not merely to spare the downtrodden and vulnerable from being oppressed; the Israelites are commanded not to show partiality in favor of the poor, either (Exodus 23:3). The concern is not that we should choose some against-the-grain group of people to treat preferentially, but rather that we should show no partiality at all. After all, God himself shows no partiality, but "makes his sun rise on the evil and on the good, and sends rain on the righteous and on the unrighteous" (Matthew 5:45).

Finally, there is this matter of faith. While James is sometimes juxtaposed with Paul on a faith vs. works spectrum, the fact is that James stands very much in the mainstream of biblical theology. Isaiah (ch. 58) alerts the people of his day to ineffectualness of ritual piety that is unaccompanied by righteous living. Samuel scolded King Saul for failing to understand that "to obey is better than sacrifice" (1 Samuel 15:22). Jesus condemned the scribes and Pharisees who were self-consciously deliberate about external and superficial obedience, while remaining corrupt within (Matthew 23:23-28). And, of course, his sheep-and-goats teaching challenges those who call him "Lord" but whose religion does not manifest itself with compassion and charity (Matthew 25:31-46).

Mark 7:24-37

We — and the people in our pews — have all sorts of pictures of Jesus that we cherish. Some of those pictures very likely adorn our church hallways and Sunday school rooms. Some are portrayed in stained glass in our sanctuaries and chapels and many of them are vivid in our hearts and minds. They are pictures of Jesus teaching the crowds on the green hills near Galilee, surrounded by the children, calming the storm, feeding the multitude, healing the sick, standing at the door and knocking, and Jesus as the Good Shepherd. We have untold numbers of pictures of Jesus that we cherish.

We do not have and do not cherish, however, a picture of Jesus turning down or turning away someone in need. Yet that is the picture Mark seems to paint for us at the beginning of this week's gospel lesson.

Mark's picture is the gentler one. Matthew also offers an account of this episode (15:21-28), and his picture presents an even more disturbing picture of Jesus at the outset. In both cases, a desperate woman's need is initially ignored. And then, when the woman is finally addressed by Jesus, it is in a language we find unacceptable.

Jesus' response to the woman is offensive to our modern ears. We are accustomed to hearing Jesus speak in metaphorical language: Indeed, we love it. We may even welcome the image of Israel as "the children" here, but when this poor, frantic mother, along with her people, is categorized as "the dogs," then we are surprised and offended. Couldn't the Gentiles have been cast as, say, "the neighbor kids" instead?

Still, though we are initially troubled by what Jesus did say, we must remember what he did not say. He did not say, "No." He did not say, "Go away." His word to the woman left room for a response, and her good response delighted Jesus.

An inescapable reality of this passage is Jesus' withdrawal from the crowds. It is not the point of either story in this passage, and yet it plays a part in both stories.

One reasonably assumes that Jesus' reason for going to the region of Tyre in the first place was to get away from the crowds. He could not go anywhere in Israel, it seems, without being pursued and surrounded (see, for example, Mark 3:7-8; 3:20; 6:31-33; 6:53-56). What is implicit in his departure from Israel to a foreign territory becomes explicit when he enters a house there "and did not want anyone to know he was there."

Likewise, in the next episode, we see Jesus take the deaf man aside, "away from the crowd." The healing is performed in as much privacy as Jesus was able to attain: a brief, undisturbed moment with a man in need.

That second event can help to cast light on the first. If we had the first only, we might think that Jesus was simply trying to avoid people and their needs, including people like the Syrophoenician woman and the deaf man. But Jesus' distancing himself from the crowds even while healing the man suggests a different purpose than merely being alone or getting away. It may be that the desires, assumptions, and intent of the crowds were getting out of hand (as in John 6:15). He had come on a particular mission, he knew what it was, and he was not going to take shortcuts (as in Matthew 4:8-10) or allow himself to be detoured by anyone else (as in Mark 8:31-33).

Application

So here are two cars in a parking lot. One is a fine-looking driving machine. The other looks like a piece of junk. Both drivers get in and turn their keys, but only the junky car actually starts and goes. The other driver is only able to sit there looking good in the parking lot because his car doesn't work.

Practically speaking, then, what good is good-looking when the car doesn't work?

The mechanic pulls up. I believe his name is James. He takes a look at the car and concludes, "Your car is dead."

The owner is offended. "It's not dead! Look at it — it's beautiful! Look at that shine, the interior, the features. How can you say it's dead?"

"Because it doesn't work," James replies. "A car that doesn't work is dead. What do you think: Will that car get you home?"

Alternative Applications

Mark 7:24-37. "Just for That." Talking back usually gets people into trouble. Many earnest parents have worked hard to prove to their children that talking back will never get them what they want.

That is so often the context of backtalk, isn't it? A child wants something, he gets turned down, and so he responds with some angry and frustrated reply. "That's not fair" seems common to almost all ages. Tantrums, pleading, whining, arguing, bargaining, and angry personal attacks are also frequent forms of backtalk.

Seldom does talking back achieve the originally desired result. And sometimes it even gets the child in more trouble. "Just for that," the mother or father sternly replies, "you go to your room" or "you can't go to that sleepover this weekend" or "no television for you tonight" or some other such punishment.

In our gospel lesson, a woman wants something — needs something — and she comes to Jesus to ask for it. Initially, it seems that he turns her down. Admittedly, his response is not a clear-cut "No." He does not simply send her away. But his response is surely discouraging. It could easily sound like "No" and prompt a person to walk away in disappointment and despair. But not this woman. No, she stays there and talks back to Jesus.

Now, certainly this isn't backtalk that in the sense of being angry or disrespectful, but it is a retort. She is saying, "Yes, but..." to Jesus. And he responds, essentially, by saying, "Just for that... just for that, you have what you came for!"

This Gentile woman is patron saint for a certain kind of faith: a faith that does not get easily discouraged; a faith that is persistent and insistent; a faith that comes to Jesus, and a faith that gets what it came for.

You and I and most of our people know what it is to be disappointed by the seeming lack of response to some prayers along the way. Let us persist with a hopeful, "Yes, but...." And perhaps, in response, we will hear him say, "Just for that, you have what you came for!"

Proverbs 22:1-2, 8-9, 22-23. "Greatest Common Factors." We observe this recurring theme, which is evident in verse 2 of our reading from Proverbs: what things various types of people have in common — the wise and the foolish (Ecclesiastes 2:14), the oppressed and the oppressor (Proverbs 29:13), the clean and the unclean (Ecclesiastes 9:2). And, in our selected Old Testament lesson, the rich and the poor (Proverbs 22:2).

At a glance, of course, and from a worldly point of view, it's easy to think that the rich and the poor have nothing in common. Stand them side-by-side as caricatures, and they seem worlds apart.

The one appears manicured and sophisticated. He seems so successful, with his importance and his influence, his corner office and his built-in pool. His neighborhood looks like a contemporary Eden, and his home a kind of palace. He is the picture of the consummate individual: well-dressed, well-bred, and well-to-do.

His opposite number, meanwhile, seems to be an undesirable character. One wonders about his competence and/or his character. He is comparatively shabby to look at, and his neighborhood makes other people uneasy. He is the sort of person no one wants to be when he grows up.

And yet, time and again, the wisdom writers of the Old Testament take the big-picture view: recognizing and identifying what these two dissimilar people have in common. And what they have in common, we discover, is always big stuff: life, death, and their creator. Compared to this, primary things that the rich and poor have in common, what they drive, how they dress, and where they live all seem quite insignificant. And if we remember that, then our churches will not fall into the trap of preferential treatment that James names and condemns.

Proper 19 / Pentecost 16 / Ordinary Time 24
Proverbs 1:20-33
James 3:1-12
Mark 8:27-38
David Davis

Setting the mind on things divine

The Sunday school teacher came up to me with a bit of a panicked looked in her face. The student from her second-grade class was following right behind. They were clearly on a mission. "Pamela has a question and I assured her you would have the answer," the teacher blurted it out as more of a request than a promise. I bent over to receive the child's question. "Where did God come from?" There was a certain intensity to her question. I explained that God has always been there and that God didn't come from anywhere. She didn't accept that and asked me if God had parents. I said no and tried to deflect that conversation toward Mary, Joseph, and Jesus. That didn't work either and the little girl walked away frustrated and I confronted my own pastoral frailties. I wished I would have thought of a better answer.

Years before that in a seminary class titled "Introduction to the Old Testament," I remember a rather demanding first-year student raising his hand after one of the lectures on the book of Genesis and asking, "So where did Cain's wife come from?" The professor paused, stroked the chin, and then said, "I believe it was somewhere east of Poughkeepsie!" The point had something to do with the nature of questions and answers. And I remember once hearing the most famous of biblical scholars respond to a question about the book of Revelation with, "I don't know."

Despite expectations to the contrary, the life of faith may not always be about having the right answer. Some have suggested that Peter's encounter with Jesus at Caesarea Philippi was something of an exam. Jesus posed that question that has always rattled around in the history of the faith. "Who do you say that I am?" From the scholarly corner where theologians wrestle to understand divinity and humanity to the pages of confirmation or youth retreat curriculum, the question is never far from front and center. It has all the trappings of a final exam question. "Who do you say that I am?" Of course Peter had an answer. Peter always had an answer. In Mark's gospel the answer comes in a predictably crisp way, "You are the Messiah." Matthew's gospel expands the answer just a bit: "You are the Messiah, the Son of the Living God!" Matthew's gospel also adds an affirmation from the lips of Jesus. Jesus offers Peter a blessing. Jesus calls Peter the Rock on which he will build the church. Jesus gives Peter the keys to the kingdom. It's pretty easy to conclude that Peter had the right answer. Indeed, Peter did have the right answer. But in Mark's gospel the conversation quickly turns to denying, following, taking up the cross. Those historic words of praise offered to Peter are not to be found in Mark.

To set one's mind on things divine is about more than just having the right answer.

Proverbs 1:20-33

The assigned lection from Proverbs 1 introduces the feminine personification of Wisdom. The reader must first work backwards to obtain the writer's sense of the meaning of Wisdom. The familiar theme of Proverbs 1:7 is what leaps to the fore. "The fear of the Lord is the beginning of knowledge; fools despise wisdom and instruction." Thus, Wisdom personified in the latter part of chapter 1 must embrace the importance of a relationship with God that is based on worship. As the writer develops this idea of Wisdom in terms of her proclamation and her place in the city, her identity rests in the characteristic of "the fear of the Lord."

246

Wisdom takes her place at the very center of life. Wisdom's voice comes from the "squares" and "busiest corners" and "entrance of the city gates." Right in the midst of society's bustle, Wisdom yearns to be heard. Her voice breaks through the white noise of everyday life there in the world. The first words from Wisdom come in the form of a stinging question to the passing crowds. "How long, simple ones, will you love being simple?" Simple here may refer more to youth than to intellect. But among those who choose to remain youthfully simple, there are scoffers and fools as well. The crowds are openly defiant toward any knowledge that reflects that godly wisdom. The voice of Wisdom calls the crowds to reproof and repentance. That call includes a promise that comes in the form of thought and words. The promise is an offering of Wisdom.

In the face of Wisdom's call, the naive, skeptical crowds refuse her counsel. They choose to receive nothing of what Wisdom has to offer. The bearer of Wisdom turns derisive in her response. She chooses to laugh and mock the panic, distress, and anguish that will surely overcome the nameless crowds of scoffers. Wisdom expresses the confidence that such calamity will surely come upon those who refuse her. At the point when the simple fools then turn to seek this reverent knowledge, she will pretend to not know them. She will refuse to answer. Like the parable of Jesus that tells of the foolish virgins who are turned away from the party when the knock is not recognized, so these scoffers will be left only to beg at Wisdom's door. Wisdom has little time for sympathy because those who stand unrecognized by Wisdom's gift did not choose the fear of the Lord.

The conclusion of Wisdom's first song heightens the contrast between the way of the simple and the way of the wise. "For waywardness kills the simple and the complacency of fools destroys them; but those who listen to me will be secure and will live at ease, without dread of disaster" (1:32-33). In content, Wisdom's voice parallels the message offered by the psalmist in the very first song. That introduction to the Psalter and the Wisdom literature of the Old Testament characterizes that same distinction. "For the Lord watches over the way of the righteous; but the way of the wicked will perish."

James 3:1-12

The reader informed by the lectionary might expect to end up here in the third chapter of James. After one encounters the personification of Wisdom in the book of Proverbs, it would make sense to come to the end of James 3 and read about that "wisdom from above." However, James 3:13ff occurs in the lectionary assignment for next week. In the continuous reading through James, this week's reading comes from the beginning of chapter 3 and the focus is "the tongue" not wisdom.

The opening verses of James 3 ought not to be read on the occasion of church school recruitment. The warning to teachers of the faith is strong and clear. "Not many of you should become teachers... for you know that we who teach will be judged with greater strictness." The writer of James goes on to argue that all of us make many mistakes and the foundation of many of those mistakes can be found in the tongue. Like bits, bridles, and rudders, the tongue functions as a small but key instrument of direction and control. It is in that control, or lack of it, that the tongue exerts its power.

The author's negative opinion about the power of the tongue cannot be overstated. Harsh images leap off the page: fire, stain, restless evil, deadly poison. Of course the irony of the tongue, according to James, is that we use it both to "bless the Lord" and to "curse those who are made in the likeness of God." The author laments the double-edged sword that is the organ of voice represented by the tongue. Such a dual purpose for the tongue works against the forces of nature as revealed in the metaphor of fresh/salt water and fig trees/olives. However, the author hesitates to conclude which is the dominant purpose of the tongue.

The reader deduces that apart from the wisdom of God, the tongue is left in service to the sinful nature of humanity. In the discipline of rhetoric, sometimes a figure of speech is used that is only a part of something intended to stand for the whole. The technical term is *synecdoche*. An example given in a textbook on preaching refers to "a ship setting out across the waves." The waves here are intended to reference the entire sea. Perhaps the writer of James intends for the tongue to evoke the sense of the broader concept of human sin and disobedience. The challenge to teachers and role models in faith is not that evil tongues full of poison are at work, but that we are all human, enslaved to the realities of the human condition.

Mark 8:27-38

It is typical of Mark's style that Jesus' teaching about his suffering and death comes in tandem with a blind man being healed. In chapter 10 the passion prediction precedes the healing of Bartimaeus. Here in chapter 8, just prior to Peter's confession and the Lord's teaching about the cross, a blind man receives his sight. It is a theme of Mark's gospel. The blind receive their sight throughout the gospel and yet, the disciples still are unable to perceive the truth about the Messiah nor understand the teaching about his death.

The conversation of the disciples must have started innocently enough. The disciples might have thought of it as casual conversation among friends. Jesus wants to know what people were saying. He wants to know the rumors. "Who do people say that I am?" The disciples mention Elijah, John the Baptist, and one of the prophets. Jesus doesn't allow the casual talk to continue. He is no longer concerned about what the polls say. With his follow up question, the stakes go higher. "But who do you say that I am?"

Peter buzzed in right away with the answer. Even as that title of "Messiah" crosses the lips of Peter, Mark's Jesus is quick to come back with that messianic secret. Then, with the fresh warning not to tell anyone still ringing in the disciples' ears, Jesus moves into the teaching about the suffering and death of the Son of Man. Mark tells us that Jesus "quite openly" talked about the Messiah's death and resurrection. Apparently not wanting to hear a word of it, Peter took the Lord aside and proceeded to rebuke him for such talk about suffering. Notice that Jesus then turns back so that the disciples are all within sight. While looking at all the disciples, he rebukes Peter for not being willing to see the bigger picture. Ever the teacher, Jesus uses Peter as something of an object lesson and broadens his teaching to include talk of the life of discipleship.

The crowds begin to grow as Jesus turns his attention to life lived in response to the suffering and death of the Son of God. His attention goes from the rumors of the world, to the response of Peter, to a lesson for the disciples, to a word intended for the crowds (which I take to mean to the church). He speaks about losing life for the sake of the gospel, about losing life in order to save. Jesus turns to speak to the crowds about life in his name. It is a life of following and serving and witnessing.

What begins with Peter's confession ends with a call to the crowds to think about life in the name of Jesus. It is the Lord's definition of setting the mind on things divine: Look to the cross of Christ and follow him with your very life.

Application

In college I learned the importance of location when taking an exam. Final exams were given in a huge hall with many classes seated at table after table. The space itself was intimidating. The sheer number of students was anxiety producing. Top all of that with a psychology professor who suggested that you should always take the test in the room where you learned the material. I figured out early on that where you take an exam is important.

In Mark's narrative, the location of Peter's exam is not to be missed. Scholars point to the location of the text in the gospel narrative itself. It is a turning point in the gospel story, a turning from the ministry of Galilee and a turning toward the passion at Jerusalem. The questioning from Jesus falls at the center of the plot. Some point out how Jesus now moves to the center and all other characters, including the disciples, fade to the shadows of the stage. In the gospel of Mark so much happens when Jesus turns to the disciples and asks, "But who do you say that I am?"

So we have to consider the location of the exam in the biblical narrative as well as the location of the exam in the plot of the story. But there is the physical location of the exam. Jesus confronted the disciples as they traveled toward the village of Caesarea Philippi. This city was a key stop geographically, a stop along the way where the traveling party could look back and look ahead. Caesarea Philippi was a Roman city named to honor the emperor, and was a place of pagan worship — a worldly stop, if you will. In terms of the Messiah's trip, in terms of his journey to the cross, Caesarea Philippi was a foreign land.

Surrounded by the trappings of power and tribute, in the area where worship was offered in many directions, at a place where adoration was seldom reserved for the almighty, Jesus asks the question. The answer came from Peter, but clearly more of a response was required. When you're standing in Caesarea Philippi, apparently there is more to the life of discipleship than what you can figure out with your mind! When you are knee deep in the powers and principalities, then the life of faith is about more than just having the right answer. When the atmosphere around you is steeped in what the world chooses to worship, then your response to Jesus, your knowledge of him, your answer to the question is less about words and more about life. It is about setting the mind, and the soul, and the heart, on things divine!

Alternative Applications
Mark 8:27-38. "As this bread is Christ's body for us, send us out to be the body of Christ in the world." That is part of a Eucharistic prayer offered from the Communion table. With Peter's affirmation about Jesus ringing in our ears, the church, called to be the body of Christ, turns to face the world. The text in Mark may be about both Christology and ecclesiology.

Years ago, at a church visioning meeting, the question I heard wasn't, "Who do you say that I am?" but "What do people say about our church?" One of the saints answered. "If you ask me who we are, I'd have to say we are the body of Christ. And I have never, ever heard anyone in this community say of this church, 'They are the body of Christ.' I've been in the Lions Club. I've coached. I've dabbled in politics, and I have sat at the tavern more than I should admit to you. And never, ever has anyone said, 'They are the body of Christ.'"

Maybe our view of Christ and our view of the church shouldn't be that different.

Proverbs 1:20-33. In the town where I live, a man has taken to reciting classic poems from memory — right in the center of everything. I have come upon street preachers before but never street poets. He doesn't shout. But he does choose a busy corner or sidewalk and stands to recite Frost, Burns, and others. The local paper even did a story on the man who said he wants to raise the bar related to the quality of conversation in the public square.

I'm not sure of the method, but I am intrigued by the image: a lone man trying to breathe some culture and wisdom on to a crowded street corner. It sounds a bit like the beginning of the personification of Wisdom here in the first chapter of Proverbs. Wisdom takes her place and raises her voice. She finds the busiest corner and then cries out. Though we preach Christ crucified as the Wisdom of the world, we more commonly offer that proclamation within the safe hallways of the sanctuary. More challenging images arise when imagining an aggressive attempt to break through the noise of the world with the wisdom of God. An eccentric street corner poet? The profound innocence of a child showing love on a crowded playground? A silent witness of grace as the world passes by? Or that voice of Wisdom crying out next to the city gate?

Proper 20 / Pentecost 17 / Ordinary Time 25
Proverbs 31:10-31
James 3:13—4:3, 7-8a
Mark 9:30-37
Craig MacCreary

Any questions? — show of hands

"Any questions?" The words hang in the air at the end of the teacher's lecture as the students play out their own pedagogical strategies. There are the usual hands that shoot up in a display of promoting the students' own eruditions. For them this will be an opportunity to display the most profound of their thoughts by asking the most arcane, esoteric questions. For others, this will be signal for a duck and cover drill as they hide from their own inabilities to take in what the teacher was talking about. Others step forward to reveal their honest confusion. Some, in effect, ask for the lecture to be repeated in simple English this time. A few, having learned something, want to know more.

When we come to the texts for preaching, where will we line up? I suspect that some of us might fall into patterns of asking little of the text because we bring such familiarity to the words. I look at the text from Proverbs and cringe. Over the years, like in the words of the letter from James, "I do not have because I do not ask." I ask little of these words other than to be the basis for a suitable funeral reflection that would capture the essence of some seriously active loving souls. There is nothing wrong in this. As a matter of fact there has been much blessing. Yet, I suspect that I have asked too little of this text over the years, considering that it was not originally written to supply my needs for funeral themes. Indeed, I suspect as the letter of James puts it, that I do not receive because I ask wrongly. I ask in a rush and on the run of a busy pastor's schedule. I ask thinking that a surface knowledge of the text will suffice; I did not take a seminary course on the Wisdom literature, yet I seek to come across with a level of rabbinic wisdom I do not have. The letter of James suggests that I might do this in order to spend what I get on my pleasures. I might get the pleasure of getting through a funeral with having squeezed something pleasing out of the text, but have I forsaken the depth that might be here? Yes, of course, maybe a funeral is not the time for such thoughts. Yet, how often does there seem to be another time in which I can begin to really ask of the text the kind of questions that, while demonstrating my limited knowledge, will get me further in the direction of knowing the ways of the Lord.

The texts for this Sunday challenge me as to what I ask for and how I do my asking. The letter of James challenges me with the words, "And a harvest of righteousness is sown in peace for those who make peace." I hear the words of the peace activist A.J. Muste, "There is no way to peace, peace is the way." I have asked for peace of mind, peace in the house, peace in the church community, and the world." My asking for peace seems to outrun the number of times I have asked to be a blessing of peace or inquired about being an instrument of the peace that passes all understanding, or for the strength to walk in peace the first mile that I may go the second mile. James may have it right here; I am missing something in my life because I do not know how to ask or I ask wrongly. When we are asked "Are there any questions?" just why are our hands shooting up or why might we be sitting on our hands?

In the Markan text we are confronted by one of Mark's basic themes. The disciples get it wrong. Indeed, if there is a way for the disciple to get it wrong, they will find it. One suspects that this theme is the result less of academic insight than of Mark's reflection on his own church life. I suspect that Mark's faith community was probably as prone to get wrapped up in these kinds of embarrassing arguments as the disciples — the kind that you might not want to take to Jesus to have him settle. Would we really want Jesus to make the call on the passionate dispute over the carpet color in the sanctuary or the new hymnal?

Or should we be coming to him in a different way about these matters — other than trying to determine who has the greatest approach? Perhaps the biggest question is just how and why we will raise our hand when the master teacher asks.

Proverbs 31:10-31

Here is a text which many of us do not ask much more of than a confirmation of middle-class domesticity. Here we have a model that fits in with many of the folks we serve. Who would not want to have an effective chief executive officer like the wife portrayed in these words? These words are quite comforting especially if you are a husband who aspires to be the chair of the board of such a corporation. How else can you be known in the city gates — known enough to be able to take your place among the elders? As I read the text, I wonder if the writer is accepting the notion that in order for the husband to take his place, the wife must know her place. In the twenty-first century I find myself at a sticking point with this text. Must it be that way? Is it okay to be that way if that is your choice? Is this a requirement for the families of those who aspire to public roles? It says that the children rise up and call her happy. It sounds like there are no phone calls forgotten on Mother's Day. Yet it seems that calling her happy is dangerous without knowing what makes her happy. The husband calls her happy, which seems a lot easier than knowing what makes her happy.

This takes me to another question. Just how can a text speak to me when it arises out a very different cultural context? In this instance, can a text from a male-dominated, hierarchical, authoritarian culture speak to me? Must I throw overboard whatever the text is saying because I find it seriously flawed? Or, is it that God uses even the profoundly flawed, in terms of current values, to bring out profound truths? In this case the more I look at it, even given the values of our day, the more it appears that there is much here that is redeeming material.

If nothing else, as we read the text, we must be astounded at the capacity of this woman to maintain a tough mindedness along with a gentle heart. Holding these two together reminds me of Jesus' instruction to his disciples to be wise as serpents as well as innocent as doves. Holding these two together affords us the capacity to be in the world but not of it. One can anticipate disaster in this house if the woman in this case did not take up this role. Perhaps even more dangerous is a flip-flop in which the manager of the household has a "tender mind and a tough heart." The text asks me to consider what is the right balance. It also pushes me to ask what happens if we also count on someone to perform the same role over and over again. In this situation, what happens when the kids are all grown up and there is an empty nest? In this case does the woman have as hard a time as men do maintaining balance when something like retirement comes? One might rewrite the text something like this, "A good wife is one who knows when to quit, she is like one who knows how to hand power on when the time comes, and she remains silent when the new ownership does things differently. She rises early for prayer and does not let the sun go down without considering whether she has had sufficient sabbath rest."

Much happens for me when I move beyond the very little that I usually ask this text to do for me. When I make that move, suddenly I find that it is as if at the end of class the teacher, rather than asking if I have any questions, turns it around and says, "Now I have questions for you to wrestle with." Suddenly I find the text calling into question, my assumptions and presumptions about life. When it does, then I find myself knowing what and how to ask of the text in return.

James 3:13—4:3, 7-8a

The letter of James poses a less than delightful thought. That we do not have because we do not ask. This hardly seems right. If anything we seem to be asking for something all the time. Our list of wants is great. Can it be that God is just waiting for us to get it right? I think I hear the voice of seminary professors challenging the notion that we have to get it right before God gets with us. Maybe Martin Luther was right in his suspicions about the worthiness of James as a vehicle of Christian proclamation. Yet Jesus said that we should seek first the kingdom of God and all else would be added unto us. My theological feathers are somewhat smoothed by the notion that the problem may be that I do not know how to ask for what I already have. The asking seems to be an essential step in appropriating what God has given me. The practical truth of what James is saying here is clear for me, because when I examine what I often ask for and how I ask for it I find much that gets in the way of my relationship with God.

One bit of the evidence of my problem is Mahatma Gandhi's list of the seven deadly sins, "Politics without principles, wealth without work, commerce without morality, pleasure without conscience, education without character, science without humanity, and worship without sacrifice." Our society seems to be able to ask for the first in each of these pairs without being prepared to ask for the latter. We find it all too easy to separate what God has joined together. We ask wrongly when we ask what it takes to win an election, not what it takes to govern a people. We ask wrongly when we make a god of the free market. We ask wrongly when we maximize pleasure and minimize responsibility. We ask wrongly when we educate for careers, not vocations. We ask wrongly when we ask about possibilities without asking about consequences. We ask wrongly when we ask for comforting worship that does not help us confront injustice.

James' claim that, "You want something and do not have it; so you commit murder. And you covet something and cannot obtain it; so you engage in disputes and conflicts. You do not have, because you do not ask" seems at first to be fairly farfetched. However, what often seems to lead to many deaths is the failure to ask about the consequences, leaving it all up to the free market, or seeking valueless education, or a science without social responsibility. I rather suspect that it may be the death of churches that we too readily seek feel-good religion that does not give us a feel for what the kingdom of God is.

The context of the letter seems to be church disputes that have gotten out of hand. This often comes when people think that they have alone seized the high ground. It seems to me that in asking wrongly there is enough foolishness to go around, and we need to be establishing common ground for our mutual forgiveness.

In a sense, we ask for much without asking about the price, not only what we have paid but what God has paid. Inquiring about the latter has a way of bringing me to my knees in gratitude for a God who has reached beyond my sins and foolishness. We do not ask about the price. If we do, we discover that we are all on a level playing field and share equally in the forgiveness of God. Inquiring about the price has a way of putting limits on our egos and toning down our conversations while lifting our spirits.

James also points out that we do not receive because we do not ask. Putting into words what we really want can be daunting. There is a personal price we wind up paying when we do ask. Saying it out loud may force us to confront some of the foolishness of what we want. Saying it out in public may be more revealing than we want. Yet putting our requests into words and putting them before others can bring needed perspective. Church could be the place where we learn to ask rightly.

Mark 9:30-37

Jesus, like most good teachers, must have recognized the pained, quizzical look on the disciple's face. It is the kind of look that students give when they don't get it, try to hide that they don't get it, and are in prayer that whatever the teacher was talking about will not be on the final exam. Of course, they were afraid to ask. The fact that they don't get it might be a judgment as much on the teacher as on the students. What student wants to inform the teacher that today's lesson might have been a bomb? It is not always obvious that when you don't understand, the appropriate response is to ask. You need to really feel the teacher out on this one. On the other hand, as I recall from school days, asking could unleash all sorts of other unwanted possibilities. Your question could let loose an answer that could go on forever. Lord help you if you have stumbled into the teacher's favorite area of expertise. You could find the teacher perceiving in you more of an interest in the course than you really have. This could lead to all kinds of interesting assignments and challenges that you might not want to take on. It could set the teacher off and send you off with a dressing down. You might be held responsible for the teacher ratcheting up the challenge level on the next quiz. There are all sorts of reasons to sit on your hands lest they impulsively leap into the air with a question.

Good teachers like Jesus know when we have hit that point. The cloud of ignorance and fear descends as the class makes its way to the door. If there are no questions from the students, Jesus has one of his own: "What were you arguing about on the way?" Were you arguing about who is going to tell the professor that we have a communication problem? He could clearly see the agitation going on.

Mark says that they were silent because they were arguing about who was the greatest among them. Maybe if they could establish a pecking order, then the least among them would be the poor soul who would have to tell Jesus that they just didn't get it this time. The disciple's conversation does not seem as odd as it might appear on the surface.

Of course, their strategy is deeply flawed. Anything that prevents us from talking with Jesus or coming to him just as we are is probably going to get us into difficulties. Jesus makes very clear that the disciples have gotten things out of line here. He puts a child into their midst as their starting point. Children are not only naturally curious but they are inherently brave. They have not learned the potential, fearful consequence of asking.

You don't get a lecture from Jesus. You get a conversation, a give and take, that can take you to insights about yourself and the world. Go ahead and raise your hand, you won't have an endless waste of your time — you will find eternity. Go ahead and ask — you will find support. Go ahead and ask — you will find yourself sorting out the difference between what you want and what you need. Welcome that child in yourself that can't wait to raise their hand and you will find yourself welcoming the God who sent Jesus into the world. Ask your questions of his stories, ask of one another, ask of the saints of old and the teachers of the church, ask in prayer with the hand waving enthusiasm of a child and you will find yourself welcoming God into your life.

Application

I think there ought to be a class on how to ask the right questions. Experience tells me that either through timidity or convenience I fail to ask enough of scripture. In doing so I miss the God that asks more of me in my study of scripture. I ought to ask more about price and consequence. I have an easier time asking about the price I might pay rather than the price that God pays or that others pay. A surefire way to fall into trouble in the asking department is to fail to put my asking into words or out loud. Kept within me my asking can lead to delusions. Asking without entering into dialogue with others can lead to serious negative consequences. Of course, a preoccupation with my asking can lead to my inability to hear what God or others might be asking of me.

I find that in the asking department I discover common ground with all sorts of people. Groups of political left or right seem to do no better job in the asking department than their opposites. I suspect that both groups would benefit from a class on asking. I suspect they would benefit even more from taking it together — "Class, any other questions?"

An Alternative Application

James 3:13—4:3, 7-8a. In verse 13 of chapter 3, the letter of James talks about the gentleness born of wisdom. What kind of wisdom leads to gentleness?

I think that it rather depends on the way you define wisdom. Certainly there is that kind of wisdom that can draw lines in the sand and define clear boundaries. One should not undersell the necessity of that kind of wisdom. How many folks have poor life outcomes because of an inadequate sense of their boundaries?

However, my gentleness also comes from the wisdom that knows how to draw inclusive circles as well as lines in the sand. One without the other is a bad bet.

The modern definition of prudence is calculated self-interest. No doubt that kind of wisdom will get us many things at the stock market, or in the corporate world, but gentleness may not be one of them. Prudence might be more accurately characterized as practical wisdom. Gentleness might come from knowing that we are all on a level playing field when it comes to the practical questions of life and getting through the day. Pooling our wisdom on these matters might lead to gentleness of spirit. No society I know of has a lock on the art of changing a diaper, encouraging a child that has just struck out for the fourth time in a baseball game, or how a man and a wife heal after inflicting emotional pain on each other. Considering such things together might lead to a real gentleness of spirit.

There is the wisdom that knows how to analyze, dissect, and classify. I can't imagine the world getting along without that kind of wisdom but I am not sure that we get much gentleness from it. Synthesizing, weaving, and knowing how to put yourself in another's place goes a long way toward creating gentle space.

The words of the letter of James from today's epistle lesson, "Show by your good life that your works are done with gentleness born of wisdom," send me scampering to consider how I define wisdom.

Proper 21 / Pentecost 18 / Ordinary Time 26
Esther 7:1-6, 9-10; 9:20-22
James 5:13-20
Mark 9:38-50
David Kalas

Public enemy

If only he had understood his real enemy.

We think of Haman as such a thoroughly bad man — one of the great villains of the Old Testament. Yet, for all of his vices and viciousness, Haman remains something of a role model for us. After all, he is no-nonsense about obliterating his enemies. He just didn't recognize who or what his real enemies were.

Recognizing the enemy is the first issue of warfare. It will not matter how well-trained and highly skilled a soldier is if he takes action against the wrong targets. You've got to know who your enemy is, and you have to be able to recognize him.

Haman did not. In his own vanity — and perhaps insecurity — Haman thought that his enemy was Mordecai. And in his impassioned effort to get rid of Mordecai, he sought to do a more thorough thing: get rid of everyone who is like Mordecai.

Again, we may be sickened by Haman, but just imagine him aiming at a different target, and suddenly we will appreciate his approach. Let us imagine, for example, that Haman identified cancer as his enemy — indeed, as "public enemy number one." If that were his target, we would applaud his passion and dedication: his single-minded investment of himself and his resources; his effective involvement of people who can help; his bringing to bear the resources of the state in defeating — eliminating! — the enemy.

Imagine Haman going after poverty, or drugs, or discrimination. Haman would be a world-class crusader. And he would be remembered admiringly by future generations for his dramatic impact in whatever field he chose.

Or, turn Haman's attention inward. Imagine him being a bit more reflective — and considerably more perceptive — than he was. If he had recognized certain personal vices (such as pride, pettiness, selfish ambition, and vindictiveness) as his enemies, and if he had gone after them with the same determination that he sought to eliminate Mordecai, Haman would have ended up as one of the great saints of scripture.

And so, with Haman as our unlikely role model, we turn in this week's lessons to a consideration of our real enemies and how to defeat them.

Esther 7:1-6, 9-10; 9:20-22

Southwest Airlines has produced a series of ingenious television commercials that portray individuals who find themselves in terribly awkward and embarrassing situations. As the person lingers in that moment of tension and discomfort, the narrator's voice asks, "Wanna get away?"

Haman could be the unhappy star of such a commercial.

The day begins as a bright one for this proud and ambitious man. He will be that night, for the second consecutive night, the special dinner guest of the king and the queen. This is not merely the privilege of appearing on the guest list for some state dinner. No, Haman has been singled out from the entire court — indeed, the entire Persian empire! — to have a private dinner with Ahasuerus and Esther.

Midway through the much-anticipated event, however, Haman is stunned to find himself singled out not as the special guest of the queen, but rather as the enemy of the queen. Moments later, the king catches him in a suspicious posture before the queen.

Wanna get away?

The book of Esther is distinctive for the absence of any explicit reference to God. Indeed, there have been voices in church history that have objected to its inclusion in the canon because of that significant deficiency. The story of Esther is useful to us precisely because of its seemingly unorthodox approach. After all, Esther's story reads the same way that our day-to-day lives read. We are not often able to point to a parting sea or a halted sun in order to prove the presence and work of God in our midst and on our behalf. Instead, more often than not, the eyes of faith are required in order to detect his provident care.

The eyes of faith surely see the unmentioned hand of God at work in Esther's life and story. Consider the improbability of an anonymous woman from a once-captive people rising to the throne and the right hand of the emperor. See how instrumental Mordecai is in saving the king's life; and then see the providential timing of that king's insomnia, how he responded to his sleeplessness, and the particular details that just happened to be read to him. See also the divine protection of God's own people in their innocence, and the fitting justice that befalls the enemy of his people.

Likewise, the eyes of faith will see God's hand at work in our own lives, too, in the ordering of circumstances, the turn of events, the holy coincidences.

Meanwhile, there is another approach to Esther's story that is especially suggested by this particular passage. Perhaps we might take a brief walk in Haman's shoes, and give some thought to what he did wrong.

The element that intrigues me especially is the contribution made by Harbona: "Look, the very gallows that Haman has prepared for Mordecai, whose word saved the king, stands at Haman's house, fifty cubits high." That is the word that leads immediately to Haman's sentence. It is not after Esther's revelation that the king orders Haman's execution, you see, but rather on the heels of the additional information supplied by Harbona.

Haman's plot against the Jews could have been, at some level, defensible. The king had not blushed at the proposal of genocide, and he seemed to have been persuaded by Haman's rationale (see Esther 3:8-11). From our contemporary perspective, we see the wickedness of Haman's plan, it was not an overtly bad move at a strategic level. The king initially endorsed it.

The unfortunate discovery for Haman, of course, was that the queen herself was a member of the very ethnic group he was arranging to exterminate. Perhaps Haman could have backpedaled enough from that mistake — if that had been his only mistake. He could, with honesty and sincerity, claim ignorance. His intent was certainly not to kill the queen. He could have reiterated his concern for the king in the face of a rebellious population within the empire.

But it was Harbona's report that was so damning. How bloodthirsty and vengeful it seemed that Haman had constructed on his own property an instrument of execution. How unseemly that it was fifty cubits high — overkill, if you will, for the execution of a single man. How juvenile and petty that Haman had personally targeted Mordecai, and how unlucky that the object of Haman's vendetta was someone who had been so personally important to the king.

Given the fact that Haman's plan had already been presented to and approved by the king, it is perhaps surprising that circumstances turn so dramatically against him. But then the turning of circumstances is very much the witness of this book, for while God is not explicitly mentioned, yet "behind the dim unknown, standeth God within the shadow, keeping watch above his own" (from *Once To Every Man And Nation* by James R. Lowell).

James 5:13-20

Churches are becoming increasingly aware of the importance of signage. If someone new and unfamiliar walks through our doors, we want to make it easy for him to find his way around. Where should they go if they're looking for the nursery? The restroom? The office? The sanctuary?

In the passage at hand, James offers to the church a still more significant set of directions. Where shall I go if I am suffering? If I am cheerful? If I am sick? Many of the people who walk through our doors qualify for those categories, and they would be well served to hear James' directions about where to go and what to do.

The New Revised Standard Version endeavors to keep these instructions inclusive (rather than gender-specific), translating the verbs as third-person plural (such as "They should pray," "They should sing songs of praise," and "They should call for the elders"). In the original Greek, however, the instructions are more individualized. Apart from the awkward "he/she" method, however, English does not make it easy to speak in the third-person singular. But singular is what it is. The individual who is suffering? He should pray. The one who is cheerful? She should sing songs of praise! And the one who is sick? He should convene the elders to anoint him and pray over him. Those are the directional signs that James offers the church, one person at a time.

The need for physical healing is a major issue in most of our churches. In my congregation, the printed prayer list is filled with phrases like "battle with cancer," "facing surgery," "recently diagnosed," "undergoing treatments," "awaiting a transplant," and so on. We gather that the need for physical healing was a part of the church's experience in James' day, as well. He assures his readers that "the prayer of faith will save the sick." Then he ponders the effectiveness of faithful prayer by turning to the example of one of the most colorful Old Testament characters, the prophet Elijah.

James says that "Elijah was a human being like us." I wonder how that statement would play on a true/false test given to our congregations. Do we really believe that Elijah was a human being like us? He who confronted kings and queens, outran a chariot, was fed by ravens, walked across the riverbed of the parted Jordan, and was carried off to heaven in a chariot of fire — just like us.

Of course, it's precisely because Elijah was a remarkable man with an extraordinary ministry that James selected him. The truth is that Elijah is just like us — we're all made of the same stuff. We all serve an extraordinary God whose power and goodness exceed our imagining. But it is not, according to James, the exceptional person who is mightily used, but rather "a human being like us" with faith. It is that faith that turns the ordinary person into a vessel for the work of our extraordinary God.

Mark 9:38-50

We must begin with this admission: We do not know who this other person was. John does not name him in his report to Jesus, and Mark, the narrator, does not supply any additional information. We are just left to wonder and theorize about this unknown individual who, during Jesus' earthly ministry but apart from Jesus' band of chosen disciples, was casting out demons in his name. While clearly that man and his actions were the issue for John, he was not the real issue for Jesus, or for Mark.

Judas, Peter, and Thomas are the disciples who are best known for their failures. John has a better reputation, though not really a very commendable track record. In addition to this episode, in which he needed to be corrected by Jesus, John is among the threesome that falls asleep at critical moments (see Matthew 26:36-46; Luke 9:28-32), he and his brother were Jonah-like in their eagerness to see others judged and destroyed (Luke 9:52-55), and they were also misguided in their ambitions (Mark 10:35-45).

John (the apostle) is seldom mentioned in the same breath with Haman, and yet we recognize again in this episode the peril of misidentifying your enemy. John's assumption was that, if a person was not "one of us," he should be stopped, even opposed. Jesus' standard, however, is a far more liberal one than John's. "Whoever is not against us is for us," Jesus said, suggesting a surprisingly narrow definition of his enemies — or at least his opponents.

John's reflex instinct remains alive and well in Jesus' followers still today. We still try to stop them, in one way or another, because they do not "follow us." It may be a point of doctrine, a behavior pattern, a political allegiance, or a matter of style. Whatever the difference, though, it is our natural reflex to oppose those who do not "follow us."

It is there, in that first-person plural pronoun, where John's great error occurs. He has established an us-them paradigm in his mind, and this renegade was to be rejected because he was not one of "us." We should not be surprised to discover, however, that the important matter turns out not to be "us" but Jesus. The issue is not this renegade's relationship to "us" but to Jesus. Of course, you and I don't know what this anonymous man's relationship to Jesus was. Apparently John didn't know, either, but Jesus wisely observed that he would not "be able soon afterward to speak evil of me."

The episode triggers several teachings, each one thematically linked to the one before. So, in the wake of John's antagonistic response to the anonymous miracle worker, Jesus offers two teachings on relations among people.

The first is the marvelous promise about the reward that will belong to someone who offers even the simplest kindness to one who bears Christ's name. This image can't help but stand in stark contrast to John's response to the man who was casting out demons in Jesus' name. Perhaps, he expected a congratulations for stopping the renegade. Instead, however, we find that he should have offered him a cup of cold water.

The second interrelationship teaching, then, is the severe warning about causing a believer to stumble. At the other end of the spectrum from offering a cup of cold water to one who bears the name of Christ, there is this deliberate opposition. And just as the earlier hospitality begets a reward, this antagonism invites unthinkable judgment.

Next, having referenced the stumbling blocks that might be placed before other believers, Jesus recognizes that an individual might have stumbling blocks of his or her own. We will return later to this hard-nosed teaching.

Finally, at the end of the passage we come to a series of quick references that seem to be only very loosely connected to each other. Some scholars argue that this almost random collection of sayings reflects the gospel writer's editorial decision to "stick" sayings of Jesus into different settings. On the other hand, it may be that Jesus is doing a very sophisticated, almost poetic thing here. Like a composer who introduces a motif, and then begins to play with and reinterpret it, so Jesus moves from teaching to teaching, always reinterpreting a prior theme. The pragmatic teaching about the choice between the kingdom of God and hell leads to an image of unquenchable fire. That turns into a cryptic reference to being "salted with fire," which almost certainly means something other than the fires of hell. Then the reference to salt is picked up and carried in a new direction, reminiscent of the familiar passage from the Sermon on the Mount (Matthew 5:13). And finally, the salt motif becomes a part of a twofold exhortation: one that is personal and internal, and another that is external and interrelational. And that two-part theme, of course, recalls issues from earlier in the lection, thus bringing the whole passage not only to a fitting conclusion but also to a kind of harmonious resolution.

Application

Haman knew how to deal with an enemy. Unfortunately, he did not understand or recognize his real enemy.

The people in our pews are not genocidal, but they may be guilty of the same fault as Haman, for it is always easy for us to misidentify enemies. Our egos have quick triggers, and our natural instinct is to target those who have hurt our feelings, offended our priorities, or impeded our progress.

While we swat vigorously at the mosquitos, however, the hungry lions stealthily surround us. The vices within are, in the long run, far more hazardous to us. Yet they may go mostly unnoticed while we devote too much energy and attention to defeating unimportant (and sometimes imaginary) human opposition.

Let us begin by recognizing and identifying our real enemies, and let's make them public enemies in the wholesome model recommended by James: "Confess your sins to one another, and pray for one another, so that you may be healed." Long before the members of Alcoholics Anonymous were wisely identifying their enemy in a group setting, James was urging brothers and sisters in Christ to stand up and say, "I'm Joe, and I'm a sinner."

And then, after identifying the enemy, we come to that all-important second step: eradicating the enemy. Here is where Haman showed his genius, albeit misguided. And if we doubt the merits of Haman as our role model, see the same ruthlessness in the teaching of Jesus.

What shall we do with the hand that causes us to stumble? What shall we do about the eye that leads us astray? The man or woman of God is challenged to live with a no-nonsense intolerance of our enemies, and a holy thoroughness in eliminating them.

An Alternative Application
Esther 7:1-6, 9-10; 9:20-22. "If the Shame Fits." The story of Esther is typically celebrated as a testimony to God's providence, and rightly so. But in the process of such a reading, we may oversimplify the character of Haman. We fit him for his black hat right from the start, and that may prevent us from taking a closer look at him — and at ourselves.

The natural reflex of the man or woman of faith is to identify with one of the story's heroes: with Esther or with Mordecai. In them, we see our role models for courage and for principle, and we recognize them as the beneficiaries of the behind-the-scenes care and protection of God.

It is quite unnatural, however, for us to identify ourselves with the genocidal Haman. If he were more famous in terms of world history, he would be among the most infamous of characters: a small man with big plans. Consequently, we may allow ourselves to read his share of the story untroubled by some of his very familiar vices.

For this Sunday, however, perhaps we should trim back the clichés and caricatures concerning Haman. It's not that his goal was anything less than monstrous; it's just that his shortcomings were so very ordinary. We might learn a sober lesson by seeing Haman in light of his terribly familiar vices.

If you are a preacher given to using alliterative lists for the sake of making sermons memorable, then I would suggest this list of four tragic errors found in Haman: pettiness, prejudice, plotting, and pride. These are the vices Haman demonstrates in his obsession with Mordecai and in his proposed resolution.

While orchestrating the annihilation of an entire group of people is far removed from your daily life and mine, Haman's underlying vices are actually very close to home. How many in our pews would say confidently that they are above all pettiness? That they have no functional prejudices? That they do not struggle with some form of pride? We and our people would be appropriately challenged, therefore, to see Haman as a villain with familiar flaws, rather than as a caricature that looks nothing like us.

Proper 22 / Pentecost 19 / Ordinary Time 27
Job 1:1; 2:1-10
Hebrews 1:1-4; 2:5-12
Mark 10:2-16
Wayne Brouwer

Defining moments

There are many benefits to pastoral ministry. We are invited to share with people their anniversaries, their successes, their laughter, and their families. Just this morning I received an email from a woman who calls me pastor, telling me of the thrill she and her family have in receiving their green cards for permanent residency in this country. We have prayed often together for this to happen, and have been stymied and disappointed by so many setbacks and challenges. But now her joy jumps, and she sends it my way as well.

Of course, pastoral ministry also brings us into the rotten places. Once I stood with a young bride as her husband marched around her calling her every horrible name possible, all the while systematically stripping her of connections with the world beyond their home — keys ripped out of her hands, locks replaced, even windows boarded up. In another setting, I used my own car as a funeral hearse, bringing three small caskets in as many years to a wind-swept cemetery, trying without success to find words of consolation to share with a couple that was systematically burying their baby sons while medical specialists offered no answer. I have lost sleep in pastoral worry, and I have aged inwardly in empathetic resonance with those enduring tragedy.

Still, while I enjoy baptisms more than funerals, and weddings better than divorces, I also know that the dark times force us to wrestle with the fundamental issues of life more than do days of light and grace. So it is that we must face the texts for this week. As we journey with Job we find ourselves caught in the millstones that grind slowly, and with him we ask whether they are the workmanship of God or machines of torture belonging to the devil. When we turn to the world of those to whom Hebrews was sent, we are sharing their persecution and seeking a road between superstition and spirituality even as their lives are threatened. And Jesus takes us, where he often does, into the defining moments of our lives where we must face our shattering imperfections in the face of divine designs.

This is a Sunday when we must stand with the oppressed and live with the hurting and cry with the weeping. But we must also rise resolutely to declare the firm teachings of scripture's hope and morality. If we do not, we will fail our people and ourselves and our God.

Job 1:1; 2:1-10
Job is a drama in which the prose of chapters 1-2 and 42 gives us an omniscient perspective from which to observe a man caught up in the terrible pain of wrongful suffering, and the poetic dialogues of the intervening chapters explore the philosophic wrestlings of theodicy in a variety of ways. According to today's opening scenes of the book, Job was one of the wealthiest men in the ancient world, with houses and servants and treasures. He had more of everything than any person could covet.

Along with that, Job was also a devout man, careful to renew his relationship with God each day. It seems, in fact, that God was rather proud of Job. When Satan came calling one time, God bragged to him about Job. "Have you seen my servant Job?" he asked. "Now there is a man whose heart you will never own!"

Satan wasn't so sure. He had cracked a lot of tough nuts in his time, and he took on Job as a special challenge. "Sure, Job loves you," Satan said to God. "But that's because you've bought his soul. You give him everything he wants. Why shouldn't he serve you? Even I would do that!"

That's when the wagering began, according to these chapters. God gave Satan permission to take everything away from Job, stipulating only that Satan could not harm Job's own body.

So Job lost everything — his children, his flocks, his buildings, his servants. He became as poor as a church mouse. Still Job loved God and served him openly.

That's when the wagering in heaven heated up, and Satan got one more shot at Job in round two. He might torment Job's body, but without killing him. Job began to writhe in pain. Satan touched Job's mind so that he could no longer clearly hear God's whisper of love. Job was truly all alone. His wife called him stupid, his friends called him a liar and a sinner, and the world didn't even call him at all anymore. On the outside, Job's horizons have collapsed. Meanwhile inside, he had become an echo chamber of despair. Where is God?

That is the hardest challenge in life, isn't it — finding God in the aching places of life? I remember sitting with a mother in a hospital corridor, praying for the recovery of her daughter. The young woman was just beyond her teen years, and only a dozen months into marriage to a wonderful man. When the doctor assisted the delivery of her first child he nicked something with his knife. Now she was turning every shade of yellow and gray, and had been flown half-way across the country to get the best medical attention possible.

The mother was unconsoled. When we prayed, she felt no peace and could not find God. And for three hours we watched her daughter's life slip away.

The mother stopped going to church. The young husband grew angry and didn't know how to care for his baby child. Where was God?

Elie Wiesel endured the horror of the Nazi death camps. He watched women and children herded into gas chambers. He cried with men beaten down by cruel soldiers. He saw a young boy hanging on a gallows. "Where is God?" he cried.

The question of Job is asked in every generation: "Where are you God?" And often, as with Job, the only answer is silence. The promises of scripture become dead fantasies. The Holy Spirit leaves and the heart grows chilly. The newspapers report events that make no sense. Where is God? Where is God when a child dies? Where is God when a mother is snatched from her family? Where is God when nuclear reactors melt down and airplanes crash and mines collapse? Where is God?

Satan looks down from heaven with glee. He knows that he has Job now. He knows that we will never get out of this one. He knows the cards in his hand are the winning draw. Can faith remain when God is silent? Can trust carry on when there seems to be no one at the other end of the line?

"No!" shouts Satan. But he doesn't have the last word.

"Yes!" whispers Job. "Even though I cannot see him, even though I do not understand what is happening, even though every human wisdom tells me God's not there, I know that my Redeemer lives, and with these eyes I shall see him!"

That is the deepest level of patience possible. James, in the New Testament, called it perseverance (5:11). Job continues to love God not for what he gets out of it, but because it is the only way life itself makes sense. We trust in God not because we always feel the wonder of the divine presence, but because, even in its absence, there is truly nowhere else to turn.

This is the patience of Job that sometimes gets bandied about in our religious conversations. It is the perseverance at the heart of the Christian faith. It is trust at its most profound level.

No one, of course, can explain it, at least not with words. Those of us who have struggled in that black pit can never really share the experience. We can talk about it later, when God seems closer again. But it is the awful agony of faith when we stand undressed and all alone.

Years ago, Dr. Arthur Gossip preached a sermon he called "When Life Tumbles In, What Then?" He brought that message on the first Sunday he returned to the pulpit of his congregation after his beloved wife had suddenly died. This is how he ended the sermon: "Our hearts are very frail, and there are places where the road is very steep and very lonely... standing in the roaring Jordan, cold with its dreadful chill and very conscious of its terror, of its rushing, I... call back to you who one day will have your turn to cross it, 'Be of good cheer, my brothers, for I feel the bottom and it is sound.' "

Somehow, by the grace of God, the perseverance of patience carries us through, and we know the end of the matter as did Job. God will never leave us alone forever. He will answer our questions in time. He will resolve the problems of life and give us a future that Satan could never manufacture. "The Lord is full of compassion and mercy," says James when reflecting on the story of Job (5:11). And the patience of faith carries us through, until we know that better than we know ourselves.

Hebrews 1:1-4; 2:5-12

Like some of the other literature of the New Testament the "Letter to the Hebrews" is not well named. For one thing, it is hardly a letter, having none of the epistolary literary conventions that might easily identify it as such. Instead this treatise jumps right into the exposition of Old Testament verses and themes, and then continues throughout to weave these seamlessly with applicatory exhortations.

Second, there is no clear indication that the first recipients were "Hebrews" in the traditional sense of belonging to an ethnic Jewish community. It is obvious that those who first read the document were well versed in the Hebrew scriptures, had an intimate understanding of the ceremonial systems that received their definition in the Levitical teachings regarding the tabernacle, and had at one time shaped their lives by the cultic calendar of the Hebrew festival year. At the same time, most of the Old Testament quotations in the book are Septuagint (Greek) readings rather than from the Masoretic (Hebrew) text. Furthermore, those who are addressed are told that they at one time were outsiders, aliens and heathens, something that would never be said to ethnic descendents of Abraham.

Recent scholarship suggests that those to whom it was initially sent were predominantly Gentile proselytes to Judaism prior to the coming of the news about Jesus. These "heathens" may have been attracted to the moral stability of the Jewish community in Rome, and sought to escape from the social corruption they viewed around them. In their quest for righteousness, the regulated religious system that pervaded the Jewish neighborhoods was very attractive, and these Gentile onlookers were willing to endure stringent initiation rites that would transform them into adoptive Jews.

When the message of Jesus as Messiah breezed in, many of this ilk traveled into the Christian church, caught up in the excitement of the movement. Now, however, great challenges threatened. New persecutions were rumored, and an increasing distinction was emerging between those in the Jewish neighborhoods who trusted in Jesus as Messiah and those who rejected this recent development.

Since many of these Gentile-cum-Jewish proselytes-cum-Christians had originally entered this narrowly defined community because of its ethical rigors and religious routines, they were now tempted to avoid persecution by slipping back into the safe and familiar strictly non-Christian Jewish environment. This treatise we call "Hebrews" was written to argue them into greater allegiance to the new way of Christianity.

In that light, we read today's passages. The first verses of chapter 1 rehearse the progression of divine revelation, showing how the Old Testament and its codes are insufficient without Jesus. Furthermore the exegesis of Psalms 8 and 22 in chapter 2 are the beginning of an exhortation that will increasingly identify the shared path Jesus took with us through suffering and persecution in order that we might find spiritual intimacy with God through him. If Jesus was able to make this pilgrimage and if Jesus was like us in every way except without sin, then we also can stay strong through persecution and chart our course to spiritual maturity on his boat.

This message can attach itself to any one of a variety of challenging experiences within the congregation. All of us, in times of struggle, are tempted to turn back or give up or rail against God without hope. These verses from Hebrews provide a hook into our lives (where and how do we hear God speak during the troubling times?) and a fellow traveler (Jesus) who can share our burdens and point a way of spiritual significance that is bigger than superstition or ritual.

Mark 10:2-16

Here is the tough one. We need to preach about divorce, but few in our gatherings will receive what we say without feeling wounds open and family troubles coming out of hiding. The lectionary does allow us to sidestep the issue, however, if we wish only to focus on the delightful story of Jesus and the children in verses 13-16. By using just those verses we can build a marvelous message about faith and childlikeness and the compassionate heart of Jesus and his church.

Yet, the teaching of Jesus on divorce is still there. But how can we tackle Jesus' words with the passion that Mark suggests was present in the original setting without undermining the message by citing too many exceptions, or otherwise ramming absolutes into the faces of truly hurting people? Here are some suggestions.

First, perhaps we might play for a bit with gender distinctions. Undergirding solid teachings on marriage is the divinely created reality of female-male sexuality. We cannot escape the genetic coding that splits us into two genders. Nor can we run from the given situation of heterosexual attractions that drive society. Often the first question asked when a baby is born is, "Boy or girl?" We are locked into sexually charged relationships from birth to death. This is why the religious leaders come to Jesus with their questions in the first place; marriage and divorce are telltale signs of our pervasive gender awareness and interaction.

Second, in light of that, we might wish to turn Jesus' words in verses 11-12 on their heads, and talk about what it is that we seek in heterosexual explorations (issues related to same-gender attractions can be brought in along the way). Perhaps a comparison might be made to learning a language other than that of our birth — as we ingest foreign vocabulary and new word order and strange syntax we begin not only to gain tools for communicating in another tongue, but we also become aware of the very makeup of culture itself, including that of our own. So it is, often, in the dating and mating rituals of our society. "Mars" and "Venus" need to investigate each other's makeup and mind in order to meet somewhere on planet Earth. Learning the language of a possible marriage partner helps us understand ourselves even better. But in this comes the rub. To explore is to disclose. To investigate is to become vulnerable. In the interaction between the sexes, all of us are looking for places of safety where we will not be ridiculed for our "otherness," nor denied for our deficiencies. Where it is possible to become "naked and not ashamed" with someone from the opposite gender, we need to find a level of trust with our partner that is not easily shaken or shattered.

Hence, the strong stance of the Bible for marriage and against divorce. Marriage is built on the predication that we are in need of finding a help-meet to our need, a counterpart like ourselves yet different enough to complement, a symbiotic partner who is as incomplete without us as we are without them. This is not a mere convenience that enables us to stumble along through the years; this is an essential part of the equation for exploring human identity to its fullest so that we might become more of the relational creatures God intended would bear the divine image (Genesis 1:26-27).

Thus Jesus' stern words against divorce are not so much a rigid standard of morality against which too many of us crash and burn. Rather they are an insistent reminder that we need to find safety in marriage or we lose something essential to society. Divorce is no more of an option for married people than is cancer a choice for how we wish our bodies to function. Divorce is a statement failure in a once-good relationship, much as cancer is a testimony of corruption in the DNA of our cells. Both happen. But both need to be dealt with as alien and unwanted. Only in that light will we remember what marriage is all about.

Application

If all three texts are used, the message must be one which uses tragedies generally as an opportunity to clarify and console and convince. Each of the passages can form an illustration that explores those defining moments we all face: pain (Job), persecution (Hebrews), and parting (Mark).

An Alternative Application

Job 1:1; 2:1-10. The Job text is a good springboard into explaining the various causes for suffering in our lives: 1) willful sinfulness which breaks the laws of morality (infidelity); 2) carelessness that violates nature's designs (substance abuse); 3) tragic happenstance in a broken world (tsunamis); 4) demonic oppression (certain forms of possession or addiction); and 5) divine chastisement (guilty conscience). All of these are expressed at one time or another in the book of Job. The goal of the message would be to raise people's awareness of the complexity of suffering so that care and empathy can go beyond simplistic reductionisms, while at the same time helping those who are currently in pain because of specific reasons to find an answer that brings healing and hope.

Tell me about it

I came home from school one day really feeling down. It had been a bad day. It started in the morning when I walked into the bathroom and looked into the mirror. There on my chin was the biggest zit in the history of medical science.

We had a pop test in English...

I left a book report home that was due that day...

My girlfriend dumped me for one of the jocks on the football team...

My name was the first one on the list of those cut from baseball tryouts...

When I came out to my car in the parking lot, a tire was flat...

When I got home that day, my father could tell right away that something was wrong, for by that time I was just about in tears. My life seemed over. No one had ever had a worse day in the history of the world!

I was on my way upstairs to collapse in bed and feel really sorry for myself when my father knocked at the door and said, "Had a rough day, huh? Why don't you tell me all about it?" I couldn't tell him right then how I felt.

Ever have a day like that? Well, you aren't alone. Just listen to Job.

Job 23:1-9, 16-17

These verses skip some of the best parts in Job, namely his three friends who come to "console" him and who do a pretty good job of it until they open their mouths. Much of the material between chapter 1 and here deal with the speeches these friends made to Job trying to explain his suffering. In other words, there had to be a reason for it. Surely Job must have sinned and this is why he was suffering. If he would but confess, then perhaps God would bless him once again. Job found none of this helpful.

Job knew that he was not suffering because of his sin. He had done nothing to deserve the calamities that had come one after another upon him. And here, in these verses, he pleads his innocence. He wants to find God and plead his case before God. He wants to know why he's suffering. Surely there must have been a mistake up there. God is reasonable. Once the situation is explained and God is reminded of how righteous Job is, then God can make things right again. But his unexplained suffering is deepened because he cannot find God at all. He's looked everywhere and God is nowhere to be found. Job goes east, west, north, south. Where's God? Job felt, like the Psalmist in today's reading, utterly abandoned by God. And he says so. He doesn't hold back anything he feels. He's in pain and lets God know it, even if it seems God isn't listening.

In addition to trying to understand his suffering, Job also seems to be concerned about his reputation. No doubt he is proud that he is known as a righteous man, a man without blame. Certainly it makes him feel good to have others think of him as such. But now all this suffering seems to suggest, as it does to even his close friends, that he is not so good after all. If he is suffering so, then he must have sinned greatly. Job wants God and his friends and everyone else to know this is not true. If he can bring God into court, which is what the language here seems to suggest, he can get his good name cleared.

Maybe Job is also confused. After all, he has done his part. He has lived the way he thought God wanted. He is a good man. He doesn't mistreat people. He obeys God's laws. But God is not sticking to the agreement. If I'm good, then God should do good things for me. That's how it works, doesn't it? Be good, God blesses you. Be bad, God punishes you. You are supposed to reap what you sow, right? But it wasn't working that way. It wasn't that simple anymore. Something was wrong.

Job is learning that being faithful to God does not mean we will avoid suffering. It does not give us immunity from the calamities common to all people. Indeed, it may well bring on more suffering. (How's that for an ad for becoming a Christian?)

Hebrews 4:12-16

The sense of verses 12-13 could be rendered as, "You can't fool God or hide from him! We may fool others and even ourselves, but not God. God sees our hearts. God knows who we really are."

Ever had someone who could seem to peer into your soul or appear to be able to read your mind? God does! God sees our motives, knows our thoughts, and knows the deepest parts of our minds and hearts. We are reminded of this when we hear God's word, which is portrayed here as the sharpest possible sword. The "word of God" here most likely means Christ and the teachings of scripture. Many people have heard the scriptures read or have studied them only to have them cut deeply into them, into their pride, bringing conviction, and showing them who they are and who they are called to be (see 1 Corinthians 4:5). But the word is not just a sword of judgment. It can also be a scalpel that ultimately brings healing.

Verses 14-16 talk about the great high priest. Because God knows all there is to know about us, God has sent Christ as our great high priest to make intercessions for us and atonement. Let's examine this concept of priest in a little more depth.

The Hebrew word for "priest" means to "draw near." This is an important clue to understanding the work of the priest. Primarily, a priest is a person God uses to draw us near to God. The priest is a mediator, an intercessor, one who cares enough for us to want to see us in a loving relationship with God where we can experience even more of God's loving care.

The Bible teaches that we are alienated from God because of sin, our willful disobedience of God's laws. Our sin has created a great chasm between us and God that we are helpless to traverse ourselves. What we need is a mediator, a go-between, a reconciler to help make things right again. That's what a priest is. In fact, the Latin word for priest is *pontifex*, which means "bridge builder."

These verses here contrast the human high priest with Jesus, the supreme high priest. Recall that the writer of Hebrews is most likely addressing Jewish Christians who are considering going back to Judaism. So he actually tells them, "Why should you wish to do that? Why go back to a human priest who must repeatedly make sacrifices and leave Christ who knows you far better and who has made one sacrifice once and for all for your sins?" No other priest has passed through the heavens into the very presence of God! Others merely passed through the curtain into the holy of holies. Jesus went directly into the heavenly presence of God — and not just once a year. He stays there, where he can make atonement and intercession for us. Not only this, Jesus is the Son of God! What access that gives him to God on our behalf! If you need to know more, then know this: This great high priest became one of us. He suffered everything we suffer (recall Jesus on the cross feeling forsaken like Job). He's been there, done that. He can identify with us and therefore convey fully to God our needs. Also, because he has been there, he is able to understand and help us in our temptations and trials.

Mark 10:17-31

Several things stand out in this well-known story. First, this rich young ruler comes and bows before Jesus, a penniless rabbi. And he calls Jesus "Good Teacher," a form of address that scholars say is very rare. Is he trying to flatter Jesus? Whatever his intentions, Jesus deflects this praise. "Don't call me 'good,' " Jesus says. "Only God is good." These words of Jesus here in Mark apparently bothered Matthew who changed the whole thing to, "Why do you ask me about what is good?" In other words, Matthew did not wish to throw any bad light on Jesus at all or call into question his character. But I think this is misguided and unnecessary. Jesus is simply doing what all good teachers do — point away from themselves to God. Personal attachment to him alone, it seems to me, as this young man was trying to do through bowing on his knees and through flattering words, was not enough. The young man was going to have to deal with God and what God demands.

Second, the young man was a good man, a godly man. He loved the law and sought to obey it. But still he lacked something and this ties in with the above — there was something in the way between him and God, something that he depended upon even more than God and perhaps loved more than God: his wealth. "Go," "sell," "give," "come follow" are the commands or imperatives Jesus gives him. Go and prove that you do not depend on or love your wealth more than God. Give up your dependence upon yourself and your own efforts and freely accept what you cannot earn: God's gift of grace and eternal life.

Third, Jesus seems to be telling him that merely not doing things so you look religiously respectable is not good enough. The young man listed what he had not done. But what of the things he needed to do? He had great wealth, but where had he used that in the service of God and in the love of neighbor? He is called upon here to think of others, and to use the blessings he has been given to bless others, especially the needy.

Fourth, it is helpful to look at this passage in light of the other readings for today, especially that from Job. This man was looking to gain or earn something. He thought that through his actions he could inherit or be given eternal life. Job seems to believe that he too, because of his own goodness, had earned the blessings he had enjoyed. If I am good, then God should bless me. That's the deal. But Jesus says otherwise. The gift of eternal life is impossible to earn. It can only be accepted freely by the grace of God. Goodness cannot earn it.

Jesus goes on to address the question of Peter, which is very much at the heart of the readings today (vv. 28ff). Peter asks, in essence, "Lord, we've done all of this for you, left all of this, given up all of this; so what are we going to get out of it?" In other words, there's a quid pro quo here. We've done all of this for you. What are you going to do for us? There should be a reward for being good. Recall how the disciples more than once argued over who among them would be the greatest, that is, get the greater rewards and the higher seats of honor. You should get something for following Jesus. That's the deal. You earn what you get. This is why the disciples are so confused with what Jesus is saying with his reference to how difficult it was for a rich person to enter the kingdom. This was exactly opposite of what they thought and most believed. The fact that the man was wealthy was, to them, a sign of God's blessings on him, that he was a good man. He was rich, you see, because he was a good man and this was God's blessings for his goodness. In other words, he had earned what he got from God because of his own righteousness. Wealth was proof of his good character and being right with God. To the contrary, Jesus says. His own way of thinking and approaching God has made it that much more difficult for him to accept the free gifts of God, the gifts that cannot ever be earned, no matter how good one can be in one's own eyes.

Application

Have you ever had a day like I described above? Job was beginning to feel that he had a whole life like that! And he was not afraid to say so. In fact, his words in today's passage are a bit shocking in their honesty and depth of emotion. Job feels abandoned and even mistreated by God. Dare anyone talk that way to God? Well, just listen to a couple more passages: Jeremiah 20:7-8, Matthew 27:46b.

Perhaps these passages are in the Bible to tell us that God wants us to be honest, to share what we truly feel and think. Why? Because God cares. God's not offended by our words. I think God's more offended by empty, meaningless prayers that mean nothing to us and are done more out of rite and ritual than honest words, even if we are angry at God.

Besides, we might as well tell God anyway, for God already knows what we think and feel, and such sharing shows that we trust God, and that, even in our pain, we still relate ourselves to God.

These people in the Bible trusted God and felt they had a relationship of love with God, and that's why they could be so honest. If you really trust someone, if you have a true and meaningful relationship with them, then you can be honest with them about your feelings and your thoughts. I do not mean being brutally honest with people all the time so that we say whatever and hurt them. I mean we trust them, we value our relationship so much that we can be who we are, we can share who we are. A real friend, someone who really loves us, wants us to be honest with them, knows that we need to be honest. And my own experience has been that when we do, that relationship is not weakened but strengthened. We grow closer to one another.

If this is true in human relationships, how much more true is it with God?

I love the drama of *Fiddler on a Roof*. Tevye could be a character right out of the Bible, for he is talking to God all the time and tells God exactly what's on his mind. In fact, he often tells God that he wished God had made him a rich man! At least he is honest. And he also talks to God a lot about his daughters (talking to God on a constant basis is not unfamiliar to many parents).

The reading from Hebrews gives us added encouragement to tell God all about what we feel. It says that Jesus, as our great High Priest, knows all that we have suffered, for he suffered too. He has faced every trial, suffering, and temptation, even death itself. He understands and he is always there ready to help us.

Imagine what it is like to have someone who has been through something that you are going through come and minister to you. That person has been there and knows. You don't have to do a lot of explaining, or when you do, you know it's understood. And that person, too, has been through it and come, hopefully, to some healing and wisdom which can then be shared with you. If this is true for us, then how much more can the Son of God know us, understand us, help us through all that life might throw at us? We can tell him anything!

Oh, I did not finish the story I started...

Later that afternoon my father came into my room and said again, "Tell me about it." I poured my heart out. He didn't say much. He just listened.

Then something happened that always happened when I really told him all about it: I felt better! Nothing had really changed. The zit was still there. My girlfriend didn't call and beg me to take her back. What had changed was me. I had a different feeling and attitude. Things didn't seem so bad any more.

I've learned as a Christian that we can go to God in much the same way. In fact, God tells us over and over in the Bible, "Tell me all about it. Anytime. Anywhere. Anything. Whatever you feel, I care. I'll listen. I'll be there for you!"

Alternative Applications
Job 23:1-9, 16-17; Mark 10:17-31. "Why Be Good?" Job is convinced that he is a good person and would be acquitted if only he could prove his case in court. In other words, he did not deserve what was happening. If you are good, you should be blessed, not suffer. The rich young ruler also thinks he can earn heaven, the kingdom. And the disciples ask what they are going to get for everything they have given up for Christ. Why follow Christ? What role do rewards play in it? What are we really seeking? If heaven were never promised to us, would we still follow Jesus? What can we expect to get from following Jesus and what should we not expect to get?

Job 23:1-9, 16-17; Hebrews 4:12-16; Mark 10:17-31. "When you feel forsaken..."
A. Realize you are in good company (Job, Jesus).

B. Don't be afraid to share your pain openly and honestly with God, like they did.

C. Know that you have someone, Jesus, as your great High Priest who is with you, understands your pain, and makes intercession for you (Hebrews reading).

D. In the midst of your own searching for God and your own pain, do not neglect others (Mark reading).

E. Find ways to reach out in practical ways to them and in so doing you may well find some answers and comfort yourself.

Proper 24 / Pentecost 21 / Ordinary Time 29
Job 38:1-7 (34-41)
Hebrews 5:1-10
Mark 10:35-45
David Kalas

My rightful place

When I was in grade school, there was not much freedom for individual children to wander the halls. If a student was seen walking alone down the hallway during school hours, a teacher or administrator was bound to stop the student and ask, "Where are you supposed to be?"

The underlying presumption, of course, was that there was seldom a good reason for a young child to be on his/her own, away from the teacher, and apart from the class. To be in the hall alone, therefore, was to be where you didn't belong. You belonged somewhere else. Hence the question: "Where are you supposed to be?"

Indeed, as that question was the instrument of teachers in my grade school, so it is also a component of so much teaching in the Bible. The psalmist, the writer of Proverbs, and the prophets all have their moments when they say to their audience, in effect, "Where are you supposed to be?"

Knowing our proper place, and then remaining there, has always been a problem for people. Our wandering eyes draw us off God's prescribed path, and our ambitious egos prompt us to pursue inappropriate heights.

All three of this week's lessons invite us to consider this matter of our proper place. The story of Job, the request of James and John, and the example of Christ all point us to the same conclusion, and that conclusion might be the message for me and my people this Sunday.

Job 38:1-7 (34-41)

Old Testament scholars offer different opinions about the composition and theology of the book of Job. Were the prose beginning and ending married from the beginning to the poetic dialogues that comprise most of the book, or did that union come later? Was the original author a skeptic, disillusioned with traditional religion, but whose caustic work was later softened by a more orthodox redactor? Does the book purport to answer the questions that it raises and reflects?

While individuals may arrive at very different conclusions about the background and interpretation of this book, no one will dispute its quality as a piece of literature. The plot, the characters, and the dialogues are filled with beauty, poignancy, drama, and even some (very dark) humor.

Among the most effective dramatic elements in the book is the appearance of the Lord, which occurs in our selected passage. The poet-theologian has, for more than thirty chapters, immersed us in the pain and the faith of Job, as well as the worldview, the doctrinal paradigms, and the judgmental assertiveness of his friends. We have heard Job say things that seem to border on blasphemy, and yet we reluctantly find that we must concede his points. And, in the next breath, we have heard his friends articulate orthodoxy in a way that makes us want to agree with what is said but not with the ones who say it.

Then, after going round-and-round with Job and his companions, chapter 38 opens with the grandest of entrances. All of the preceding human talk — full of bluster, certainty, and self-importance — is now as dim as penlights when the sun comes up. The Lord, who has been spoken of and spoken for plentifully by Job and his three (or four) companions, has now arrived on the scene to speak for himself, and everyone else, including especially Job, is dwarfed by his arrival.

The entire passage is a spectacle. "The Lord answered Job out of the whirlwind."

It is perhaps noteworthy that this "whirlwind" appears on only occasion in the history books of the Old Testament, and that was the event of Elijah's rapture (2 Kings 2:1, 11). It is not a word, therefore, that describes so common an occurrence — so routine a meteorological event — that it appears frequently in the Old Testament's stories. Instead, it is a word reserved almost exclusively for the writings and the prophets, used to paint stunning pictures of spectacular events (see, for example, Psalm 107:25; Psalm 148:8; Isaiah 29:6; Jeremiah 23:19; Ezekiel 1:4; Zechariah 9:14).

This was no ordinary breeze. The human windbags are suddenly blown away by this breathtaking storm. Perhaps Job has to fall down in order to hold his ground in the face of this wind. There is a great noise, perhaps like that sound of a thousand freight trains that tornado survivors sometimes describe. Yet, in the end, we discover that the awesome storm is merely nature's entourage — the warm-up act — for the one who is truly spectacular.

There is some irony, of course, in the fact that our translation reads, "The Lord answered Job out of the whirlwind." We have a notion about what it means to answer someone. Goodness knows that Job had a great many questions. An answer from the Lord would be most welcome! But the Lord's answer, it seems, is only more questions. Impossible, relentless, put-you-in-your-place questions. If the Lord were a prosecutor, the defense attorney would object that he was badgering the witness, for the Lord literally overwhelms Job with his questions.

Interestingly, Job may have anticipated this very experience near the beginning of the book. "How can a human being win a case against God?" he asks. "How can anyone argue with him? He can ask a thousand questions that no one could ever answer" (Job 9:2-3 TEV). Still, it might be argued that Job is better off when he is overwhelmed by God's questions than when he is overwhelmed by his own.

The first of God's questions may be the most difficult of all. The litany of questions that follows about nature, animals, legendary beasts, and outer space combine to form a majestic poem and a daunting exam. But the first question is the toughest, for it is the personal one. It is not "out there," pointing to distant constellations and unseen warehouses of snow; rather, it points directly at Job, as well, perhaps, as at his companions. "Who is this that darkens counsel by words without knowledge?"

The mother finds some part of the house in disrepair and calls out to everyone within earshot, "Who made this mess?" Some family member is expected to come forward, then, and take responsibility for his or her actions.

Likewise, here; Job and his friends are invited to come forward and identify themselves specifically, as ones who have spoken unwisely. In the end, it is Job who responds (40:3-5; 42:1-6), though God's ultimate verdict is that the friends, not Job, are the ones whose speech needs to be forgiven (42:7-9).

Hebrews 5:1-10

I lived for several years in a small, rural town in southern Virginia. As a newcomer, I often needed help finding my way around. From time to time, one of the folks who had lived there all of their lives would give me directions like this: "You turn right by where the Watkins' farm used to be" or "You go one mile past the old Johnson place." Those were suitable landmarks for the local lifers, but they were not much help to the unoriented.

Our congregations may have something of the same experience with the epistle to the Hebrews.

The unknown writer of the letter to the Hebrews revealed the good news about Jesus in light of what his audience already knew: the familiar territory of the Old Testament Law, the design of the Tabernacle, and the Levitical rituals. His audience was full of locals and lifers when it came to a Jewish heritage. Because that material is largely foreign to the people in our pews, they may need some orientation to the landmarks.

The "old Johnson place" of this passage is priesthood. And for a Jewish audience, priesthood was associated with Aaron and the tribe of Levi.

271

Through my years of parish ministry, I have led probably hundreds of youth and adults in through-the-Bible classes. For first-time readers, there is always a bit of surprise at how much material is devoted to these Levitical matters. Church folks who have not read the Bible are usually only familiar with the materials commonly preached and taught. Noah, Abraham, Joseph, Moses, David, Elijah, Daniel, Peter, Paul, and Jesus — these are the folks whose stories have emerged as familiar. But Aaron, Eleazar, and Phineas are not so well known. And Noah's is the best-known ark in scripture, though it receives much less attention in the Old Testament than that later box that resided in the holy of holies. Furthermore, the details of sacrifices, offerings, and tabernacle rituals are mostly uncharted territory for our folks.

Yet this is the world of Hebrews, and the writer finds the gospel there. For in an approach to the Old Testament that betrays the influence of Greek philosophy, the letter to the Hebrews understands the Old Testament tabernacle, rituals, holy days, sacrifices, and priesthood as types that reflect and anticipate the eternal and true realities found in Christ.

Before our people will be able to appreciate the beauty of the comparison made between Christ and the Aaronite priests, of course, that Old Testament priesthood will need some introduction. Then, while most of this "gospel according to Leviticus" is concerned with Levitical material, in our selected passage the Levites and the Aaronite priests are eclipsed by another priesthood: the order of Melchizedek. Melchizedek himself will almost certainly require an introduction, for he hardly makes the list of the ten most familiar Old Testament characters.

Of course, he is never formally introduced to us within the Old Testament. Rather, he appears, mysteriously and unannounced, in a brief encounter with Abraham (Genesis 14:18-20). The encounter is tightly packed with significance, and yet the character of Melchizedek comes and goes without introduction or explanation. He disappears from the scene as suddenly as he had appeared in the first place, and we are left wondering, like the beneficiaries of the lone ranger, "Who was that masked man?"

A thousand years or so later, the psalmist reminds us of the mysterious Melchizedek (Psalm 110:4), but the cryptic reference only adds more mystery, not more explanation. It is left to the New Testament writer of the letter to the Hebrews — 1,000 years after the psalmist's allusion and 2,000 years after Abraham's encounter — to introduce us officially to Melchizedek.

Melchizedek is identified as the king of Salem (hence, king of peace), and his name means king of righteousness. In addition to being a king, he is identified in both the Genesis and Psalms passages as a priest. He appears out of nowhere and disappears without a trace. He precedes the Levites and the Aaronite priesthood by generations, greeting and blessing Levi's great-grandfather. And he receives from Abraham a tithe.

This magnificent and mysterious character, then, reveals Christ to us. He is one of those Old Testament landmarks (familiar to the lifers who received this epistle) that are part of how we find our way to Christ.

Mark 10:35-45

You have to like their candor. James and John, affectionately nicknamed "the sons of thunder" (Mark 3:17), don't pull any punches. "Teacher, we want you to do for us whatever we ask of you." It is the admission very few of us would be willing to make, although it might be a perfectly accurate statement.

A certain philosophical sort would exempt themselves from such blatant self-interest. "I do not always know what is best," one might say, "and so I would not actually want him to do for me whatever I ask of him." But among honest people, that is probably a minority position. It may not be so much the voice of one redeemed from fallen human selfishness as it is the voice of a warranted skepticism about humanity.

James and John are unashamed to admit what they want: that Jesus should do for them whatever they ask of him. And while their undisguised self-interest is unbecoming, and their Jesus-as-genie Christology is offensive, Jesus remarkably does not chide them for what they have said.

We should note, by contrast, that on other occasions Jesus doesn't shrink from taking issue with what someone has said (see, for example, Mark 3:22-26; 12:13-15; John 9:1-3), including even a seemingly harmless salutation (Luke 18:18-19). Here, when James and John have said something so obviously misguided, Jesus simply meets them where they're at: "What is it you want me to do for you?" What an encouraging image of the gracious way that the Lord hears our prayers!

Encouraged by Jesus to continue, the brothers reveal their desire: "Grant us to sit, one at your right hand and one at your left, in your glory." It is a level of audacity that we find hard to imagine, on the one hand, and yet we should also note that their request shows a high level of faith, on the other. This is pre-resurrection, after all. Jesus has thus far only proven himself to be a remarkable human being, and yet the request of James and John suggests a higher recognition and expectation.

Their request may have been misguided, but their expectation was not. Jesus does not dispute their premise: he does not say "there will be no glory" or "there will be no such seats at my side." Instead, he reminds them of the painful path between here and there, between now and then.

Jesus' language is conspicuously sacramental. What James and John have requested is embodied in the verb "sit." Jesus' response, however, leaves that image temporarily behind, speaking instead in terms of "drink the cup" and "be baptized." We can hardly miss the allusion to the two most widely recognized sacraments. And the consequent association of both sacraments with Jesus' suffering may add a new layer of insight, especially to the sacrament of baptism.

Jesus asked the "are ye able" question of Zebedee's sons, and "the sturdy dreamers answered" (from "Are Ye Able" by Earl Marlatt) that they could, indeed, drink the cup he would drink and be baptized in his baptism. And, again, we are struck by the fact that Jesus does not take issue with them. Indeed they will follow him through that suffering, but the substance of their request remains in doubt, for it "is not mine to grant, but it is for those for whom it has been prepared."

What follows, then, is a teaching moment for the disciples. The request of James and John is gently revealed to be the usual and customary way of thinking in this world, but Christ's followers are challenged to think — and live — differently. We are reminded of Paul's counsel to the Philippians: "Let the same mind be in you that was in Christ Jesus" (see Philippians 2:5ff).

In the end, we see that the passage is framed by two very different pictures of Jesus. James and John picture him in his glory, and they are eager to associate themselves with him there. But Jesus reveals himself as a servant, and invites his followers to associate themselves with him in that way. Do not aspire to sit next to his throne where he reigns; aim, rather, to get on your hands and knees next to him on the floor where he washes feet.

Application

How appropriate it is for God's people to ask themselves and one another, "Where are you supposed to be?" Our egos, our appetites, and the prevailing winds of a fallen world can so easily — and so subtly — derail us. It's a good question for us to consider.

Job, we gather, had gotten a bit out of place. The implication of God's response to Job is not so much that Job had sinned, but rather that Job had lost his proper perspective on where he stood in relation to God, and Job was duly humbled.

James and John, likewise, misunderstood where they were supposed to be. Perhaps they pictured themselves on thrones next to Christ — co-regents with him in glory. But Jesus redirected their focus to suffering and servitude, "For whoever wishes to be first among you must be slaves of all."

And the description of Christ offered by the writer of Hebrews reminds us of where we are supposed to be. For if the Son of God must humble himself in servitude and suffering, then surely the mortals who follow him should expect to travel the same road.

Our instincts (and our culture's emphasis) are to pursue for ourselves comfort and honor. But, as followers of Jesus Christ, is that where we're supposed to be?

An Alternative Application

Mark 10:35-45. "When I Don't Need to Forgive." Even the most cursory review of Jesus' teachings will reveal the great importance of forgiveness. Free and gracious forgiveness is one of the hallmarks of the Heavenly Father that Jesus reveals, and that same kind of forgiveness is what he teaches us to practice. Indeed, the principle is one of the most familiar to the people in our pews since, every Sunday, so many of them pray to be forgiven by God as they forgive others.

As we consider our obligation and opportunity to forgive other people, however, it is important to recognize the occasions when we don't need to forgive. I don't mean some occasion when the sin is so great, so heinous, so inexcusable that we are reasonably released from our command to forgive. But rather, I think of those occasions when no sin has been committed.

If you do something terribly wicked, I need to forgive you. But if you haven't done anything wrong, then I don't need to forgive you. The mere fact that I am hurt, disappointed, or annoyed by what you've done is not the final arbiter of whether you've done something wrong. And if you haven't, then you do not need to be forgiven. Instead, perhaps I need to be forgiven for my selfish or irritable response to what you've done.

This may be the case in our gospel lesson. When the other disciples heard about the request made by James and John, "they began to be angry" with them. The striking fact, however, is that there's no indication that Jesus himself was angry with them.

Jesus did not condemn James and John for what they did; why, then, should the other disciples be so indignant? Perhaps they are the ones who need to be forgiven for the selfishness and faithlessness of their response.

The face at the center of history

My friend is an agnostic. He grew up in a Christian family where church participation was as common as air and mealtime prayers were daily ritual. He went to Sunday school and gained familiarity with all the great Bible stories. During his high school years, he had a charismatic conversion and became a rabid evangelist. Many were bit by his incisor words and became children of eternity.

My friend read his Bible every day. He even bought an audio version on tape so that he could listen to it through earphones while he worked his third-shift factory job. At break time, in the wee hours of the morning, he convicted and convinced his fellow workers, and started a growing Bible study in the lunchroom.

By the time he finished high school, he wanted to get a degree in geology so that he could disprove those who were debunking Christianity through evolutionary teachings. He set out to become the world's foremost scientist who, as a Christian, would be able to write the final geological textbook on young earth theory and convincingly endorse what he believed to be the only valid creationist hypothesis. Meanwhile he brought scores to church and displayed a personal life of radical discipleship.

Along the way, he began to lose his faith. Pastors and his parents disappointed him first because they were not as committed to Christ as he thought ought to be natural. Their lives betrayed constant compromise and theological wishy-washiness. Then his converts let him down. They became Christians, but argued with him about lifestyle issues. Next, theology and church history turned against him. He devoured early apologists of the faith and found them contradicting one another, and often interpreting the Bible in simplistic ways that didn't square with obvious modern, scientific explanations of the way things were or worked.

Finally, his academic world conspired against him. Those who were most honest in the field of geology seemed to have ample reason to undermine flood theory geology and young earth cosmology. Meanwhile, those who seemed most adamant about faith were regularly playing mind games with scientific data until they appeared to bend it to their own ends.

Now my friend is lonely and lives in the rarified agnostic world between theism and atheism. If left to his jilted and scandalized church experiences, he would easily step across the line and capitulate to an existence without God, but he can't get past the face of Jesus. He respects Jesus, regardless of what the gospel writers or the church might have done to him. He wonders about Jesus — so manly and yet so religious; how could he be brutally honest and still express trust in God?

Jesus is the hinge, the hook, the weft in the warp and woof of the fabric of the universe. Each of today's lectionary passages reminds us that we can't live in a world without God, and that only a messiah like Jesus can keep us connected.

Job 42:1-6, 10-17

This culmination to the drama of Job may seem at first glance to bring about a happy conclusion, but great care must be taken in its explication. First, God never gave a clear answer to Job's question as to why he suffers. Although Job confesses his finitude over against God's infinity, he does not jump up and down shouting "Eureka!"

Second, there is a hint of cause-and-effect judgment against Job's friends (the actual indictment falls in verses 7-9, which are not included in today's reading, but the outcome of that assessment clearly underlies v. 10, so it needs to be dealt with) that seems to go against the very heartbeat of the dramatic dialogues earlier in the book. Job's friends saw a direct and specific correlation between improper actions and divine judgment, but Job protested otherwise, and Elihu supported a more complex understanding of suffering. Here there is a kind of poetic justice which appears to demand a pound of flesh from those who are deemed wrong for their earlier actions.

Third, the tie-up of loose ends is too neat. In the opening of the drama, Job lost a bunch of stuff; now he gains back a whole lot more. At the beginning, Job offered sacrifices on behalf of his children who might have uttered an inappropriate word or considered a wrong thought; now he makes similar atonement for his friends who have spoken inappropriate words and considered wrong thoughts.

Fourth, Satan is not in the picture. Since the whole matter of Job's suffering was predicated on a wager between the unseen powers, it would stand to reason that there should be a divine declaration of a winner here at the end. It does not appear, and the scoreboard of heaven which clocked tragedy so mercilessly at the start, now stands dark, with no trophies awarded.

Fifth, while the entire dramatic dialogue of the book railed against a mechanical understanding of the universe, the final prose verses seem deftly to restore that perspective to prominence. So many things were taken from Job, therefore so many similar things must be added back to Job (with interest, of course).

To preach this text carelessly is to tell people, in the words of the classic Bobby McFerrin song, "Don't Worry! Be Happy!" since it is all going to turn out fine in the end. But such oversimplification directly opposes the complex theodicy woven through the inner chapters.

Job 42 should be approached as if it were the final scene of a morality play. The goal of the medieval morality plays was to summarize value systems broadly and apply them to specific daily behaviors. Here the primary value system put forward is that the creator God remains in charge, despite snippets of evidence to the contrary as touted by our newspapers. Evidence of this is seen in three things: Job, God's marvelous friend and the test-case for spiritual faithfulness, is vindicated in his refusal to give in either to Satan's challenges or to his own friends' simplistic theology; prayers and offerings overcome expected mechanistic outcomes; and evil is not co-terminus with good. When Job's fortunes are restored at the close of the book, it is an eschatological flag of hope waving for all who continue to live somewhere between Job 2 and 37.

The message must echo with mature hope which neither oversimplifies pain and suffering in heavy-handed judgments, nor wallows too long in the empathetic mire of the distressed. There is a God who will not allow evil to run wild forever. There is a right way of living, even in tough times. There will be a resolution to all these things that trouble us, although it might not come according to our schedules or bring the outcomes we might believe most appropriate from our limited vantage points.

Hebrews 7:23-28

The lectionary deftly steps around Melchizedek in picking these verses to explain Jesus' unique role as high priest. Combining rabbinic teaching and philosophic argumentation, Jesus is identified as a superior intercessor for the people of God. There are two reasons for this. First, Jesus offers the sacrifice of himself, which provides a more fitting in-kind substitutionary atonement than does even the best of unblemished lambs. Second, because Jesus came back to life after death, and now lives forever, he can reaffirm his single great offering in perpetuity.

What is not so obvious, at first, is the cosmological worldview informing this short passage within the whole of the work. Visually, all of the theology in Hebrews is based upon the architectural layout of the tabernacle. Created at the foot of Mount Sinai, the tabernacle was intended to provide a residence for Yahweh among the people of Israel, in a dwelling as portable as were their own. It was part of the

Suzerain-Vassal covenant agreement — in order for Israel to fulfill its destiny as the divinely appointed ambassador for blessing to the nations (see Genesis 12:1-2), the nation had to embody Yahweh's presence on earth (see Exodus 33).

The layout for the tabernacle, although much grander and elaborate, was essentially that found in any Israelite tent. A fire pit and utensils for washing sat in front. A common area included lamps for illumination, dishes for eating, and other household tools. At one side or end, hidden from public view by a cloth or skin, was a sleeping area. This was the place of most privacy and infinite intimacy between those who belonged to the household. The tabernacle duplicated these areas and equipment on a larger scale. The courtyard was more clearly defined by an outer perimeter of royal-colored hangings. It had a large altar for fire, and a super-sized washbasin called the laver or bronze sea. These symbolized processes of cleansing and reconciliation, just as the fire pit and washing utensils did in other tents. In the "common area" of the tabernacle, identified as "the Holy Place," were the lampstand (always lit), the table (always set), and the altar of incense (always smoldering). These represented the equipment of hospitality, and assured Israel that there was always a welcome for them in Yahweh's home. The place behind the screen, known in the tabernacle as "the Most Holy Place," was the intimate residence of God. It housed a portable throne (the Ark of the Covenant, which was topped by the "Mercy Seat" and guarded by two Cherubim), which visualized Yahweh's identity and relationship with the community.

All of the theology in Hebrews is designed to move us from external places (heathen conditions and unbelief), past the altar of burnt offering (the cross of Christ) and laver (baptism), into the church (the holy of holies) where prayers are offered (altar of incense) and insight is gained (lampstand) and the fellowship meal is celebrated (the Eucharist), finally to be received into the very presence of God (The Most Holy Place). For a brief summary of this see Hebrews 10:19-25.

Moreover, the image of the tabernacle is tipped on end in the book of Hebrews, so that the place behind the curtain or veil, the Most Holy Place, is actually heaven, and the rest is terrestrial. Jesus is the great high priest who comes from behind the curtain (heaven) to our world in order to bring us back through the barrier with him to the other side (see Hebrews 4:14-16).

The point of these descriptions is to remind Jewish believers (many of whom may well have been proselytes from among the Gentiles) to remain in the messianic fellowship of Jesus rather than slipping back into the old ways of the earthly tabernacle. That ancient expression of religion had been appropriate until now, but it has recently been superseded by the better expressions of intercession expressed in and by Jesus.

A contemporary application of this message might be to address forms of traditionalism in the church which often reduce it to ritualized acts of self-preservation. A focus on the person and mission of Jesus could re-energize a church's purpose for existence, even in the face of persecution.

Mark 10:46-52

Jesus is on his way to Jerusalem. In the synoptic gospels, Jesus only makes one trip to Jerusalem during his adult ministry, so the journey there is critical because it explains the reason for Jesus' existence (messianic death) and reactions to that purpose. As Jesus passes through Jericho, he gives sight to blind Bartimaeus. In so doing, Jesus identifies himself as the Messiah promised by the prophets. Throughout the Old Testament there is no incident recorded of a blind person having sight restored (there is a brief story in 2 Kings 6:8-23 of Elisha being instrumental in producing a temporary blindness to an army of Aram, but this is very different from having a congenitally blind person or a person who lost sight because of an accident suddenly receiving the ability); this healing gift is reserved for the Messiah (see Isaiah 42:7).

This is why Mark reminds us several times over that Jesus is the "Son of David." Family records had been kept through the years of exile and restoration, and there were many others who could trace family lines back to David's royal house. Jesus is not merely one of the shirttail relation that linger on in third-rate apartments and hope for some windfall patronage position and pension when their favorite rises to the throne. Jesus is in fact the true heir to David's kingly greatness. Bartimaeus, though blind, can see what sighted folks are ignorant about. He witnesses the character of Jesus' link to the family founder. He knows the power that flows through Jesus' veins. He understands who Jesus is and what Jesus is about as Jesus travels this last cruel leg of the journey to the cross. In order for Jesus to be the Messiah, he must have the healing graces of heaven at his disposal, and he must also walk the road of the suffering servant. Blind Bartimaeus sees both these things as he calls out to the one who is about to change the course of human history.

Preaching on this passage must explore both the level of the miracle as evidence of Jesus' divine character and also the underlying theme of faith as more than sight. Bartimaeus lived in a world where his senses had failed him; yet he is able to understand things that those who still exist in a world ruled by scientific empiricism are blind to.

Who among us can truly see? Who among us is able to get behind the limits of the senses and experience with the mind and the heart? Who today needs a miracle, and who is able to pray appropriately for it to take place? Only those who understand Jesus' true pedigree.

Application

We are nearing the end of the liturgical year. We have passed through Advent anticipations that God will act among us, Christmas carols announcing God's faithfulness in the incarnation, Epiphany reminders of the uniquely revelatory character of Jesus, Lenten journeys with Jesus through the valleys of anguish, Holy Week reminders of redemptive suffering on our behalf, Easter excitement and Pentecost empowering. Now we are getting ready to do it all over again.

What have we learned? What do we know each time around this cycle of the seasons? In the end, it comes down to this: It all depends on Jesus. Without Jesus, God remains hidden and we drift between agnosticism and superstition. Without Jesus, there is no solid revelatory hook on which to hang our faith. Without Jesus, suffering is never redemptive and there is no exit from the grave. Without Jesus, the warmth of the Spirit never comes and we are left to seek substitutionary thrills in experiential consumerism that kills us before we can satisfy our addictions.

Without Jesus, Job's story is merely a nice fairy-tale in which "they lived happily ever after" but we don't. Without Jesus, Gentile proselytes to the Jewish faith who embraced the Messiah are sent back to the rituals because they found that no one was really at home in the house of God. Without Jesus, Bartimaeus remains blind and unfortunately his sighted neighbors live in the only land of reality, and it isn't very pretty.

It all hinges on Jesus.

An Alternative Application

Mark 10:46-52. It might be possible to deal with the gospel lesson in terms of Jesus' compassion. C.S. Lewis said that there are two ways to be impartial in our relationships with others. The first was by reducing each one we meet to the lowest common denominator and disdaining them all equally. In prison, for example, each inmate is the same and thus each is treated "impartially"; names are replaced with numbers; clothing for all is identical; living quarters are reduced to exactly the same size for each person; even the schedule of the day is harmonized until none is given special privileges over another. Impartiality rules.

The second way of impartiality, said Lewis, was that of individualized esteem. Here the goal is not to treat each person equally but to treat each person uniquely with a focus on caring. In illustrating his point, Lewis said that he was upset with the way that some of his friends invited their children to call them, as parents, by their first names. While he understood their motives, he feared the outcome. The result of such social conditioning, said Lewis, is far worse than its benefit. The beauty of family life is found precisely in the inequalities present. In a family, we learn that people are not to be loved "equally," but "uniquely." A wife does not love her husband because he is just one of the crowd that hangs about. Nor does a father treat one child completely the same as any other child. True love discriminates. Any parent who tries to love all the children in exactly the same way becomes frustrated to the point of incompetence. It is in the family that we learn to esteem each person greatly not because each is another cloned pea in a pod, but because each is unique and different.

In this lies the secret of Jesus' relationship with Bartimaeus. A person who cares with an impartial love does not look at all people the same. Rather, a person who cares impartially begins with the assumption that each person is different, and each person is worthy of individual love. Bartimaeus could see the uniqueness of Jesus and declared it in his shouting. Jesus, also, could see the uniqueness in Bartimaeus that required a special act of grace to bring him along the road to the kingdom. In such ways Jesus sees each of us. And when we are so seen, we begin to have the capacity to see others in turn.

Continual reformation

On October 31, 1517, a young Catholic priest nailed to the door of Castle Church in Wittenberg, Germany, a list of 95 theses or statements concerning practices and teachings of the church for which he had grave misgivings. He was not looking for some world-shaking reformation, just a debate and discussion about them. But many trace to this event the beginnings of what would come to be known as "The Protestant Reformation." His name was Martin Luther. So, as a way to remember and celebrate the whole Reformation, the Sunday before October 31st each year is observed as "Reformation Sunday."

All the readings for today relate to key themes that inspired and were highlighted by the Reformation. The Jeremiah passage speaks of humanity's need for a new beginning, a reformation, a new covenant or relationship with God beyond what obedience to laws could bring. Paul takes up this theme throughout Romans, sharing from his own experience what this new covenant is based on — God's unmerited favor or acceptance through grace and our response of faith. The gospel lesson presents Jesus as the means of "truth," the one through whom God helps set us free for a whole new relationship with God, with others, and even within our own selves.

In a way, what Reformation Sunday is all about is taking the time to rediscover just what it means to be a Christian, to be the church, and what our role is in the world. We too easily forget who we are, sink into a kind of spiritual loss of identity and purpose. It is a challenge to always seek to be re-formed, re-newed by that "truth" Jesus shares which can set us free.

So, Reformation Sunday would ask us two great questions: One, where or how in my own walk with God do I most need reformation, change, renewal right now? Two, though I might not have 95 of them, what or how does the church need such reformation? The order is important. Perhaps if we focused on answering the first one, the other might well take care of itself!

Jeremiah 31:31-34

The theme of covenant has been prominent throughout the Bible. We see it first on in the story of the covenant made with Noah and all creation after the flood (Genesis 9), the covenant made with Abraham (Genesis 17), the covenant at Sinai through the giving of the Law (Exodus 20), the covenant with David and so on. God, it seems, never tires of trying to reach out to us, to renew a relationship with us. Jeremiah talks about a day when a whole new relationship with God will be created, one unlike any other before it. Jesus would use language from Jeremiah here to say that this new covenant or relationship with God is exactly his own mission. (Something we are reminded of each time we take the cup and the bread. See 1 Corinthians 11:25 and Luke 22:20.)

The covenant between God and the people had been broken by the sins and unfaithfulness of the people, bringing judgment upon them. That covenant, based on the Law given through Moses, had in essence, been annulled by the actions of the people. It was no longer in force. In fact, it is as if God and the people had been married (note the image of God as "husband" in v. 32) and the people (the bride/wife) had been unfaithful, thus breaking the marriage covenant. If the relationship was to be restored, it would take something new, something radical — a whole new covenant (vv. 31-34). (Note this language of marriage is used very much in Hosea, who sees the nation through the light of his own failed marriage. Yet, he takes back his unfaithful wife and hears God saying the same thing. Here it is as if God is saying that the relationship has to start all over again, but based on a real and true love for God within the hearts of the people.)

The problem was not the law but the human heart. What is envisioned here is a covenant in which the people will truly wish to love and obey God, from within, not because the law says so. Marriage vows, for example, do not make a marriage. They must be written on the hearts of the couple, that is, be based on a mutual love and desire to love, honor, and cherish one another. Love of God cannot be legislated. It must come freely from within. The Law provides ways to help show that love.

Verse 34a continues this marriage image. What God truly desires is a depth of intimacy to truly be known. "To know" in the Bible is also used as a way of referring to sexual intimacy (recall how in Genesis it says "Adam knew Eve" and she conceived). What God wants is not a marriage in name or form only, just vows, some promises made, but a true marriage, a union of heart and mind, a daily relationship of love that deepens and grows. Once again, especially in the gospel of John, we see how Jesus is seen as the one who makes God known to humanity, the one who becomes the door, the gate, the way, the bridge to God.

But this new covenant is really not based on human love. It is based on the grace and forgiveness of God (last part of v. 34). God takes the initiative to reach out in gracious forgiveness to make this new relationship possible, to write the law on their hearts (the ink being love itself). Christians believe that this was ultimately fulfilled in the life of Christ. God does in Christ what the human heart and the law could not do. Grace is God's answer to human sin, a grace that is most fully expressed in the one whom the writer of Hebrews calls our great high priest and who, in the gospel lesson, gives up his life to bring life. In the heart of Jesus we see that perfect obedience and love for God and through him we find forgiveness for our failure to love and serve God and the power to receive new hearts, ones growing, hungering daily to know, love, and serve God.

Romans 3:19-28

Something is very wrong with human beings. Surely that is beyond dispute. Just pick up a newspaper, watch the news on television, or give an honest look in the mirror. The Bible calls this something wrong "sin." Isn't it interesting that the middle letter for this word is an "I"? For at the heart of sin is a radical self-centeredness, a desire to look out only for number one, for one's self. According to the scriptures, this placing of self above all else has resulted in a brokenness in our relationship first and foremost with God but also with others and even within ourselves. The question then becomes, "What is the cure?" How can this brokenness be healed? How can we be made right again with God, with one another, and become whole within ourselves?

Ask Paul those questions before his conversion, and as a Pharisee, he would have said that keeping the law (the teachings in what we call "the Old Testament") was the way to become right again or righteous. But what a reformation Paul had experienced! Now he had come to understand that the law could not save or restore or cure what ailed humanity. At best what it could do was make us aware of our sin, that we are, in fact, guilty (see v. 19). It's as if we are all standing before God in a courtroom and the law is laid down, showing beyond any doubt that we are all sinners (v. 23), so that we cannot even speak a word in our defense (v. 19). All we can do is await the judgment/punishment, which is surely coming.

But hold on a moment. Expecting to hear the judge condemn us, we hear instead, "You are aquitted! You are free!" (see the gospel reading where Jesus talks about the truth setting us free).

How can this be?

There is a new covenant that has been made (see the Jeremiah reading today). There is a new law, not written on stone like the ten commandments, but written in our hearts. There is a whole new relationship made possible because of Christ and it is based, not on our obedience to the law, which no one could ever really accomplish, but on grace. We are "justified," set free by the loving, free acceptance and mercy of God.

It was impossible to restore this relationship, this brokenness on our own. We needed something or rather someone to do for us what we could not do for ourselves. We needed an advocate, a mediator to restore or bring about reconciliation. That one was Jesus. It was as if we were about to be condemned by the judge but one, Jesus, stood up and took our place, took upon himself our guilt, and gave to us his perfect life and love.

So it is that we do not or cannot say or do anything to defend ourselves. We don't have to any longer because our relationship with God is no longer based on our works, our attempts to make ourselves righteous, which we could not do, but solely on the unmerited acceptance and love of God — grace!

All we need do in response is trust, is have faith that what God has done in Christ, has accepted us, forgiven us, set us free is, in fact, true — and live in that truth (see the gospel reading). Faith is accepting that we are accepted! This emphasis on grace and faith is at the heart at what reformed, changed Paul, Martin Luther, and helped bring about the Great Reformation.

John 8:31-36

This is a powerful passage about what it means to be a disciple of Jesus.

First, it involves belief or trust. Faith. This is trusting that what Jesus teaches about God and humanity is true, reliable. That the primary goal of one's life is to love God above all else and one's neighbor as one's self. Jesus not only taught this, he embodied it. He is the one who makes such a life possible. He not only shows that it can be done but empowers us to live that way.

Second, this involves growing or "continuing" in the "word" or "truth" Jesus brings. A disciple is literally a "learner" or student. But unlike in a public education, this school never ends. To "abide" in his word is to have a hunger to sit always at his feet, to always be listening to him, learning from him, following him. No matter how much we can hear and know, there is always more to learn.

Third, discipleship like this "will make you free." Perhaps the main thought is that devoting one's life to loving God and others sets one free from self-centeredness, sin. What God offers us in Christ is "freedom" from one thing — sin — and freedom for another thing — to be and become the human beings God wants us to be, to become like Christ.

The Jews who were listening to him protest. They say two things. First, that they are the children of Abraham. Second, that they are not slaves. To the first Jesus doesn't directly respond here. But elsewhere, like John the Baptist, Jesus refutes the view that their roots in Abraham give them special status. What God looks for is not roots but fruits. As for the second, they misunderstand Jesus. He's not talking about physical slavery but spiritual. They are slaves to sin. They are depending on the law for their righteousness and that somehow by their own will or works they can make themselves acceptable to God. But such living is to be a slave to a master, not the child or son of the Father! Thinking that they had to obey all the laws pictures God as some tyrant, some slave master. But the revelation God is making in Christ, this "truth" they have yet to see or believe is that now there is a new righteousness, one that frees them from the yoke of the law, from being slaves to being sons, children of a heavenly Father. What Paul says in today's readings is a wonderful commentary on how he, once a Jewish Pharisee, now sees the law in light of grace. The result was freedom! The freedom of being a child of God made so by the Son of God.

Application

Jeremiah 31:(27-30) 31-34. "A God of New Beginnings." The more you read the Bible, the more you begin to see patterns in it, that is, threads woven from book to book. One such thread or theme goes from Genesis to Revelation — God is a God of new beginnings. In Genesis alone, a word that means "beginning," we see God creating new things, new creatures, and constantly giving them new beginnings — with

Noah, Abraham and Sarah, then with all who followed. In the book of Revelation we see the new Jerusalem and a new heaven and new earth. Between these books we read story after story of the God of new beginnings. So it is hardly a surprise that Jeremiah adds to this never-ending story of new beginnings.

A New Beginning for Judah. The land of Judah had been devastated by the Babylonians. The people had been exiled. Even the animals had been taken but Jeremiah sees a new beginning, a second Genesis as God will repopulate the land with people and animals. God will give them a new start (v. 27). The words about plucking up and breaking down given when Jeremiah was commissioned (1:10) are now reversed as God will plant the people and build them up. Though it took decades, many did return to the land and the nation of Israel began anew.

New Beginnings in Faith. But something else would be new too. The people had believed a new beginning impossible. Indeed, how could they escape their fate for they believed they were suffering for the sins of their ancestors? So what was the use in even thinking about a new beginning? Such was the depth of their despair. Jeremiah says here that confession and repentance do matter (vv. 29-30). Accepting responsibility for their own sins and repenting in the present were meaningful actions that turned their hearts back to God and opened them to new beginnings for the future.

Indeed, a whole new beginning is what Jeremiah sees. It will be a "new covenant," or relationship unlike the one they had known based solely on obedience to laws. They had failed that one miserably. This new covenant would be more personal, written on their hearts. For they would come to "know God" intimately and deeply. They will then seek to serve and obey God out of love and out of that knowledge.

As Christians, we believe that in Christ this promise has been fulfilled and that the world has been given a whole new beginning. Paul goes so far as to say that we have in Christ been made new creations, the old has passed away, the new has come. Think of the many people who met Jesus who must have thought that new beginnings were impossible. How many, like the blind, the lame, the outcasts, the sinners, the demon possessed found a power in Jesus that gave them a new beginning? Remember the woman at the well? Think of the disciples themselves. Christ gave them many new beginnings. Peter especially. After the death of Jesus, who would have ever thought that he or the others could hope to start again? But Easter came, the ultimate of new beginnings, and gave them and us a new beginning.

Many of us will take and drink from the cup of Christ this day and eat the bread. Whenever we do, we are reminded of the God of new beginnings, of new covenants, a God who just does not want to give up on us or let us give up on ourselves. For this God of new beginnings loves us, forgives our sins, and remembers them no more.

An Alternative Application

"I, Martin." A very effective way to talk about the Reformation and its themes as shared in today's readings would be to come as Martin Luther and tell your story (or, if you have someone in your church or community who could do this). It would also be good to even dress as he did. Or, since there are many video resources available on his life, show an excerpt from one and then build a sermon based on it. Yet another way is to share your own experience of the grace of God, of how in Jesus you have been set free (or ask someone else to share their testimony). Such personal testimony or story sharing goes beyond just talking about grace but demonstrating it and what it looks and feels like.

"What's that Sound?" Have someone ready outside the front door of the church with a hammer. Have the person knocking, of course, on a piece of wood against the door not the door itself. Respond with something like, "I wonder — what's that sound? Is someone knocking to come in? Or, is it the echoes of that hammering that took place on October 31, 1517 by a priest named Martin Luther? (Then explain or tell the story.)

Share with the congregation that our texts for today are knocking first and foremost on our own hearts (Jeremiah passage). Have our hearts grown into cold stone? Do we need new hearts, a whole new relationship with God? Is the knocking the very Spirit of God seeking a new and fresh entrance into our hearts and lives? Share with the people Luther and Paul's experience of reformation through grace and faith. Share your own story of how God came knocking on your own heart.

Could the knocking also be about our church? Where do we need reform? What might be the notes from God left on our church, the ways in which we, too, as a church, as a people need re-forming?

All Saints
Isaiah 25:6-9
Revelation 21:1-6a
John 11:32-44
Craig MacCreary

Do you really want to be in that number?

I have to admit that *Monty Python's Flying Circus* is an acquired taste. Yet, those who have found themselves hooked by this groundbreaking British comedy series of the '70s often find theological truth jumping out at them in the midst of the odd humorous bits and pieces that has now become a cult comedy classic. One of the sketches, titled "How Not to Be Seen," featured a series of failed attempts at hiding that met with the characters being shot and blown up on sight. Being seen involved folks taking a potshot at you.

In that circumstance who would not want to have a means of camouflaging their way through life? One of the ways of doing that is to be dead. The stench alone will keep people away. Sometimes it seems that in some of our struggles in the church we have found a pretty good way of keeping people away and of keeping our vitality fairly well hidden. Some time ago, there was an unending string of controversial headline church stories that seemed guaranteed to keep the gospel under wraps and hidden away. Some churches have lost conferences over equal marriage rights. The Episcopal church is set for a rendezvous with schism over the ordination of openly gay bishops. The Presbyterians apologized for their previous stand on divestment from the State of Israel.

Like Martha in the story of Lazarus, no matter what side you take on certain questions, you get the feeling that we may not be seeing some people because of what is in the air. The saints have outvoted, outmaneuvered, outsmarted, outlasted, and outfoxed each other. On All Saints, this does not feel like what is meant by the communion of saints. Given some of the fearsome statistics that are facing many of our communions, some of us wonder if Mary and Martha are not on to something when they speculate, "Lord, if you had been here, my brother would not have died." Perhaps a sign of what the communion of saints means is the pain and sorrow that surrounds these events cause us all to weep. If we do not quite "Live in harmony with one another" — not being haughty, we still "Rejoice with those who rejoice, weep with those who weep."

In such circumstances, our mood contrasts sharply with the tone set in Isaiah and the book of Revelation. Isaiah writes in the midst of the precarious political world where nations and people are swallowed up by empires, never to be seen again. This was not a world in which it was easy to believe you would not be eaten up. For most, life was about keeping invisible to the powers that be. For your effort you might get some longevity if not ultimate safety. Of course, John saw a new heaven and earth descending. However, I suspect that there were at least a few who saw just more of the same old world where people got swallowed up by events, never to be seen or heard from again. Keep a low profile, keep your head low, keep your faith under wraps, and keep out of sight: It might not be what we mean by keeping the faith but it would keep you alive. The claims of both Isaiah and John are no less incredible than the claim of the gospel reading that, under the right circumstances, the stone could be removed and people under wraps could walk out into a new day.

When many want to do a duck-and-cover drill from being outmaneuvered, outvoted, and outtalked, we wonder if there can be a new day, let alone a new heaven and earth, for the saints. It seems that much is being kept out of sight and under wraps. Like Martha, we take the measure of what is in the air before we get too far into conversations with the saints less a pleasant moment be turned into a battle zone. We become careful and cautious rather than connected. This does not seem to be what is meant by the communion of saints.

I read my way through the literature on denominational turnarounds and revitalizations. I find much truth in their analyses and recommendations. Yet, I get the feeling it will take something like a new heaven and earth if we are to come out from the mode of outsmarting, outmaneuvering, outtalking, and outvoting each other. Wrapped up in such things, we may find that we have hidden much of who we are and can be for each other.

I find the first task of being part of the communion of saints is never to take a holier-than-thou attitude. I, too, have my issues that I believe in. I, too, have my agenda; yet I find All Saints pushing for a deeper understanding of what it means to be part of the saints.

Isaiah 25:6-9

Boldly put, it is party time on Mount Zion. One cannot escape the massive effort devoted to the analysis of religion and its influence on our society. For Isaiah, the triumph of God ends in a party on Mount Zion — in short, it is not over until the party begins for all people of all nations. Nothing is stinted: rich food, not fast food; well-aged wines, not last week's *muscatel*; rich food for all tastes: vegans and vanquished; the vanguard and the rear guard will be able to gather at this feast. This does not exactly feel like the coffee and fellowship hours that I find in many churches. Indeed many are too cautious to engage in this kind of irrational exuberance. For many, there is too much to be hidden, too many victories to be won, and too many points to be made or avoided. If you are at the head of the parade, it is better not to reveal that you might not be on the top of your game. If your church is seriously divided over any of the current controversies, fellowship hour can feel more like a minefield than a field of dreams. Knowing "that there is nothing hidden that will not be revealed," does not prevent us from trying to keep things under wraps.

Isaiah helps us to measure the gap between present reality and where we can be. I recently purchased a home in a retirement community. I am 57 years old and have run a personal best of 56:43 minutes for six miles. I was shocked, therefore, to find myself being treated like an old person. The phone installer patronized me by explaining in my native English as if it were my second language how to use the pretty buttons and make long-distance phone calls. I felt as if I was being swallowed up by stereotypes and pander, feeling my life doomed to a series of condescentions. Not on Mount Zion — party on! What swallows us up is swallowed up. All faces will find the tears wiped away. Among the saints, when this happens for those who have just lost in the latest denominational maneuvering then we will be on to something. When the tears of joy that can come in victory are wiped away and replaced with a deep sympathy and affection for those who feel they are losing it as they lose their sense of place in the world, then we will be approaching something of Zion-like proportions.

Then we will be saying that we are talking about God stuff here. Of course, this is not to say issues that divide us do not matter. It is not to say that we should not seek the mind of the church on these matters or that for many our consideration of these issues is part of their chance at making it up Zion's hill. It is not over until we are all sitting down to the feast. Then the disgrace of God's people will be taken away.

The prophet focuses on our disgrace -- the shame of those who want or claim to be in that number when the saints go marching in. There is a long list of folks being swallowed up in our world; a recent urban conference reminds us that many will be swallowed up in urban slums in the midst of globalization. If you live in Bangladesh, large parts of your country may be swallowed up by the rising tide of global warming. Americans find their lives swallowed up by working longer hours than any other people on the face of the earth. If you live in India your family life might be swallowed up serving the computer needs of those in the opposite time zone on the other side of the globe. Let us make no mistake about it. This is not the Zion hill that Isaiah is writing about. The challenge for the saints: Can we model a behavior and devotion that provide an alternative to the path that nations are going down? How can we do that if we do not know how to so identify with each other that we are not satisfied until our own tears are wiped away? When coffee and fellowship hours begin to look like what is happening on Zion's hill where no sorrow is hidden and no one need fear that they must hide, only then can we proclaim victory.

Revelation 21:1-6a

John says God's strategy is to reveal God's purpose and plan. There can be no doubt that there has been much spiritual damage done by those who claim more insight to the plan and purpose of God than God has offered up. To paraphrase Calvin, God has given us sufficient knowledge for our salvation but has never revealed enough to satisfy our unending curiosity. What is revealed here is a God whose will is to make all things new — not to do away with all things but make all things new. God's intention is a new and different kind of city than the one that is swallowing up people. God's ultimate purpose has massive implications for the penultimate lives of the saints. Eugene Peterson might not be far off the mark when he translates the verse, "I heard a voice thunder from the throne: 'Look, Look! God has moved into the neighborhood.' "

A different kind of neighborhood might be one in which a young couple is not swallowed up in the kind of deadly work schedule they must maintain in order to have the heavenly house conventionally understood, as opposed to a place where they feel at home with the growth in maturity and wisdom that God has planned for them. It might be a neighborhood where people don't have to live anonymous lives lest their sexual orientation is found out and they be invited out of the social life of community and church. A new neighborhood might be where people of color do not find themselves stopped by the police because their presence suggests that something is amiss. A new neighborhood might be a place where it is less about being protected from each other and more about being connected to each other.

Sometimes I wonder if the church is ready to receive this bride adorned and if it is ready to party on as a result of what God has joined together. In literature on church growth and renewal there is in some quarters an emphasis on the need for uniformity and similitude among church members — good sociology, good theology? There is much evidence that many are seeking safe enclaves among the similar. I would not pretend that there are simple, easy answers here. However, the text here drives us in the direction of rethinking what neighborhood should mean in the age to come. Will it be highly segregated or highly variegated? I go downtown in my new hometown, Manchester, New Hampshire, and I find many folks clearly in Arabic dress. I ran this past weekend in a 10k race accompanied by a woman in Arabic headdress and long pants. I ate dinner recently in an Ottawa pub during the playing of the World Cup soccer tournament. The singing of various national anthems suggested scenes from the movie, *Casablanca*.

What is the role of the communion of saints in this heady mix — segregation or variegation? Does it mean seeking out and learning from the saints, conventionally understood, in other faith communities, groups, and peoples? Might we learn something in the discovery of what is considered a saint in different faith communities? Certainly, this is a new heaven and would result in a new earth. It is enough to take your breath away as the former things and understandings pass away. Of course, it might be enough to breathe new life into the communion of saints. John makes clear that the voice he hears is both alpha and omega. We might find out that the end might be quite different from the kind of neighborhoods in which many of us had our beginnings! John notes that the sea is no more in the new vision. The old boundaries have passed away and made way for new possibilities.

John 11:32-44

As this story opens, there is no mistaking the fact that family and friends have worked their way through the denial phase of grief and are well on the way into serious anger. "Lord, if you had been here, my brother would not have died." On the whole, here the saints do not seem to do too well in living up to our expectations of sainthood. Some of the crowd also found Jesus' stay for two days in another place unforgivable. Mary (in the section not included in the lectionary passage) got the ball rolling in venting anger at Jesus (John 11:21). Of course, our sympathy moves in the direction of the two sisters but not for long. As Jesus makes his move against the force of death Martha tries to call a halt to the proceeding by reminding Jesus of the potential stench. It is her brother, for crying out loud! Can't she cut Jesus some slack here? You can feel the room temperature rise as Jesus responds with what seems less than the best counseling skills, "Did I not tell you that if you believed, you would see the glory of God?" Jesus is thankful that at least God hears him even if Mary does not.

What we have here is not a counseling session but a confrontation with the reality of the kind of death that we can do something about. If Jesus had been there, Lazarus would not have died. In John's ironical way we already know the answer. If Jesus is there, whatever the stench, there is the potential that folks can come out from their wrappings and live. Jesus shouts for Lazarus to come out before the wrappings are removed. The unwrapping will be left to the gathered saints. Unwrap folks that we may see they need their souls taken care of and they need acceptance, they need accomplishment, they need forgiveness, they need to know and be known. Unwrap folks and see them as flawed but not the sum total of the stupidest things they have ever done.

Whatever else in this story, when the saints get it right it comes when they hold their nose and engage in the unwrapping process that frees people and that lets them go their way. Not necessarily being our way, this can cause some elevated stress. Whatever the stench are we ready to unwrap people that they may go their own conservative, liberal, evangelical, intellectual, social action way? Or must they keep their way under wraps in our presence? Which way will make the church alive and give vitality to the communion of saints?

Application

As my years in ministry grow, I find myself revisiting the fundamentals of the faith. I find that I am seriously Trinitarian, undeniably evangelical, and totally a believer in the communion of saints. Although I must admit that the doctrines of the church function for me less as a description of metaphysical realities and more as reflections of people who have had similar experiences to me in their Christian journey. The celebration of All Saints, in light of past history and future hope, causes me to reflect on the gathering of the saints that has come as a result of the birth, life, and death of Jesus Christ. Protestants are normally not quite as comfortable as Roman Catholics when we get to talking about saints. Regretfully, on the Protestant side we see the concept as getting in the way as much as facilitating our relationship with God. However, we would do well to consider the high calling to sainthood and the responsibilities it entails. Some days, I find my thoughts ruminating on how the saints are really communing with each other in the here and now. As saints we have the power to unbind and let people go. We can give new meaning to neighborhood that might make all things new and prevent many people being swallowed by death. Folks who can do that are candidates for sainthood in my book.

An Alternative Application

Isaiah 25:6-9. The traditional understanding of a saint is one whose life is so virtuous that it is a clear example of Christian living that can bring people to faith. When All Saints hits, I find myself reflecting on those who have brought me to faith and pondering just what qualities of their lives move me to Christian living. More often than not they are the folks who I do not want to let down. There is something about them that engages me in a way that causes me not to just emulate them but to find my own way in a manner that is faithful to their example. They are more often than not the voice that comes to me in sermon preparation that will not let me be satisfied with something less than a full effort. Sometimes, I recognize their voice as demanding and challenging. At times, saints are those who, with no questions, still let me into their lives even when I have failed to build on the standards they have given me. Other times, saints are those who let on to enough of their own wanderings in their lives that I can accept my own. Saints do not let me get away with anything. I can fool myself but not them. They are willing to stand with me and up to me at the same time.

Sometimes it seems to me that saints specialize in one or the other of these categories. Sometimes they are packaged together in various combinations. However, their presence always forces me to consider what I have been specializing in lately as I go off on various paths or to think just what I have packaged together. I understand that the official Roman Catholic understanding of saints is that they can intervene for you with God. I don't know. However, I do know that they cause me to intervene in life in ways that I would not have without their presence in my life. This is a day to name them, thank God for them and perhaps even apply to be one of them.

Values clarification

Sometimes in conversation with friends, we will amuse ourselves — or torment ourselves — by wondering what we would do when confronted by certain kinds of choices. If you inherited enough money to become independently wealthy, would you keep working your current job? For what one thing would you like to be remembered after you die? If you could go back and change one thing that you said or did in the past, what would you change? If you could only rescue one item from your burning house, what would it be? And so on.

Such questions are more than a mere amusement. They help reveal what things are most important to us.

Jesus was asked a similar sort of question. "Which commandment is the first of all?" The episode is perhaps so familiar that we have lost our sense of wonder at either the question or the answer. Imagine, therefore, that same question in a more extreme form: "If you had to toss out all of the commandments from God except one, which one would you keep?"

It's a dramatic question that asks the Son of God to prioritize the commands of God. He does so, apparently without hesitation, and his marvelous answer reveals what is most important to God.

The star of the show this week is love. Ruth embodied it. Jesus came, lived, and died because of it. And we discover that love is the thing that is most important to God.

Ruth 1:1-18

If you're reading the Bible cover-to-cover, the book of Judges is still fresh in your mind when you read the opening lines of Ruth. Immediately in the wake of the candid report of Israel's dismal and violent frontier days, the opening line of the book of Ruth rings true. "In the days when the judges ruled, there was a famine in the land." That famine is just one more grim detail from a harsh, even gruesome era in Israel's history. Furthermore, that famine may read like a metaphor for the spiritual and moral destitution that seems to have characterized the land all of the days between Joshua and Samuel.

The author of Judges concludes his book with his terse verdict on the times: "In those days there was no king in Israel; all the people did what was right in their own eyes" (Judges 21:25). And when we turn the page, the author of Ruth begins with a comparably bleak summary of the era: "In the days when the judges ruled, there was a famine in the land."

And if the setting is inhospitable when the curtain opens on the story, the plot soon matches scenery. Within just a few verses, we see a series of tragedies that is reminiscent of Job. Naomi and her family are forced to flee their famine-stricken homeland to make a new life for themselves elsewhere, only to have her life partner die there in that foreign place. She is not left alone, however, for her two grown sons are with her. They marry local girls, and it seems that there is promise for new life and a future in the adopted place. Then, unbelievably, both of Naomi's sons die. This seemingly cursed woman finds herself to be a grieving, childless widow in a foreign country.

Absent some physical ailment, it's hard to draw a much more desperate picture. The sorrow of a woman who has lost her whole family to premature deaths. The alienation of a person who is forced to live as a refugee in a foreign land. The helplessness and vulnerability of a woman in that time and place with no father, husband, or son to support her. Naomi is a portrait of sadness and desperation.

The great pivotal moment of the passage, of course, comes when the three widows are about to part company. Naomi says significant things to her daughters-in-law.

She tells each of them to go back to their mother's house. Why not to their father's house? Were their fathers also already dead? Were men such an uncertainty that the mother was a greater image of stability and comfort for these three women? Or was she reminding them that, while she was a kind of mother to them, they had their actual mothers back home, ready to receive them?

Next, Naomi pronounces a kind of blessing over them: "May the Lord deal kindly with you, as you have dealt with the dead and with me." It is a blessing conspicuously tied to their goodness rather than to the Lord's. In other words, may they be properly rewarded by the Lord for their goodness to others. But Naomi is unable to say, "May the Lord deal kindly with you, as he has with me," or some such. And, a moment later, she reveals more straightforwardly her issue with God: "The hand of the Lord has turned against me."

Then Naomi launches into a bit of exaggerated reasoning. Mindful that her connection to these two young women was through their marriage to her sons, she explains at length that she can no longer provide for them in that way. The whole proposal is a preposterous one, but it reflects a kind of resignation that the rationale for their relationship with her is permanently ended, and they should move on with their lives.

The one daughter-in-law, Orpah, is persuaded, and she says her tearful good-bye, but the other daughter-in-law, Ruth, pledges her allegiance to Naomi. In the process, Ruth articulates a whole-hearted loyalty that becomes a metaphor for conversion, a model for discipleship, and a historic turning point with ramifications that could not have been imagined by those two destitute widows on their way between Moab and Judah.

Hebrews 9:11-14

Our selected lection from Hebrews for this Sunday is not one of the conventionally beautiful passages of scripture. This is not the cherished territory of Psalm 23 or John 14. It does not have the familiar loveliness of the Beatitudes or the fruit of the Spirit. But there is great beauty in these verses, and skillful preaching will reveal that beauty to congregations that may be mostly unfamiliar with this epistle and its contents.

I am imagining a jigsaw puzzle. The finished product may be a very lovely picture of some beautiful scene, yet the individual pieces, by themselves, are not especially beautiful. Indeed, taken individually they are completely incoherent.

So it may be with this passage from Hebrews. It is a single piece or two from a much larger picture, and those pieces may make little sense to the person who is unfamiliar with that picture. Our task, then, is to help our people see the whole picture and thus discover the beauty contained and reflected in this one small passage.

The beauty of the passage is seen within three larger contexts.

First, there is the larger context of the Old Testament. That, of course, may be the most unfamiliar puzzle to so many of the people in our pews, but that is precisely the larger picture that the author of Hebrews has in mind as he writes. The beauty of the passage — as with the entire epistle — is found in the author's marvelous translation from law to gospel. He takes the dots of rituals, symbols, figures, and themes from the Old Testament Levitical code, and he connects them to reveal a picture of Christ. The particular pattern seen in this passage is characteristic of the book as a whole: namely, what Christ is and does was anticipated by Old Testament people and practices, yet what Christ is and does is far superior to those antecedents.

Second, then, there is the larger context of the person and work of Christ. This goes hand-in-hand, of course, with the first matter, for it is that Old Testament context that reveals to us the person and work of Christ. Here, specifically, Christ is understood as both the high priest who offers blood and the sacrifice whose blood is offered. Within the original Old Testament context, the mixed roles would seem ridiculous. In Christ, however, they are mysteriously combined, and the very mixture bears witness to how wonderful and superior he is.

In this regard, we do well to remember — and to remind our people — that this is arguably the central beauty of the entire New Testament. From the gifts of the wise men to the song of Simeon, from the confession of Peter to the preaching of Paul, and from the writings of the evangelists to the Revelation of John, the person and work of Christ is the central issue, message, and beauty of the entire New Testament.

Finally, the image of Christ as both high priest and sacrifice leads us to the third larger context of this passage, that is, our relationship with God.

The author's original audience understood the role of the high priest and of the blood. The former was the go-between: the one who, on the day of atonement, entered into the presence of God on behalf of the people. The latter was the actual means of that atonement: the blood that purifies and sanctifies. The beauty of Christ's work, then, is that he is the one who does all of these things for us: he represents us before God, he sanctifies us, and he purifies us. Our entire relationship with God is by him and through him.

The initial context of that relationship, of course, is sin. That is the condition in which we find ourselves. Filthy humanity at odds with its holy creator. Men and women afflicted with a fatal disease they cannot treat or cure by themselves. Humankind hopelessly, helplessly distant, until God himself lovingly comes to the rescue. And, at his own expense, Christ offers "eternal redemption," "sanctifies those who have been defiled," and purifies both their flesh and their consciences. That is the third beauty: the sublime beauty of what is available to us in Christ.

Mark 12:28-34

We know from Mark's gospel in particular, and from all of the gospels in general, that the final week of Jesus' life was an eventful one.

He entered the city to a conspicuous and triumphant welcome on Sunday. It was no doubt an unnerving development for the Jewish leaders who were already antagonistic toward and suspicious of Jesus. And it may have caught the attention and raised the concern of the Roman officials in Jerusalem, as well.

Monday may have been the day when he cleansed the temple. That disruption was a condemnation of and challenge to the leaders of the people, including especially the chief priests. If Jesus had wanted to lay low and stay out of trouble, he would not have made this move in the temple. That dramatic act was surely sticking his hand into the hornets' nest.

Still, each day that week Jesus and his disciples, who were apparently spending their nights outside of town on the other side of the Mount of Olives, came into Jerusalem, and he taught daily in the temple.

From early in the gospel story, we see evidence that the leaders who were antagonistic toward Jesus were restrained by their fear of the crowd. Jesus' great and growing popularity created a nearly impossible situation for them. As a result, they ultimately had to do their dirty deed under the cover of night, and without the presence or knowledge of the crowds. Indeed, given the low-profile nature of the arrest, the clandestine late-night meeting of the council, the expedited process, and the detail that Jesus was on the cross by nine o'clock on Friday morning (Mark 15:25), one wonders how much of the adoring crowds even knew that Jesus was being executed until it was too late.

During that eventful week, therefore, the leaders were seeking a way to get Jesus without incurring the wrath of the crowd. Their first method of choice was to ask Jesus challenging questions. The questions were designed to be traps, forcing Jesus to say something that would either get him in trouble with Rome, cut across the grain of scripture and the Mosaic law, or offend and alienate the crowds. In each case, however, Jesus responded with a wisdom and skill that both kept him out of trouble and dumbfounded his opponents.

Immediately prior to our gospel lection, Mark records three such question-traps, which prompts the scribe in our passage to pose a question of his own to Jesus. This particular scribe, about whom we know nothing, is an interesting case within that larger context. While others — including, no doubt, some colleagues and associates of this scribe — had been trying to trick Jesus with the questions, only to be confounded by his wisdom, this man was differently motivated. His question was no trap. Rather, he was attracted to Jesus' wisdom, and so he asked a legitimate and earnest question.

On the one hand, "Which commandment is the first of all?" may have been a kind of theological *shibboleth.* Perhaps (as we will explore further) the question is designed to reveal just where an individual is in terms of theology, ethics, and priorities. In our day, we might ask a person, "Which amendment in the Bill of Rights do you think is most important?" and we would no doubt find that how a person answered that question would reveal a good deal about that person.

On the other hand, "Which command is the first of all?" may have been a very personal, even tortured, kind of a question.

A scribe in that day was regarded as an expert in the scriptures. That made the scribes both theologians and legal scholars. They were looked to for the proper interpretation of scripture in general, as well as the authoritative interpretation and application of the Mosaic law. This particular man, therefore, was asking Jesus a question from his own area of expertise, his own field of study.

How easy it is for experts to become almost lost within all the minutiae of their expertise. And how easy it is for those who become professionals in the things of God to become disoriented — needing to be reminded of the basics, needing to return to the simple faith and truth they once knew before they came to know so much more.

Perhaps this scribe needed Jesus to throw him a lifeline, rescuing him from the endless theoretical debates of his profession. Perhaps he needed Jesus to provide him with a compass, reminding him which way was up and where to find God.

In any case, what Jesus said rang true for the scribe. He enthusiastically echoes Jesus' answer, adding an emphasis of his own: "This is much more important than all whole burnt offerings and sacrifices."

That sort of theological triage — conferring a greater importance and urgency on matters of the heart than on prescribed rituals — is not new. We see the same priority reflected periodically in the psalms and the prophets. Still, it was a significant insight for the scribe to articulate, and perhaps especially right there within the confines of the temple.

Jesus, who had answered wisely so many questions himself, "saw that (the scribe) answered wisely." Jesus said to him, "You are not far from the kingdom of God." Interestingly, while the proximity of the kingdom is the theme of the early preaching in the gospels (see, for example, Mark 1:15), here Jesus depicts it the other way around: that is, in terms of the individual's proximity to the kingdom.

Application

On the one hand, we should be properly shocked by Jesus' answer to the scribe's question. With all of the detailed ritual and rigid regulations of the Levitical code, how does an ethereal instruction to love God rate the top spot? With all of the emphasis, in law and prophets alike, on idolatry and the exclusive worship of God, why doesn't "have no other gods" keep its designation as the first commandment? And with all of the trouble caused by Adam and Eve, why not make a simple "obey God" the most important command of all?

On the other hand, we shouldn't be at all surprised by Jesus' answer. It is absolutely consistent with what we know about this God. Love is his chief motivation (John 3:16) and his quintessential attribute (1 John 4:8). It is the most important gift of the Spirit (1 Corinthians 12:29—13:13) and ranks first among the fruit of the Spirit (Galatians 5:22-23). It is Jesus' new commandment (John 13:34) and the telltale characteristic of his followers (13:35).

Ask God the questions that clarify and reveal what is most important to him, and we will be delighted to discover the answer. Love. If it were anything else — holiness, perfection, obedience, doctrine, purity, faith, works — we'd be in trouble. But love is number one with God; and that is very good news for us, indeed.

An Alternative Application

Mark 12:28-34. "Personal Best." The question that the scribe asked Jesus may have been a theoretical question. Perhaps this Sunday we should turn it around and make it a very personal question.

Which commandment is first? There are hundreds and hundreds of commandments in the scriptures; but which one shall we regard as most important?

An individual's answer to that question may serve as a kind of x-ray: a revealing, even diagnostic glimpse into a person's soul. Assuming that we regard all of God's commandments as important, the one that we consider most important reveals a great deal about the kind of person we are. Perhaps my answer would show that I am a legalist, or a libertarian. Perhaps it would reveal my sentimental side, or a certain vindictiveness. Perhaps it would demonstrate whether I lean more toward justice or more toward mercy.

Of course, if I know this story, then I know the answer to the question. If I know this story, then when someone asks me which commandment is most important, I can simply quote Jesus' answer.

But that does not automatically make it my answer, does it? Just knowing Jesus' answer is not quite the same as recognizing my answer. For, you see, my answer to that question is not found in what I say but in how I live. What I regard as the most important commandment is more revealed than replied.

That Jesus identified the commandment he did reveals volumes about him and about God's will. We can learn so much from considering the answer he gave and the answers he didn't give. However, a look in the mirror may be in order. Based on how I live my life — my priorities, my emphases, my decisions, my nonnegotiables — what is apparently the most important commandment to me?

Beyond compare

Much of the rest of our culture is unapologetic about sacrifice. In fact, much of the world around us is proud of it. Sports drink makers and sneaker manufacturers prominently feature images of personal sacrifice and discipline in their television commercials. The armed forces promote their opportunities with strong boasts about what it takes to be one of them. Competitive graduate schools make it clear to would-be applicants that prohibitive sacrifice will be essential. Likewise, so many big companies and major firms unapologetically preach sacrifice to their junior executives as an essential component of success.

We preach sacrifice, too, but ours is different.

Most proponents of popular sacrifice in our culture sell sacrifice for self's sake. I'm invited to make sacrifices in order to benefit myself in the end. My employer or my school or my health club promise me that my sacrifices will lead to my success, to my fitness, to my self-improvement, to my promotion. Sacrifice in popular culture is a calculated investment, and the return is all about self.

The kind of sacrifice described — for that matter, demanded — in scripture, however, is not about self. Quite the contrary: scriptural sacrifice is selfless. Forgetting your self (Matthew 16:24ff) may be the quintessential sacrifice required of the person who would be a disciple of Jesus Christ. It may yield a reward in the end, but that is God's grace and providence, not human manipulation.

In the three passages we consider this week, sacrifice is a recurring theme. Ruth's selfless sacrifice for the sake of her mother-in-law is the backdrop for the Old Testament passage. The widow's sacrificial giving is at the heart of the gospel lection. And Jesus' atoning sacrifice is the centerpiece of the gospel message explicated in Hebrews.

Ruth 3:1-5; 4:13-17

The sweet story of Ruth is a refreshing change from the rough-and-tumble period from which it comes. The book of Judges portrays a lawless time, place, and people. It was an era when "all the people did what was right in their own eyes" (Judges 21:25). That is the final verdict of the biblical author on that period in Israel's history.

But then we turn the page, and the scene brightens considerably. We find ourselves face-to-face with two women whose love and devotion to one another cut across the grain of the prevailing selfishness.

The story, whose happy ending is part of our lection for this Sunday, does not have a happy beginning. Naomi, her husband, and their two sons are forced by famine to leave their home in Bethlehem and seek refuge in Moab. Before the family's sojourn in Moab is over, Naomi's husband dies. No explanation or cause of death is given. From the terse reporting, one senses that the death was sudden and unexpected. Naomi is a widow now, but not desolate, for she has two grown sons to provide for her.

The two sons marry Moabite women, but within a few years the young men die. Again, no explanation is given, but the rapid-fire tragedies and unrelenting troubles make Naomi's story reminiscent of Job's.

Now Naomi's situation is desperate. She is in a foreign land, a widow, and without any sons, sons-in-law, or grandsons to provide for her. A widow in that culture was nearly helpless, and so she had to depend upon the remaining males in her family for her sustenance. The plight of widows in that world is implicit in the Old Testament Law (Deuteronomy 10:17-18; 24:19), in Jesus' teachings (Mark 12:40;

Luke 18:2-8), and in the efforts in the early church to care for the widows in their midst (Acts 6:1; 1 Timothy 5:3-16; James 1:27). The potential for widows to become destitute is also graphically illustrated by the gospel reading for this Sunday.

Naomi begins to return to Judah, where the famine is now past. It seems she will return home in a very different condition than she was when she left — a solitary, tragic figure who lost her whole family in a foreign land.

Naomi urges her two daughters-in-law to return to their homes, for they are young enough to have hopes of remarrying and bearing children. The one daughter-in-law says a tearful good-bye, and returns to her home and family. The other daughter-in-law, Ruth, however, refuses to leave Naomi.

This is Ruth's first great sacrifice of love. Naomi is no doubt correct — at least in terms of probability — that Ruth's future looks brighter if she stays in her homeland and returns to her family. But Ruth dismisses what is in her own best interest in order to stay with her mother-in-law.

Here is where biblical sacrifice and popular sacrifice part company. Popular sacrifice is doing precisely that which is in my own best long-term interest. Biblical sacrifice, however, challenges me to swim upstream against the current of my fallenness and dismiss what is in my own best interest for the sake of someone else. That was Ruth's brand of sacrifice, and it is the background for the Old Testament lection.

Another fundamental component of biblical sacrifice is obedience. Abraham was being obedient when he took Isaac up the mountain to sacrifice his only son. Christ was "obedient to the point of death, even death on a cross" (Philippians 2:8). And the quality of Ruth's obedience to Naomi is evident in our selected passage for this week.

The end of the passage — the end of the story — is all exclamation points. Naomi and Ruth, whose futures looked so very bleak in chapter 1, are now secure. The son born to Boaz and Ruth is reckoned by Naomi's friends as her son. And the providential hand of God is beautifully apparent as the story of Ruth anticipates the reign of David.

A later descendant of Ruth said, "Unless a grain of wheat falls into the earth and dies, it remains just a single grain; but if it dies, it bears much fruit" (John 12:24). So it is that Ruth's sacrifices, in the end, bore much fruit.

Hebrews 9:24-28

Any passage from Hebrews needs to be read with an understanding of the hermeneutic approach to scripture that lies behind the whole letter. The letter to the Hebrews explains the gospel to those steeped in the Jewish Law. It is not a refutation or setting aside of the law. Rather, Hebrews understands the law as a kind of connect-the-dots puzzle, and the coming of Christ has connected those dots. In Christ, the law is completed. In him, we are able to see clearly the whole picture contained in the law.

While we do not know who wrote the epistle to the Hebrews, many scholars assume that the author was a product of Alexandrian Judaism, such as Apollos (Acts 18:24). Alexandria, at once both the home of so many Jews in the Diaspora and a stronghold of Hellenism, produced a distinctively Greek method of interpreting the Jewish scriptures. Reminiscent of the Platonic notion of a heavenly plane, of which all earthly realities are merely shadows, the writer of Hebrews understood the Old Testament law and all its component parts as shadows of a heavenly reality. Our more commonplace term, foreshadowing, is a picturesque way of understanding the Hebrews hermeneutic.

High school and college English teachers often give "compare and contrast" essay assignments. That is essentially the approach of the letter to the Hebrews. The author compares and contrasts the person and work of Christ to elements of the Old Testament. Christ compares to those, for they foreshadowed him. Christ also stands in contrast to those, however, for he is what they were not and achieves what they could not.

Several comparisons are suggested in our brief passage, all springing from one basic premise: The work of Christ stands in contrast to the work of the high priest. While the high priest entered a man-made sanctuary, Christ entered heaven. The high priest performed his duty again and again, while Christ's offering was once and for all. The high priest made an offering that was unrelated to himself, while Christ made an offering of himself. And then, moving beyond the Old Testament comparisons, the author of Hebrews contrasts Christ's first coming with his second: two comings, two purposes.

Obedient self-sacrifice is once again the underlying theme of the passage, but this sacrifice is different. Ruth's sacrifice bears much fruit, to be sure. And the widow (in the gospel lection) is exemplary for her sacrificial giving. But Christ's sacrifice is more than just one in a series of examples, more than just another illustration of sacrifice. This is a sacrifice with implications that are both universal and eternal. It is not a sacrifice, the writer of Hebrews might say. It is the sacrifice.

Mark 12:38-44

We don't live in a culture where an ostentatious religiosity would be much admired, and so we are perhaps immune from some of the temptations that afflicted the religious folks of Jesus' day. It may be, however, that in the smaller context of a given church or fellowship group there does exist a temptation to make a spectacle of one's spirituality.

In mainline American Christianity today, perhaps the temptation is a different one. The underlying issue — an unwholesome preoccupation with what others see and think — is the same, even if the manifestation is different. I think of the respectable facade that so often covers us in church. It is not so much driven by a desire for admiration of one's spirituality, but rather a fear of judgment of one's shortcomings. And so the show we put on is not the "long robes" and the "best seats." Our show is the pretense that we have our act together, and an unwillingness to "confess your sins" (or "faults") "to one another" (James 5:16).

The other prominent issue, beyond the ostentatious religiosity, is the hypocrisy that accompanies it. The hypocrisy of the scribes is reflected in the juxtaposition of their "long prayers" with their cruel and unjust treatment of the weakest in that society (v. 40). The notion of the scribes devouring widows' houses becomes especially poignant a few verses later when we see the destitute widow bringing her tiny contribution to the temple. Could it be that her condition is so desperate because of the greed and injustice of the religious leaders? If so, she managed to keep clear a distinction in her own mind between God, on the one hand, and his ministers and representatives, on the other.

Jesus offers a lengthier, more detailed, and more passionate commentary on the hypocrisy of the religious leaders in his six "woe" statements (Luke 11:39-52).

The other issue of hypocrisy in this passage is the implicit hypocrisy of those who make a show of offering large gifts at the temple when, in Jesus' view, their gifts are actually quite small. Anything we pretend to do for God that is, in reality, for our own glory, praise, or applause, is hypocrisy, for it indicates a lack of integrity between what goes on at the surface and what goes on in the heart. The "surface," of course, is the constant preoccupation of the world in which we live, but we are challenged to live for a God who looks on the heart (see 1 Samuel 16:7; Matthew 6:4).

Those of us who are in professional ministry may be especially susceptible to this brand of hypocrisy — not just the commonplace hypocrisy of actions that don't square with words, but rather the more subtle and invisible form of hypocrisy mentioned above. For in professional ministry, it is easy for us to lose clarity about our motivation. Exactly for whom do I do what I do each day? In terms of my original sense of calling, it is all for God. And in terms of people's assumptions, it is all for God. But the reality is that I can fall into the trap of doing what I do for my church or my people or my supervisor or reputation, success, or survival, fear of criticism, or what have you.

Jesus "sat down opposite the treasury, and watched the crowd putting money into the treasury" (v. 41a). The image is a compelling one. Clearly some of the giving that day was animated by the presence of an audience. The image of Jesus sitting and watching, however, reminds us that the only audience that matters in our giving — or in any other act of worship — is the Lord.

Other teachings of Jesus (e.g., Matthew 6:1-6, 16-18) remind us of this fundamental truth. All of our piety has an audience of One. And if we do what we do for anyone's approval but his, we leave ourselves open to a double risk: First, that our Christianity will not really be for Christ's sake; and, second, that when our human audience begins to *disapprove* of our Christianity, we will betray or deny our Lord.

As we ponder the image of Christ watching our giving, we are also reminded of the much-neglected theme in scripture of unacceptable worship. It is a foreign concept to most folks in the pews, for if worship is to be judged as pleasing or displeasing in our culture, that judgment is the prerogative of the worshipers. We have largely lost sight of the biblical truth that God is or is not pleased by our worship. And, at the extreme, that God does or does not accept our worship. When we imagine Christ watching our giving — and all our acts of worship — we are forced to face the question of whether our worship is pleasing and acceptable in his sight or not.

It is worth noting in this episode to whom Jesus addresses himself. He does not make his point to any of the givers there at the temple: neither as a corrective to the majority, nor as a commendation to the widow. Rather, he uses it simply as a teaching point for his disciples. That approach may be instructive for us as we preach this passage.

Application

Just as Hebrews compares and contrasts Christ with Old Testament figures and events, so we may embark this week on a little comparing and contrasting of our own.

The first level of consideration, as mentioned above, is popular sacrifice versus biblical sacrifice. We must be aware, though, that both kinds of sacrifice are present in every generation. There are examples of the phenomenon we are calling "popular sacrifice" — that is, sacrifice for the sake of self — in the pages of scripture. Likewise, there are surely examples of biblical sacrifice in the world around us — very probably in the pews around us.

The ostentatious public giving of those who "contributed out of their abundance" may be a biblical example of popular sacrifice. It was likely a sacrifice motivated mostly by the attention and applause it enjoyed. Or the public display of affliction, as it were, that Jesus warned about when fasting (Matthew 6:16-18) is another.

Meanwhile, the biblical models of sacrifice seen in Ruth and the poor widow are duplicated in our generation. The person who so quietly and generously serves his or her church without anyone's notice. The day-in-day-out faithfulness of an individual who cares for an ill or disabled loved one. The heroic sacrifice of those who live out their witness for Christ in an antagonistic environment.

Then there is the second level of compare-and-contrast: Christ's sacrifice compared to all others.

In terms of comparisons, there are these great similarities between his sacrifice and our best sacrifices: it was selfless, it was on others' behalf, and it was fundamentally motivated by love.

In terms of contrast, meanwhile, these observations:

First, there is the element of fault. Ruth's sacrifice was on behalf of an innocent Naomi. Christ's sacrifice, by contrast, was on behalf of a guilty humankind. Paul makes the point that a rare individual would die for a righteous person, but Christ died for sinners (Romans 5:6-8).

Second, there was love's great gamble. It was in his love for us — and his desire for us to freely love him — that God created humankind with free will. In our freedom, however, we distanced ourselves from his love. Then, at the cross, his love gambled on us again — gambled in the sense that he risked everything with no certain return.

And, finally, we must confess that there is no adequate human comparison for what God did. The incomprehensible condescension of the Incarnation (see Philippians 2:6-8), followed by the inconceivable death of the Son of God. None of our sacrifices can approach that. As Charles Wesley said, " 'Tis mystery all: th' Immortal dies! Who can explore his strange design? In vain the firstborn seraph tries to sound the depths of love divine. 'Tis mystery all! Let earth adore; let angel minds inquire no more."

An Alternative Application

Mark 12:38-44. If your congregation is made up of people who have been in church most of their lives, then they have no doubt heard the story of the widow's mite. And, truth be told, the story may have become an unwelcome one, for it can so easily be used by a preacher to wag a finger at the congregation. After all, most of our people, like the majority of givers in the gospel episode, give out of their abundance.

It might be a refreshing approach, therefore, for your congregation to hear you preach this story to yourself rather to them. That is to say, rather than overtly challenging them to give differently, invite them into your struggle to think differently. For surely the shock value of what Jesus said to his disciples was in how differently he thought of giving than everyone else did.

The budgetary pressures in the average church make us rather more favorably disposed toward the "big givers." We need them. We need their support. And for the purposes of the annual budget, the building program, the special needs, those folks who give out of their abundance are, in fact, the big givers.

In the kingdom of heaven, however, it seems that those folks are not the big givers. While we are tempted to view giving always in terms of the church's budget, Jesus seems to view giving in terms of the giver's budget.

And so the preacher — and the congregation he or she leads — is left with a quandary. Shall we think in terms of the world in which we live, or in terms of the kingdom for which we live and the Lord for whom we live? Which is the greater reality? And which reality will animate and motivate us — as preachers, as committees, as congregations, and as worshipers?

Proper 28 / Pentecost 25 / Ordinary Time 33
1 Samuel 1:4-20
Hebrews 10:11-14 (15-18) 19-25
Mark 13:1-8
Craig MacCreary

Propping up or opening up

It is never a good place to be when you feel that you are losing it. When clearly marked though, such times can be moments of creativity and renewal. However, there are times when things are slipping away and falling apart and panic sets in. Jared Diamond, in his book, *Collapse*, tells the tale of the Easter Islanders. The island was found abandoned, with only the remains of the huge stone statue heads of their gods left in place staring out to sea. The Islanders, unbeknownst to themselves, were planting the seeds of their own destruction as they kept carving and setting in place the huge stone heads. The different sections of the Island were in a sort of competition to carve bigger and better heads. Of course, the problem was that as they went about propping up their gods, they required more and more wood to transport the stone and set it into place. Eventually, they reached a tipping point and the Island forests could no longer replenish themselves.

The conversation between Jesus and one of his disciples as they came out of the temple suggests that this is a fate that might not just befall the South Pacific Islanders. As he came out of the temple, one of his disciples said to him, "Look, Teacher, what large stones and what large buildings!" Then Jesus asked him, "Do you see these great buildings? Not one stone will be left here upon another; all will be thrown down." Jared Diamond's work suggests that the cracks in the cultural facade begin to show when minority voices are silenced, there is a radical indifference to the surrounding environmental realities — a particular downfall of the islanders, and a preoccupation with war. In the face of such things, you can anticipate the kind of cracking that if undetected and uncorrected can bring down whatever gods we might prop up.

When folks say it can't happen here, look out for falling rocks and be prepared to do some duck-and-cover drills as the building blocks that we thought were in place begin to show their age and the need for some serious maintenance or significant replacement. Of course, not all will tumble down. "For truly I tell you, until heaven and earth pass away, not one letter, not one stroke of a letter, will pass from the law until all is accomplished." Of course, Jesus' words point out that heaven and earth will at some point pass away. If heaven and earth can pass away, what chance do our propped-up gods have?

Each of these texts deals with the experience of finding one's own world suddenly at risk. Perhaps by now we are a little more likely to believe that one's world might be tumbling down. Still, it does come as somewhat of a shock when there is indisputable evidence the cracks have widened to the point that familiar patterns of life are in jeopardy. It seemed that the wisdom of the world did not prevent the fissure in the environmental facade that appeared when evidence was found in the Yukon of polar bears cannibalizing each other because, due to global warming, they can no longer reach their traditional feeding ground. The crack seems to widen as one of the leading seminaries of our denomination must put its historic campus on the auction block because the support dollars are drying up. It feels like a hairline crack has seriously widened when more young couples report that they work longer hours, and have less in the bank in order to buy starter homes that are more expensive than ever before. They feel that the social net may not have enough to take care of their retirement.

In each of the texts for this Sunday, there is evidence of hairline cracks that might fissure into chasms. The text from Samuel shows a family at risk. The Hebrew text calls into question a religious system that no longer delivers. The text from Mark calls into question a national epic as nation rises up against nation.

Like the disciples, we find ourselves asking when these things will happen and what the signs will be. Give us some way of handling this that will see us through the crisis.

1 Samuel 1:4-20

Allow for a bit of serious cultural diversity and this could be a family that could be living on your street. Jealousy, a sense of failure, and a husband that is cloddish in his response to the feelings of his wife seem to be indicators that folks are in over their heads. Hannah does some serious bargaining with God. When she hears, "Hannah, why do you weep? Why do you not eat? Why is your heart sad? Am I not more to you than ten sons?" she knows it is time to start drawing on her faith tradition to see her through. She knows that her husband cannot meet all her needs. In this she has both psychology and some sociology on her side. After all, if Elkanah is not around, her goose is going to be cooked. It is time for some theology. Unfortunately, the authorized religious representative reads the situation thoroughly wrong as he mistakes her form of devotion and prayer for drunkenness. With a wonderful husband like Elkanah who, thinking the world of her, cuts her an extra ration of food and who clearly thinks his devotion can cover her needs, what could be the problem?

Unfortunately, this will not be the last time that an official religious representative brings some serious insensitivity to a family situation. When Eli does hear her voice, he gets it right in a very big way. He hears her out, and hears in a way that elicits a significant response. But Hannah answered, "No, my lord, I am a woman deeply troubled; I have drunk neither wine nor strong drink, but I have been pouring out my soul before the Lord. Do not regard your servant as a worthless woman, for I have been speaking out of my great anxiety and vexation all this time." Hannah hits it right on the head: Do not regard me in the usual cultural way as a hysterical woman assuaging her pain with too many long afternoons of boozing. Eli has choices here. He can try and prop up the usual gods that would put Hannah in her place. "Go home, talk it out with you husband, try harder, be thankful to the almighty that you have what you have. Adopt the gratitude attitude. Have you considered a hysterectomy?"

Eli responds to her insistent voice of integrity with a voice of his own in a different key. Then Eli answered, "Go in peace; the God of Israel grants the petition you have made to him." The operative word here is peace — *shalom*. My Bible dictionary offers these synonyms — "completeness (in number), safety, soundness (in body), welfare, health, prosperity, peace, quiet, tranquility, contentment, peace, friendship of human relationships with God, especially in covenant relationship, peace (from war), peace (as adjective)." He does not tell her to go home and work things out. Her petition was for a male child. We assume that it was with Elkanah. We do not actually know how she felt about Elkanah. In soundness of body, in way of justice, in equality: she is a composed, competent woman. She makes the choice to begin again with Elkanah. Having come to the end of her rope she will now walk on in shalom that will lead to a new future for her and her family.

Walking in shalom has made the difference here. Shalom has made a way where it appeared that there was no way. In the midst of chaos, the breakdown of old ways, the breaking in of stress and strain into all homes: walk in shalom. Here old gods of male superiority that dismiss women and diminish their stories are not propped up for the sake of the voice of the God of shalom.

In reading this story, I find myself wondering what gods I have propped up that have caused me to diminish and not hear others? Have I propped old ways that have caused me, unlike Eli, not to hear the truth in others' experience? Comfortable in my ways, am I cruising toward an unanticipated tipping point? Replenishing my life and the world's life means a return to walking in shalom.

Hebrews 10:11-14 (15-18) 19-25

The text begins with the unsettling notion that the religious community has reached a dead end. "And every priest stands day after day at his service, offering again and again the same sacrifices that can never take away sins." If you have taught a confirmation class that is from somewhere other than heaven and you feel like you are just going through the motions, then you can identify with this experience. No doubt many a pastor can readily point to aspects of church life that seemingly have lost the power to redeem. Preaching as taught in seminaries where I attended has in a visual age been challenged by new modes of communication. Great battles over what hymns to include in denominational hymnals are eclipsed by those who call into question the very notion of hymnals. Trained to think in terms of finding the inputs for the support of any church project, the literature now speaks of the need for all concerned to focus on outputs.

There seems to be no aspect of church life that is as it was when I began in ministry and has not come into serious question. I read the current literature and I feel like the priest in this passage, as one who may have been standing at the wrong altar all these years. I am part of a denomination that is considering alternative paths to ordination that demand far less effort than the one that was expected of me. Having just made a move that required me to pare down my library, I was astounded that there were few takers for the great classics of the Christian faith that I have managed to amass. Okay, I expected that I would reach an age when I would find myself a bit behind the curve. Nothing prepared me for this! I find the letter to the Hebrews a bit too facile in failing to take account of what the priest must feel like if he is found to be standing, perhaps through no fault of his own, at an altar that is no longer deemed to be too effective in taking away the sins of the world.

I find my experience somewhat parallel to the crisis that is taking place in journalism, as shrinking circulation and increasing competition from the internet and blogging is causing many to question their commitment to print media. One major Boston newspaper has even considered switching its operation entirely over to an internet format — scary.

My initial response to feeling like a dinosaur is to want to prop up the old gods that I am most comfortable with. No, ministers should be professionally trained just like doctors and lawyers — being called doctor should matter. My credentials and experience matter. Yet, I look at the state of the church and wonder whether standing at these altars and having made the sacrifice to get here has much to do with taking away the sin of the world as I think.

Ben Bradlee, former editor of the *Washington Post*, confronting the crises in journalism said that the answer here is "stories, good stories." It might not be the whole answer but he is onto something. It is certainly the conclusion that the letter to the Hebrews makes. "But when Christ had offered for all time a single sacrifice for sins, he sat down at the right hand of God," and since then has been waiting until his enemies would be made a footstool for his feet. For by a single offering, he has perfected for all time those who are sanctified. The letter sets before us the primary task of being able to narrate a saving experience. This past year my confirmation class came alive as they sought to narrate the saving experiences in their lives. Looking at their lives they could identify places where only something that could be named as grace had occurred.

This invites me less to consider my credentials and more to consider how I can name and communicate the saving experiences in my life. Having been raised in the mainline religious milieu I was not strongly encouraged to think this way. Yet, telling my story may help others identify their story. The letter invites one to consider how God has written the law in our minds and upon our hearts. How God will go so far as the shedding of blood not to allow my sins and foolishness to be the final word over my life.

In my defensive mode, I focus on my sacrifice. When I read the letter to the Hebrews, I focus on God's sacrifice for me. In my defensive mood I call others into question. When I focus on the sacrifice of God I realize that all in Christ have some serious blood ties. When I am standing at my altars, I focus on what I know. When I consider the letter to the Hebrews, I experience the God who has understood me.

The letter suggests what ought to be the starting point when we feel that we have come to a dead-end.

"Let us hold fast to the confession of our hope without wavering, for he who has promised is faithful. And let us consider how to provoke one another to love and good deeds."

Mark 13:1-8

As he came out of the temple, one of his disciples said to him, "Look, Teacher, what large stones and what large buildings!" Standing downtown, in the local mall, or on the mall in Washington DC, it can sure look like it does to the disciples. It can look that way to the millions that now flock to the cities of the world in search of fame, wealth, or employment. It is quite a beguiling vision. Jesus saw another aspect to the enthralling show. If you manage to get to the top of the pile, the center ring, the corporate board room, you might find yourself at the place you are most likely to be led astray, particularly if thinking that you have finally arrived you think the journey is over. Interestingly enough, both the secular community and the religious community make the same claim. You have arrived, there is nothing more in store than this order of things — history is over. Or, history is over, watch what God has in store.

Recently, on Pentecost, I had the opportunity on the day we confirmed some of our youth to reflect on what it might mean to find yourself at the center of culture, on top of things, and in general, in center ring. This year's confirmation class was composed of students who, in many ways, had already won the gene pool. Through their native talents and their positive upbringings, they had their tickets punched for the train ride to the top. Here in part is what I said: "As I look at this confirmation class, I have no doubt that many of you will find yourselves at the center of many things — some center stage, some center court, some the center of attention, some at the center of controversy, some in center field or playing center."

The problem will not be getting there. Your talents and character will lead you and the Holy Spirit will push you there. But the danger in our world is that once you get there it is hard to stay centered in the right things and people can get burned. Just look at what politics seems to do to people at the center of power, or what the Hollywood set can do to people who find themselves center stage. The Enron Corporation executives, thinking they were the center of the universe, are facing stiff prison sentences for their self-centeredness. More than a few teachers I have known face burnout after standing at the center of a classroom for years.

If you find yourself standing at the center of a sanctuary somewhere taking wedding vows, call on the name of the Lord. At that place the family name, the name of common sense, matters much less than the name of the one who will take your sorrows, your grief, and your disagreements and turn them into growth and wisdom and make more of you by teaching you how to give and receive love.

If you get to center stage, and I think some of you will, remember, in his name you are nothing without the people who are downstage or offstage. Living in his name will keep you centered as you walk through the fiery furnace. As a matter of fact, that seems to be the world's problem. We have forgotten the people who are downstage and offstage and out of sight and mind as if we are no longer all in it together. We have done it in the name of the free market, the right of some to drive gas guzzlers, you name it. But everyone who calls on the name of the Lord shall be saved.

I know some of you will one day step to the center of a classroom and all eyes will be on you. Remember, behind those eyes are human souls that fear rejection, long for their place, and who need someone to see more in them than they can see in themselves. Remember, you have those souls in your hands and you will live. Some of you will find yourselves the center of attention. You just have the knack of doing that. I have seen it. When you do find yourself at the center, call on his name that you might take this gift to heart before you let it go to your head. Jesus often found himself the center of attention and from there he could see the hurting and the wounded, the too angry and the not angry enough, as nobody else could because everyone was looking at him. What will be important here is not that all eyes are on you, any fool can get that, what will matter is what your eyes see from that privileged position.

When you are standing at the center of things looking up at all those magnificent buildings and what the world has to offer, call on the name of the Lord less you be led astray.

Application

In each of these texts there is the temptation to remain on the surface. Yet, each text causes the reader to take a second look at one's domestic arrangements, theological stance, and acceptance of the order of things. This can be particularly difficult on the Sunday before Thanksgiving. As I look back at the Thanksgivings of my youth, they were affirmations of my culture. We gave thanks for the brave triumph of the Pilgrims, thanks that we were Christians not pagans, thanks for traditional domestic arrangements that at the time did not include the strong role of women, and thanks for our shot at being center stage. Since then it seems that there has been a lot of nation rising against nation, and earthquakes on the social landscape. The theological understandings, domestic arrangements, and political certainties I began with are no longer there. The props have been knocked out from a lot of the assurances of my youth. Thanksgiving is a little tougher than I thought it would be. However, Jesus suggests that we need not put away the turkey and cranberries quite yet, for "This is but the beginning of the birth pangs."

An Alternative Application

Hebrews 10:11-14 (15-18) 19-25. Verse 22 of chapter 10 of the letter to the Hebrews invites us to approach the throne of grace with hearts "sprinkled clean from an evil conscience." I wonder what an evil conscience could mean in the life of most churchgoers. Can it mean more consciousness of what can go wrong than of how God can turn even our worst mistakes into something that can give glory to God and blessing to the world? Can it mean more consciousness of past certainties than future opportunities, more conscious of our differences than our commonalities?

The language of the verse suggests that one's heart does not need a power wash. The gentle sprinkle of the blood, sweat, and tears that fall from the cross might be sufficient to do a miracle wash.

He doth provide

Henry Alford's familiar hymn, "Come, Ye Thankful People, Come," so often sung at this season of year, includes this testimony: "God our Maker doth provide for our wants to be supplied."

Such affirmation and recognition of the provident care of God are at the heart of Thanksgiving. For Thanksgiving does not begin with our gratitude, or even with our bounty. The first principle is the generous providence of God. He is the source of our bounty. And he is the proper recipient of our worshipful gratitude.

In the three scripture readings for this day, we are rightly reminded of the many and various ways that our God doth provide.

In both the Joel and Matthew passage, we are assured of his willingness and ability to provide for us materially. His care extends to our most basic needs, and he demonstrates his loving inclination to provide in abundance.

The material needs that tend to be primary in our minds, however, are not the extent of his repertoire. The prophecy from Joel speaks of God providing for his people's vindication and compensation. He provides what they need for their dignity. And his comprehensive care covers past, present, and future.

Finally, the most significant gift of God is our salvation. We are reminded of the prophetic words and images that emerge from Abraham's near sacrifice of Isaac. In a poignant moment on the way up the dreaded mountain, Abraham makes his great statement of faith: "God himself will provide a lamb" (Genesis 22:8). And after he has been stopped from offering his own son, and has offered instead the ram provided by God, "Abraham called that place 'The Lord will provide'; as it is said to this day, 'On the mount of the Lord it shall be provided' " (v. 14).

The Ephesians passage bears witness to this most important providence of God. And when we see all things clearly, that is the gift that dwarfs all of the others, and it is the high point of our thanksgiving.

We want to let all of today's scripture readings speak to us about thanksgiving. And as they do, we will discover that the focus of our attention — and of our gratitude — is on the God who "doth provide."

Joel 2:21-27

Joel is perhaps the trickiest Old Testament prophet for Old Testament scholars. While many other prophets offer very helpful contemporary landmarks — referencing specific historical events or people — Joel defies such easy dating. As such, he is open to much speculation about the exact threats that his judgment messages anticipate.

Judgment is not Joel's only message, however. As is the case in so many of the canonical prophets, judgment is not God's final word. He has a plan for goodness and blessing on the other side of the predicted calamities. The judgment is a means to an end, not an end in itself. And this excerpt from Joel reflects some of that hopeful message — the good news of what God will do when the judgment is passed.

In order that they might appreciate fully the imagery of this passage, we ought to give our congregations a taste of some of those earlier judgment passages from Joel. For the prophet describes in compelling language a complete and unstoppable destruction (2:4-11). Absolute devastation will be left in judgment's wake (1:9-20; 2:3). The countryside will be a wasteland, with every tree stripped and every green thing consumed.

It is in dramatic contrast and response to those images, then, that this message is presented. God paints a picture of the entire land as a kind of glorious cornucopia. The fields and trees burst with their produce, and the wine and oil overflow with abundance.

One of the hallmarks of God's provident care in scripture is the uncontainable quality of his generosity. Jesus does not merely satisfy the appetites of the 5,000 hungry men; he so over provides that there is more food leftover than there was food to begin with. The manna and the quails in the wilderness were supplied in a measure that exceeded the need even of that vast multitude of Israelites. His reward is not merely adequate, but "pressed down, shaken together, running over" (Luke 6:38), and his work within us is "far more than all we can ask or imagine" (Ephesians 3:20).

So, too, here in the promises made through Joel. The picture is not merely of people who have enough to eat again. No, but rather a people who are immersed in the flood of God's generosity.

And then the good news gets still better. The goodness of God is not limited to the promise of a bumper crop. It goes deeper than that. Just as the former devastation and scarcity had a spiritual cause and meaning, so also the abundance is about more than just bushels and vats.

Part of the promise and picture, for example, is a return to healthy normality of nature's seasons. The Lord guarantees "the early and the later rain, as before." Symbolic of the deeper meaning, however, is that the early rain is specifically identified as "for your vindication." Not just for their fields, but for their vindication.

Moreover, God promises to cover their losses. "I will repay you for the years that the swarming locust has eaten, the hopper, the destroyer, and the cutter, my great army, which I sent against you." It's a remarkable grace that compensates us for the punishment that we deserved. And it is a beautiful testimony to his strong and versatile goodness that his generosity reaches back, as well as forward. The promises are not just for tomorrow; remarkably, they are for yesterday, too!

Finally, the promise that began with simple things like rain and grain concludes with three profound goals: 1) "You shall know that I am in the midst of Israel"; 2) "You shall know... that I, the Lord, am your God and there is no other"; and 3) "My people shall never again be put to shame."

1 Timothy 2:1-7

By the time the New Testament opens, the Roman Empire had been occupying Palestine for more than a generation. Roman soldiers were ubiquitous. Roman officials — and/or locally appointed puppets — were the civil authorities. And taxes were collected by Rome to subsidize the whole occupation.

Meanwhile, by the time the New Testament era closes, the presence and impact of Rome is even more sinister. Rome is no longer just the unwelcome and oppressive foreign occupier for the Jews in Palestine. Now Rome has set itself up as the persecutor of the church throughout the empire, and as such Rome is seen by Christians as the enemy of Christ. The question of an individual's ultimate allegiance was embodied by these two competing claims: Caesar is lord; Jesus is Lord.

It is in the face of that, then, that the apostle urges that "supplications, prayers, intercessions, and thanksgivings be made for everyone, for kings and all who are in high positions." It is a remarkable instruction, given the fatal antagonism of some of those kings toward the believers of Timothy's day. One might expect a more subversive or bitter exhortation. Or if one were to invoke one's gods at all in regard to those "kings and all who are in high positions," it would be in the manner that Balak sought from Balaam: a divine curse on one's enemy.

It is noteworthy that the apostle so specifically mentions those civil authorities. He generically refers to "everyone," but he does not leave the instruction so general. Instead, he goes out of his way to specify a particular — and probably resented — category of people.

Our natural human tendency, it seems, is to include in our prayers — that is, in our supplications, in our thanksgivings, and in our intercessions — the people we love. No one has to go out of his way to teach me that I should pray for my wife, children, and other family members. But I do need someone to instruct me to pray for those who are antagonistic — perhaps even threatening — to me, for I would not do it naturally.

Interestingly, Paul's stated rationale for his extraordinary instruction has nothing ultimately to do with those civil authorities. Rather, his goal is "that we may lead a quiet and peaceable life in all godliness and dignity." The paradigm is reminiscent of Jesus' "audience of One" instructions in the Sermon on the Mount (see, for example, Matthew 6:1-6, 16-18). Those kings and others in high positions will not likely know one way or the other whether we are praying for them or cursing them under our breath. No matter, for it's not really about them. Rather, the issue is living faithfully before our God.

Meanwhile, Paul's statement about Jesus — "there is also one mediator between God and humankind, Christ Jesus, himself human" — brings to mind the plight of Job. Feeling distanced from God, and unable to reach him, Job laments, "He is not a mortal, as I am, that I might answer him, that we should come to trial together" (Job 9:32). And so Job expresses the need for a mediator: "There is no umpire between us, who might lay his hand on us both" (v. 33).

It may well be that someone in your pews or mine will be feeling that God is far away and unreachable. They might resonate with Job's wish that there was someone who could serve as a go-between: some rare individual who was able to lay a hand on God himself, and yet not also be distant and untouchable. They would welcome the good news Paul brings that there is just such a mediator: Jesus Christ — both God and man — able to touch both and bring the two together.

Finally, an observation about Paul's literary style in this passage.

Like Noah's animals boarding the Ark two-by-two, here in this passage it seems that Paul makes his points "two-by-two," for virtually everything he says comes in sets of two. Consider the following phrases: "kings and all who are in high positions," "quiet and peaceable," "godliness and dignity," "right and acceptable," "to be saved and to come to the knowledge of the truth," "a herald and an apostle," and "faith and truth." If I were going to preach an expository sermon on this passage, I would organize my message around these theological couplets.

Matthew 6:25-33

Jesus was Jewish. His disciples were all Jewish. The multitudes that flocked to hear him in Galilee must have been predominantly, if not exclusively, Jewish. And Matthew's particular gospel has often been nicknamed, "The gospel for the Jews," because of the apparent audience for which Matthew was writing.

In light of all of that, what does it mean when Jesus, in the Sermon on the Mount, makes reference to the Gentiles?

See the startling thing that Jesus said to his audience. It is a kind of verbal slap in the face, for he implies that they are being like "the Gentiles." Referring to a concern for food, drink, and clothing, Jesus observes, "It is the Gentiles who strive for all these things."

For our purposes, of course, the term is a problematic one. Most of us — and most of the people in our pews — are Gentiles. And so we will need to find some way of translating the message anew to make it meaningful. What shall we say instead of "the Gentiles"? How can we capture for our congregations the strong, even offensive thing that Jesus is saying? Is it "the unbelievers" who strive for all these things? Is it those people who have no knowledge of God? Those who have no faith in him? Those who have no relationship with him? Are they the ones who strive for all these things?

Of course, they are not. Not exclusively, at least. These are standard fare human concerns. This is not the stuff of either immorality or heresy. It is a quite ordinary and natural human instinct to be concerned about how the basic needs of life are going to be met. And yet Jesus chides his audience for their preoccupation with these matters, for that is not how the people of God should operate.

The passage cuts across our grain right from the start. "Do not worry about your life," Jesus says. Don't worry about my life? What kind of impossible and unnatural instruction is that? How can a person not worry about his life? Candidly, Jesus seems a bit out of touch with reality.

In truth, however, Jesus is entirely in touch with — a different reality. And his teaching is designed to put us in touch with that reality, as well.

If I am an adult man making a drive from Wisconsin to Tennessee, then I must be concerned about directions, fuel level, toll roads, speed limits, and such. That's the reality if I am an adult.

On the other hand, if I am a child and my dad is the driver, then I do not need to be concerned about such things. The directions, fuel, and the rest are still just as important as before, mind you; but they are not my concern.

That is the kind of reality Jesus presents to us. It's a reality about our heavenly Father. It's a paradigm that does not focus on the need but on the source.

In day-to-day life, when someone tells us not to worry about a thing, it can seem like a minimization of something important to us. If my five-year-old daughter is all upset about one of her toys being missing, her older sister may say dismissively, "Oh, don't worry about it!" And so, when Jesus first says to us, "Do not worry about your life," it may seem to us that he is minimizing something that is important to us.

In reality, though, Jesus' words are most life-affirming. His teaching values our lives more highly than our worrying does, for he insists that life is "more than food, and the body more than clothing." Then, at the end of the passage, he reveals the real value of life.

If the chief concern of my life is food and clothes, then they become my purpose, my *raison d'être*. And such a purpose devalues my existence, confining me to that which is temporal and passing. But Jesus points beyond the myopia of my physical needs to a much farther horizon: "Strive first for the kingdom of God and his righteousness."

You and I may set aside our concerns for fuel levels and toll roads, leaving them to our Father. And, instead, we may elevate our concerns — and thus our reason for being — to things high and eternal: the things of God.

Application

God our maker doth provide. That is the testimony of the hymn, and each of today's lections bears witness to that same truth. They invite us to ponder together the implications of how he provides.

The fact that he provides becomes the source of our peace. We do not need to worry, Jesus assures us, because our Father already knows our needs and can be trusted to provide for them.

The fact that he provides becomes our liberty. We are not sentenced to live in constant and meaningless pursuit of things temporal. Rather, we are called to strive for higher things. The highest! Far from God minimizing our basic needs, he enables us to minimize them: that is, to keep them from becoming all-important in our lives because we leave them to him.

And, finally, the fact that he provides becomes the cause and the context of our worship and thanksgiving. God promised the people of Joel's day, "You shall eat in plenty and be satisfied, and praise the name of the Lord your God, who has dealt wondrously with you." If there is a phrase that could serve as the caption for our Thanksgiving holiday, it is the first part of that verse. Let the whole verse be true in our lives and our homes this Thanksgiving holiday.

An Alternative Application

Matthew 6:25-33. "Enter Your Destination." When I was a child, my parents would plan a family trip by getting out maps and atlases, spreading them out on the kitchen table, evaluating possible routes, and adding in their heads the tiny little red and black numbers along the highways to determine the total mileage.

It's all a far cry from how I plan trips for my family today.

I use my computer and go to one of several websites; I enter my starting address; I enter my destination; and, in a matter of seconds, I have a complete itinerary, with total mileage, estimated travel time, and detailed directions. With just a little more effort and only a few more minutes, I can add in specific stops on the way, make motel reservations, identify favorite restaurant chains, and locate points of interest along my route.

Many of the folks in your congregation will also be accustomed to this more high-tech method of planning a trip. They will understand, therefore, what it means to "enter your destination."

Arriving at your destination, of course, comes at the end of the trip. But entering your destination comes at the beginning. Indeed, before the beginning. For when you first start to plan your journey, you have to identify where you intend to go.

Jesus challenges us to enter our destination, and to be wise about it. On a family car trip, your destination is about where you drive. In life, your destination is about where you strive.

On the one hand, there is a very ordinary sort of human destination. We may, like "the Gentiles," strive for routine things like food, drink, and clothing. In the process, however, we choose for ourselves such a small and temporal destination.

On the other hand, there is that peculiar goal and focus of Jesus' followers: the kingdom of God. Strive for that and you choose for yourself a magnificent and eternal destination. And, by the way, you'll have all the rest of those routine needs provided, too.

So let's invite our people to enter their destinations today: to make a conscious decision about where and for what they want to strive, to steer clear of the common detours, and to take the steps required to get there.

Majesty

Several generations ago, King George and Queen Elizabeth went to a London theater to see a Noel Coward/Gertrude Lawrence production. As they entered the royal box, the whole audience rose to its feet to honor them. Standing in the wings, Gertrude Lawrence said, "What an entrance!" Noel Coward added, "What a part!"

Today's lectionary readings, on this "Christ the King" Sunday, look at the marvelous part that king Jesus has to play in the drama of time and space. Says Joan of Arc in the first installment of Shakespeare's *King Henry VI*: "Glory is like a circle in the water, which never ceaseth to enlarge itself" (I.ii). For human rulers, she pointed out, that was disastrous. Eventually, the reach would exceed the substance.

But what a part for the Lord of the universe! David builds upon this theme in his "last words" as he draws comparisons between the ever-expanding circles of God's glory and those of a ruler whose heart beats in tune with divine music. Similarly, the book of Revelation opens with shock waves of glory emanating from the risen Christ. And even during the humiliation of Jesus' trial, as John notes in his review of the Passion story, the glory of divinity could not be hidden away.

Still, despite the fact that every element of creation, from the star-spangled skies to the goo-slurping slug, stands and shouts at Jesus' entrance, one ring among the circles of expanding glory, heaves only a mixed applause toward heaven. It is the orb of humanity. Elizabeth Barrett Browning put it this way:

Earth's crammed with heaven,
And every common bush afire with God;
But only he who sees takes off his shoes;
The rest sit round and pluck blackberries.

What we need to remember today is that our ability to see God is quite directly related to our understanding of ourselves and the qualities and values of life around us. Those who carelessly toss aside human life will never worship God as they stuff blackberries into their mouths. Indeed, John Calvin started his magnificent survey of the Christian faith, *The Institutes of the Christian Religion*, by reflecting that our knowledge of ourselves and our knowledge of God are so intertwined that the one has little power to grow without the other. So today we need to recover the twin knowledges of ourselves and our God in order to celebrate rightly the rule of our true sovereign.

2 Samuel 23:1-7

Being the leader of a community isn't easy. A cartoon shows a man near death lying on a hospital bed. Two visitors sit next to him, and one hands him a card. "The good news, pastor," she says, "is that the women's club at the church decided to get this 'Get Well' card for you. The bad news is that the vote was 23 to 22!"

That could be the picture of any of 100 different leaders in our world today. A prime minister skates at the bottom of the popularity polls. A president wins a Nobel Peace Prize from those outside of his country and buckets of complaints from those within it. Another world leader seems intent on courting the disfavor of the whole world.

If one of them were to be taken to hospital, Hallmark Card Company stock wouldn't go up a penny! The ancient Greek philosopher was right: "Authority is never without hate."

A few years back, Jim Lundy wrote a book called *Lead, Follow, or Get Out of the Way*. According to Lundy, the most common message circulating in many organizations is this lament: We the uninformed, working for the inaccessible, are doing the impossible for the ungrateful. To put it another way, he says, "Most people feel like the mushrooms being grown in one of those long, low barns: We feel we're being kept in the dark. Every once in a while someone comes around and spreads manure on us. When our heads pop up, they're chopped off. And then we're canned!" Do you ever feel like that?

The opening of 2 Samuel 23 is a song of royal leadership. It has no hint of the tired frustration we so often feel about heads of state and leaders of corporations. Enthusiasm builds, till it seems as if the sun rises and sets on the king. We are told that these are "the last words of David." Is this one of David's final poems or psalms? Was this David's dying testimony about himself or about kings in general? Did David intend this to be the coronation hymn for the celebration that would install his son and successor to the royal seat? We do not know.

Yet, it is obvious that David understands leadership, at least within the context of the people who are under divine care. His themes are echoed in what Jim Kouses and Barry Posner call *The Leadership Challenge*. A righteous leader will 1) challenge the status quo (v. 6), 2) inspire a shared vision for the people (v. 3), 3) enable others to act in this manner (v. 5), 4) encourage the hearts of those under his or her care (v. 4), and 5) model the way in his or her own personal dealings (v. 5).

When Isaac Watts pondered the qualities of leadership put forward in one of David's psalms, he penned a hymn that resonates with today's celebration:

Jesus shall reign where'er the sun
Does its successive journeys run,
His kingdom stretch from shore to shore,
Till moons shall wax and wane no more.

If the last words of David stir in us noble thoughts about David or Solomon or other such great rulers, they do well. Moreover, if they point us to king Jesus, so much the better. But if they fill us with a desire to participate actively in such a kingdom ourselves, then the word of God is doing its best work. For every child of God is a king or queen who shares the possibilities of restoring righteousness and dignity to relationships on earth.

Revelation 1:4b-8

The book of Revelation is used too often by those enamored by its weirdness and too little by those who understand its good purpose. There are many reasons why it is a hard book to preach on, of course, and for that reason the lectionary sidesteps major interpretive issues by choosing only a few pericopes like this one which are unambiguous in their presentation. No matter which primary school of Revelation interpretation one follows (Preterist — the book is code language for the religious and political struggles of the day and speaks mostly about first-century times; Historicist — the book expounds on the whole of church history and it is possible, if done with care, to identify the current location of our contemporary existence on its 22-chapter timeline; Futurist — the bulk of the book is a prophetic unfolding of near-future events and will culminate in the millennial reign of Jesus on earth; Idealist — the book is intended primarily as representational and allegorical, exposing the clash of powers and worldviews, but also assuring those who trust in Jesus of the divine victory), this word about Jesus is clear and unambiguous. John announces a blessing on all who know that Jesus is the divine Son of God who has risen victorious from death, reigns in majesty in heaven, and is coming soon to make all things new. It is both a call to worship and a call to arms. It is an encouragement to faithful service of an unseen king.

Before C.S. Lewis became a Christian, he was quite taken aback by such language in the Bible and the church. He wondered, on the one hand, why we humans, who have so much to live for here, might ever be enticed to long for "heaven" or "eternal life." Furthermore, he questioned why religion seems often to turn the worship of God into a duty that exacts a tax of begrudging acknowledgment from us. We *have* to go to church. We *must* be good. We are *obligated* to pray. In fact, in places like this call of the apostle John, there appeared to Lewis to be a rather profound browbeating that requires obescience to the overpowering deity who impacts his senses.

What Lewis only began to understand over time is that his feelings of antipathy to presumed religious coercion arose from a pagan notion that we can somehow increase the majesty of our tribal gods in the clash of worldly power plays. The religion of the Bible, Lewis began to find out, is actually quite different. The vantage point of scripture is that of transcendence looking into our limited existence, and not the other way around. It is God who creates us in his image. It is God who loves us when we are unlovely. It is God who declares us to be kings and queens. It is God who thinks wonderful thoughts about us, even when we can't be bothered to think much of ourselves. So the worship of God is not about obligations placed upon unruly peons to toe some arbitrary line drawn by a vain and self-absorbed deity, but rather a reminder to those on planet earth who are too quickly enamored with themselves and their capacities that a great good can be had when they are caught up in the divine splendor which shines over them all.

When the German prince, George II, became king of Great Britain, he had a special fondness for the music of his fellow countryman, George Frideric Handel. At the premiere concert of Handel's *Messiah* in 1743, the king and the crowds were deeply moved by the glory and grace of the masterpiece. When the musicians swelled the "Hallelujah" chorus, and thundered those mighty words, "And he shall reign for ever and ever!" King George (whose English wasn't all that great) jumped to his feet, thinking they sang of him! The whole crowd followed suit — for a different reason, of course, and a different king!

The comedy of that moment reflects what will become the ultimate theme of the rest of the book of Revelation. God in heaven claps his hands and shouts of our greatness in the shared honor Jesus has brought into our world. And in the expanding circles of God's glory, we rise, singing the "Hallelujah" chorus.

John 18:33-37

"Politics are almost as exciting as war, and quite as dangerous!" said Winston Churchill. "In war you can only be killed once, but in politics many times." He might well have been reflecting on the centuries of religious conflict that were at their initial crisis in the encounter between Pilate and Jesus in today's text.

Politics is about power, as both the governor and the prisoner knew. The question was not about whether each had power, but what kind of power each had to wield. Dale Carnegie was well aware of the differing dimensions of power when he created his popular seminars on "How to Win Friends and Influence People." Generations earlier, in his famous treatise on politics, *The Prince*, Machiavelli charted a course for all who would seek political power when he wrote, "All the armed prophets conquered, all the unarmed ones perished!" In the end, it seems, what matters is your ability to create your dream, not the rightness of the dream itself. Napoleon even confided in his journals that "justice means force as well as virtue." Your ideal can be noble, but you must be able to force it upon others you consider less noble than yourself.

So the confrontation between Jesus and Pilate. Who is ruler? Who exercised authority? Who can lead the masses and what will that take? Jesus understands Pilate and his precarious position in the power plays of the day, but can Pilate understand Jesus?

In one of his essays, Albert Camus describes a powerful scene that replays something of the irony in today's gospel lectionary verses. John Huss, the great Czech reformer of the church, is on trial. His accusers twist all his ideas out of shape. They refuse to give him a hearing. They maneuver the political machine against him and incite popular passion to a lynch-mob frenzy. Finally, Huss is condemned to be burned at the stake. As the flames surround him, people who couldn't possibly have read his writings and who have no interest in either his perspectives or those of the governing authorities, line up to assist in the murder. "When they were burning John Huss," writes Camus, "a gentle, little old lady came carrying her fagot to add it to the pile."

The tragedy of politics often lies in passions, not platforms. "Private passions grow tired and wear themselves out; political passions, never!" says Lamartine. That is why many communities have an unwritten rule that when all the in-laws and out-laws get together for the annual "family rebellion" none can talk about politics or religion. Both topics grab a person too deeply and vent emotions too enormously.

Yet maybe, when it comes right down to it, politics and religion are much the same thing. The kingdom of God is *very* political. It is, as Jesus indicates, a perspective on all of life. It is a way of holding things together and giving them meaning. It is a movement that is out to change the world, to reclaim lost territory in the civil war of the universe.

That's why Jesus' followers soon got into trouble with both the political and religious leaders of their day. Two visions of reality collided. Two perspectives on life challenged each other. Six times over in the book of Acts, the Christian community is called "The Way." Not "The Society," nor "The Institution," but "The Way"!

The church of Jesus Christ is a political movement. It is *on the way* to somewhere. Every worship service is a political rally: a time when we refocus our energies, study our political platform and policies, and pay homage to the party leader. Especially on "Christ the King" Sunday.

Application

The year was 1934. Times were difficult around the world, especially in the repressed economic and political climate of post-World War I Germany. But recovery was in sight. A group of theologians at Wurtemburg saw a rising star of hope and penned together a declaration of faith that would be signed by 600 pastors of churches and fourteen theology professors at seminaries.

Their promising statement included these words: "We are full of thanks to God that he, as Lord of history, has given us Adolf Hitler, our leader and savior from our difficult lot. We acknowledge that we, with body and soul, are bound and dedicated to the German state and to its Fuhrer."

Astounding, isn't it? In retrospect we can only shudder at the demonic twists of history that could produce such unqualified devotion to a man who would later rip God's world apart, and destroy, insofar as he was able, both the church and children of God.

That same year, 1934, Hitler summoned a group of church leaders to his office. Martin Niemoller was among them. He had been a great hero in the German Navy during World War I, commanding a submarine that caused great destruction to the Allied fleet. Now he was a pastor, much loved in his new vocation.

The meeting with Hitler began cordially enough. Suddenly, however, Hermann Goering burst into the room with a charge of treason against Niemoller. Hitler raged in angry tirade. Finally, he regained his composure and told Niemoller, "You confine yourself to the church. I'll take care of the German people!"

But Niemoller knew what "Christ the King" Sunday meant, and he marched to its challenging beat. He stood quietly and replied, "Herr Reichskanzler, you said just now: 'I will take care of the German people.' But we, too, as Christians and churchmen, have a responsibility toward the German people. That responsibility was entrusted to us by God, and neither you nor anyone in this world has the power to take it from us."

Hitler knew a showdown when he saw it. Niemoller went to trial, and was convicted of misusing his pulpit for political purposes. Hitler refused to pardon him, declaring, "It is Niemöller or I."

Not all political confrontations are that dramatic. No current government leader would ask North Americans to make a choice between themselves and God. But the gray area of compromise, whether social, economic, emotional, physical, or political, always takes place with the slow staccato of drumbeats in the background. Conflicting rhythms tear at our souls until we find a way to isolate the heartbeat of the God we will follow.

"Onward, Christian Soldiers" may sound too combative in an age of growing world accommodation and pluralism. But the community of God's people that speaks "Peace!" while the final armistice has not yet been signed before the judgment seat of heaven has capitulated to the enemy.

Alternative Application

Using the doxological blessing in Revelation, today might be a wonderful Sunday to build a service around the themes of Jack Hayford's modern classic "Majesty." Hayford is the founding pastor of the Church on the Way in Van Nuys, California. When he visited Sir Winston Churchill's boyhood home in Oxfordshire, England, he was captured by its grandeur. As Hayford walked through the beauty of Blenheim Palace's landscaped grounds, he said to his wife: "In a place this magnificent, it's easy to see how a person raised here could imagine himself to be a person of destiny. There's something about the environment that makes you feel: 'I am significant.' "

This was the inspiration for "Majesty." Hayford reflected: "I thought about the majesty and dignity we've been endowed with in Christ. If that would dawn on all God's people, if they would sense their significance in him, then we all could become aware of his purpose in us" (*The Power of Hope*, p. 57).

About the Authors

Wayne Brouwer teaches Religion, Theology, and Ministry Studies at both Hope College and Western Theological Seminary in Holland, Michigan. He holds degrees from Dordt College (A.B.), Calvin Theological Seminary (M.Div., Th.M.), and McMaster University (M.A., Ph.D.), and spent three decades as a pastor and international missionary teacher. Along with hundreds of published articles, Wayne Brouwer has authored thirteen books, including *Covenant Documents: Reading the Bible Again for the First Time* (Cognella), *The Literary Development of John 13-17: A Chiastic Reading* (SBL), and *Being a Believer in an Unbelieving World* (Hendrickson).

Timothy B. Cargal currently serves as Associate for Preparation for Ministry with the General Assembly of the Presbyterian Church (USA). For some twenty years he combined pastoral ministry with teaching biblical studies in universities and seminaries. He is the author of two books, including *Hearing a Film, Seeing a Sermon: Preaching and Popular Movies* (Westminster John Knox Press), and has contributed to several other books, study bibles, dictionaries, and journals in the areas of New Testament studies and preaching. He holds a Ph.D. in Religious Studies from Vanderbilt University.

David A. Davis is currently the senior pastor of the Nassau Presbyterian Church in Princeton, New Jersey. He has served that congregation since 2000. David earned his Ph.D. in Homiletics from Princeton Theological Seminary where he continues to teach as a visiting lecturer. His academic work has focused on preaching as a corporate act and the active role of the listener in the preaching event. Before arriving in Princeton, he served for fourteen years as the pastor of the First Presbyterian Church, Blackwood, New Jersey. David grew up in Pittsburgh and did his undergraduate work at Harvard University where he was a member of the University Choir singing weekly in Memorial Church and listening to the preaching of Professor Peter Gomes. David is married to Cathy Cook, a Presbyterian Minister who is currently Director of Student Relations and Senior Placement at Princeton Seminary. They have two children Hannah and Ben. David is a regular contributor to the *Huffington Post* and various journals in the discipline of preaching and has had published a collection of his sermons. His book is titled *A Kingdom We Can Taste: Sermons for the Church Year* (Wm. B. Eerdmans).

David Kalas is the pastor of First United Methodist Church in Green Bay, Wisconsin. Before moving to Green Bay, he pastored churches in Whitewater, Wisconsin; Appleton, Wisconsin; and Hurt, Virginia. He also led youth ministries in Cleveland, Ohio, and Richmond, Virginia. David earned his undergraduate degree from the University of Virginia in Charlottesville and his Master of Divinity degree from Union Theological Seminary in Richmond, Virginia. He has also done coursework at Pittsburgh Theological Seminary and Asbury Theological Seminary.

In addition to the present volume, David has also contributed to other preaching resources published by CSS, is a regular contributor to *Emphasis: A Lectionary Preaching Journal* (CSS Publishing Company, Inc.), and has also written curriculum materials for the United Methodist Publishing House. David and his wife, Karen, have been married nearly 30 years and have three daughters, Angela, Lydia, and Susanna.

The late **R Craig MacCreary** was pastor of South Congregational Church, United Church of Christ in Newport, New Hampshire. He held pastorates in Pennsylvania, West Virginia, and Massachusetts. He earned degrees from Elon University (B.A.), Lancaster Theological Seminary (M. Div.), and Hartford Seminary (D. Min.). His work appeared in *Colleague*, *Pulpit Digest*, and *The United Church News*. He was a guest on National Public Radio and was a contributor to *Candles in the Dark: Preaching and Poetry in Times of Crises*, edited by James Randolph.

Bass Mitchell is an elder in the United Methodist church, Virginia Conference. Bass is currently pursuing a doctorate in higher education and religion at George Mason University. He is the author of numerous articles and books. Mitchell coauthored a book for CSS Publishing called *Bit Players in the Big Play*. Bass lives with his wife Debbie in Virginia. He and his wife have two grown children. Bass enjoys writing, being a workshop and retreat leader, and being a teacher.

CPSIA information can be obtained at www.ICGtesting.com
Printed in the USA
BVOW051657171111

276339BV00004B/4/P